2018

Social Panorama
of Latin America

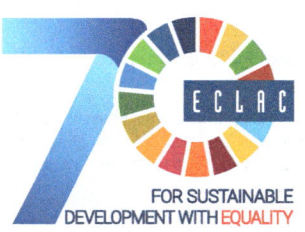

Alicia Bárcena
Executive Secretary

Mario Cimoli
Deputy Executive Secretary

Raúl García-Buchaca
Deputy Executive Secretary
for Management and Programme Analysis

Laís Abramo
Chief, Social Development Division

Ricardo Pérez
Chief, Publications and Web Services Division

Thanks are owed for the valuable collaboration of Pascual Gerstenfeld, former Chief of the Statistics Division, Mario Castillo of the Division for Gender Affairs, Xavier Mancero, Officer in Charge of the Statistics Division, and Alberto Arenas and Wilson Peres, Regional Advisers.

The following worked on the preparation of the chapters of this document: Verónica Amarante, Miguel del Castillo Negrete, Simone Cecchini, Ernesto Espíndola, Álvaro Fuentes, Rodrigo Martínez, Claudia Robles, Daniela Trucco, Iliana Vaca Trigo, Varinia Tromben, Soledad Villafañe and Pablo Villatoro. Ignacio Carrasco, Nicolas Dinerstein, Fabiana del Popolo, Verónica Ortiz, María Jesús Silva, Guillermo Sunkel and Heidi Ullmann prepared substantive inputs; while Amparo Bravo, Miguel del Castillo Negrete, Nicolas Dinerstein, Andrés Espejo, Ernesto Espíndola, Fabiola Fernández, Álvaro Fuentes, Michael Hanni, Carlos Howes, Carlos Kroll, Felipe López, Rocío Miranda, Verónica Ortiz, Ana Catalina Valencia and Daniel Vega worked on the statistical processing. Valuable contributions and comments relating to different sections of the document were received from Fabiana del Popolo, Jürgen Weller and Pablo Yanes.

United Nations publication

ISBN: 978-92-1-122009-4 (print)

ISBN: 978-92-1-058650-4 (pdf)

ISBN: 978-92-1-358102-5 (ePub)

Distribution: G

Sales No.: E.18.II.G.7

LC/PUB.2019/3-P

Explanatory notes:
- Three dots (...) indicate that data are not available or are not separately reported.
- A dash (-) indicates that the amount is nil or negligible.
- A full stop (.) is used to indicate decimals.
- The word "dollars" refers to United States dollars, unless otherwise specified.
- A slash (/) between years (e.g. 2013/2014) indicates a 12-month period falling between the two years.
- Individual figures and percentages in tables may not always add up to the corresponding total because of rounding.

This publication should be cited as: Economic Commission for Latin America and the Caribbean (ECLAC), *Social Panorama of Latin America, 2018* (LC/PUB.2019/3-P), Santiago, 2019.

Figures

Boxes

Diagrams

Introduction

The eradication of poverty and extreme poverty, as well as the reduction of inequality in all its dimensions, continues to be a core challenge for the countries of Latin America. Although the region made great strides in this regard from the start of the last decade to the middle of the present one, setbacks have occurred since 2015, particularly in extreme poverty. This is a matter for concern and a warning signal, especially amid low economic growth and profound demographic and labour market changes in the region. In this context, it is imperative to develop and strengthen social protection and labour market policies, including employment and social inclusion measures, as well as income redistribution policies. To this end, it is essential to protect and preserve social spending, strengthen social and labour institutions, and specifically tackle the causes of poverty and exclusion that disproportionately affect children, adolescents and young people, women of working age and indigenous and Afrodescendent people.

Since the middle of the past decade, labour income, pensions and cash transfers to the poorest households have played a key role in reducing poverty and income inequality. From 2015 onward, major labour indicators deteriorated: unemployment rates increased and the process of employment formalization seen in several countries in previous years was interrupted. In that context, the social protection network, whose expansion and solidification in the region since the early 2000s had contributed to the improvement observed until the mid-2010s, has been fundamental in containing distributional deterioration and avoiding further setbacks in levels of poverty, extreme poverty and income inequality.

In turn, social spending by central governments, even amid fiscal adjustments, remains significant within total public expenditure and in 2016 was slightly up on 2015, reaching one of its largest percentage shares of GDP since 2000. In per capita terms, social spending by the countries of Latin America almost doubled between 2002 and 2016, an encouraging sign and a key factor in the expansion of social and labour market policies during this period. However, in both absolute and relative terms, the region's social spending remains significantly lower than in the countries of the Organization for Economic Cooperation and Development (OECD) and the European Union. That includes spending on labour market policies, in particular on unemployment protection.

Furthermore, levels of social expenditure in the region are still very uneven between subregions and countries. It is precisely the countries where the greatest efforts are required to combat poverty and which are most in need of services to ensure social rights and achieve the social targets of the 2030 Agenda for Sustainable Development that have the least resources, both per capita and in relation to GDP. This means that, despite the progress made, there are still major challenges of social policy financing, especially in countries with higher levels of poverty and other social development shortfalls. Higher social expenditure has been key to achieving the progress made in reducing poverty and inequality and other social development indicators. Bolstering social spending is thus all the more imperative in times of increased instability and economic volatility.

Between 2002 and 2016, Latin America also made significant progress in terms of social and labour inclusion, but structural gaps persist, with a sharper impact on women and youth, as well as persons with disabilities, indigenous people and persons of African descent. Social inclusion indicators related to education, health and basic infrastructure have improved significantly, but large gaps in service access and quality persist. Labour inclusion indicators are also evolving positively, despite the persistence of structural challenges, such as insufficient generation of productive and good-quality employment, low incomes, high levels of informality and lack of protection at work. Social protection and labour market policies have been instrumental in achieving the above-mentioned advances, but should be strengthened in view of changes in the world of work driven by the new wave of technological innovations and the necessary transition to an environmentally sustainable economy.

In this context, gender inequalities must be explicitly addressed if they are not to worsen. Without adequate public policies to address key issues, such as the promotion of women's training and employment in science, technology, engineering and mathematics (STEM), to avoid job insecurity and to promote co-responsibility in care systems, women could not only lose out on the benefits of future jobs, but also run the risk of perpetuating existing gaps and the existing shortfalls of decent work.

In a scenario of uncertainty and change, it must be a priority to reinforce social and labour market policies with a universalist perspective, and to build the capacities to seize new opportunities, not merely address risks. Social policy must promote the simultaneous advancement of social and labour inclusion, and be guided by the principle of universalism sensitive to difference, with a focus on equality and rights. Although the commitment made by all the region's countries to definitively eradicate poverty is important, this is not the sole objective of social policy. In addition to this, and even to make poverty eradication possible, it is necessary to advance along the path of equality and build welfare States for the entire population, in which social protection is an effective right.

Summary

A. Socioeconomic inequalities: income and wealth distribution

Inequality is a historical and structural characteristic of Latin American and Caribbean societies that has been maintained and perpetuated even at times of growth and economic prosperity. Although significant progress has been made over the past 15 years, Latin America and the Caribbean remains the most unequal region in the world, ahead of sub-Saharan Africa (the second most unequal region), with an average Gini index almost a third higher than that of Europe and Central Asia.

High levels of inequality conspire against development and pose a barrier to the eradication of poverty, the expansion of citizenship, the exercise of rights and democratic governance. Equality is a necessary condition for the dynamic efficiency of the economy in that it creates a framework of institutions, policies and efforts conducive to capacity-building. This facilitates local innovation, the absorption of technological advances generated in other parts of the world and the dissemination of innovations in the productive fabric, which translates into the narrowing of technological gaps, increased productivity and the creation and sustainability of investment opportunities.

Chapter I focuses on the analysis of the level and trends of income concentration from three complementary perspectives: the distribution of current income of households and individuals on the basis of household surveys; trends in the functional distribution of income, on the basis of systems of national accounts and derived estimates; and the concentration of wealth, particularly the ownership of physical assets and of fixed- and variable-income financial assets.

As noted in previous editions of the *Social Panorama of Latin America*, income inequality between households and individuals has declined significantly in the region since the early 2000s. The simple average of the Gini index for 18 Latin American countries decreased from 0.543 in 2002 to 0.466 in 2017. However, the average annual pace of decline has slowed in recent years: from 1.3% between 2002 and 2008 to 0.8% between 2008 and 2014, and to 0.3% between 2014 and 2017 (see figure 1).

The decline in income inequality between 2014 and 2017 is explained, as in previous periods, by the fact that the average income in the first quintile increased proportionally more than that of the fifth quintile, or at least decreased to a lesser extent. The factors that determine increases or decreases in income in the lowest and highest resource groups over the period differ from country to country. Although in some cases the variation in income largely reflects changes in the distribution of labour income (which represents on average 72% of total household income), pensions and transfers also played a significant role, particularly in the lower income strata. This testifies to the importance of social protection networks, which were expanded and strengthened from the early 2000s in Latin America to contain distributive deterioration and, in more recent years, to avoid further setbacks in poverty reduction. These instruments include cash transfers and non-contributory pensions targeting families with limited resources, in some instances complemented by migrant workers' remittances.

Inequality in the capital and labour shares of the income generated in the production process, which is reflected in the low share of wages in national income, has long been a hallmark of Latin American and Caribbean economies. However, as has been observed in the distribution of households' current income, since the mid-2000s the share of the wage bill in total income increased in 8 of the 15 countries in the region for which this information is available, thereby reversing the fall that had occurred since the 1970s; a similar dynamic occurred in the developed countries, but from considerably higher levels. The improvement was more significant in the South American countries (see figure 2).

Figure 1

Latin America (18 countries): Gini coefficient of income inequality, 2002–2017[a]

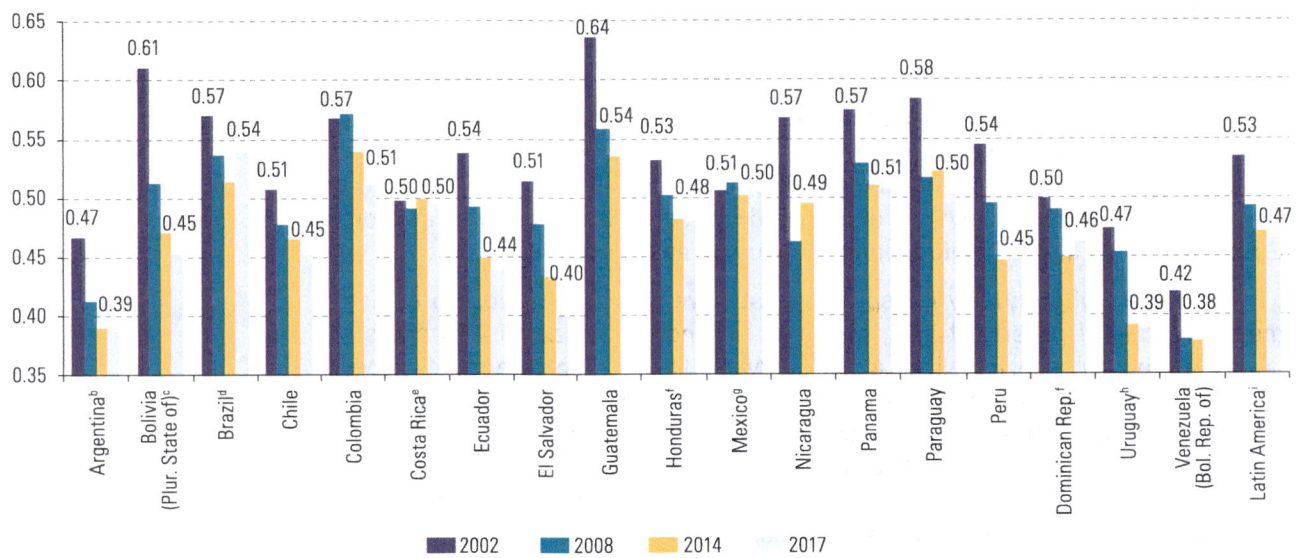

Source: Economic Commission for Latin America and the Caribbean (ECLAC), on the basis of data from the Household Survey Data Bank (BADEHOG). The figures by country shown in the graph may be consulted in annex table I.A1.1 at the end of chapter I.

[a] The calculation of the Gini coefficient included zero incomes.
[b] Urban total.
[c] Figures for 2017 refer to 2015.
[d] Figures for 2017 not comparable with those of previous years.
[e] Figures from 2010 onward not comparable with those of previous years.
[f] Figures for 2017 refer to 2016.
[g] Figures for 2016 estimated on the basis of the 2016 statistical model for MCS-ENIGH continuity.
[h] Figures for 2002 refer to the urban area.
[i] Average based on nearest available year's data for each of the 18 countries.

Figure 2

Latin America (15 countries): share of wages in GDP (at market prices), weighted average for the total region and subregions[a]
(Percentages)

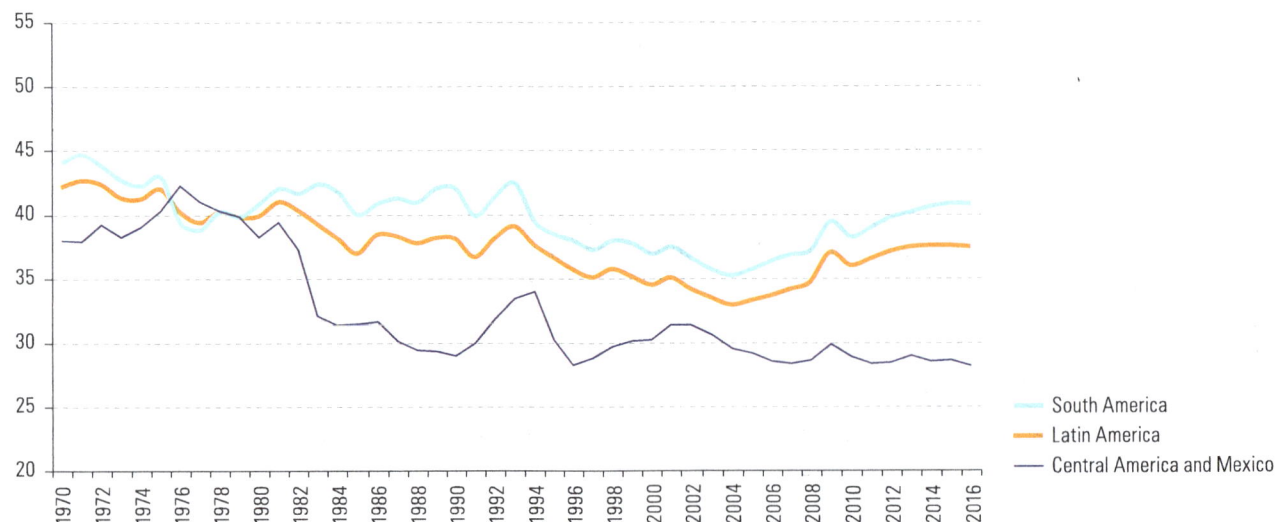

Source: Economic Commission for Latin America and the Caribbean (ECLAC), on the basis of official information from the countries and United Nations, UNdata [online database] http://data.un.org.

[a] Average weighted by current GDP in dollars.

Since 2005, the region's average economic growth has gone hand-in-hand with an increase in the wage share, a trend that was interrupted by the 2009 crisis but then continued until 2014, when the lowest rates of unemployment and poverty were recorded. Public policies contributed to this result: countries where this dynamic was more intense not only experienced strong economic growth, but implemented a significant set of policies to promote job creation, the reduction of informal labour activity, wage growth (including the minimum wage) and the strengthening of labour institutions, especially labour oversight, collective bargaining and social dialogue mechanisms. Since 2014, however, the increase in the wage share of GDP has weakened on average in the region, although this varies greatly among countries.

Given the configuration of labour markets, it is essential to also consider the labour income of the non-wage-earning employed (own-account workers and employers). Chapter I presents estimates that show the share of labour income participation over 25% higher, on average, than the wage share traditionally published in the national accounts.

Another key to understanding socioeconomic inequality is the analysis of the structure of ownership of physical and financial assets, since wealth and extreme wealth are central issues of development and public policy. The distribution of assets between the State, families and companies is a significant indicator of the level of polarization, concentration or inequality of the social structure, and in turn a key component of the socioeconomic inequality matrix in the region. Studies on Chile, Uruguay and Mexico presented in the chapter show that inequality among families in the wealth distribution is higher than inequality measured by income, while asset ownership inequality is greater for financial than for physical assets. In Chile, the Gini coefficient of total assets (physical and financial) has a value close to 0.72, which contrasts with the 0.45 Gini coefficient of the distribution of households' current income. In Uruguay, the Gini index of physical and financial assets is 0.67, much higher than the 0.39 for current per capita income, according to 2014 data. In Mexico, the Gini concentration was 0.69 for the value of dwellings and 0.78 for contracts in brokerage firms (value of investment in financial assets), compared with 0.50 for the distribution of current per capita household income.

In short, Latin America has made major strides in reducing household and individual income inequality since the early 2000s, as well as in improving the functional distribution of income (increasing labour's share of GDP) since the middle of that decade. However, both processes slowed from 2014 onward. Studies on the distribution of ownership of physical and financial assets in three Latin American countries show that inequality in this area is greater than in the distribution of current income. It is essential to refine the traditional instruments and methodologies for measuring inequality in these areas in order to analyse the factors that reproduce or mitigate inequalities in Latin American societies and to design policies that will underpin progress towards greater equality.

B. Recent and long-term poverty trends

Chapter II offers an updated review of the magnitude and trends of poverty and extreme poverty in Latin America and the factors relating to these. After 12 years in which poverty and extreme poverty rates in the region decreased significantly, in 2015 and again in 2016 both rates rose. The figures for 2017 show a further rise, albeit a small one, in extreme poverty, while the overall poverty figure shows no variation from 2016. For 2018, GDP growth is expected to support a small reduction in the poverty rate, while the extreme poverty rate will remain unchanged (see figure 3).

Figure 3
Latin America (18 countries): poverty and extreme poverty rates, and persons living in poverty and extreme poverty, 2002–2018[a]
(Percentages and millions of persons)

A. Percentages

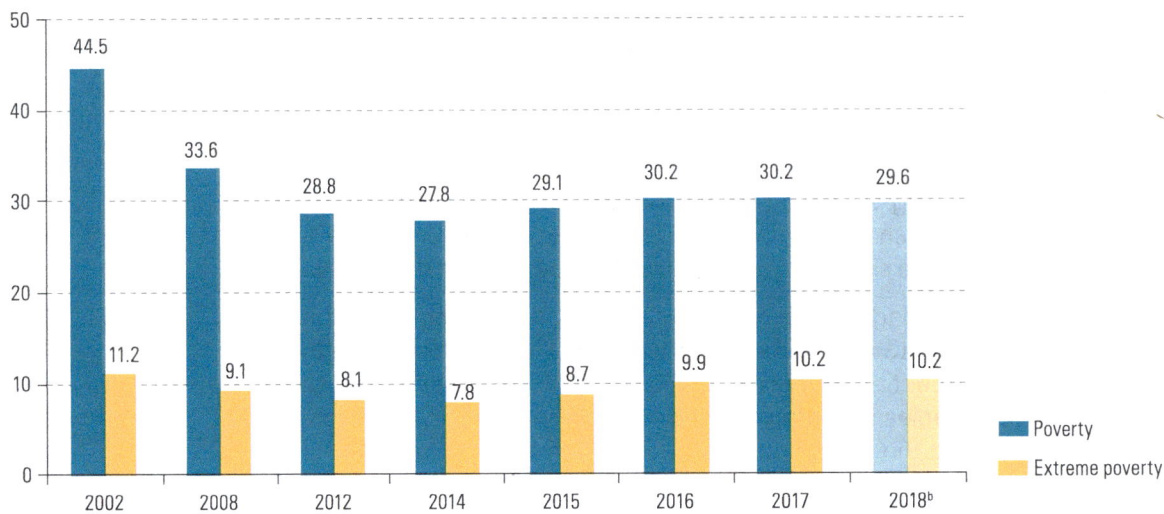

B. Millions of persons

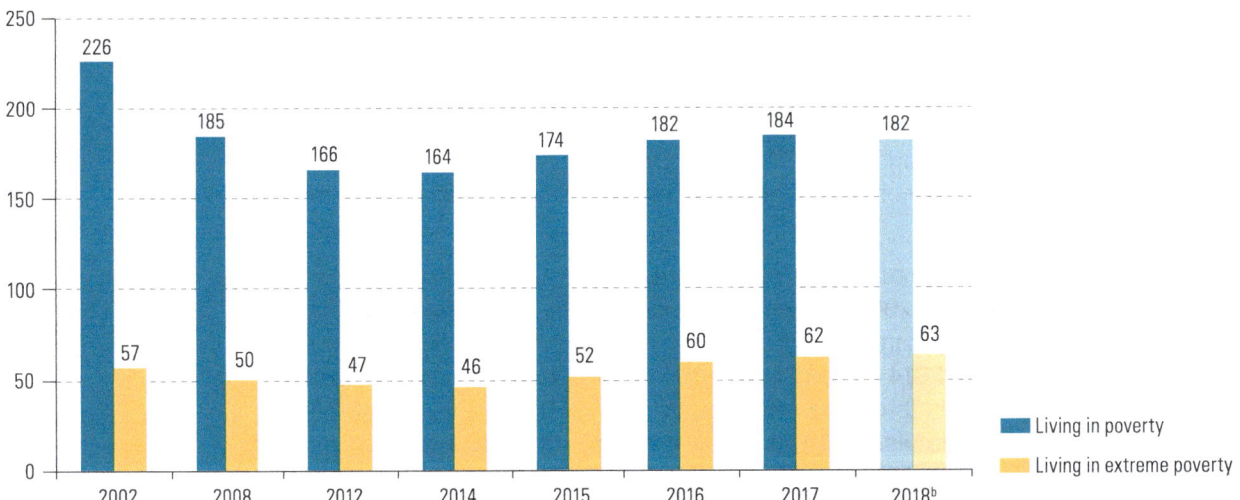

Source: Economic Commission for Latin America and the Caribbean (ECLAC), on the basis of data from the Household Survey Data Bank (BADEHOG).
[a] Weighted average for the following countries: Argentina, Bolivarian Republic of Venezuela, Brazil, Chile, Colombia, Costa Rica, the Dominican Republic, Ecuador, El Salvador, Guatemala, Honduras, Mexico, Nicaragua, Panama, Paraguay, Peru, Plurinational State of Bolivia and Uruguay.
[b] The figure for 2018 is a projection.

The increase in the number of poor in the region in 2017 reflects the combined variations in different directions seen or projected in the countries. According to estimates by the Economic Commission for Latin America and the Caribbean (ECLAC), of the 12 countries with information available to 2017, poverty fell by more than 1 percentage point in six, and increased in one. In two other countries which do not have household survey data available for 2017, the variations in per capita output suggest that poverty rates have increased.

It is important to analyse the prospects for reducing poverty in the context of the Sustainable Development Goals. The first target of Goal 1 is to eradicate extreme poverty for all people everywhere by 2030, and the second is to reduce at least by half the proportion of men, women and children of all ages living in poverty in all its dimensions by that same year. The behaviour of monetary poverty is directly related to the way in which household income grows and is distributed; accordingly, it is possible to project how poverty would evolve in different scenarios of income growth and distributive change. If both variables followed a similar trajectory to the average observed from 2008 to 2017, a group of 10 countries could reduce extreme poverty by up to 3% and 11 countries could halve poverty by 2030 (see figure 4).

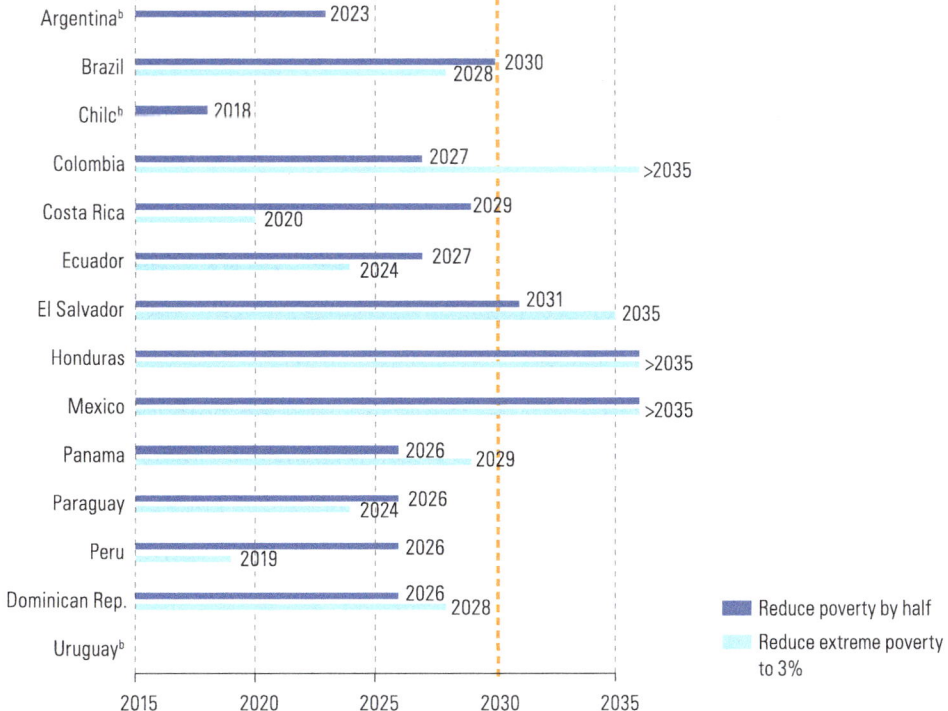

Figure 4
Latin America
(14 countries): year in which poverty reduction targets would be reached, if income growth and inequality reduction trends continue to follow their current trajectories[a]

Source: Economic Commission for Latin America and the Caribbean (ECLAC), on the basis of data from the Household Survey Data Bank (BADEHOG).
[a] Countries with information available to 2016 or 2017.
[b] The absence of horizontal bars signifies that the target has been achieved.

These results offer two different perspectives. On the one hand, it is encouraging that the changes in income distribution and levels needed to meet poverty reduction targets are consistent with the regional trajectory of the last decade, assuming past performance is an indicator of feasibility. However, it is also a wake-up call to strengthen social protection systems, because some countries of the region will not meet the targets and because several countries performed much worse over the last three years than in the period 2002–2014.

Poverty and extreme poverty affect the population of Latin America differently depending on where they live and their sociodemographic characteristics. Poverty rates among people living in rural areas are around 20 percentage points higher than those in urban areas. Although poverty is measured at the household level, both poverty and extreme poverty are more prevalent among women than among men (in the case of people aged 20–59). Another widespread feature is that the lower the age group, the higher the incidence of poverty. The poverty rate among children and adolescents up to the age of 14 years is 19 percentage points higher than for those aged between 35 and 44, and 31 percentage points higher than for those aged 65 or over. Ethnicity also shows a clear association with poverty incidence. According to data from nine countries where household surveys allow self-identification of indigenous people, the poverty rate in this group is almost double that of the non-indigenous, non-Afrodescendent population. Lastly, employment status is another factor highly related to poverty status.

In sum, reducing poverty and extreme poverty continues to be a key challenge for the countries of Latin America, in a context of social, political and economic change. Although the region made great strides over the period between the 2000s and mid-2010s, setbacks have occurred since 2015, particularly with regard to extreme poverty. The region's poor performance in recent years, coupled with the weak economic cycle, calls for public policies on social protection and the labour market to be developed and strengthened, particularly with regard to social and labour inclusion and income redistribution measures. Efforts must be redoubled to promote high-quality jobs and to build and expand comprehensive and effective social protection systems, that would allow the population overall to rely on having the resources to live a decent life.

C. Social spending: public policies and trends in the labour market

Chapter III gives an updated analysis of the series of public social spending by central governments of the countries of the region in the period 2000–2016.[1] As a simple average, central government social spending in 17 Latin American countries was 11.2% of GDP in 2016, a small increase on the previous year and the highest level since 2000 (see figure 5A).[2] Social spending accounted for 51.4% of total public expenditure by central governments, a figure similar to that of 2015 and among the highest for the fiscal priority of social policies since 2000. This situation is estimated to have remained unchanged in 2017, on average. In the English-speaking Caribbean, the average social expenditure of the central governments of five countries (Bahamas, Barbados, Guyana, Jamaica and Trinidad and Tobago), at 11.6% of GDP in 2016, reflected strong growth since the beginning of the 2000 decade (see figure 5B). The Caribbean countries have allocated a smaller proportion of central government public resources to social issues (38% of total spending) than the Latin American countries, as public spending on other priorities accounted for a larger share.

Analysis by government function shows that, at the central government level, education and health remain the most significant functions in terms of the funding allocated. On average, these functions accounted for 4.1%, 3.9% and 2.2% of GDP, respectively, in the Latin American countries in 2016. These are also the functions whose resources expanded most between the early 2000s and 2016. Although the amounts involved are smaller, the housing and community amenities function almost doubled its proportion of GDP over the period analysed.

In the five English-speaking Caribbean countries analysed, the education function is the one that accounts for the most resources (ranging from 3.8% of GDP in 2008 to 4.1% of GDP in 2016), followed by social protection, with values of between 2.2%

---

[1] The data presented here relate only to central government coverage and the amounts may change significantly if broader coverage, such as general government or the non-financial public sector, is taken. This is particularly relevant in the case of countries that have federal structures or subnational governments with high levels of autonomy, such as Argentina, Brazil, Colombia and Mexico.

[2] No information is included for the Bolivarian Republic of Venezuela, Cuba or Haiti because they do not have up-to-date figures for the whole series.

and 3.4% of GDP in this decade, and health, which presents an upward trend that has taken it to 3.0% of GDP in 2016. The housing and community amenities function represents an average of between 0.8% and 1.3% of GDP in this group of countries.

Figure 5
Latin America and the Caribbean (22 countries): central government social spending, by function, 2000–2016
(Percentages of GDP)

A. Latin America (17 countries), 2000–2016[a]

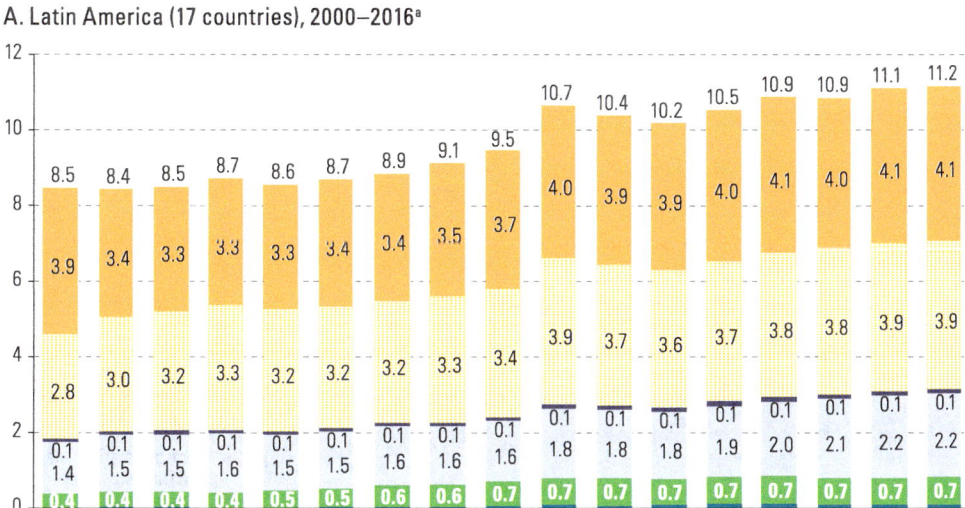

B. The Caribbean (5 countries), 2008–2016[b]

Legend:
- Social protection
- Education
- Recreation, culture and religion
- Health
- Housing and community amenities
- Environmental protection

Source: Economic Commission for Latin America and the Caribbean (ECLAC), on the basis of official information from the countries.
[a] The averages are arithmetic means of the values for 17 countries: Argentina, Brazil, Chile, Colombia, Costa Rica, Dominican Republic, Ecuador, El Salvador, Guatemala, Honduras, Mexico, Nicaragua, Panama, Paraguay, Peru, the Plurinational State of Bolivia and Uruguay.
[b] The averages are arithmetic means of the values for 5 countries: Bahamas, Barbados, Guyana, Jamaica and Trinidad and Tobago.

Average per capita central government social spending in the Latin American countries almost doubled between 2002 and 2016, to reach US$ 894, although this was very mixed across subregions and countries (see figure 6). The average for South America is twice as high as that of the group comprising Central America, Mexico and the Dominican Republic. Chile and Uruguay stand out as the countries allocating most resources per capita for social policies (US$ 2,387 and US$ 2,251, respectively), followed by Brazil, Argentina and Costa Rica (which spend US$ 1,631, US$ 1,469 and US$ 1,176, respectively). By contrast, El Salvador and the Plurinational State of Bolivia reach averages of about US$ 310, and Guatemala, Nicaragua and Honduras less than US$ 220.

Figure 6
Latin America (17 countries): per capita central government social spending, by subregion, 2000–2016[a]
(Dollars at constant 2010 prices)

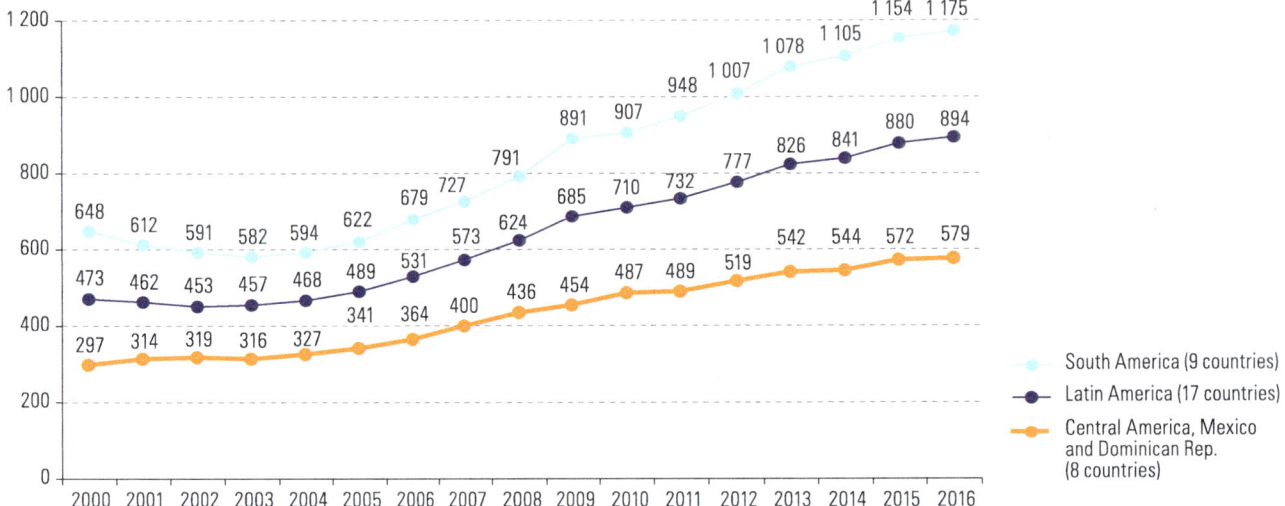

Source: Economic Commission for Latin America and the Caribbean (ECLAC), on the basis of official information from the countries.
[a] The averages are arithmetic means of the values for the countries. The 17 countries included are: Argentina, Brazil, Chile, Colombia, Costa Rica, the Dominican Republic, Ecuador, El Salvador, Guatemala, Honduras, Mexico, Nicaragua, Panama, Paraguay, Peru, the Plurinational State of Bolivia and Uruguay.

The region lags far behind in the availability of resources for social spending, both in absolute terms and in relation to the countries of the Organization for Economic Cooperation and Development (OECD) and the European Union. At the same time, the Latin American countries where the greatest efforts are required to combat poverty and which are most in need of services to ensure social rights and achieve the social targets of the 2030 Agenda for Sustainable Development have the fewest resources, both in absolute terms and as a proportion of their GDP.

Chapter III also offers a quantification by ECLAC of public expenditure on labour market policies, which allows analysis of its structure and recent trends in six countries of the region (Argentina, Chile, Colombia, Costa Rica, Mexico and Uruguay).[3]

Information by country shows various situations in terms of the level as well as the structure and trends of public spending on labour market policies. In relation to GDP, Costa Rica and Uruguay spend twice as much as the other four countries studied. While spending on labour market policies showed an upward trend between 2012 and 2016 in five countries, Mexico was the exception, as its public spending in that area fell from 0.91% to 0.35% of GDP between those two years. Regarding the structure of spending, Argentina focuses its fiscal effort on training and direct job creation, Colombia and Costa Rica on training and Uruguay on income protection in the event of

---

[3]   The analysis uses the classification of public measures aimed at the labour market developed by Eurostat, which has eight categories: (i) labour market services, (ii) training, (iii) employment incentives, (iv) sheltered and supported employment, (v) direct job creation, (vi) start-up incentives, (vii) out-of-work income support and (viii) early retirement.

unemployment. Chile and Mexico have more diversified structures: in Chile, the three main measures are training, direct job creation and employment incentives, while in Mexico they are start-up incentives, direct job creation and employment incentives.

The average public spending on labour market policies in the six countries was 0.45% of GDP in 2016, when the average for 28 OECD countries was almost triple that (equivalent to 1.31% of GDP). The great difference lies in out-of-work income maintenance and support programmes. Whereas in the six countries of Latin America this intervention category averages barely 0.1% of GDP, the figure rises to 0.72% of GDP in the OECD countries. This difference is explained by the lower level of development of these programmes in the countries of the region and the high degree of informality in their labour markets, in which a large proportion of workers do not have protection covering part of their income if they lose their jobs, even if there is a public system in place to cover that risk in their country.

In conclusion, despite the significant progress the region has made in terms of the level of social spending (both in terms of averages and per capita spending) since 2008, major challenges persist in financing for social policies, especially in the countries with the highest levels of poverty and other social development shortfalls. In addition, spending levels remain much lower than those in developed countries. If progress is to be made towards meeting the targets of 2030 Agenda for Sustainable Development, social spending will have to be protected and strengthened. It is also necessary to strengthen and expand the coverage of labour market policies and programmes, especially with regard to unemployment protection, as a fundamental part of integrated social protection systems. This will require policies to drive the formalization of employment and production units.

D. Structural challenges of inclusion and the labour market

Chapter IV examines some key dimensions of social and labour inclusion dynamics in the region and identifies gaps in access to social rights and services and to decent work. The Latin American and Caribbean region is confronting a complex social and economic situation, in which persistent structural challenges and disparities are compounded by new challenges. Stalled progress on poverty reduction, in conjunction with emerging dynamics associated with the technological revolution and demographic changes, as well as more frequent disasters and other factors, raise uncertainty levels and put sustainable development processes in Latin America and the Caribbean under threat. To turn a risk scenario into one of opportunities, it is important to analyse the dynamics of social and labour inclusion, and to identify the persisting areas of structural deficit. In particular, there is a need to address the inequalities faced by various groups in accessing social and labour inclusion mechanisms, which requires the implementation of policies which, while seeking to guarantee universal rights in these areas, are formulated in a way that is sensitive to differences.

In recent decades, the region has made great progress in various areas of social inclusion, such as the right to education, health care and access to basic infrastructure (water, sanitation, electricity and the Internet). Nonetheless, glaring inequalities persist both in the coverage of the services that uphold these rights and in their quality. Despite progress in enrolment and completion in secondary and tertiary education, profound socioeconomic gaps persist in these indicators (see figure 7). The gaps in the right to a quality education leave the region ill-prepared to confront technological challenges; and they make the school-to-employment transition more difficult, since there are major shortcomings in skills training.

Figure 7
Latin America
(18 countries): young
people aged 20–24
years with complete
secondary education,
and young people aged
25–29 with complete
tertiary education
(four years of study),
by income quintile,
2002–2016[a]
(Percentages)

A. Young people aged 20–24 years with complete secondary education

B. Young people aged 25–29 with complete tertiary education
(four years of study)

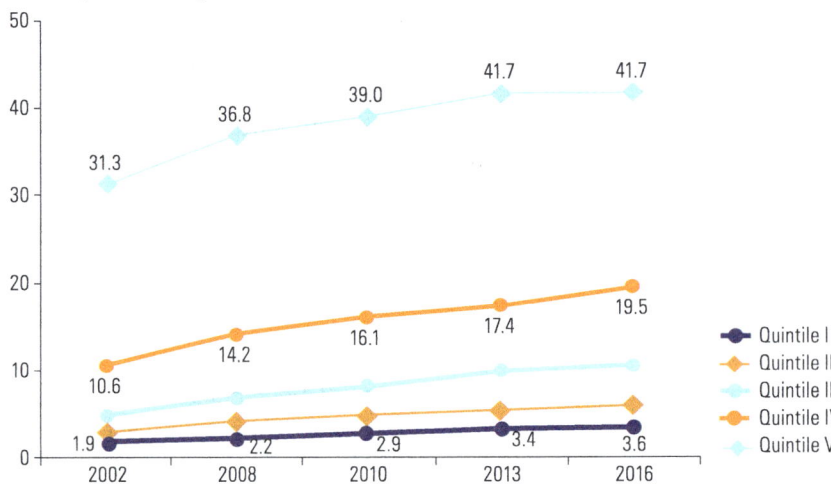

Source: Economic Commission for Latin America and the Caribbean (ECLAC), on the basis of data from the Household Survey Data Bank (BADEHOG).
[a] Simple averages.

As in education, advances in health are diverse and highly segmented along the main axes of the social inequality matrix. Economic and social contexts have a major influence on the development of diseases, and on their detection and treatment. Poverty, inequality and social exclusion have serious consequences for the population's health.

Access to basic infrastructure has improved continuously in the region, and its coverage has expanded into increasingly remote areas. Although the gaps have narrowed, there are still both quantitative and qualitative disparities in access between geographical areas and socioeconomic levels. In the case of access to more advanced services, such as digital infrastructure —which is increasingly important for social inclusion, given the rapid technological transformations and their penetration into the different areas of people's lives— growth has been accompanied by gaps that may exacerbate inequalities and entrench cores of exclusion.

ECLAC has often stated that work is the key to equality and a central means for people to access income to enable them and their families to achieve adequate living standards. Despite advances in labour market indicators between 2002 and 2014, which played an important role in reducing poverty and inequality, major labour inclusion challenges persist. The region's labour markets are characterized by an insufficient supply of jobs, significant gaps in the quality of those jobs, in access to social protection and in labour incomes, which are often below the legal minimum wages and insufficient to overcome poverty and achieve adequate levels of well-being, as a result of which a significant proportion of employed persons work long hours. The challenges are even greater for women, the youth population in transition from education to the labour market, indigenous peoples, persons of African descent and persons with disabilities.

As noted earlier, high rates of informality are a key feature of labour markets in Latin America and the Caribbean. Informality usually implies a lack of access to social security coverage in the areas of health and pensions; defined working hours (including weekly rest and paid annual leave); insurance against unemployment, workplace accidents and diseases; and maternity and paternity protection; among other rights under labour legislation. One of the least protected forms of labour market participation is unskilled self-employment, which is a major source of employment and income in the region's labour markets. This is a heterogeneous occupational category, but with tendencies towards precariousness, since it is usually concentrated in low-productivity sectors with little access to social benefits, especially to contributory social protection. Changes in the world of work, associated with the technological revolution, could further increase the proportion of self-employment.

In Latin America, a high proportion of employed persons have income below the respective national minimum wage. On average, around 40% of the working population is in this situation and that proportion is much higher among young persons, those aged over 65 and women at all stages of the life cycle (see figure 8).[4] Another sign that part of the employed population does not earn enough income to achieve adequate levels of well-being is the existence of significant income underemployment —in other words individuals who have to work very long hours to earn labour incomes above the relative poverty levels in their country. In 2016, around 20% of employed persons were in this situation, with a much higher proportion in rural (35%) than in urban areas (16%).

In order to move towards increasing levels of inclusion and participation in the benefits of development and in the exercise of rights, it is necessary to progress simultaneously in social inclusion and labour inclusion. Chapter IV also offers an exercise of measuring dual social and labour inclusion, which draws attention to persisting debts in Latin America in ensuring basic rights for large segments of the population, and emphasizes the interlinkages between access to social services and decent work. Dual inclusion refers to the ability of States to simultaneously guarantee universal access to rights to social services and basic infrastructure, regardless of income level and other household characteristics, as well as to people's engagement in paid work under dignified conditions, with decent jobs that give them access to labour rights and social protection and enable them to escape poverty. The proportion of households in a situation of dual social and labour market inclusion has risen continuously since 2002, while there has been a decline in the percentage of households in dual exclusion. Nonetheless, only one in four Latin American households is in a situation of dual inclusion; and the gaps are widening for the rural population, households headed by indigenous or Afrodescendent persons, and persons with disabilities.

---

[4]   Strictly speaking, minimum wage legislation applies only to wage-earning workers with an employment contract, so part of the employed population (informal wage-and non-wage-earners or those without a contract) is not legally covered by this regime. Nevertheless, the percentage of employed earning less than the minimum wage proxies for the proportion of workers who do not earn enough from their work to sustain a decent standard of living. Moreover, the minimum wage usually has a "beacon" effect, since it also serves as a benchmark for the income of the self-employed and part-time workers.

Figure 8

Latin America (18 countries): employed persons aged 15 years or over whose average earnings are below the national minimum wage, by gender and age group, around 2016[a]

(Percentages)

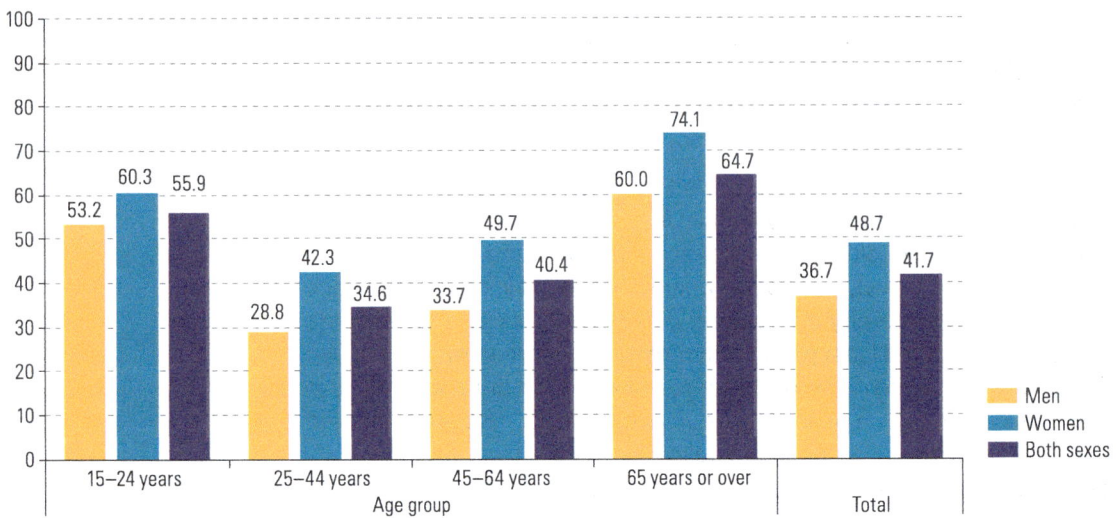

Source: Economic Commission for Latin America and the Caribbean (ECLAC), on the basis of data from the Household Survey Data Bank (BADEHOG).
[a] Simple averages. The countries included are: Argentina (urban areas), Bolivarian Republic of Venezuela, Brazil, Chile, Colombia, Costa Rica, the Dominican Republic, Ecuador, El Salvador, Guatemala, Honduras, Mexico, Nicaragua, Panama, Paraguay, Peru, Plurinational State of Bolivia and Uruguay (urban areas).

In short, these indicators confirm a panorama that raises issues for a region facing major challenges in ensuring social and labour inclusion for its population and in which deep inequalities persist —especially in the current context and the transformations currently unfolding in the world of work. In terms of access to social services, the region will face additional demands in the health and care sectors, associated with population ageing, while it is still consolidating universal opportunities in these dimensions and in access to education and its quality. In terms of labour inclusion, the improvements made in pension coverage, for example, or the capacity of labour incomes to sustain adequate living standards, are insufficient to close gaps. At the same time, phenomena such as the weakening of typical employment structures and the emergence of new modes of employment are intensifying. These directly affect requirements for training, education and digital inclusion, social protection systems and the quality of workers' labour force participation. A scenario is thus formed in which pre-existing deficits are compounded by emerging tensions, with uncertain results for the population's well-being.

In order to address persistent and emerging gaps in well-being, it is essential to adopt a universalist approach in public policies, contributing to the construction of welfare States. This will require mobilizing specific strategies that are sensitive to differences, to close access gaps that affect certain population groups and recognize the scenario of new and pre-existing risks that have an impact on society as a whole. In particular, it requires recognizing that social and labour inclusion are central and complementary dimensions of inclusive social development and of ensuring a basic level of well-being for all people. Social policy must foster progress in both areas simultaneously. Strengthening policies that increase coverage and access to education (at the various levels) and to health and infrastructure, while enhancing the quality with which these services are supplied, needs to be an active public policy in the region's countries, if they are to make headway on social inclusion. In turn, labour market institutions play a key role in improving working conditions and promoting decent work, both in terms of employment opportunities and unemployment protection, and in terms of remuneration, access to social security and observance of rights at work.

ECLAC recommends strengthening inclusive labour and labour market policies in conjunction with social security, to create good-quality jobs, encourage formalization, promote social dialogue and strengthen union organization and collective bargaining. The strengthening of universal and integrated systems of social protection is doubly linked to social and labour inclusion, insofar as its instruments promote access to social services and decent work. In short, States have available to them a range of public policies to address this twin challenge, which must be tackled in the light of the intertwined gaps that have been identified in terms of the axes that structure social inequality, lack of decent work and changes in the spheres of technology, economy and employment, demography and the environment.

E. Women's economic autonomy in a changing labour market

Chapter V employs statistical data to give an account of some of the structural constraints preventing gender equality in the sphere of labour. In Latin America and the Caribbean, there are structural barriers that limit women's full enjoyment of rights and progress towards gender equality. Globalization, changing demographic patterns, climate change, economic conditions and inequality in technology access and use within and between countries pose additional challenges to the achievement of gender equality.

The world of work plays a key role in eliminating or perpetuating inequality. From a gender perspective, a comprehensive analysis of the world of work is required: observing the dynamics of employment in the market but not disregarding unpaid work done in the home. The overburden of unpaid work acts as a barrier to women's full inclusion in decent work and deepens existing gaps.

The increase in the female participation rate in the past decades has not been matched by greater participation by men in unpaid work. There is a large group of women who are impeded from entering the labour market by family situations, especially care of dependants. This has brought the rise in women's participation rate to a standstill; at 50.2%, the female participation rate in 2017 remains lower than the male rate of 74.4%. In addition, women's unemployment is still higher than men's (10.4% and 7.6%, respectively, in 2017).

Latin American labour markets are also characterized by marked horizontal segmentation which restricts women's labour market participation and leaves them concentrated in certain sectors of the economy, such as care (education, health, social assistance and domestic employment), which makes up their largest source of employment (27.7%). This overrepresentation of women in the care sector is an extension to the labour market of the role assigned to them as caregivers. Another significant form of occupational segregation is women's high concentration in less-skilled occupations (see figure 9).

The emergence, interaction and confluence of a whole series of disruptive technologies have all the features of a new technological revolution that generates opportunities and challenges for societies and economies, reshaping the world of work. Technological changes could deepen gender gaps in the labour market, as the sectors where most jobs are expected to be lost are those in which women tend to be mostly employed, such as the service sector. Women are also likely to face greater difficulties in accessing the jobs that will be created from new technologies, because they are underrepresented in the sectors and occupations with the potential to expand the most.

Figure 9
Latin America (weighted averages of 9 countries): distribution of the employed population and wage gaps
between women and men, by occupation type and sex, around 2016[a][b][c]
(Percentages)

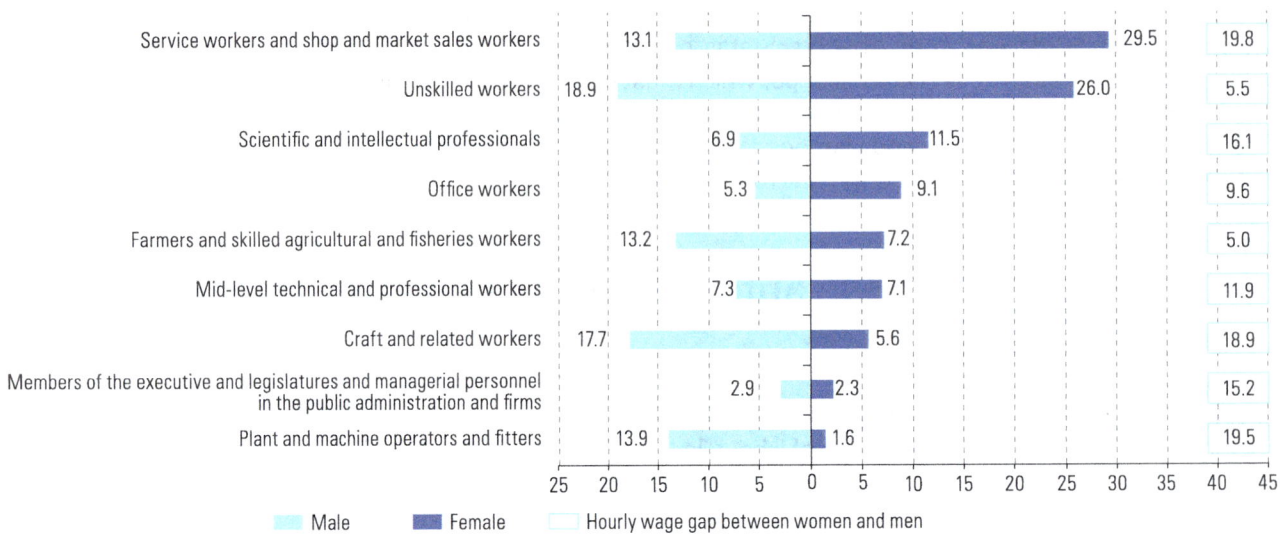

Source: Economic Commission for Latin America and the Caribbean (ECLAC), on the basis of data from the Household Survey Data Bank (BADEHOG).
[a] The left side of the figure refers to the total employed population of 15 years of age and over. The right side refers to the waged population. The wage gap refers to the
  difference in labour earnings between waged women aged 20–49 working 35 or more hours per week in urban areas and men with the same characteristics.
[b] The data are for 2016 in the cases of Argentina, Costa Rica, Ecuador, El Salvador, Panama, Peru and Uruguay and 2015 for Chile and the Plurinational State of Bolivia.
[c] Occupations were standardized for countries with information organized in accordance with the International Standard Classification of Occupations (ISCO-88).

The new technologies have enabled the emergence of new forms of work that have altered labour relations by establishing more flexible arrangements, but with weaker links between employer and worker and lacking access to traditional mechanisms of social protection. If the cultural forms and allocation of household and care tasks remain unchanged, these new types of work organization could further entrench traditional gender roles and jeopardize the progress made regarding equality between men and women.

To address the impact that technological changes will have on employment, the technological revolution will need to be accompanied by a transformation of education and technical and vocational capacity-building. These changes must occur in synergy with the demands of new markets and the challenges that persist in the region. In this context, it is important to develop new skills in advanced technologies associated with science, technology, engineering and mathematics (STEM) disciplines; socio-emotional skills for the resolution of complex problems; critical thinking and creativity among others. Women are underrepresented in these areas, representing only 34.6% of STEM graduates in the region (see figure 10).[5]

There is also persistent gender segmentation in the provision of technical and vocational education and training that is reproduced in the production system and employment opportunities, especially in good-quality employment.

Greater incorporation of women into the labour market would not only have a significant impact on economic activity, but would also improve the distribution of income and reduce poverty, while increasing women's economic autonomy. However, women's contribution to economic sustainability is not confined to labour market: they also contribute significantly to the economy through unpaid work. The economic contribution of unpaid work done in the household is equivalent to between 15.2% and 24.2% of GDP: in many countries a greater contribution than any other economic activity.

[5] Simple average for 2015 in 12 countries of the region (except Argentina, whose latest figure is for 2010), on the basis of UNESCO, "Data for Sustainable Development" [online] https://sdg.uis.unesco.org.

Figure 10

Latin America (12 countries): graduates in science, technology, engineering and mathematics (STEM) subjects, by sex, and graduates in STEM subjects as a proportion of all graduates, both sexes, between 2002 and 2015 [a] [b]
(Percentages)

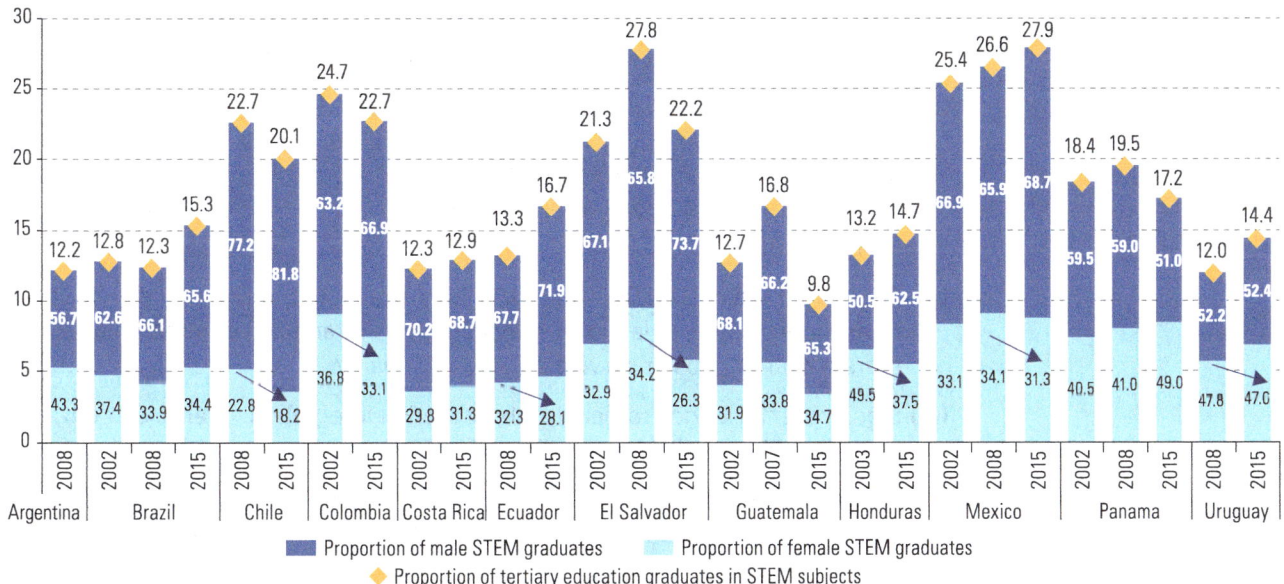

Source: Economic Commission for Latin America and the Caribbean (ECLAC), on the basis of United Nations Educational, Scientific and Cultural Organization (UNESCO), "Data for Sustainable Development" [online] https://sdg.uis.unesco.org/.

[a] STEM graduates by sex are calculated as the respective female and male proportions of all those graduating in STEM subjects each year.
[b] Tertiary education graduates in STEM subjects are calculated as a proportion of all tertiary education graduates.

Without public policies to promote women's engagement with STEM subjects, avoid employment impoverishment and precariousness, and increase co-responsibility in care systems, women not only risk being excluded from the benefits and opportunities of the jobs of the future, but might find that they continue to face the gaps and shortfalls in decent work that exist today. To avoid such outcomes, it is necessary to create an agenda of relevant policies suited to the regional context that takes account of the production structure, development strategies and interactions with the global economy and, most importantly, that mainstreams the gender perspective and is supported by prospective studies that can generate timely proposals for anticipating and keeping up with change.

F.   Concluding remarks

In short, the main messages of this edition of *Social Panorama of Latin America* are:

(i)   Poverty eradication continues to be a core challenge for the countries of Latin America. Although the region made major strides in this regard between the 2000s and the mid-2010s, setbacks have occurred since 2015, especially in extreme poverty.

(ii)   Particular attention needs to be afforded to the factors that lead to poverty disproportionately affecting children, adolescents and young people, the rural population and indigenous and Afrodescendent persons.

(iii) Income inequality decreased considerably between 2002 and 2017, but the pace of this process has slowed in recent years. The wage share in GDP has risen, but this too began to slow from 2014 onward.

(iv) Labour income, pensions and transfers to the poorest households play a key role in reducing poverty and income inequality. Social protection is essential to contain distributive deterioration and to avoid further setbacks in these indicators.

(v) Social spending has held steady as a proportion of total public spending and expanded faster than output between 2015 and 2016. This made a key contribution to progress over the period, but financing of social policies remains a major challenge. In a more adverse context, efforts will need to be made to strengthen social spending.

(vi) The period between 2002 and 2016 saw significant improvements in social inclusion indicators relating to education, health and basic infrastructure, but there are large gaps in service access and quality.

(vii) Significant challenges remain to labour market integration: unemployment, low income, high levels of informality and lack of protection at work.

(viii) Structural gaps in inclusion operate to the detriment of the rural population, women, young people and indigenous and Afrodescendent persons.

(ix) Given the changes occurring in the sphere of work, economic uncertainty and a weak growth cycle in the region, it is imperative to strengthen social and labour policies, in order to reduce poverty and inequality and tackle shortfalls in social and labour inclusion.

(x) In this context, gender inequalities must be addressed explicitly to prevent them from becoming further entrenched and to make progress in eliminating them.

(xi) It is crucial to develop universal, intersectoral policies that are sensitive to difference and geared towards increasing the coverage and quality of social services, social protection and decent work.

(xii) These policies need to be linked with the challenges of the changes needed in the production structure in order to achieve sustainable development with equality.

Socioeconomic inequalities in Latin America: recent trends in the distribution of income and wealth

Introduction

Inequality has been a long-standing structural characteristic of Latin American and Caribbean societies, which has been maintained and reproduced even in periods of economic growth and prosperity. Significant progress has been made in reducing inequality in the past decade, as reported in successive editions of *Social Panorama of Latin America;* nonetheless high levels of economic and social inequality persist. Latin America and the Caribbean remains the world's most unequal region, ahead of sub-Saharan Africa, with an average Gini coefficient that is nearly a third higher than in Europe and Central Asia.

The region's high levels of inequality hinder development and act as a powerful barrier to poverty eradication, expansion of citizenship, exercise of rights and democratic governance (ECLAC, 2016a). Significantly reducing inequality is a global commitment embodied in the 2030 Agenda for Sustainable Development, which recognizes equality as a key factor for international stability and conflict reduction. The Agenda's aim of ensuring that "no one is left behind" clearly reflects its universalist and inclusive motivation (ECLAC, 2018b).

While economic growth is fundamental for poverty reduction and for economic and social inclusion, high levels of inequality can significantly frustrate these processes. Inequality generates very marked barriers that make it difficult for people to rise socially, achieve higher levels of well-being than their parents, or aspire for their children to attain those levels, because the social structure tends to self-replicate through a differential structure of opportunities and a huge disparity of outcomes, which restricts mobility, particularly towards higher social strata. Inequality is perceived as particularly harmful when opportunities to improve the socioeconomic situation vary widely and when those at the top of the income distribution have gained that position through inheritance backed by a "culture of privilege" (Bárcena and Prado, 2016). Under these conditions, inequality can lead to social instability and delegitimize resource-allocation mechanisms, along with the systems that regulate them and the social groups that control them (ECLAC, 2016b).

For the Economic Commission for Latin America and the Caribbean (ECLAC) equality is a fundamental value of development and an unassailable ethical principle, not only because it provides policies with an ultimate foundation in rights, but also because it is a condition for moving towards a development model focused on innovation and learning. Such a model has positive effects on productivity, economic and environmental sustainability, dissemination of the knowledge society, and the strengthening of democracy and full citizenship. This emphasis stems from the recognition that inequality imposes high efficiency costs, since it results in economic agents having unequal access to capacities and opportunities; and it shapes rules of the game and incentives which can obstruct their full participation (ECLAC, 2018b).

Equality thus serves as a necessary condition for dynamic efficiency in the economic system, by creating an environment of institutions, policies and efforts for capacity building, speeding up innovation, the absorption of innovations generated elsewhere in the world and hence the closing of technological gaps, their dissemination in the productive fabric and, consequently, increased productivity and the opening of sustainable investment opportunities. Not only does equality promote efficiency in supply, but it also has positive effects on effective demand: a better distribution of income fuels demand growth and drives an increasingly diversified and competitive production structure (ECLAC, 2018b). Progress towards equality of resources, rights, opportunities, capacities, autonomies and recognition are necessary conditions for achieving the national and international social agreements that are essential for moving towards a sustainable style of development that fosters long-term economic growth that is compatible with social development and environmental stewardship.

This chapter analyses the level and trend of concentration in the income distribution, which is one of the key factors underlying the region's high inequality and serves as an obstacle to a sustainable development model. It approached this task from three different but complementary perspectives. First, it analyses recent and medium-term trends in the distribution of the current income of households and individuals, based on the household surveys conducted in each country. Secondly, it makes a long-term review of the trend of the functional distribution of income, in other words of changes in the shares of labour and capital in the incomes derived from the production and value added of the countries' goods and services (GDP), based on the systems of national accounts and derived estimates. Thirdly, it analyses the concentration of wealth, particularly the ownership of physical and financial assets that generate fixed and variable incomes, in three countries for which information is available from financial and similar surveys.

A.   The distribution of household income

Since the early years of the 2000 decade, income inequality has decreased sharply in the region, albeit more slowly between 2014 and 2017. The evolution of the gaps between lower and higher income groups largely reflected the changes that occurred in the distribution of labour incomes (which accounts, on average, for 72% of total household income), although pensions and transfers also played a significant role, particularly at the lower income levels. This indicates that the existing social protection systems have helped reduce income concentration since 2002, as noted in previous editions of *Social Panorama;* and, in recent years, they have helped to contain deteriorating distributional trends and avert major setbacks in the fight against poverty.

1.   Inequality as measured by traditional indicators

Continuing with the systematic monitoring of income inequality performed by ECLAC, this section describes its current status and evolution in recent years, based on information obtained from the most recent household surveys (which in most of the countries analysed were conducted in 2017).[1] The level and trend of inequality in the income distribution can be quantified using synthetic indicators that consider the relative situation of all individuals. The most widely used of these is the Gini coefficient, which takes values between 0 (total equality) and 1 (total inequality).

According to the most recent information available, the Gini coefficient averages 0.466 for Latin America as a whole.[2] In the 15 countries with data for 2016 or 2017, it ranges from over 0.5 in Brazil, Colombia, Mexico and Panama to below 0.4 in Argentina, El Salvador and Uruguay (see figure I.1).

---

[1]   The information used to measure distributional inequality is obtained from the various household surveys implemented in the region's countries to measure income. These may be employment, multipurpose and income and expenditure surveys. They are compiled and harmonized regularly by ECLAC to form part of the Household Survey Data Bank (BADEHOG).

[2]   Average for 18 countries based on 2017 data, except in the Plurinational State of Bolivia (2015); Honduras, the Dominican Republic and Mexico (2016); and the Bolivarian Republic of Venezuela, Guatemala and Nicaragua (2014)

Figure I.1

Latin America (18 countries): Gini coefficient of income inequality, 2002–2017[a]

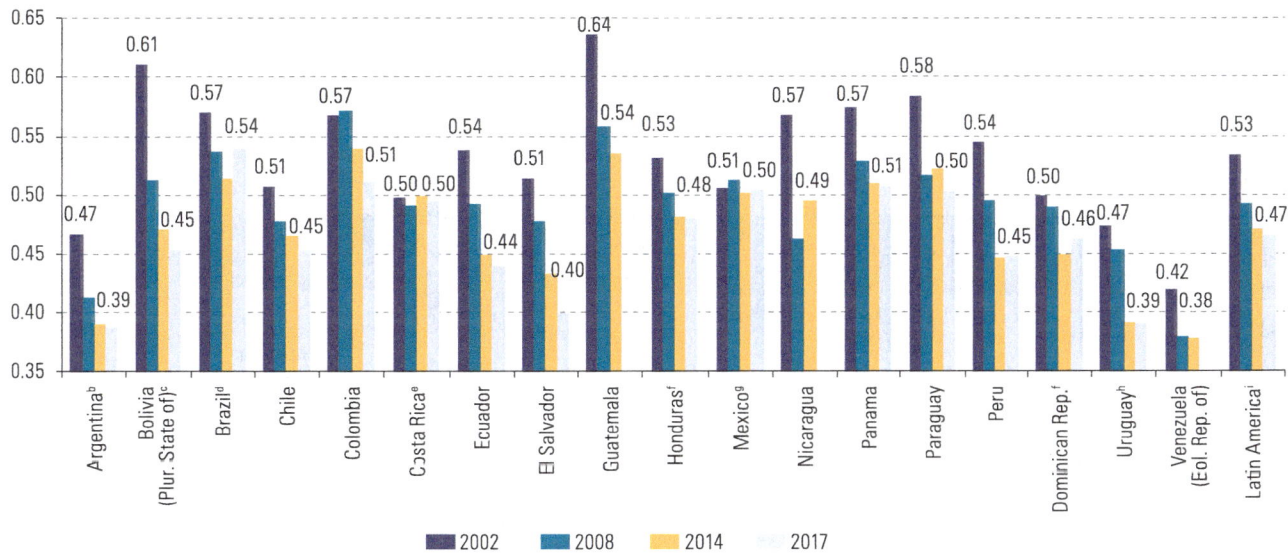

Source: Economic Commission for Latin America and the Caribbean (ECLAC), on the basis of Household Survey Data Bank (BADEHOG). The figures by country shown in the
graph may be consulted in annex table I.A1.1 at the end of the chapter.
[a] The calculation of the Gini coefficient included zero incomes.
[b] Urban total.
[c] Figures for 2017 refer to 2015.
[d] Figures for 2017 not comparable with those of previous years.
[e] Figures from 2010 onward not comparable with those of previous years.
[f] Figures for 2017 refer to 2016.
[g] Figures for 2016 estimated on the basis of the 2016 statistical model for MCS-ENIGH continuity.
[h] Figures for 2002 refer to the urban area.
[i] Average based on nearest available year's data for each of the 18 countries.

Although current levels of inequality are considerably lower than in the early 2000 decade (ECLAC, 2018a), in the last three years the regional average of this indicator has not changed significantly. The simple average of the Gini coefficients of the region's 18 countries fell from 0.534 in 2002 to 0.493 in 2008, and then to 0.471 in 2014 and 0.466 in 2017. The annual rates of reduction were 1.3% between 2002 and 2008, 0.8% in 2008–2014 and just 0.3% between 2014 and 2017.[3]

The variations recorded in 13 countries between 2014 and 2017 reveal heterogeneous situations. In Colombia, El Salvador and Paraguay the coefficient dropped by more than 1% per year, while Chile and Ecuador registered annual reductions of just above 0.5%. This indicator stayed broadly constant in the remaining countries analysed, except for the Dominican Republic where inequality actually increased, at least until 2016 (see figure I.2 and annex table I.A1.1).

---

[3]　The average for the 18 countries includes household surveys that are not comparable over the entire period. If just the surveys of the
13 countries that maintain comparability between 2002 and 2017 were used (those of Argentina, Chile, Colombia, Dominican Republic,
Ecuador, El Salvador, Honduras, Mexico, Panama, Paraguay, Peru, the Plurinational State of Bolivia and Uruguay), the rates of reduction
would be 1.2% per year between 2002 and 2008, 1.0% between 2008 and 2014 and 0.6% between 2014 and 2017.

Figure I.2
Latin America (13 countries): annual variation of the Gini, Theil and Atkinson inequality measures, 2014–2017[a][b]
(Percentages)

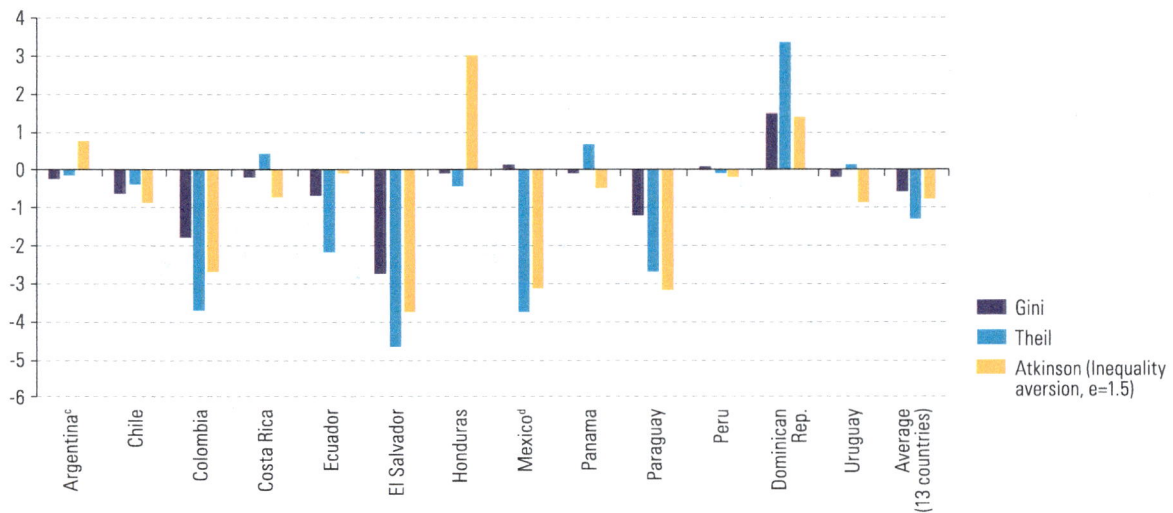

Source: Economic Commission for Latin America and the Caribbean (ECLAC), on the basis of Household Survey Data Bank (BADEHOG).

[a] The initial year used to estimate the variation was 2014, except in Chile (2013). The final year was 2017, except in Honduras, Mexico and the Dominican Republic (2016).

[b] The calculation of the Gini coefficient included zero incomes. To reduce the effect of extreme values, the Theil and Atkinson indices were calculated excluding values close to 0 and the three highest per capita incomes.

[c] Urban area.

[d] Figures for Mexico for 2016 were estimated on the basis of the 2016 statistical model for MCS-ENIGH continuity, prepared by the National Institute of Statistics and Geography (INEGI), to mitigate the lack of comparability between the 2016 survey and the 2008–2014 series.

The use of complementary indicators of income inequality, such as the Theil and Atkinson indices (with an inequality aversion coefficient of 1.5), makes it possible to assess whether the variations in the Gini coefficient adequately describe the trend of the income distribution.[4] Both of these indices corroborate the decreases and increases in inequality revealed by the Gini coefficient. Nonetheless, the Atkinson index, which is more sensitive to changes occurring in the lower part of the distribution, reports a distributive deterioration in Honduras that is not captured by the other two indicators. Moreover, the two complementary indices find that Mexico's income distribution improved in the period, but this is not detected by the variation in the Gini coefficient.[5]

Another common way to characterize the income distribution is through household shares in total income. The highest-income quintile (quintile V) accounts for about 45% of total household income, while the lowest-income quintile (quintile I) receives, on average, just 6%. The gaps between income groups are particularly pronounced at the higher end of the distribution, with the richest decile receiving 30% of total income, or twice the share captured by the ninth decile and five times that of the first quintile (see table I.1).

---

[4]   For a more detailed explanation of how to calculate and apply the inequality measures, see Atuesta, Mancero and Tromben (2018).

[5]   The figures for Mexico in 2016 are obtained from the "2016 statistical model for MCS-ENIGH continuity". The divergence between the results of the Gini coefficient and other inequality indicators may be affected by the characteristics of that model.

Table I.1
Latin America (18 countries): share of total income, by income quintile, most recent year[a]
(Percentages)

Country	Year	Quintile I	Quintile II	Quintile III	Quintile IV	Quintile V	
						Decile IX	Decile X
Argentina[b]	2017	10	16	17	22	14	21
Bolivia (Plurinational State of)	2015	5	12	18	25	16	25
Brazil	2017	5	10	12	20	15	38
Chile	2017	8	12	15	20	14	31
Colombia	2017	5	11	15	21	15	33
Costa Rica	2017	5	10	15	22	17	31
Dominican Republic	2016	7	11	16	21	15	30
Ecuador	2017	7	12	17	23	15	27
El Salvador	2017	8	13	18	23	15	24
Guatemala	2014	5	10	14	20	16	35
Honduras	2016	5	10	15	22	16	31
Mexico[c]	2016	6	11	15	21	15	33
Nicaragua	2014	5	10	16	21	14	34
Panama	2017	5	10	16	22	15	32
Paraguay	2017	5	10	15	21	14	35
Peru	2017	5	11	17	24	16	27
Uruguay	2017	10	14	17	22	14	23
Venezuela (Bolivarian Republic of)	2014	8	14	19	23	14	22
Latin America (simple average)		6	11	16	22	15	30

Source: Economic Commission for Latin America and the Caribbean (ECLAC), on the basis of Household Survey Data Bank (BADEHOG).
[a] Household income deciles ranked by per capita income.
[b] Urban area.
[c] Figures for Mexico for 2016 were estimated on the basis of the 2016 statistical model for MCS-ENIGH continuity, prepared by the National Institute of Statistics and Geography (INEGI) to mitigate the lack of comparability between the 2016 survey and the 2008–2014 series (see [online] http://www.beta.inegi.org.mx/proyectos/investigacion/eash/2016/).

Although the level of household income differs widely between the different quintiles, its composition by source is relatively homogeneous throughout the distribution, except in the first quintile. The main source of household income is pay for work, both wage-earning and self-employment, which jointly account for 72% of all income, on average. Income from paid work has a similar share in the second and higher quintiles; but it is a smaller proportion in the first quintile (64%); and, within paid work, the contribution of wage employment is lower. This is also the quintile in which monetary transfers (public and private) are most important, representing an average of 16% of per capita income (see figure I.3).

Pensions and transfers received by households represent between 13% and 19% of income in the different quintiles, with the composition varying throughout the distribution. In the first quintile, income from transfers (including non-contributory pensions, transfers from poverty reduction programs and remittances from households living abroad, among others) predominate, while in the fifth quintile, incomes from contributory retirement and other pensions are more important.

Other income, such as that obtained from asset ownership and imputed rent, represent between 12% and 16% in the various quintiles. Naturally, property income only gains a significant share in the fifth quintile (see section C), although this source is generally underreported in household surveys (see ECLAC, 2018a, chapter I).

Figure I.3

Latin America (18 countries): income sources, by quintiles, most recent year[a]

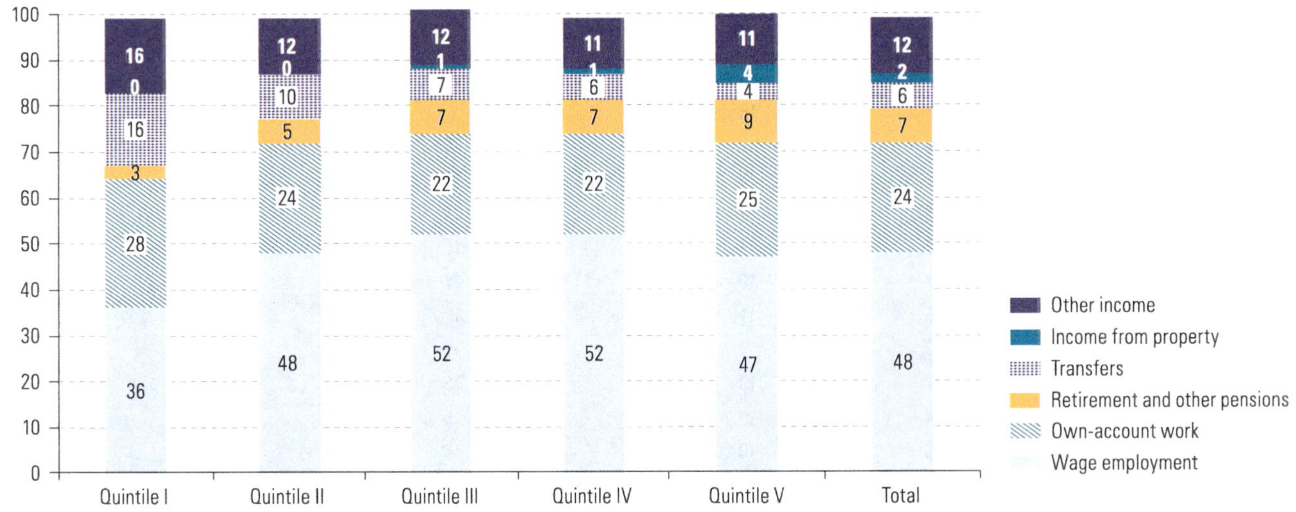

Source: Economic Commission for Latin America and the Caribbean (ECLAC), on the basis of Household Survey Data Bank (BADEHOG).

[a] Average based on available data for the year nearest to 2017 for each of the 18 countries. The countries included are: Argentina, the Bolivarian Republic of Venezuela, Brazil, Chile, Colombia, Costa Rica, Dominican Republic, Ecuador, El Salvador, Guatemala, Honduras, Mexico, Nicaragua, Panama, Paraguay, Peru, the Plurinational State of Bolivia and Uruguay.

Changes in the main income sources in the extreme quintiles of the distribution point to the factors that explain the recent trend in income inequality. In the five countries where the Gini coefficient fell by at least 0.5% per year between 2014 and 2017 (Chile, Colombia, Ecuador, El Salvador and Paraguay), the average income in the first quintile grew proportionally more than that of the fifth, or at least decreased by less. In Chile, the higher income growth in the first quintile was driven by income from work, transfers and other income. In El Salvador, the first quintile experienced real growth in average income from pensions and transfers and labour earnings, while the fifth quintile lost income on average, mainly owing to a reduction in labour income. In Colombia, the average income of the first quintile increased thanks to growth in labour income, which in the fifth quintile decreased in real terms, leading to a decrease in the average income of that group. In Paraguay, the first quintile's income rose owing to pensions and transfers and other income, while the fifth quintile lost income mainly owing to a fall in labour income. In Ecuador, average incomes in the first and fifth quintiles both declined because labour income fell by less in the first quintile (see figure I.4).

Of the remaining countries in which the Gini coefficient either decreased slightly or else increased in 2014–2017, in Argentina, Costa Rica, Mexico, Peru and Uruguay, average income in the first quintile grew by more than in the fifth quintile. Although these increases are largely explained by labour income (owing mainly to its share in total household income), increases in pensions and transfers explain between 10% and 20% of the variation in income in the first quintile. In Costa Rica and Uruguay, however, it accounted for half of the income growth of the poorest 20% of the population). Lastly, in Panama, although the total income of the highest quintile was similar to that of the lowest, the improvements recorded in the latter are mainly the result of increases in pensions and transfers. In contrast, reductions in these same sources explain most of the deterioration in total income of the first quintile in Honduras.

These data highlight the importance of the social protection network that has been set up and consolidated in the region since early in the 2000 decade (especially monetary transfers and non-contributory pensions targeted on low-income families and, in some cases, remittances), to mitigate the distributional deterioration of recent years and avoid further setbacks in the fight against poverty.

Figure I.4

Latin America (13 countries): annual variation of per capita income and contribution of the main income sources, first and fifth quintiles, 2014–2017[a]
(Percentages)

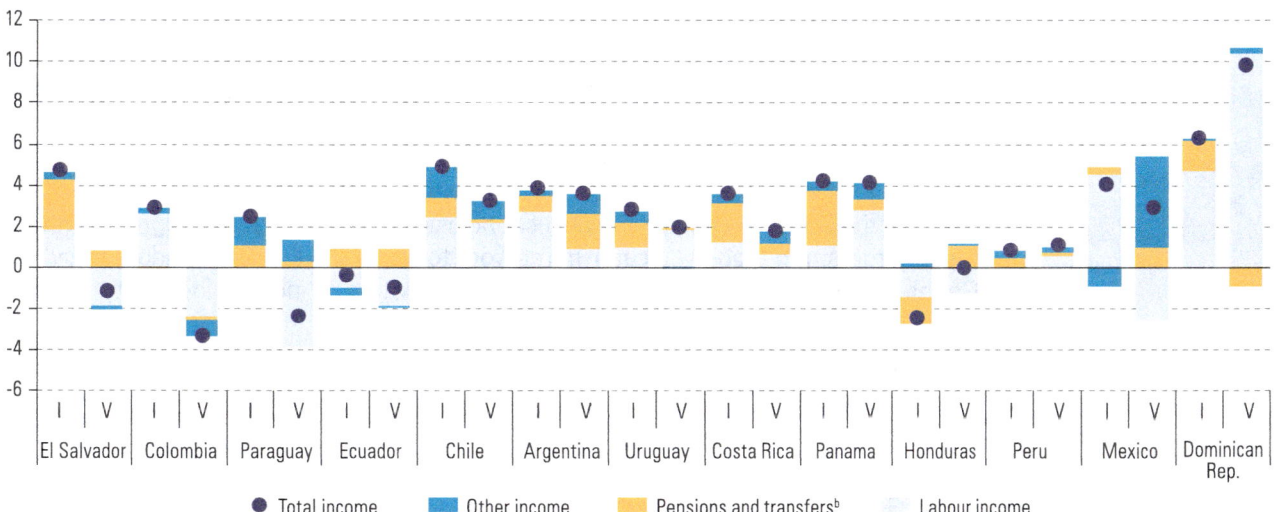

Source: Economic Commission for Latin America and the Caribbean (ECLAC), on the basis of Household Survey Data Bank (BADEHOG).
[a] Countries in which the Gini coefficient fell by more than the regional average, ranked by the size of the reduction. The initial year used to estimate the variation was 2014, except in Chile (2013). The final year was 2017.
[b] Refers to public and private transfers including, in the latter case, remittances from abroad and from other households within the country.

As noted above, the large share of labour income in households' total income suggests that distributive changes in both income streams are likely to be closely related. Indeed, the variations in the Gini coefficient of labour income per employed person recorded between 2014 and 2017 are very similar to those of the Gini coefficient of per capita income described above. Only in Mexico does the distribution of labour income show a clear improvement, which is not reflected in the result for the population at large, since it is offset by a deterioration in the distribution of other income (see figure I.5).

Figure I.5

Latin America (13 countries): annual variation of the Gini coefficient of per capita income and labour income per person employed, 2014–2017[a]
(Percentages)

Source: Economic Commission for Latin America and the Caribbean (ECLAC), on the basis of Household Survey Data Bank (BADEHOG).
[a] The initial year used to estimate the variation was 2014, except in Chile (2013). The final year was 2017, except in Honduras, Mexico and the Dominican Republic (2016).

2.   Reducing inequality in the context of the Sustainable Development Goals

The Sustainable Development Goals (SDGs), adopted in September 2015 by the United Nations General Assembly, are a benchmark for monitoring the income distribution. Goal 10 consists of reducing inequality both within and among countries; and its various targets include two that concern inequality between individuals. The first of these is to progressively achieve and sustain income growth of the bottom 40 per cent of the population at a rate higher than the national average; the second is to empower and promote the social, economic and political inclusion of all. To quantify progress towards these targets, the global indicator framework to follow-up the Goals, adopted by the General Assembly in July 2017, includes two indicators of income inequality that are relevant to the analysis of this section.

The first target of SDG 10 requires that the income of households in the lower part of the distribution grow at a faster rate than the rest of the population. If the 2014 figures are taken as a reference, one year before SDG adoption, six of the region's countries had advanced towards that target. In the three countries with the largest fall in the Gini coefficient in this period (Colombia, El Salvador and Paraguay), income in deciles I to IV grew by at least 2 percentage points more than average income, even though average income fell in real terms in two of the countries. Chile, Costa Rica and Mexico also experienced income growth in the first four deciles of about 1 percentage point above the average, even though the Gini coefficient did not fall in two of those countries. In Argentina, Panama and Peru, income growth in the lower part of the distribution was similar to the average, while in the Dominican Republic it was below average (see figure I.6).

Figure I.6

Latin America (13 countries): annual variation of the income of the first to fourth deciles and of the total population, and annual variation of the Gini coefficient, 2014–2017[a]

(Percentages)

Source: Economic Commission for Latin America and the Caribbean (ECLAC), on the basis of Household Survey Data Bank (BADEHOG).

[a] The initial year used to estimate the variation was 2014, except in Chile (2013). The final year used was 2017, except in Honduras, Mexico and the Dominican Republic (2016).

[b] Urban area.

[c] Figures for Mexico for 2016 were estimated on the basis of the 2016 statistical model for MCS-ENIGH continuity, prepared by the National Institute of Statistics and Geography (INEGI) to mitigate the lack of comparability between the 2016 survey and the 2008–2014 series.

The second key indicator of the income distribution is the proportion of the population living with incomes below 50% of median per capita income. This indicator is commonly used in the European Union and the countries of the Organization for Economic Cooperation and Development (OECD) to identify the population at risk of poverty or social exclusion (European Union, 2017).[6] Although the indicator does not conform to the notion of "relative poverty" when its incidence is similar to or lower than the absolute poverty rate, as is the case in several of the region's countries (ECLAC, 2013a), it indicates the size of the population with incomes far below the average of the society in which it lives. From this standpoint, albeit incompletely, the indicator is used globally to represent the target of empowering and promoting the social, economic and political inclusion of all.

According to the most recent information available for 14 countries around 2017, the proportion of the population with incomes below 50% of the median varies between 13.6% (in Argentina, urban area) and 24.8% (in Panama); and the simple average is 18.8% (see figure I.7). This measure of inequality has improved since the start of the millennium, albeit more slowly than the Gini coefficient; but the pace of improvement has slackened recently. While 21.9% of the population (14 countries) had per capita incomes below 50% of the national median around 2002, by 2008 the proportion had dropped to 20.3% and in 2014 to 19.0%; but it only decreased by a further 0.2 of a percentage point between then and 2017.

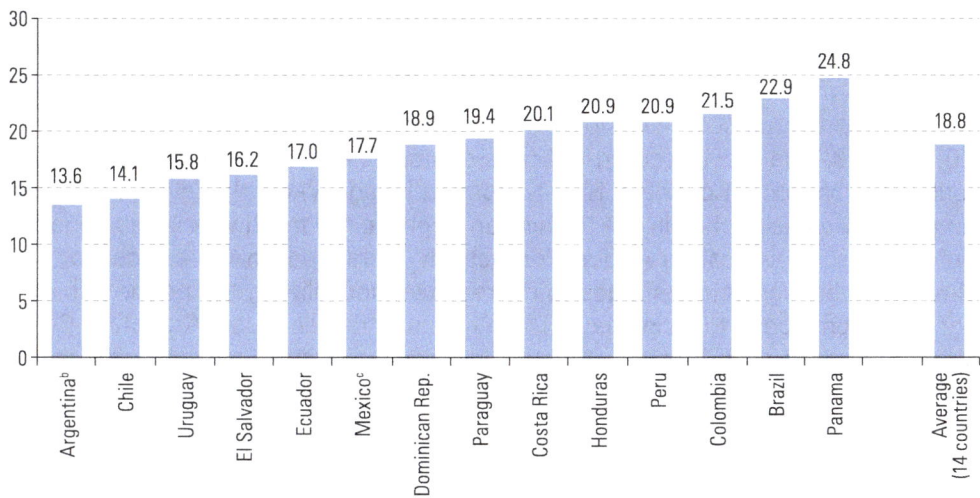

Figure I.7
Latin America
(14 countries): population
with per capita incomes
below 50% of the
median, 2017[a]
(Percentages)

Source: Economic Commission for Latin America and the Caribbean (ECLAC), on the basis of Household Survey Data Bank (BADEHOG).
[a] Data correspond to 2017, except in Honduras, Mexico and the Dominican Republic (2016).
[b] Urban area.
[c] Figures for Mexico for 2016 were estimated on the basis of the 2016 statistical model for MCS-ENIGH continuity, prepared by the National Institute of Statistics and Geography (INEGI) to mitigate the lack of comparability between the 2016 survey and the 2008–2014 series.

The changes that occurred between 2014 and 2017 produce a more heterogeneous situation than what emerges from the indicators analysed previously. Firstly, there was an improvement in the relative position of lower-income populations in Colombia, El Salvador, Mexico and Paraguay, where the proportion with per capita incomes below 50% of the national median fell by at least 2% per year. In Chile and Ecuador, where the Gini coefficient decreased, the proportion with incomes below half the median remained unchanged in the first case and increased in the second. In contrast, this indicator rose in Honduras and in the Dominican Republic; but only in the latter was this reflected in the variation of the Gini coefficient (see figure I.8).

---

[6]   The indicator "Population at risk of poverty or social exclusion" is calculated on the basis of "adult-equivalent" income. When the existence of economies of scale in household consumption are taken into consideration, adult-equivalent income implies an increase in purchasing power relative to per capita income (which is the measure used in the Sustainable Development Goals).

Figure I.8
Latin America
(13 countries): annual
variation in people with
incomes lower than 50%
of the median,
and Gini coefficient,
2014–2017[a]
*(Percentages and
percentage points)*

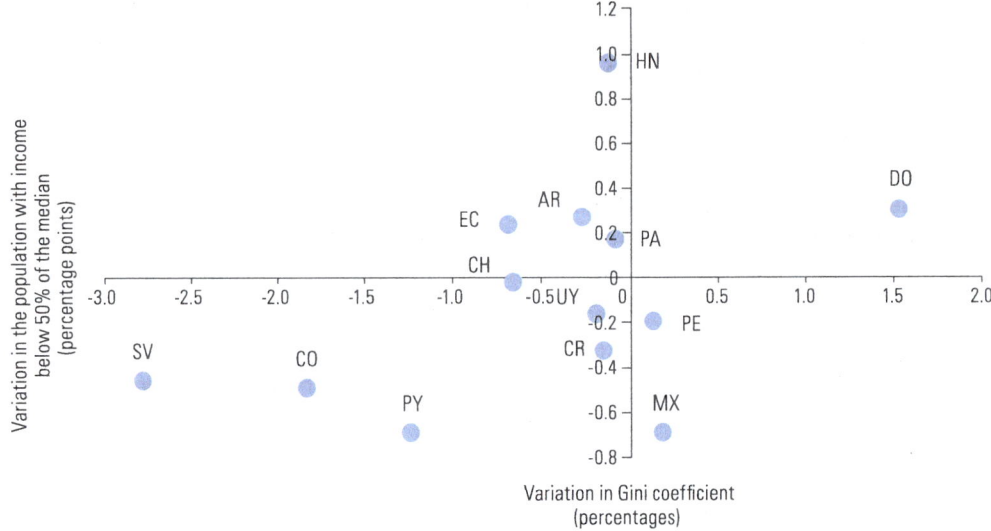

Source: Economic Commission for Latin America and the Caribbean (ECLAC), on the basis of Household Survey Data Bank (BADEHOG).
[a] The initial year used to estimate the variation was 2014, except in Chile (2013). The final year was 2017, except in Honduras, Mexico and the Dominican Republic (2016).

In summary, this section uses different indicators to confirm the significant reduction in income inequality that has occurred in Latin America since 2002, and the fact that this process has slowed most recently. Considering the latest years (2014 and 2017) in the 13 countries where comparable figures are available for the period, only in three (Colombia, El Salvador and Paraguay) did the levels of income inequality decrease, while in the Dominican Republic the trend was in the opposite direction, as the indicators in question actually worsened. In Chile, Ecuador and Mexico, several indicators suggest a decrease in inequality in the period, while in Honduras some point to an increase. The other countries analysed (Argentina, Costa Rica, Panama, Peru and Uruguay) did not generally display significant variations in their levels of inequality.

The data presented in the section also show the important role played by labour incomes in the increase or decrease in the concentration of income during the period. This is closely related to the share of this income source in total household income (72% on average). The analysis also reveals the importance of the social protection network that has been set up and strengthened in the region since the early 2000 decade (especially monetary transfers and non-contributory pensions targeted on the lowest-income families) to mitigate the concentration of income that has occurred since 2002. An analysis of what happened in the 13 countries with comparable data for 2014–2017 shows that these transfers have helped to contain distributional setbacks and avoid major reversals in the fight against poverty in recent years.

In the following paragraphs, inequality is analysed from a second perspective: the functional distribution of income, in other words the distribution of the remuneration received by labour and capital from the production of GDP in the different countries. The analysis not only takes a long-term view, but also uses the most recent data, to describe a trajectory similar to that observed in the distribution of household income, which largely depends on the trend of labour income in the different socioeconomic strata.

B. The functional distribution of income

Since the middle of the 2000 decade, the functional distribution of income has improved: the share of wages in total income has grown in eight out of 15 countries in the region, thus reversing the decline seen since the 1970s (which was similar to the trend in developed countries, but starting from much lower levels). This positive trend in the functional distribution of income has been more accentuated in the South American countries. Since 2014, however, the pace of improvement has slackened in terms of the regional average, despite wide variations between countries. Given the way the region's labour markets are structured, it is also crucial to consider the incomes of employed persons other than wage earners (own-account workers and employers), which also represent remuneration for work. Including this income category raises the labour share of national income by nearly 25%, on average, above the wage share traditionally published in the national accounts.

1. Share of wages in total income

Interest in the functional distribution of income has been growing among numerous researchers and institutions, partly because of the sustained decline in labour's share of total income in developed countries since the 1980s. The past decade has witnessed a proliferation of studies analysing the factors associated with this dynamic. Many of them explain this declining trend (with different emphases) in terms of the roles played by globalization, technological change, financialization and institutional changes —the latter mainly in the labour market, such as the unionization and collective bargaining processes (Guscina, 2006; ILO, 2010; OECD, 2012; Stockhammer, 2013; Giovannoni, 2014; Berg, 2015; Dao and others, 2017; Ciminelli, Duval and Furceri, 2018). In contrast, other studies warn of the potential effects of this trend, in particular, on the business cycle or the personal distribution of income (Lavoie and Stockhammer, 2013; ILO, 2013; Alarco Tosoni, 2014). They also analyse the characteristics of the phenomenon on the production structure (Giovannoni, 2014; ECLAC, 2016b; Dao and others, 2017) and in the distinction between what is happening between wage earners and other workers (Gollin, 2002; Young, 1995; Giovannoni, 2014; Abeles, Amarante and Vega, 2014).

Inequality in the capital and labour shares of the income generated in the production process, which is reflected the low share of labour in national income, has been a historical feature of Latin American and Caribbean economies. The absence of homogeneous and systematic long-term information has made research in this field more difficult; but, in recent years, there has been a renewed effort to generate data and analysis (Lindenboim, 2008; Frankema, 2009: Bértola and others, 2008; Alarco Tosoni, 2014). In particular, ECLAC (2017) shows that the contribution of Alarco Tosoni consists not only of the systemization of the available data on the functional distribution of income, but also its historical characterization. It drew attention to the declining trend in the wage share since the 1970s, along with the high levels of heterogeneity among the region's countries in terms of both levels and dynamics. ECLAC has also made contributions that incorporate the income of non-wage earners (Abeles, Amarante and Vega, 2014); it has analysed the functional distribution with a production approach (Abeles, Arakaki and Villafañe, 2017); and it has considered the relationship between the primary and secondary phases of income distribution either empirically (ECLAC, 2017) or conceptually (Cimoli and others, 2017; ECLAC, 2018b).

This section systemizes and updates the available information (for methodological details and data sources, see box I.1) to examine the dynamics of recent years, while maintaining the long-term perspective of *Social Panorama of Latin America 2016* (ECLAC, 2017). As noted in that publication, the share of wages in total income has decreased since the 1970s in most of the region's countries for which information is available, although with high degrees of heterogeneity.[7] Costa Rica and Honduras depart from the general trend; and, in the former, the wage share has increased since the mid-1980s. In the other countries, current levels are lower than at the start of the period analysed, but with widely differing magnitudes (see figure I.9). In some cases, the wage share in income is less than 5 percentage points smaller than in the early 1970s (El Salvador, Argentina, Brazil, Colombia and Paraguay). In others, the fall exceeds 10 percentage points (Bolivarian Republic of Venezuela, Chile, Mexico, Nicaragua, Panama and Peru).

Box I.1
Construction of long-term series of the share of wages in GDP

Reconstructing homogeneous long-term series of wage earners' GDP share in the region's countries raises a number of methodological issues, including the type of indicator to be used, how series of this type should be spliced, and the data sources in each country.

The indicator most frequently used in studies on this subject is the ratio of "doubly gross wages" (the sum of employed workers' wages, and the employee and employer social security contributions) to GDP at current prices. Although analyses of each country are normally based on gross value added at basic prices, whereas gross value added at factor cost is currently being used, in this exercise the series relative to GDP at market prices are published to provide a dataset that is more homogeneous between countries (following Alarco Tosoni (2014). The estimation based on gross value added at factor cost is only used in figure I.15 to standardize the comparison with the labour income share estimated by OECD. The estimations for the average of the region and its subregions are weighted by GDP in dollars at current prices, as published in UNdata.

As successive changes have been made to the base year in systems of national accounts, the splicing method applied is crucial. In this exercise, three alternatives were considered. The first and most widely used is to apply the growth rates that arise from the series of the previous base year to the level established by the new base year. This procedure was performed on labour income, gross value added at factor cost and GDP at market prices, to obtain gross operating surplus, taxes on production and imports net of subsidies, as residuals. This technique is commonly used, but for constant price values. Given the need to splice the series at current prices —which in the region's countries raises an additional difficulty owing to the effects of high-inflation processes and currency changes— it was decided to consider other methods.

One of these involves interpolation between base years, which consists of respecting the estimated values for the year chosen as the base and estimating values for the intervening years by linear interpolation. The trend of the previous series is used as an indicator of changes between the base years. Although there is consensus that this is the recommended method for splicing series at current or nominal values, in countries where there is a very marked difference between two different bases for the same year, the interpolated wages-to-GDP values might always be in the same direction (increase every year or decrease every year) when the original series indicates otherwise, due to the large size of the correction factor.[a] Moreover, in the region's systems of national accounts, it is usual for the official estimates of a new base year to include updated information from the previous years, consistent with the new methodology. If the linear interpolation methodology were strictly observed, part of the information consistent with the last base year would be lost. For both reasons, but especially because of the magnitude of the correction factor between bases in some countries, it was decided to make a third estimate.

With the estimate finally chosen, steps were taken to maintain the level of the wages/GDP ratio according to the most recent base year in each country's national accounts and to backcast it based on the percentage point difference relative to the previous base. This means respecting the percentage point differences in the original data for each of the base years. When data for the same year or period under two or more base years overlap, the data for most recent

---

[7]　The long-term dynamics in each country are shown in the annex.

Box I.1 (concluded)

base year was always used. Lastly, it should be noted that the estimates made using this methodology, as well as the results obtained from splicing using the growth rates technique, produce small differences in all countries (less than one percentage point), except for Chile and Peru.

The general data sources used were the digital data held in CEPALSTAT, official information from the countries in question and, in some cases, the figures estimated by Alarco Tosoni (2014) to complete the periods that lacked official data from some countries. The sources and specific considerations for each country are detailed below.

In Argentina, the data for 1970–1992 were obtained from Kidyba and Vega (2015); and information for 1993–2007 came from the 1993 income generation account (CGI93) published by the National Institute of Statistics and Censuses (INDEC, 2018a). The data corresponding to 2004, 2016 and 2017 came from the 2004 income generation account (CGI04) of INDEC (2018b). Given the absence of official information between 2008 and 2015, an estimate was made similar to that reported by Kennedy, Pacífico and Sánchez (2018). This methodology consists, firstly, in performing a splice between CGI04 and CGI93 by linear interpolation. Secondly, the data contained in CGI04 for 2004, 2016 and 2017 were used to perform an estimation for 2005–2015, using as inputs the number of private registered workers and the number of private and public non-registered workers, along with their respective remunerations. The data on wages and the number of registered wage earners in the private sector are taken from the statistics of the Argentine Integrated Pension System (SIPA). The information on non-registered private employment, public employment and the respective remunerations is obtained from the processing of the Permanent Household Surveys (EPH) published by INDEC. In the Plurinational State of Bolivia, the data source for 1970–1977 is National Accounts Bulletin, No. 3 (INE, 1989). Data for 1978–1986 were obtained from the definitive 1978–1986 national accounts of the National Institute of Statistics (INE, 1989a). Data for 1987 was approximated on the basis of the rate of growth of nominal average wages and the employed population, according to data contained in the 1987 and 1988 annual reports of the Central Bank of Bolivia (1987 and 1988). For the period 1988–1997 the data source is ECLAC (2013b), and for 1998–2016 the statistics published by the National Institute of Statistics (INE, 2018). In Brazil, the data source for 1970–1989 is Alarco Tosoni (2014), and for 1990–1999 ECLAC (2008 and 2013b). The data for 2000–2015 are based on statistics published by the Brazilian Institute of Geography and Statistics (IBGE, 2018). In Chile, data for 1970–1995 were obtained from ECLAC (2013b); and those for the period from 1996 to 2016 were completed with the *Cuentas Nacionales de Chile* statistical yearbooks published by the Central Bank of Chile (2006 and 2018). In Colombia, the data for 1970–1999 were obtained from ECLAC (2013b); and data for 2000–2016 are based on statistics published by the National Administrative Department of Statistics (DANE, 2018). In Costa Rica, data for 1970–1990 come from ECLAC (2013b), and for 1991–2016 from the Central Bank of Costa Rica (2018). In Honduras, data for 1970–1999 were obtained from ECLAC (2013b), while those for 2000–2016 come from the statistics published by the Central Bank of Honduras (2018). In Mexico, data for 1970–2002 come from ECLAC (2013b), and for 2003–2016 the statistics published by the National Institute of Statistics and Geography (INEGI, 2018). In Panama, data for 1970–2006 were obtained from ECLAC (2013b), while those for 2007–2016 are based on statistics published by the National Institute of Statistics and Census (INEC, 2018a and 2018b). In Paraguay, data for 1970–1990 come from ECLAC (2013b), and for 1991–2016 they come from the statistics published by the Central Bank of Paraguay (2018). In Peru, the data source for 1970–1990 is ECLAC (2008), while data for 1991–2016 are based on statistics published by the National Institute of Statistics and Information (INEI, 2018). In Uruguay, data for 1970–1996 were obtained from Alarco Tosoni (2014). The information corresponding to 1997–2016 was provided by the ECLAC office in Montevideo, on the basis of official information from the country up to 2005 and estimates since that year based on the trend of the average nominal wage index, the employment rate and GDP. The data for the first two of these variables come from the National Institute of Statistics (INE), while the GDP figures were obtained from the Central Bank of Uruguay (2018). Lastly, in the Bolivarian Republic of Venezuela, the data source for 1970–1996 is ECLAC (2013b), while data for 1997–2014 are based on statistics published by the Central Bank of Venezuela (2018). Information for 2015 was taken from the United Nations database (2018).

Source: Economic Commission for Latin America and the Caribbean (ECLAC), on the basis of official information from the countries.

[a] This happens in the case of Peru, which for 1991 has a wages/GDP ratio of 25% according to the 1979 base year, but 33% according to the 1994 base year. For 1994, it has a wages/GDP ratio of 28% according to the 1994 base and 38% according to the latest 2007 base. The situation in Costa Rica is similar, but the difference in this case is 6 percentage points.

Figure I.9
Latin America
(15 countries): share of
wages in GDP (at market
prices) between the
early 1970s and the
latest available data[a]
(Percentages)

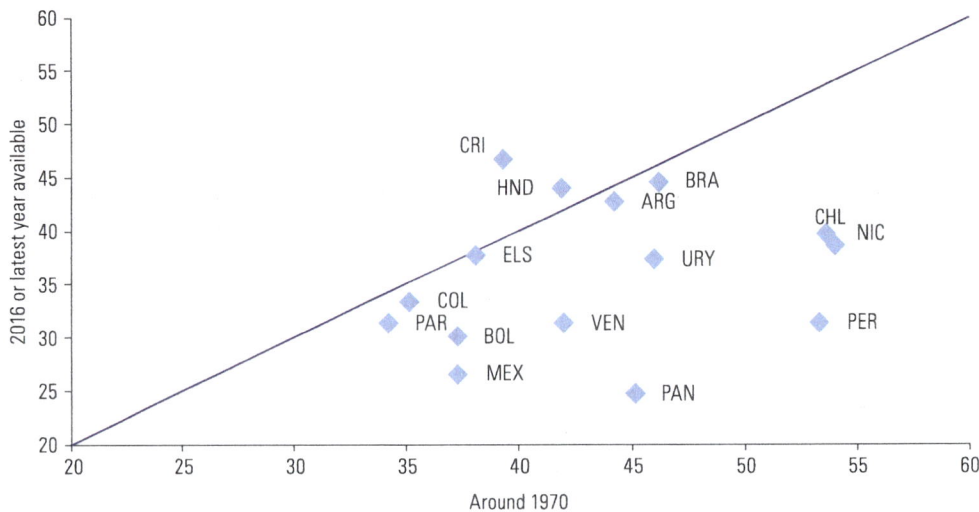

Source: Economic Commission for Latin America and the Caribbean (ECLAC), on the basis of official information from the countries.
[a] For most countries 2016, except for the Bolivarian Republic of Venezuela and Brazil (2015).

Heterogeneity in the levels and dynamics of the wage share also applies for different subperiods, thereby reflecting the complexity of structural factors related to the accumulation, economic, social and political models that determine GDP shares. In a stylized reading, as noted by Alarco Tosoni (2014), the highest shares were attained in the 1960s or early 1970s, during intensive industrialization processes or in sociopolitical conjunctures favouring workers that prevailed in the different countries. The changes that occurred in the region thereafter (growth models, the 1980s debt crisis, the weakening of workers' bargaining power, higher levels of unemployment and job insecurity, among other factors) are associated, in differing degrees, with the declining share of wages observed until the 1990s. For the region as a whole, the wage share declined by an average of over 4 percentage points in the two decades, with steeper falls particularly in South America: wage earners in Chile, Argentina, Paraguay and Peru ended the 1980s with their share of total income down by more than 10 percentage points. In the group of countries comprising Central America and Mexico, the largest falls were recorded in Mexico, Nicaragua and Panama.

Although in the first half of the 1990s the share of wages in total income grew in several countries (Argentina, Brazil, Chile, Costa Rica, Mexico, Paraguay and Uruguay), at the end of that subperiod and following the crisis of 2002, the average pace of growth faltered, particularly in South American countries. In contrast, Central America and Mexico performed more strongly as a group in those years, thanks to the trend in Mexico, owing to its relative size.

The 2016 edition of *Social Panorama of Latin America* (ECLAC, 2017) notes that, in several countries of the region, the average wage share has increased by nearly 4 percentage points since 2004 (in some cases since 2005). Once again, there are differences between individual subregions and countries. Much of this growth is explained by developments in South America (see figure I.10). Between 2004 and 2014, wage earners in eight of the 15 countries with data available gained a larger share of total income (particularly in Argentina, Uruguay, the Bolivarian Republic of Venezuela and Brazil in South America, and also Costa Rica and Nicaragua in Central America); in two others the changes were minor, while in the remaining five the wage share decreased significantly (by over 1.5 percentage points, see table I.2).

Figure I.10
Latin America (15 countries): share of wages in GDP (at market prices), weighted average for the total region and subregions[a]
(Percentages)

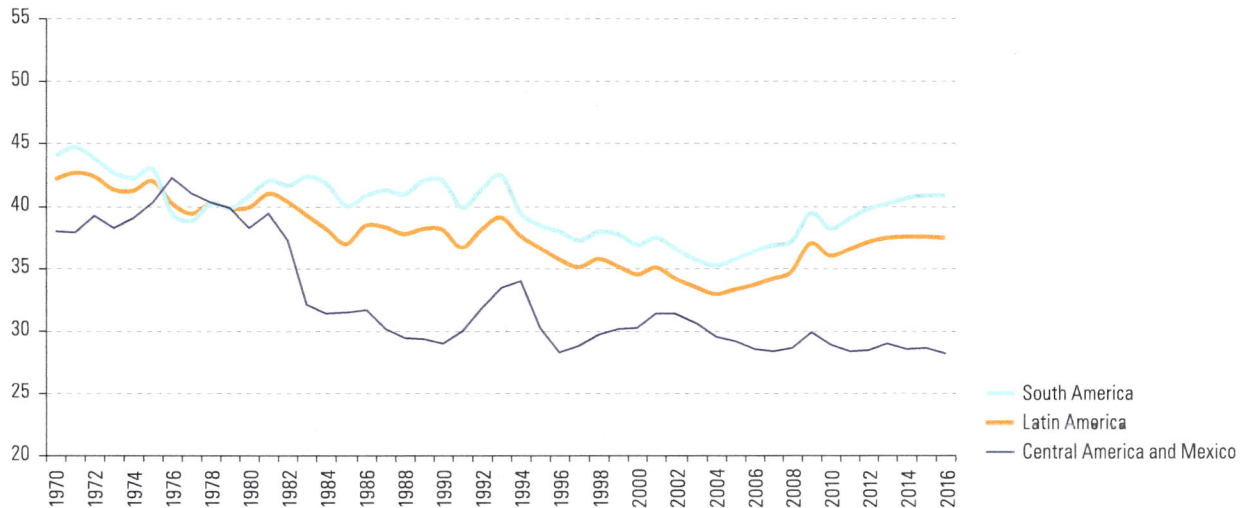

Source: Economic Commission for Latin America and the Caribbean (ECLAC), on the basis of official information from the countries and United Nations, UNdata [online database] http://data.un.org.
[a] Average weighted by current GDP in dollars.

Table I.2
Latin America (15 countries): variation in the share of wages in GDP (at market prices), selected periods
(Percentage points)

	1970-1980	1980-1990	1990-2003	2003-2014
Argentina	-8.1	-2.3	-6.8	15.0
Bolivia (Plurinational State of)	2.6	-3.0	-0.3	-8.4
Brazil	-2.6	4.9	-9.9	5.0
Chile	-4.6	-7.0	5.4	3.0
Colombia	2.6	-4.3	1.5	-1.3
Costa Rica	2.6	1.1	0.7	4.8
El Salvador	15.3	-7.3	-2.6	-1.9
Honduras	4.9	2.5	-1.5	0.2
Mexico	0.4	-10.1	2.2	-2.5
Nicaragua	-11.4	9.7	-18.1	6.1
Panama	-5.1	1.8	-5.7	-10.1
Paraguay	0.5	-10.5	6.6	2.8
Peru	-6.1	-3.0	-7.5	-3.8
Uruguay	-12.8	3.3	-0.4	3.6
Venezuela (Bolivarian Republic of)	0.8	-8.1	-4.0	5.7
Latin America[a]	**-2.3**	**-1.9**	**-4.6**	**4.0**
South America[a]	**-3.3**	**1.0**	**-6.2**	**4.9**
Central America and Mexico[a]	**0.3**	**-9.2**	**1.6**	**-2.1**

Source: Economic Commission for Latin America and the Caribbean (ECLAC), on the basis of official information from the countries.
[a] Average weighted by current GDP in dollars.

To compare the two periods, it is useful to study whether the increase or decrease in the share of wages in total income occurred in an economic-growth context. During the first half of the 1990s, the region's economic growth was accompanied by an increase in the share of wages, particularly in Central America and Mexico (see figure I.10). Nonetheless, the characteristics of the capital accumulation models, in conjunction with the growth of unemployment and the precarious nature of the jobs created, led to a subsequent period of economic growth in which the relative situation of workers deteriorated. This reached its lowest point with the crisis in the first few years of the twenty-first century, which involved a substantial fall in the wage bill that lasted until 2004.[8]

When considering short-term dynamics, it is important to analyse the growth of wages in relation to the phase of the economic cycle. In general, recessions (including economic crises) can occur when the wage share of total income is increasing, because economic activity adjusts more quickly than employment and workers' pay. In several episodes of this type, employment adjusts with a lag, associated with the effects of "labour hoarding".[9] As economic crises deepen, the wage share declines as a result of lay-offs or wage cuts.

Figure I.11 illustrates this phenomenon, by comparing the (weighted average) share of wages in the region with per capita GDP (in purchasing power parity (PPP) dollars). The years of economic growth (recession or crisis) are read to the right (left) on the horizontal axis while the increase (decrease) in the wage share is measured up (down) on the vertical axis. The effect in question is clearly visible in 1998, 2001 and 2009, when economic activity declined but the wage share increased. After each of these years, the share of wages decreased, with the 2001 crisis having the greatest and longest impact (with falls in three consecutive years up to 2004).

Figure I.11
Latin America (15 countries): share of wages in GDP (at market prices) and GDP per capita in PPP dollars,[a] weighted average for the whole region, 1990–2016

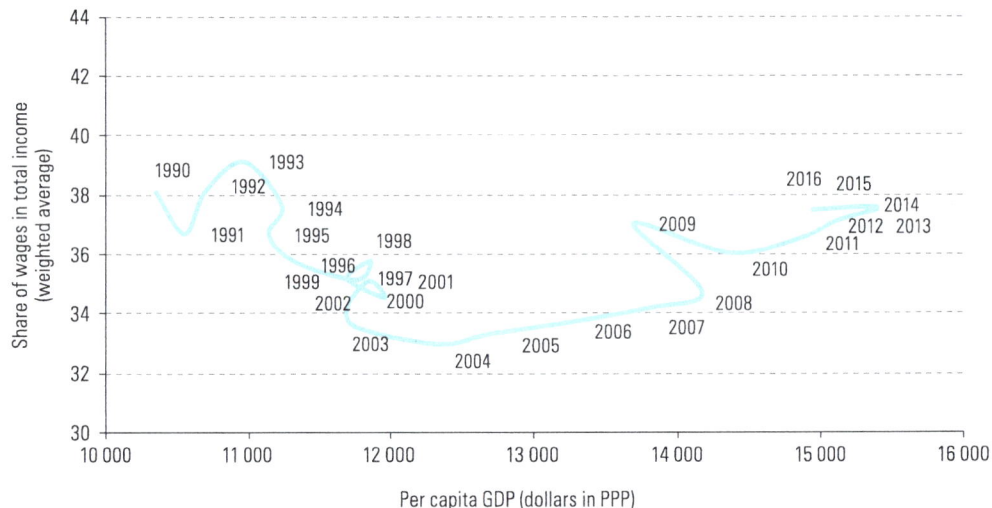

Source: Economic Commission for Latin America and the Caribbean (ECLAC), on the basis of official information from the countries and United Nations, UNdata [online database] http://data.un.org.
[a] Average weighted by current GDP in dollars.

As noted above, since 2005 the region's average economic growth has gone hand-in-hand with an increase in the wage share, a trend that was interrupted by the 2009 crisis but then continued until 2014, when the lowest rates of unemployment and poverty were recorded. Public policies contributed to this result. In particular, countries where this dynamic was more intense not only experienced strong economic growth, but implemented a significant set of policies aimed at strengthening labour institutions (labour law, minimum wage hikes, increased labour inspection and the creation or revival of social dialogue mechanisms, among others), along with job creation, the reduction of informal labour activity, wage growth and the strengthening of collective bargaining processes.

---

[8]   The long-term trajectory of each country's share of wages in GDP is shown in annex figure I.A1.1.
[9]   When confronted by a cyclical downturn, firms often postpone decisions to lay off staff and, in particular, keep the most skilled workers on, while awaiting a reversal of the cycle. This phenomenon is accentuated the higher the cost of staff adjustment (not only monetary cost, but also in terms of loss of worker skills and knowledge) and expectations regarding an upturn in the business cycle.

Since 2014, in a context of weaker economic growth (contraction of per capita GDP) the improvement process has slowed on average, owing to developments in some of the larger economies, particularly Mexico and Argentina, and also in Colombia and Peru.[10] The only country to diverge from this trend is the Plurinational State of Bolivia, where wage earners' share in total income has grown more strongly since 2013, although from a significantly lower level than in most of the countries analysed (see figure I.12).

Figure I.12
Latin America (14 countries): share of wages in GDP (at market prices), 2014–2016
(Percentages)

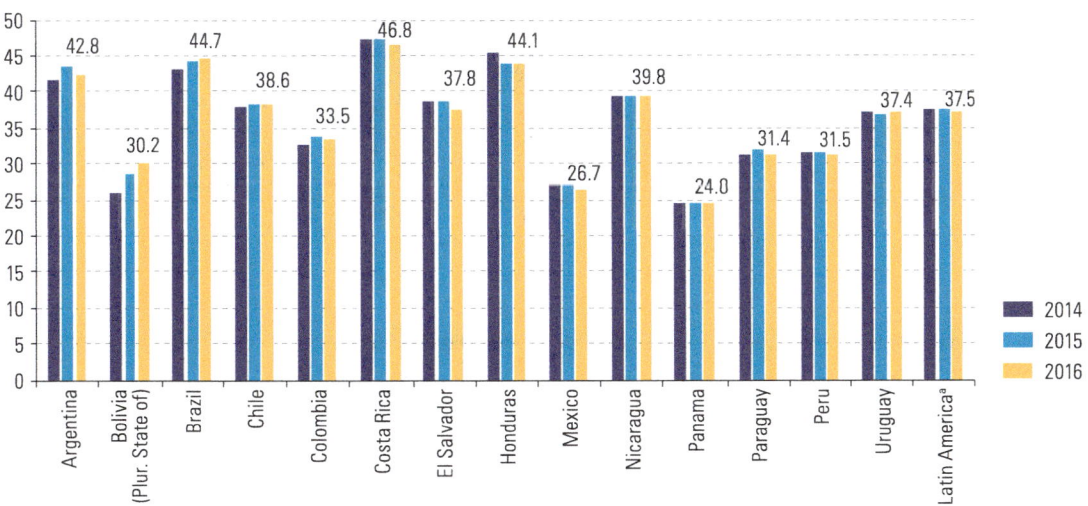

Source: Economic Commission for Latin America and the Caribbean (ECLAC), on the basis of official information from the countries and United Nations, UNdata [online database] http://data.un.org.
a Average weighted by current GDP in dollars.

A comparison with extraregional dynamics shows that, despite the growth of the wage share of total income, both on average and in certain countries of the region, the levels in question are significantly lower than those of the vast majority of developed countries. Figure I.13 shows the distribution of the wage earner income shares for the OECD countries (excluding Chile and Mexico) and a subset of the most developed countries (Group of Seven (G7) relative to those of the Latin American countries analysed. This box diagram shows the average levels (orange bars) and the degree of heterogeneity between countries (height of the boxes and vertical lines, showing the highest and lowest value of the distribution), for 2006 and 2016 (or the latest year with data available).

The diagram firstly draws attention to differences in level. Even with the increases mentioned above, Latin America continues to lag well behind the wage share levels of OECD countries and, particularly, those of G7. Secondly, the levels vary greatly, and the dispersion widens in 2016. The same can be seen in the OECD countries, albeit with less intensity but at higher wage share levels.

---

10   There are no official data on this indicator for Brazil or for the Bolivarian Republic of Venezuela, although employment and wage trends suggest a reduction.

Figure I.13
Latin America (15 countries) and other regions: dispersion of the share of wages in GDP (at market prices), 2006 and 2016 or latest year available
(Percentages)

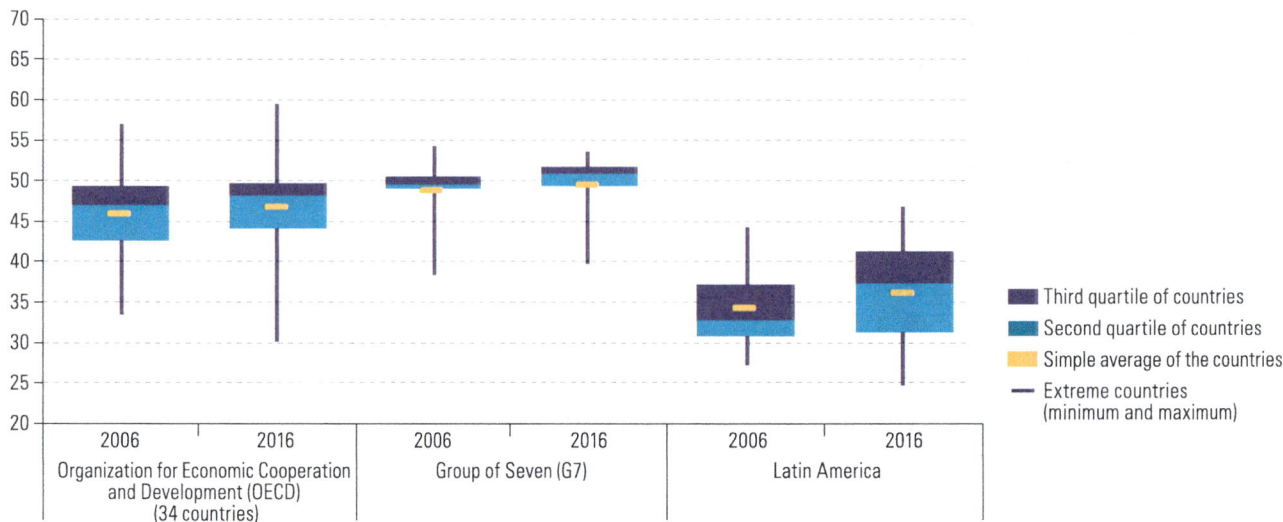

Source: Economic Commission for Latin America and the Caribbean (ECLAC), on the basis of official information from the countries.

It is important to note the limitations of this comparison, given the different productive structures prevailing in the countries involved,[11] and the significantly greater structural heterogeneity among the economies of the region compared to the other two groups of countries. This is related to a significantly larger proportion of self-employment, the income from which is not captured by this indicator. This effect is addressed below.

2. Share of total labour income

Analysis of the GDP share of total labour income is hampered by serious data constraints, apart from those already mentioned. Although the national accounts have recently been providing more information on the wage bill (wage-earner remuneration), not all cases include the concept of mixed income (or mixed gross income), which reflects the remuneration of persons who are not wage earners and implicitly contains a component representing remuneration for work and another for the capital involved in the productive activity in question. Thus, to correctly calculate the labour share, quite complex estimates need to be made to measure the labour income of non-wage earners (own-account workers and employers). This has been done approximately, by assuming that they receive remuneration similar to the average wage (see, for example, Gollin, 2002); and it has also been done in a more refined manner, by estimating the labour income that non-wage earners would receive according to their personal characteristics and sector of economic activity (instead of taking the overall average wage), following the proposal made by Young (1995).

For Latin America, Abeles, Amarante and Vega (2014) have performed estimations based on these two methodologies, and conclude that including the income of non-wage-earning employed persons increases the labour share considerably —by between 60%, assuming that these workers receive an income similar to the average wage, or by 25%, in the case of the more refined estimate that takes account of the different characteristics of individuals and jobs.

---

[11] See Abeles, Arakaki and Villafañe (2017) for a discussion on issues arising when comparing this indicator between countries, considering differences not only in workers' income share per se, but also in the composition of the production structure.

This chapter uses that methodology to present current estimates of the labour share including income from self-employment. Figure I.14 compares the three results: the share of wages in GDP analysed in the previous subsection (obtained from the system of national accounts); the correction made by assuming independent workers receive an income similar to the overall average wage (estimation 1); and the more detailed correction (estimation 2). The selected years reflect the availability of information based on the gross income data published by the countries and the availability of household surveys.

Figure I.14
Latin America (17 countries): shares of wages and estimated labour income in GDP (at market prices), around 2002 and 2016
(Percentages)

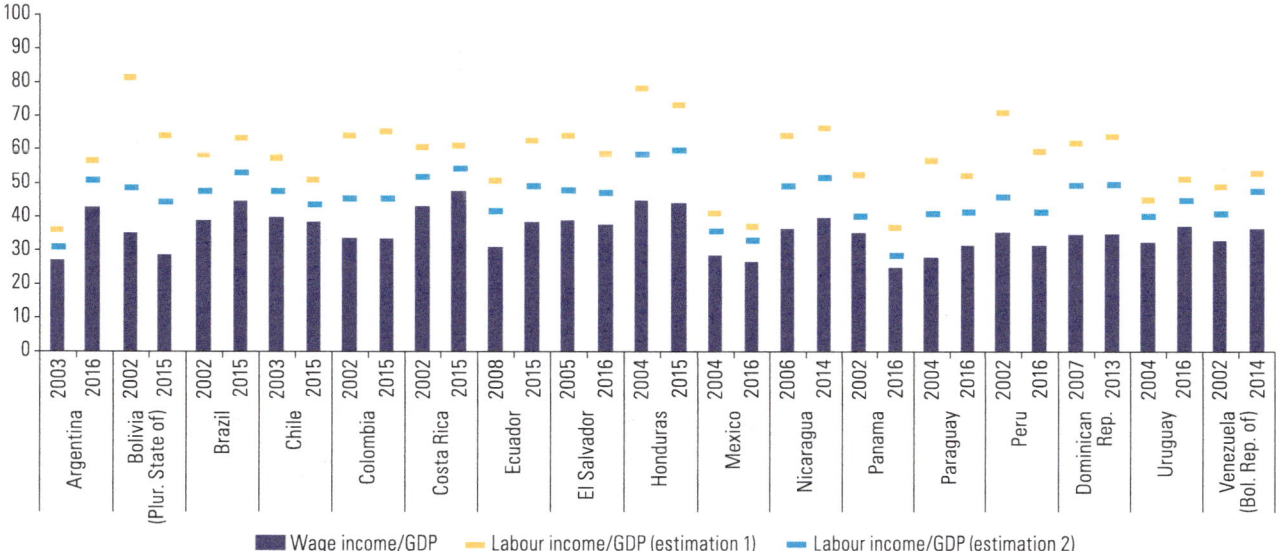

Source: Economic Commission for Latin America and the Caribbean (ECLAC), on the basis of CEPALSTAT, Household Survey Data Bank (BADEHOG) and official information from the countries.

The results are consistent with the proportions reported in Abeles, Amarante and Vega (2014), especially those of the second estimation, which confirms that, when non-wage income is included, the labour share increases by more than 25%, or by 10 percentage points. In terms of trend, when considering the GDP share of total labour income (including the income of own-account workers and employers) the trend that was observed in the share of wages is maintained, but at a higher level. The heterogeneity that exists between countries reflects their different labour market structures, in particular the importance of employed non-wage earners, their income and the sectors of activity in which they work, among other factors.

Lastly, when the share of labour income as a whole is considered in an international comparison similar to that performed above, higher levels are observed for all countries, although the differences in levels are maintained (see figure I.15). The average levels recorded in Latin America are almost 10 percentage points lower than the average of the OECD countries and more than 15 percentage points below the G7 average.

In short, following a period of growth in the GDP shares of wages and labour income (including the income of employed non-wage earners), which occurred in several of the region's countries after 2004 or 2005 (depending on the country), the pace has slackened since 2014 and in some countries (the larger ones) the trend has reversed. Only the Plurinational State of Bolivia diverges from this trend, although from much lower levels. Given the lower economic growth rates of recent years and the impacts on the labour market (such as higher unemployment and the interruption of employment formalization processes), this may result in steeper falls.

Figure I.15
Latin America (17 countries) and other regions: dispersion of the labour share in GDP (at factor cost), around 2012
(*Percentages*)

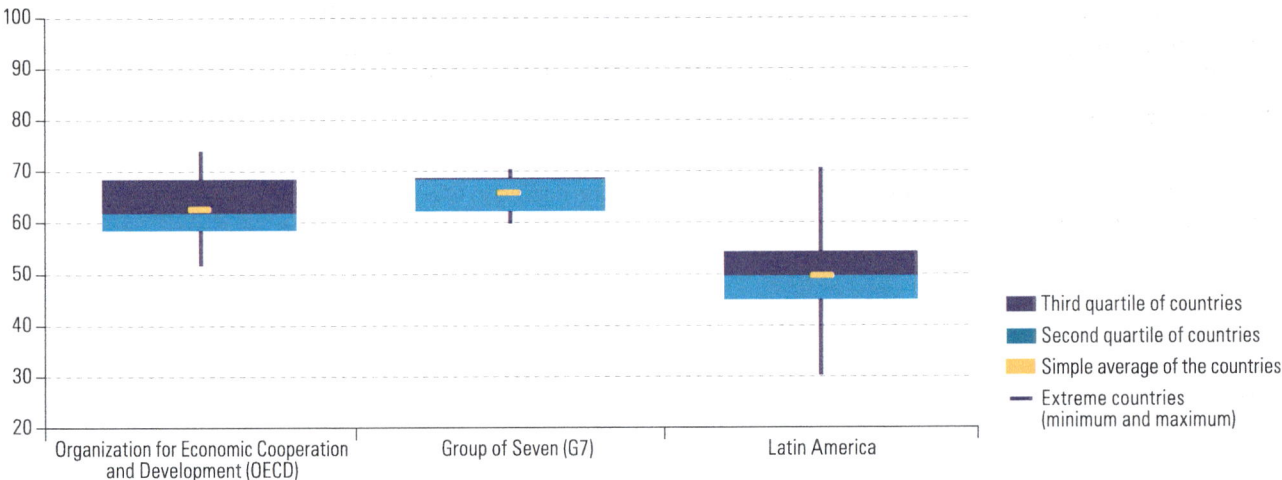

Source: Economic Commission for Latin America and the Caribbean (ECLAC), on the basis of CEPALSTAT, Household Survey Data Bank (BADEHOG), Organization for Economic Cooperation and Development (OECD) and official information from the countries.

These trends are important because, from a structuralist standpoint, the relationship between productivity, employment and the labour share in total income —which results from the way the production structure is organized— is one of the key domains of the income distribution. The other important area is the institutional one, which also influences the secondary distribution of income through the tax structure, labour institutions and social protection policies, among other mechanisms. The combination of different production structures (hence, different levels and dynamics of the labour share in GDP), with different institutional frameworks, is likely to produce different distribution outcomes. More diversified economic structures with a larger share of knowledge-intensive activities are essential for a better income distribution, given their proven capacity to sustain economic growth and employment and because they provide a broader policy space for adopting institutional redistribution mechanisms (Cimoli and others, 2017).

The following paragraphs analyse another aspect of economic inequality, related to the concentration of wealth: in other words, the degree to which the ownership of physical and financial assets is concentrated among the population and, hence, the amount and concentration of capital. The analysis, which is restricted to three cases owing to data constraints and the complexity of the available instruments, reveals the high concentration of asset ownership in the higher-income strata, a situation that is not detected in household surveys (see the first section) through the declaration of current income.

C. Inequality and wealth: distribution of physical and financial assets

As a domain of analysis and reflection for the design of public policy, income inequality needs to be analysed in its multiple dimensions. This means working with new instruments and approaches aimed at capturing aspects that are not always adequately identified by traditional tools. One of the keys to understanding this inequality is to examine the concentration of wealth in general and, more specifically, the ownership structure of physical and financial assets. Studies of the realities prevailing in Chile, Uruguay and, partially, Mexico, find that the distribution of wealth between families is more unequal than the distribution of income alone; and also that the ownership of financial assets is more highly concentrated than that of physical assets.

The countries of Latin America and the Caribbean have abundant natural wealth. According to World Bank data, the region had US$ 35.2 trillion in physical assets in 2014. If this amount were distributed equally, each inhabitant would have US$ 57,000 in natural and produced capital. Although the region only has 8.6% of the world's physical assets, the proportion grows to 30% in terms of non-timber forest resources (edible seeds, fungi, fruits, fibres, spices, wildlife, resins, gums, vegetable and animal products), 29% in terms of protected areas (mainly due to the contribution of the Amazon) and 26% in mining resources (see tables I.3 and I.4).

Table I.3
Physical assets in the world, 1995–2014[a]
(Millions of dollars at constant 2014 prices and percentages)

Region	1995	2000	2005	2010	2014	Percentage by region 2014
East Asia and the Pacific	39 454 030	49 673 442	65 839 595	93 439 225	115 702 668	28.2
Europe and Central Asia	84 774 494	88 754 212	101 523 371	116 124 164	121 065 511	29.5
Latin America and the Caribbean	20 316 539	21 340 717	25 959 411	31 599 660	35 226 711	8.6
Middle East and North Africa	8 682 878	9 342 096	13 495 273	20 690 773	25 055 938	6.1
North America	48 382 945	57 678 319	71 594 383	80 465 762	86 516 212	21.1
South Asia	6 185 428	7 041 545	8 627 842	12 797 100	15 924 869	3.9
Sub-Saharan Africa	9 441 659	8 270 200	9 880 549	11 029 595	11 484 053	2.8
Total	217 237 973	242 100 530	296 920 425	366 146 279	410 975 961	100.0

Source: Economic Commission for Latin America and the Caribbean (ECLAC), on the basis of G. Lange, Q. Wodon and K. Carey (eds.), *The Changing Wealth of Nations 2018: Building a Sustainable Future*, Washington, D.C., World Bank, 2018.
[a] Physical assets encompass natural capital (energy, minerals, agricultural land, protected areas and forests) and produced capital (machinery, structures, equipment and urban land). The value of non-renewable resources is estimated from the present value of the expected flow of income from the stocks that can be extracted until the resource runs out.

Table I.4
Physical assets in the world, by type, 2014
(Percentages of the global total)

Region	East Asia and the Pacific	Europe and Central Asia	Latin America and the Caribbean	Middle East and North Africa	North America	South asia	Sub-Saharan Africa	Total
Produced capital	27.7	34.5	6.5	2.1	25.4	2.7	1.1	100.0
Forest, timber resources	33.6	16.6	18.6	0.2	9.7	2.3	19.0	100.0
Forest resources, non-timber	25.3	15.2	29.5	0.1	27.3	0.7	1.9	100.0
Protected areas	24.8	18.6	28.7	3.0	9.2	3.0	12.7	100.0
Cropland	49.6	10.1	10.0	2.2	6.0	12.7	9.5	100.0
Grazing	25.4	16.2	16.8	4.8	6.6	19.3	10.8	100.0
Petroleum	5.5	17.5	8.8	56.4	5.3	1.1	5.6	100.0
Natural gas	10.0	56.5	3.3	23.7	1.7	2.8	2.0	100.0
Coal	56.0	7.4	1.2	0.0	23.3	9.2	2.9	100.0
Metals and minerals	45.7	11.0	26.2	1.4	5.5	4.6	5.6	100.0

Source: Economic Commission for Latin America and the Caribbean (ECLAC), on the basis of G. Lange, Q. Wodon and K. Carey (eds.), *The Changing Wealth of Nations 2018: Building a Sustainable Future*, Washington, D.C., World Bank, 2018.

Most of the region's produced assets are located in six countries: Brazil (33%), Mexico (25%), the Bolivarian Republic of Venezuela (11%), Argentina (8%), Colombia (7%) and Chile (4%). The largest non-timber forest resources are held by Brazil (62%) and Mexico (10%); the largest metal and mineral resources are situated in Brazil (46%), Chile (29%), Peru (12%) and Mexico (6%) (see figure I.16).

Figure I.16
Latin America and the Caribbean: countries with the most physical assets, 2014
(Percentage shares of regional total)

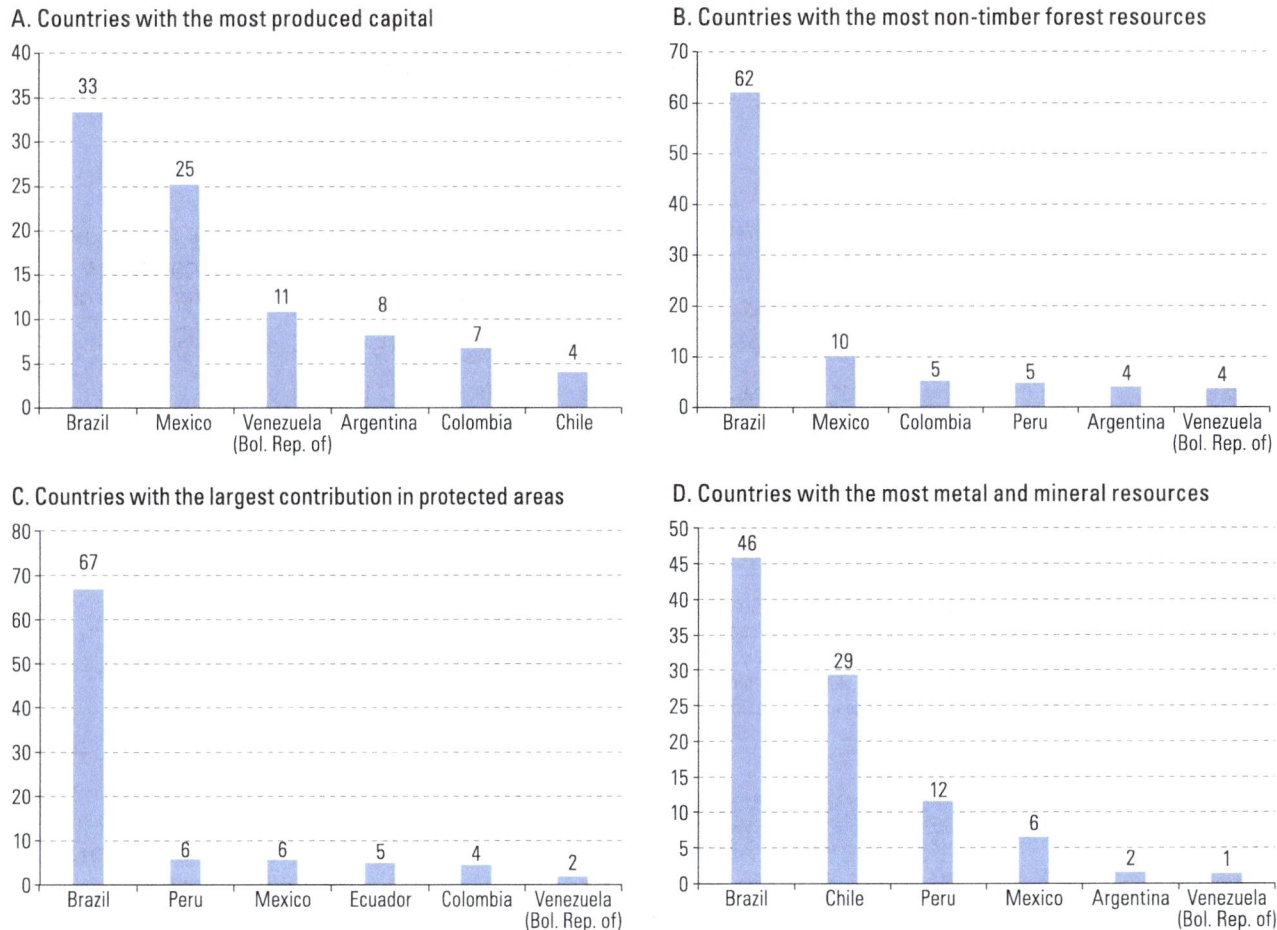

A. Countries with the most produced capital

B. Countries with the most non-timber forest resources

C. Countries with the largest contribution in protected areas

D. Countries with the most metal and mineral resources

Source: Economic Commission for Latin America and the Caribbean (ECLAC), on the basis of G. Lange, Q. Wodon and K. Carey (eds.), *The Changing Wealth of Nations 2018: Building a Sustainable Future,* Washington, D.C., World Bank, 2018.

In 2016 Brazil was the world's largest tantalum producer, the third largest producer of bauxite (and, hence, of alumina) and iron ore, and ninth in terms of crude oil. Chile was the world's leading copper producer and the fourth largest silver producer. Peru ranked second in the production of copper, silver and zinc; fourth in lead, and sixth in gold. Mexico ranked first in silver production, fifth in lead and zinc, and eighth in gold (BGS, 2018). The Bolivarian Republic of Venezuela, which owns a quarter of the world's proven oil reserves (OPEC, 2017), was the world's tenth largest producer of crude oil (Brown and others, 2018).

A country's wealth also consists of the financial assets of companies, government, households and institutions that provide services to households.[12]

Brazil, Chile, Colombia and Mexico[13] are the only Latin American countries to have published financial-account figures by institutional sector, as part of their system of

---

[12]   The assets owned by financial institutions are not included in the analysis because, by nature, the counterpart of a bank asset is a liability contracted with the institution by firms, government and households.
[13]   According to OECD, 36 countries have published balance-sheet data for financial assets, four of them from Latin America: Brazil, Chile, Colombia and Mexico.

national accounts.[14] Brazil has the largest amount of financial capital; its non-financial firms, government, households and institutions that serve households possess US$ 11 trillion in financial assets (not including debt). Mexico follows closely behind with US$ 7.9 trillion; and Colombia and Chile have just over US$ 2 trillion (in all four cases, dollars expressed in purchasing power parity terms). Nonetheless, these differences are due largely to the size of each country's population. If financial capital (excluding debt) is divided by the number of inhabitants, Chile ranks first with US$ 120,000, followed by Mexico with US$ 61,000 (see table I.5).

Year	Millions of current dollars in PPP				Current dollars per capita in PPP			
	Chile	Mexico	Brazil	Colombia	Chile	Mexico	Brazil	Colombia
2003	714 469	2 447 785		548 636	45 221	23 171		13 016
2004	781 110	2 669 519		542 391	48 900	24 950		12 695
2005	827 658	2 963 532		626 151	51 257	27 321		14 466
2006	1 043 929	3 644 294		708 239	63 967	33 102		16 157
2007	1 188 128	3 987 235		775 021	72 044	35 652		17 465
2008	1 202 693	4 271 146		850 307	72 182	37 578		18 937
2009	1 210 961	4 200 520	9 251 198	912 157	71 955	36 366	47 467	20 084
2010	1 371 326	4 627 688	8 988 868	981 269	80 698	39 445	45 676	21 370
2011	1 636 975	5 374 868	9 257 897	1 090 327	95 432	45 133	46 595	23 495
2012	1 731 324	5 880 665	9 981 616	1 150 836	100 020	48 670	49 768	24 548
2013	1 840 028	6 161 401	10 316 420	1 313 485	105 367	50 282	50 968	27 744
2014	2 055 847	6 847 449	11 096 723	1 625 183	116 718	55 123	54 339	34 005
2015	2 120 481	7 193 775	11 184 921	2 200 767	119 378	57 143	54 306	45 632
2016	2 153 471	7 903 332		2 522 469	120 240	61 967		51 846
2017	2 222 989				123 125			

Table I.5
Latin America (selected countries): financial assets of firms, government, households and institutions that serve households, 2003–2017[a]
(Millions of dollars at current prices and PPP dollars per capita)

Source: Economic Commission for Latin America and the Caribbean (ECLAC), on the basis of Organization for Economic Cooperation and Development (OECD), OECD Stat [online database] https://stats.oecd.org/ [accessed on: 13 September 2018]; and United Nations, *World Population Prospects: The 2017 Revision* [DVD edition], 2017.
[a] Does not include financial liabilities.

When the value of financial assets grows by more than the economy at large, families and individuals with financial capital (a small proportion of the population) see their income and, hence, their assets increase. In contrast, for the majority of wage earners and own-account workers the only income source is their work, which is why they are directly affected by the impact of a slowdown in the pace of production and productivity, and do not always benefit proportionately from the upswing. Although this impact can be assessed through surveys of household income and assets, only three countries in the region have conducted financial surveys: (i) Mexico, which implemented the National Survey on Household Living Standards (ENNViH) in 2002, 2005–2006 and 2009–2012; (ii) Chile, which carried out the Household Financial Survey (EFH) in 2007, 2011–2012, 2014 and 2017; and (iii) Uruguay, with the Financial Survey of Uruguayan Households (EFHU), covering 2012–2014 and 2017.[15]

---

[14]   As happens in the national accounts with respect to non-financial corporations, government, households and institutions that provide services to households.

[15]   The surveys of Mexico and Chile use panel data, in which a representative number of households is randomly selected in the first survey and then revisited in the next round. To replace households that have moved or were not located, a random refreshment sample is added. In the case of Chile, only the 2007 and 2017 surveys are analysed, because in this latter year the refreshment sample was 62% (for a more detailed explanation, see box I.2).

1.   Inequality and wealth in Chile

According to the Chilean Household Financial Survey, in 2017 households had an average net wealth of about US$ 115,000 (physical assets plus financial assets generating fixed and variable income, minus short and long-term financial liabilities).[16] That average was distributed very unevenly: while the poorest 50% of households had an average net worth of US$ 5,000, the figure for the wealthiest 10% averaged US$ 760,000, and the richest 1% owned US$ 3 million (see table I.6).

Table I.6
Chile: distribution of adjusted net household wealth, 2007 and 2017[a]
(Averages in dollars, PPP dollars and percentages)

Deciles	Dollars *(average exchange rate for the period)*				Dollars in PPP				Distribution *(percentage)*			
	2007		2017		2007		2017		2007		2017	
	Without imputation	Imputed	Without imputation	Imputed	Without imputation	Imputed	Without imputation	Imputed	Without imputation	Imputed	Imputed	Imputed
I	-41 643	-37 656	-26 596	-22 649	-67 139	-60 710	-42 694	-36 358	-6.3	-5.5	-2.3	-2.0
II	-1 586	-1 123	-617	-141	-2 556	-1 810	-991	-226	-0.2	-0.2	0.0	0.0
III	57	192	522	3 125	91	309	838	5 017	0.0	0.0	0.1	0.2
IV	4 820	5 289	8 291	14 865	7 771	8 527	13 309	23 862	0.7	0.8	0.7	1.3
V	12 626	12 719	24 170	30 371	20 357	20 507	38 799	48 753	2.0	1.9	2.2	2.6
VI	20 675	20 824	40 213	44 390	33 332	33 574	64 552	71 257	3.2	3.1	3.6	3.8
VII	29 820	29 909	54 862	60 826	48 077	48 221	88 068	97 641	4.6	4.4	4.6	5.2
VIII	45 127	45 171	84 327	93 456	72 755	72 827	135 366	150 021	6.8	6.6	7.4	8.0
IX	75 734	76 685	154 425	165 701	122 101	123 633	247 891	265 993	11.8	11.3	13.5	14.3
X	509 338	529 724	804 162	769 339	821 172	854 038	1 290 885	1 234 985	77.6	77.7	70.2	66.5
Total	65 455	68 272	114 220	115 862	105 529	110 070	183 353	185 988	100.0	100.0	100.0	100.0
Richest 5%	867 402	905 528	1 307 322	1 222 746	1 398 453	1 459 921	2 098 586	1 962 820	66.3	66.3	57.2	52.8
Richest 2%	1 654 162	1 688 787	2 386 101	2 111 938	2 666 892	2 722 717	3 830 302	3 390 200	49.9	49.5	41.6	36.4
Richest 1%	2 399 843	2 437 298	3 713 384	3 070 849	3 869 102	3 929 489	5 960 930	4 929 497	36.8	35.8	32.4	26.5

Source: Economic Commission for Latin America and the Caribbean (ECLAC), on the basis of Central Bank of Chile, "Encuesta Financiera de Hogares" [online] http://www.bcentral.cl/web/guest/financiera-de-hogares.

[a] Figures adjusted in line with the national accounts. The imputed column shows the average of the 30 imputed databases in the two years, 2007 and 2017 (for further details see box I.2).

Wealth in Chile is highly concentrated. While the poorest 50% of households owned just 2.1% of the country's net wealth in 2017, the richest 10% held two thirds (66.5%) and the richest 1% accounted for 26.5% (see table I.6). Accordingly, the Gini coefficient of total assets (physical and financial) has a value close to 0.72 (see table I.7),[17] which contrasts sharply with the 0.45 Gini coefficient of the distribution of households' current per capita income (see section A).

Nonetheless, the upper strata of the distribution (the tenth decile) saw its appropriation of net wealth and physical and financial assets decline relatively between 2007 and 2017, probably due to the adverse effect of the 2008 crisis on the long-term value of equity investments. In contrast, the eighth and ninth deciles saw a slight improvement in the same period: the eighth decile's share of physical and financial assets grew from 7.1% to 8.6% (average of the imputed databases), while the ninth decile's share increased from 11.0% to 14.8% (average of the imputed databases) (see table I.7). The methodology of the Chilean Household Financial Survey is described in box I.2.

---

[16]   Average for the 30 imputed bases (for further details, see box I.2).
[17]   Great care is needed when analysing the changes occurring between 2007 and 2017, because, firstly, while all the households of the 2007 survey were selected randomly, in the 2017 survey a third of them were not. They were included because they had been interviewed in the previous year (2014). Secondly, the extent to which the change in the Gini coefficient is due to sampling needs to be estimated; and, if the imputed databases are used, so does the statistical error associated with this process.

Table I.7
Chile: distribution and concentration of adjusted physical and financial assets of households, total and by type, 2007 and 2017[a]
(Percentages and Gini coefficient)

Deciles	Total assets				Assets by type, 2017					
	2007		2017		Base without imputation			Average of the 30 imputed databases		
	Without imputation	Average of the 30 imputed databases	Without imputation	Average of the 30 imputed databases	Physical assets	Financial assets (fixed income)	Financial assets (variable income)	Physical assets	Financial assets (fixed income)	Financial assets (variable income)
I	0.0	0.0	0.0	0.0	0.0	0.0	0.0	0.0	0.0	0.0
II	0.0	0.0	0.0	0.1	0.0	0.1	0.0	0.1	0.2	0.0
III	0.6	0.6	0.4	0.6	0.5	0.8	0.1	0.8	1.3	0.1
IV	1.6	1.6	1.5	1.9	2.0	1.4	0.1	2.6	1.2	0.2
V	2.7	2.6	2.5	3.0	3.7	0.9	0.2	4.3	1.1	0.1
VI	3.6	3.5	4.4	4.1	6.6	1.3	0.2	5.7	1.5	0.3
VII	5.0	4.4	5.4	5.8	8.0	1.8	0.4	8.1	2.0	0.3
VIII	6.9	7.1	8.5	8.6	12.6	2.7	0.7	11.6	3.4	1.5
IX	11.3	11.0	14.0	14.8	18.5	10.0	4.6	18.3	11.8	5.4
X	68.2	69.1	63.3	60.9	48.0	80.9	93.8	48.6	77.4	92.2
Total	100.0	100.0	100.0	100.0	100.0	100.0	100.0	100.0	100.0	100.0

Households with the most assets				
Richest 5%	57.4	58.0	50.0	47.1
Richest 2%	42.8	42.3	35.3	31.7
Richest 1%	31.5	30.4	27.1	22.8
Gini	0.7219	0.7327	0.7436	0.7206

Source: Economic Commission for Latin America and the Caribbean (ECLAC), on the basis of Central Bank of Chile, "Encuesta Financiera de Hogares" [online] http://www.bcentral.cl/web/guest/financiera-de-hogares.
[a] Figures adjusted in line with the national accounts.

Box I.2
The Chilean Household Financial Survey

The Household Financial Survey (EFH) has been conducted by the Central Bank of Chile since 2007, when the Microdata Centre of the University of Chile was contracted to implement its first edition. Four surveys were carried out in urban areas nationwide, in 2007, 2011–2012, 2014 and 2017; and three more, in 2008, 2009 and 2010, covering the urban area of the Metropolitan Region. Chile's population is 87.4% urban.[a]

The 2007 survey interviewed the family member who made the largest monetary contribution in 4,021 randomly selected urban households, based on the 2002 census and the tax base of the Internal Revenue Service (SII) (income statements for 2006). The 2017 survey chose the individual aged 18 years or older with greatest knowledge of household finances, or who claimed to be the head of the household.[b] The sample comprised 4,500 households, and was calculated on the basis of the Real Estate Cadastre of December 2016 and SII.[c] The Household Financial Survey is a panel type survey; in other words, it revisits the households interviewed in the previous round and also refreshes with new homes. This panel type sampling does not admit probabilistic data for the years 2011–2012 and 2014. In the most recent survey, held in 2017, 38% of households in the 2014 sample were included, and the majority (62%) were selected randomly for that year's survey, thus making it somewhat more representative. For this reason, it was decided to work only with the 2007 and 2017 surveys.[d]

Box I.2 (concluded)

Sample size of the Household Financial Survey

Survey year	Total	Panel			
		2007	2011	2014	2017
		Number			
2007	3 828	3 828			
2011-2012	4 059	1 970	2 089		
2014	4 502	994	766	2 742	
2017	4 500			1 700	2 800
		Percentage			
2007	100	100			
2011-2012	100	48.5	51.5	0.0	0.0
2014	100	22.1	17.0	60.9	0.0
2017	100	0.0	0.0	37.8	62.2

Source: Economic Commission for Latin America and the Caribbean (ECLAC), on the basis of Central Bank of Chile, *Encuesta Financiera de Hogares 2014: principales resultados*, Santiago, 2015, and *Encuesta Financiera de Hogares 2017: metodología*, Santiago, 2018.

In order to improve the coverage of wealthier households, the Central Bank of Chile performed an oversampling. As a result, in the 2017 EFH, households in the ninth and tenth deciles represented 39% of the sample (29% in the final database), while the poorest 50% of households accounted for 37% of the sample (42% in the final database), an effect that was corrected for when applying the expansion factors. As surveys of this type tend to produce a large number of unanswered questions, because the respondent either does not reply or does not know the answer, the Central Bank of Chile imputed the missing data, by replacing the unreported values with randomly generated ones. A total of 30 imputed databases were thus generated. Analysing the imputed bases is complex: the statistic must be calculated for each imputed database, and the average of the statistic is obtained following Rubine's rules.[e] The data imputation process mainly helps solve the problem of involuntary underreporting of data (that is, as a result of forgetting rather than intentionally). Nonetheless, income and wealth surveys are also subject to willful underreporting. Rich families tend to underreport their assets, particularly financial ones. The scale of this underreporting can be gauged with information obtained from the national accounts, provided institutional sector data are available.

As Chile has published figures with this level of disaggregation, it is possible to make the comparison between the value of assets and liabilities declared in the household financial surveys, and the amounts recorded in the national accounts. For example, in 2017, while the national accounts report just over 40 billion pesos in fixed income financial assets (mainly cash and demand deposits), families declare just 6.1 billion pesos in the financial survey (an amount that rises to 7.8 billion pesos on average after the imputation process). The difference is greater in the case of financial assets of variable yield (short- and long-term bonds, plus shares and other equity): 98 billion pesos in the national accounts, compared to just 9.5 billion pesos in the survey.

This bias was corrected by applying adjustment factors, estimated from national accounts data, to the records that reported an amount greater than zero, in both assets and liabilities. To estimate the coefficient, a database was generated by household centiles (100 groups), according to physical and financial assets (without debt).[f] It should be noted that Gini coefficients estimated with more granular data tend to be slightly higher; so the Gini coefficient based on deciles would be slightly lower than that calculated for quintiles.

Source: Economic Commission for Latin America and the Caribbean (ECLAC), on the basis of Central Bank of Chile, *Encuesta Financiera de Hogares: metodología*, Santiago, 2018.
[a] National Institute of Statistics (INE) of Chile, *Compendio Estadístico*, Santiago, 2017, p. 108.
[b] If no one with these characteristics was able answer the questionnaire, the individual with the largest debt was selected. If no one was in debt, the person with the most assets was selected; if no one had assets, the individual with the highest income was chosen, always subject to interviewee being 18 years of age or older.
[c] Central Bank of Chile, *Encuesta Financiera de Hogares: metodología*, Santiago, 2018, pp. 11–12.
[d] Bearing in mind that the latter may have some bias, although less, when households selected in 2014 are included.
[e] D. Rubin, *Multiple Imputation for Nonresponse in Surveys*, J. Wiley & Sons, New York, 1987.
[f] The DescTools package of the R statistics program was used. Gini coefficients were estimated for the original base and the 30 imputed bases.

A breakdown by type of asset reveals greater inequality in the distribution of financial assets, mainly those yielding variable returns. In 2017, the richest 10% of households accounted for 92.2% of investments in shares and mutual funds, other equity holdings in firms and investment funds (variable income assets), and 77.4% of deposits in savings accounts and time deposits (fixed income assets). In contrast, real estate and household vehicles (physical assets) were less biased: although the poorest 50% of households owned just 7.7% of total physical assets, the rest was distributed, in almost equal proportions, between the sixth to ninth deciles (43.7% of the total) and the tenth decile (48.6%) (see table I.7).[18]

2.　Inequality and wealth in Uruguay

In 2013–2014, the average net wealth of households in Uruguay was US$ 66,800 (US$ 83,400 in PPP terms). While this is less than in Chile, household wealth in Uruguay is more equally distributed: although the richest 1% of families had net wealth of US$ 1.2 million (US$ 1.5 million in PPP terms), this segment's share of total wealth is 17.5%; and, at the other extreme, the poorest 50% owned 5% of the country's total net wealth (see table I.8).

Deciles	Dollars (average exchange rate for the period)		Dollars in PPP		Distribution (percentage)	
	Without imputation	Imputed	Without imputation	Imputed	Without imputation	Imputed
I	-7 337	-6 259	-9 156	-7 810	-1.3	-0.9
II	249	475	310	593	0.0	0.1
III	1 028	2 644	1 283	3 300	0.2	0.4
IV	4 452	11 220	5 556	14 001	0.8	1.7
V	13 924	23 741	17 376	29 627	2.5	3.6
VI	28 787	37 736	35 924	47 091	5.2	5.6
VII	45 059	54 033	56 229	67 427	8.1	8.1
VIII	66 142	76 140	82 538	95 015	11.9	11.4
IX	100 259	116 815	125 113	145 773	18.0	17.5
X	305 373	351 746	381 074	438 943	54.7	52.6
Total	55 789	66 819	69 619	83 383	100.0	100.0
Richest 5%	442 138	517 312	551 743	645 553	43.3	42.0
Richest 2%	698 258	832 765	871 355	1 039 205	23.3	24.9
Richest 1%	951 356	1 169 321	1 187 195	1 459 193	17.4	17.5

Table I.8
Uruguay: distribution of net household wealth, 2013–2014[a]
(Averages in dollars, PPP dollars and percentages)

Source: Economic Commission for Latin America and the Caribbean (ECLAC), on the basis of University of the Republic, *Encuesta Financiera de los Hogares Uruguayos (EFHU-2): descripción y resultados,* Montevideo, 2016.
[a] The imputed columns report the average of the values of the 10 imputed databases (for further details, see box I.3).

The Gini coefficient of physical and financial assets (excluding debt) in Uruguay was 0.6696 (with a pre-imputation value of 0.6948). These figures are much higher than the 0.392 Gini coefficient of the country's current per capita income in 2014 (see annex table I.A1.1).[19] As in Chile, variable income financial assets are more highly concentrated; the richest 10% accounted for 89.5% of these assets (average of the ten imputed databases). In contrast, fixed income financial assets were less concentrated, with the richest 10% accounting for 63.5% (average of the imputed databases). In the case of physical assets (movable and immovable property), the distribution was slightly more balanced, with the wealthiest 10% owning half (see table I.9). Box I.3 provides further details of the treatment of the Uruguayan Household Financial Survey.

---

[18]　Simple averages of each decile's share in the 30 imputed databases.
[19]　The Economics Department of the Faculty of Social Sciences at the University of the Republic of Uruguay, has estimated a slightly higher Gini coefficient for asset ownership, at 0.71. Nonetheless, it does not specify whether this Gini was estimated with the unimputed data or from the imputed databases (University of the Republic, 2016, p. 27). It should also be noted that the Gini coefficient estimated in the present document does not include the assets and liabilities of household businesses, loans made to family members and friends, or individual pension fund capitalization accounts (see box I.3)

Table I.9
Uruguay: distribution
and concentration of
household physical and
financial assets, total and
by type, 2013–2014
*(Percentages and
Gini coefficient)*

Deciles	Total assets		Assets by type					
			Without imputation			Average of imputed databases		
	Without imputation	Average of imputed databases	Physical assets	Financial assets (fixed income)	Financial assets (variable income)	Physical assets	Financial assets (fixed income	Financial assets (variable income)
I	0.0	0.0	0.0	0.0	0.0	0.0	0.0	0.0
II	0.1	0.1	0.1	0.0	0.0	0.1	0.1	0.1
III	0.3	0.6	0.3	0.2	0.3	0.6	1.5	0.1
IV	1.0	2.1	1.0	2.1	0.0	2.0	3.5	0.4
V	2.9	3.9	2.8	5.3	2.0	4.0	3.2	1.2
VI	5.5	5.8	5.5	5.7	1.7	6.0	2.8	0.8
VII	8.3	8.2	8.5	5.2	0.0	8.5	3.9	1.1
VIII	12.0	11.3	12.4	4.8	2.6	11.7	5.6	2.8
IX	17.8	17.3	18.1	12.6	1.0	17.5	15.9	4.1
X	52.1	50.5	51.4	64.0	92.5	49.5	63.5	89.5
Total	100.0	100.0	100.0	100.0	100.0	100.0	100.0	100.0

Households with the most assets		
Richest 5%	37.4	36.9
Richest 2%	23.6	23.7
Richest 1%	16.2	16.6
Gini	0.6948	0.6696

Source: Economic Commission for Latin America and the Caribbean (ECLAC), on the basis of University of the Republic, *Encuesta Financiera de los Hogares Uruguayos (EFHU-2): descripción y resultados*, Montevideo, 2016.

Box I.3
The Uruguayan Household Financial Survey

The Financial Stability Committee of Uruguay tasked the Economics Department of the Faculty of Social Sciences of the University of the Republic and the National Institute of Statistics (INE) with conducting the Uruguayan Household Financial Survey (EFHU). To date, two surveys have been held: 2012–2014 and 2017. The survey for 2012–2014 was implemented in two stages. In the first (EFHU-1), 28 questions were added by the INE to the Continuous Household Survey (ECH) of the last quarter of 2012. In the second stage (EFHU-2) a specific questionnaire was applied (with 122 questions), which gathered a very detailed picture of the financial situation of Uruguayan households. The field work in this stage was undertaken by the aforementioned Economics Department, through interviews held between October 2013 and July 2014, using a sample based on the INE Household Survey.

An additional weighting was assigned to households in the two highest income quintiles of the population (representing 57% of those interviewed). The assets of home businesses (microenterprises) were also included.

The response, or interview acceptance rate, was 76%, reaching 80% among the poorest households and dropping to 71% in the richest 20%. Once the households were contacted, not all of them answered all the questions, either because they did not know the answer or preferred not to reply. Accordingly, an imputation process was performed, which generated an additional 10 databases.

The Uruguayan survey is very complete and includes a broader range of information than Chile's. In order to make it comparable with the Chilean survey, a selection was made of the variables. The correspondence may not be exact because, for example, the Chilean case includes educational loans (both with private banks and with a credit supported by a State guarantee (CAE)). In contrast, the Uruguayan survey does not consider these as a separate item, and loans with the State are related to electricity, water and other utilities (debts with government agencies such as the National Power Plants and Transmission Administration (UTE)), State Sanitary Works (OSE), the National Telecommunications Administration (ANTEL) or municipal governments). Accordingly, it was decided not to include credits with government agencies, in the case of liabilities; and, similarly, the value of any loans granted to a relative, friend or neighbour in the last 12 months was excluded, as were individual capitalization accounts held with Pension Savings Fund Management Companies (AFAPs). The value of the assets comprising the business and the total value of the business were also excluded.

As in the case of Chile, the Gini coefficient was estimated from the data on physical and financial assets (excluding debt), ranked in centiles from the lowest level of wealth to the highest.

Source: Economic Commission for Latin America and the Caribbean (ECLAC), on the basis of University of the Republic, *Encuesta Financiera de los Hogares Uruguayos (EFHU-2): descripción y resultados*, Montevideo, 2016.

3.   Distribution of physical and financial assets in Mexico

Although there are no recent surveys of physical and financial assets in Mexico, their distribution can be estimated from two data sources that represent a large proportion of household wealth. The first is the National Household Survey (ENH), which has been conducted annually since 2014 by the National Institute of Statistics and Geography (INEGI). Its second edition (2015) included a question on the value of owner-occupied housing (whether or not mortgaged). In that year, 46% of families did not own their own home, but were living in rented or borrowed accommodation; so the value of these physical assets was nil. At the other extreme, there were just under 400,000 families with homes valued at 2 million pesos or more, which accounted for 62% of the total value of physical assets in this category. The relevant Gini coefficient was 0.6924 (see table I.10).

Ranges (value of home in pesos)	Homes		Value of homes	
	Number	Percentage	Millions of pesos	Percentage
Without own home	10 641 447	46.1	-	0.0
Below 50 000	1 006 859	4.4	50 343	0.4
50 001 to 100 000	1 726 295	7.5	129 472	1.0
100 001 to 300 000	3 648 595	15.8	729 719	5.8
300 001 to 500 000	2 922 791	12.7	1 169 116	9.3
500 001 to 1 000 000	1 942 097	8.4	1 456 573	11.6
1 000 001 to 2 000 000	816 022	3.5	1 224 033	9.8
Over 2 000 001	389 048	1.7	7 780 960	62.0
Subtotal	23 093 154	100.0	12 540 216	100.0
Not known	8 119 432	Gini=	0.6924	
Total	31 212 586			

Table I.10
Mexico: value of own housing, 2015
(Number of units, millions of current pesos and percentages)

Source: Economic Commission for Latin America and the Caribbean (ECLAC), on the basis of National Institute of Statistics and Geography (INEGI), "Encuesta Nacional de los Hogares (ENH): principales resultados 2015" [online] http://www.beta.inegi.org.mx/contenidos/proyectos/enchogares/regulares/enh/2015/doc/enh2015_resultados.pdf.

The second data source that makes it possible to approximate the distribution of wealth in Mexico is the number of accounts held in brokerage firms and their investment amount, as published by the National Banking and Securities Commission of Mexico (CNBV).[20] In 2016, there were about 177,000 contracts held by Mexican individuals in Mexico, to invest in the purchase and sale of shares through brokerage firms, with a total investment representing 56.9% of total household financial assets. Most of these contracts represented an investment amount of less than 5 million pesos. In contrast, about 20,000 contracts (10% of the total) accounted for 76% of total investment in brokerage houses. The Gini coefficient of the contracts, not including individuals who do not have investments in the stock market, is 0.7769 (see table I.11).

Mexican society is relatively unbanked. Although the 2015 National Survey of Financial Inclusion (ENIF) found that 44.1% of the population had a bank account, most of these are transactional and used merely to receive wage or pension payments, so the balance at the end of the fortnight or month tends to zero in most cases. The penetration rate is even less in the case of other types of account. Only 17.6% of the population has a savings account; 1.5% has a term investment account (fixed income, with an accumulated balance representing 14% of household financial assets, according to the national accounts); and 0.5% has an investment fund account (variable income). The small proportion of families and people with physical and financial assets shows that wealth in Mexico is highly concentrated.

---

[20]   See National Banking and Securities Commission of Mexico (CNBV), "Portafolio de información" [online] www.cnbv.gob.mx/Paginas/PortafolioDeInformacion.aspx [accessed on: 22 October 2018].

Table I.11
Mexico: distribution
of contracts held by
individuals in brokerage
firms, 2015–2017
*(Percentages of the
number and value
of contracts, and
Gini coefficient)*

Ranges in millions of pesos	2015		2016		2017	
	Number	Value	Number	Value	Number	Value
Below 15	79.7	1.1	79.5	1.1	80.4	1.2
15–49	2.6	1.2	2.8	1.2	2.7	1.3
50–99	1.8	1.9	1.9	2.0	1.9	2.1
100–249	2.0	4.8	2.2	5.3	2.1	5.4
250–499	2.6	13.3	2.7	14.1	2.5	13.8
Over 500	11.3	77.8	10.9	76.2	10.4	76.1
Total	100.0	100.0	100.0	100.0	100.0	100.0
Gini		0.7855		0.7827		0.7769

Source: Economic Commission for Latin America and the Caribbean (ECLAC), on the basis of National Banking and Securities Commission (CNBV), "Información operativa: cuentas y empleados" [online] https://portafoliodeinformacion.cnbv.gob.mx/cb1/Paginas/infcuentasemp.aspx.

D. Closing remarks

The region has made major strides in reducing household income inequality and increasing labour's share of GDP since the start of the 2000 decade, although progress has slowed in recent years. In three countries for which information is available (Chile, Mexico and Uruguay), there is evidence that the distribution of wealth is highly concentrated than household per capita income.

Latin America and the Caribbean remains the most unequal region in the world, with still significant levels of poverty and large sectors which, although they have moved above the poverty and extreme poverty thresholds, are still highly vulnerable to the economic cycles. Within this framework, expanding social protection systems have played an important role in reducing income inequality since 2002 and in containing the distributional deterioration that has occurred in more recent years. Nonetheless, they provide often insufficient coverage and benefits; and discrimination and exclusion persist, based on membership of social class, gender, ethnicity or race, life cycle, zone of residence and country of origin, among other factors (ECLAC, 2018a).

The culture of privilege and the current style of development accentuate the differences between the territorial and social centres and peripheries, while at the same time generating an unsustainable degree of polarization of income and wealth, which increases the power of the more privileged groups to establish and maintain rules of the game that favour them. Persistent inequality in access to well-being and in the exercise of political, economic, social and cultural rights fosters social instability, which hinders social coexistence, the consolidation and deepening of democracy and economic stability. Overcoming these problems is increasingly complex in an international economic scenario in which expectations of growth are deteriorating because of the uncertainty associated with major trade tensions, the geopolitical changes implemented by the United States and the leading countries in Europe and Asia, and signs of possible wars. In addition, climate change is increasingly evident and its effects are more frequent, which adversely affects not only economies, but also large population centres, especially the most vulnerable. This scenario makes global progress more difficult within the framework of the 2030 Agenda for Sustainable Development; and it poses a major challenge for the ever more urgently needed transition towards a sustainable style of development.

Inequality remains the key —in terms of resources, rights, opportunities, capacities, autonomies and recognition. It is essential to move towards a more equitable distribution of income and wealth, with labour receiving a larger share of output; towards the elimination of discrimination of any kind in access to social, economic or political positions; towards the wholesale acquisition of abilities, knowledge and skills; towards greater participation by diverse actors in care, work and power, and towards a more equitable distribution of costs and benefits between present and future generations. A better distribution is a necessary condition for achieving the essential social agreements at the national and international levels, which will make it possible to move towards a sustainable style of development that makes long-term economic growth, social development and environmental stewardship both viable and mutually compatible. This requires cooperative strategic decisions at the global, regional and national levels, under a multilateral approach and with all actors participating. In this context, ECLAC reaffirms its belief that the countries of Latin America and the Caribbean need to launch a new development paradigm based on an environmental big push. The current generation is the first that cannot deny the scale of these changes; and it is also possibly the last that can lay the foundations for, and launch, a new economic, social and political regime capable of making more egalitarian economic growth compatible with environmental stewardship, since the speed of the technological revolution and the deepening of the environmental crisis are shortening the time horizon for action (ECLAC, 2018b).

The study, analysis and measurement of wealth offers a promising path of research towards a better understanding of the multidimensional nature of inequality, and to obtain a more consistent analysis of the challenges for the region in substantively reducing it. Wealth and extreme wealth are central issues of development and public policy. It is, therefore, crucial to obtain the deepest possible knowledge of the characteristics, magnitude and dynamics of both flows and assets, and also of the correlation between them. The structure of ownership of physical and financial assets, and the way they are distributed between the State, families and firms is one of the key indicators of the degree of polarization, concentration or equality of the social structure. It is also one of the key components for understanding the matrix of socioeconomic inequality in the region. In this connection, it is necessary to promote more regular national studies on the possession of physical and financial assets, and also liabilities, and to promote greater transparency —while preserving data privacy and security— in access to available information on investment banks, brokerage houses and institutions that record financial transactions, as well as on business and personal taxes.

Another challenge is to refine traditional instruments and methodologies for measuring inequality. The improvements that can be made to household surveys to enable them to capture high incomes more accurately should be accompanied by an analysis of other information sources, which can connect these data and complement the intuitions gleaned from the analysis of survey data. Lastly, it is important to revive the classical analyses of the functional distribution of income and its contributions, including the link between market structures and the share of wages in GDP. In this connection, this chapter has made progress in developing estimates for analysing the mixed income of the non-wage-earning employed (own-account workers and employers). This is useful for monitoring the functional distribution of income and for gaining a better understanding of the new class dynamics, particularly regarding the growing heterogeneity of the middle classes and their interests.

This process is full of conceptual and methodological challenges, for which increasingly robust and creative solutions need to be found in the years to come. This would make it possible to discern promising links between economic, social, cultural and environmental analyses to enable all the region's countries to make headway in fulfilling their commitments under the Sustainable Development Goals.

Bibliography

Abeles, M., V. Amarante and D. Vega (2014), "The earnings share of total income in Latin America, 1990–2010", *CEPAL Review*, No. 114 (LC/G.2629-P), Santiago, December.

Abeles M., A. Arakaki and S. Villafañe (2017), "Distribución funcional del ingreso en América Latina desde una perspectiva sectorial", *Studies and Perspectives-ECLAC Office in Buenos Aires series*, No. 53 (LC/TS.2017/39-LC/BUE/TS.2017/2), Santiago.

Alarco Tosoni, G. (2014), "Wage share and economic growth in Latin America, 1950–2011", *CEPAL Review*, No. 113 (LC/G.2614-P), Santiago, August.

Atuesta, B., X. Mancero and V. Tromben (2018), "Herramientas para el análisis de las desigualdades y del efecto redistributivo de las políticas públicas", *Project Documents* (LC/TS.2018/53), Santiago, Economic Commission for Latin America and the Caribbean (ECLAC).

Bárcena, A. and A. Prado (2016), *El imperativo de la igualdad: por un desarrollo sostenible en América Latina y el Caribe*, Buenos Aires, Economic Commission for Latin America and the Caribbean (ECLAC)/Siglo XXI.

Berg, J. (ed) (2015), *Labour Markets, Institutions and Inequality: Building Just Societies in the 21st Century*, International Labour Organization (ILO).

Bértola, L. and others (2008), "Income distribution in the Latin American Southern Cone during the first globalization boom, ca: 1870–1920", *Working Papers in Economic History*, No. 08-05, Madrid, Carlos III University, April.

Brown, T. and others (2018), *World Mineral Production 2012–2016*, Keyworth, British Geological Survey (BGS).

Central Bank of Bolivia (1988), *Memoria 1988*, La Paz.

___(1987), *Memoria 1987*, La Paz.

Central Bank of Chile (2018), *Cuentas Nacionales de Chile 2013–2017*, Santiago.

___(2006), *Cuentas Nacionales de Chile 1996–2005*, Santiago.

Central Bank of Costa Rica (2018), "Cuentas nacionales período de referencia 2012" [online] https://www.bccr.fi.cr/seccion-cuentas-nacionales-periodo-2012/cuentas-nacionales-periodo-de-referencia-2012.

Central Bank of Honduras (2018), "Producto interno bruto enfoque del ingreso en valores corrientes, 2000–2017" [online database] http://www.bch.hn/pib_base2000.php.

Central Bank of Paraguay (2018), "Sistema de Cuentas Nacionales del Paraguay: serie 2008 al 2017" [online] https://www.bcp.gov.py/nuevo-ano-base-2014-i642.

Central Bank of Venezuela (2018), "Cuentas consolidadas de la Nación: base 1997" [online] http://www.bcv.org.ve/estadisticas/cuentas-consolidadas-de-la-nacion.

Ciminelli, G., R. Duval and D. Furceri (2018), "Employment protection deregulation and labour shares in advanced economies", *IMF Working Paper*, No. WP/18/186, Washington, D.C., International Monetary Fund (IMF).

Cimoli, M. and others (2017), "Productivity, social expenditure and income distribution in Latin America", *Brazilian Journal of Political Economy*, vol. 37, No. 4, São Paulo, Centro de Economia Política.

DANE (National Administrative Department of Statistics) (2018), "Cuentas Nacionales anuales: base 2015" [online] http://www.dane.gov.co/index.php/estadisticas-por-tema/cuentas-nacionales/cuentas-nacionales-anuales.

Dao, M. C. and others (2017), "Why is labour receiving a smaller share of global income? Theory and empirical evidence", *IMF Working Paper*, No. WP/17/169, Washington, D.C., International Monetary Fund (IMF).

ECLAC (Economic Commission for Latin America and the Caribbean) (2018a), *Social Panorama of Latin America, 2017* (LC/PUB.2018/1-P), Santiago.

___(2018b), *The Inefficiency of Inequality* (LC/SES.37/3-P), Santiago.

___(2017), *Social Panorama of Latin America, 2016* (LC/PUB.2017/12-P), Santiago.

___(2016a), *The social inequality matrix in Latin America* (LC/G.2690(MDS.1/2)), Santiago.

___(2016b), *Horizons 2030: Equality at the Centre of Sustainable Development* (LC/G.2660/Rev.1), Santiago.

___(2013a), *Social Panorama of Latin America, 2012* (LC/G.2557-P), Santiago.

___(2013b), *Statistical Yearbook for Latin America and the Caribbean, 2013* (LC/G.2582-P), Santiago.

___(2008), *Statistical Yearbook for Latin America and the Caribbean, 2007* (LC/G.2356-P), Santiago.

European Union (2017), *Monitoring social inclusion in Europe*, Luxembourg.

Frankema, E. (2009), "*Reconstructing Labour Income Shares in Argentina, Brazil and Mexico, 1870–2000*", Utrecht, Utrecht University.

Giovannoni, O. G. (2014), "What do we know about the labour share and the profit share? Part III: measures and structural factors", *Working Paper*, No. 805, Annandale-on-Hudson, Levy Economics Institute of Bard College.

Gollin, D. (2002), "Getting income shares right", *Journal of Political Economy*, vol. 110, No. 2, Chicago, The University of Chicago Press.

Guscina, A. (2006), "Effects of globalization on labour's share in national income", *IMF Working Paper*, No. 294, Washington, D.C., International Monetary Fund (IMF).

IBGE (Brazilian Geographical and Statistical Institute) (2018), "Sistema de Contas Nacionais - SNC" [online database] https://www.ibge.gov.br/estatisticas-novoportal/economicas/contas-nacionais/9052-sistema-de-contas-nacionais-brasil.html?=&t=resultados.

ILO (International Labour Organization) (2013), *Global Wage Report 2012/13: Wages and equitable growth*, Geneva.

___(2010), *Global Wage Report 2010/11: Wage policies in times of crisis*, Santiago.

INDEC (National Institute of Statistics and Censuses) (2018), "Cuenta de generación del ingreso para el total de la economía" [online] https://www.indec.gob.ar/informacion-de-archivo.asp.

INF (National Institute of Statistics) (2018), "Cuentas consolidadas de la Nación" [online database] https://www.ine.gob.bo/index.php/producto-interno-bruto-departamental-4/producto-interno-bruto-departamental-5.

___(1989a), *Cuentas nacionales definitivas 1978-1986*, La Paz.

___(1989b), *Boletín de Cuentas Nacionales*, No. 3, La Paz.

INEC (National Institute of Statistics and Census) (2018a), "Cuadro 36. Producto interno bruto en la República y su composición porcentual, según el enfoque del ingreso a precios corrientes: años 2007-15" [online] https://www.contraloria.gob.pa/inec/archivos/P8361PIB%20seg%C3%BAn%20el%20enfoque%20del%20Ingresos.pdf.

___(2018b), "Cuadro 1. Relaciones entre agregados de contabilidad nacional, en la República: años 2013–16" [online] https://www.contraloria.gob.pa/inec/archivos/P8371Relaciones%20%20entre%20%20%20Agregados%20%20de%20Contabilidad%20Nacional.pdf.

INEGI (National Institute of Statistics and Geography) (2018), "Por actividad de los bienes y servicios. Base 2013. Serie anual detallada desde 2003" [online] https://www.inegi.org.mx/app/tmp/tabuladoscn/default.html?tema=CBS.

INEI (National Institute of Statistics and Informatics) (2018), "Cuentas nacionales" [online database] https://www.inei.gob.pe/estadisticas/indice-tematico/national-accounts/.

Kennedy, D., L. Pacífico and M. Sánchez (2018), "La masa salarial y su composición según el vínculo laboral. Argentina. 1993–2017: propuesta de estimación en el marco de la base 2004 (2005–2015) y empalme con la base 1993", *Documentos de Trabajo*, No. 24, Buenos Aires, Research Centre on Population, Employment and Development (CEPED).

Kidyba, S. and D. Vega (2015), "Distribución funcional del ingreso en la Argentina, 1950–2007", *Studies and Perspectives-ECLAC Office in Buenos Aires series*, No. 44 (LC/L.4091-LC/BUE/L.223), Santiago, Economic Commission for Latin America and the Caribbean (ECLAC).

Lavoie, M. and E. Stockhammer (eds.) (2013), *Wage-led Growth: An Equitable Strategy for Economic Recovery*, Palgrave Macmillan/International Labour Organization (ILO).

Lindenboim, J. (2008), "Distribución funcional del ingreso, un tema olvidado que reclama atención", *Problemas del Desarrollo*, vol. 39, No. 153, Mexico City, National Autonomous University of Mexico.

OECD (Organization for Economic Cooperation and Development) (2012), *OECD Employment Outlook 2012*, Paris.

OPEC (Organization of Petroleum Exporting Countries) (2017), *OPEC Annual Statistical Bulletin 2017*, Vienna.

Stockhammer, E. (2013), "Why have wage shares fallen? A panel analysis of the determinants of functional income distribution", *Conditions of Work and Employment series*, No. 35, Geneva, International Labour Organization (ILO).

United Nations (2018), UNdata, "National accounts official country data" [online database] http://data.un.org/Data.aspx?d=SNA&f=group_code%3a401.

University of the Republic (2016), *Encuesta Financiera de los Hogares Uruguayos (EFHU-2): descripción y resultados*, Montevideo.

Young, A. (1995), "The tyranny of numbers: confronting the statistical realities of the East Asian growth experience", *The Quarterly Journal of Economics*, vol. 110, No. 3, Oxford, Oxford University Press.

Annex I.A1

Table I.A1.1
Latin America (18 countries): indicators of personal income distribution, 2001–2017[a]

Country	Year	Gini coefficient[b]	Theil index[c]	Atkinson index[c] (e=0,5)	Atkinson index[c] (e=1.0)	Atkinson index[c] (e=1.5)	Population with incomes below 50% of the median
Argentina[d]	2003	0.467	0.348	0.157	0.289	0.410	18.7
	2008	0.413	0.292	0.134	0.250	0.357	13.8
	2012	0.389	0.258	0.120	0.226	0.325	13.9
	2014	0.391	0.264	0.121	0.224	0.317	12.8
	2016	0.393	0.270	0.123	0.226	0.319	12.9
	2017	0.388	0.263	0.121	0.225	0.324	13.6
Bolivia (Plurinational State of)	2002	0.611	0.732	0.313	0.550	0.738	29.0
	2008	0.513	0.493	0.219	0.401	0.566	23.5
	2012	0.474	0.394	0.187	0.363	0.538	23.6
	2014	0.471	0.403	0.185	0.349	0.506	22.6
	2015	0.453	0.362	0.171	0.333	0.503	21.4
Brazil	2002	0.570	0.650	0.262	0.432	0.548	21.7
	2008	0.536	0.574	0.234	0.394	0.510	21.1
	2012	0.523	0.555	0.223	0.377	0.492	21.5
	2014	0.514	0.526	0.217	0.370	0.486	21.6
	2016[e]	0.540	0.560	0.233	0.397	0.519	22.7
	2017[e]	0.539	0.570	0.235	0.400	0.524	22.9
Chile	2003	0.507	0.514	0.211	0.359	0.478	18.7
	2009	0.478	0.453	0.188	0.323	0.434	15.8
	2011	0.469	0.430	0.181	0.313	0.419	15.1
	2013	0.466	0.424	0.178	0.306	0.408	14.2
	2015	0.453	0.408	0.170	0.293	0.392	14.1
	2017	0.454	0.417	0.172	0.295	0.394	14.1
Colombia	2002	0.567	0.663	0.266	0.447	0.586	23.5
	2008	0.572	0.652	0.268	0.456	0.600	25.1
	2012	0.539	0.573	0.240	0.414	0.553	23.3
	2014	0.540	0.577	0.240	0.412	0.547	23.0
	2016	0.521	0.541	0.225	0.388	0.520	21.9
	2017	0.511	0.515	0.216	0.375	0.504	21.5
Dominican Republic	2002	0.498	0.461	0.197	0.342	0.453	20.5
	2008	0.489	0.452	0.193	0.335	0.445	20.0
	2012	0.469	0.412	0.179	0.316	0.425	17.9
	2014	0.449	0.351	0.160	0.293	0.404	18.3
	2016	0.463	0.375	0.168	0.303	0.415	18.9
Costa Rica	2002[f]	0.497	0.462	0.198	0.349	0.475	20.0
	2008[f]	0.491	0.461	0.195	0.339	0.451	18.7
	2012	0.502	0.450	0.200	0.359	0.493	21.4
	2014	0.498	0.440	0.197	0.356	0.488	21.1
	2016	0.500	0.448	0.200	0.358	0.488	20.7
	2017	0.496	0.445	0.197	0.351	0.478	20.1
Ecuador	2001	0.538	0.643	0.244	0.395	0.502	18.1
	2008	0.493	0.458	0.195	0.337	0.448	18.6
	2012	0.464	0.393	0.171	0.303	0.412	19.0
	2014	0.449	0.400	0.168	0.291	0.388	16.3
	2016	0.445	0.391	0.165	0.290	0.392	16.2
	2017	0.440	0.375	0.161	0.284	0.386	17.0
El Salvador	2001	0.514	0.481	0.209	0.371	0.503	23.3
	2009	0.478	0.428	0.186	0.327	0.440	19.9
	2001	0.514	0.481	0.209	0.371	0.503	23.3
	2014	0.434	0.340	0.151	0.273	0.373	17.6
	2016	0.420	0.313	0.141	0.257	0.357	17.7
	2017	0.399	0.295	0.13 1	0.239	0.332	16.2

Table I.A1.1 (concluded)

Country	Year	Gini coefficient[b]	Theil index[c]	Atkinson index[c]			Population with incomes below 50% of the median
				(e=0,5)	(e=1.0)	(e=1.5)	
Guatemala	2000	0.636	0.883	0.341	0.558	0.714	27.0
	2006	0.558	0.608	0.253	0.432	0.567	25.5
	2014	0.535	0.664	0.248	0.407	0.533	22.2
Honduras	2001	0.532	0.526	0.226	0.392	0.519	23.2
	2009	0.502	0.480	0.204	0.353	0.467	21.3
	2013	0.515	0.579	0.225	0.374	0.487	19.9
	2014	0.481	0.428	0.185	0.325	0.435	19.0
	2016	0.480	0.424	0.187	0.336	0.462	20.9
Mexico	2002	0.506	0.489	0.209	0.362	0.476	20.7
	2008	0.513	0.535	0.219	0.376	0.498	20.8
	2012	0.499	0.499	0.207	0.359	0.486	19.9
	2014	0.502	0.511	0.209	0.357	0.475	19.1
	2016[g]	0.504	0.473	0.195	0.335	0.446	17.7
Nicaragua	2001	0.568	0.536	0.231	0.408	0.561	22.5
	2009	0.463	0.400	0.175	0.314	0.440	19.9
	2014	0.495	0.511	0.207	0.355	0.476	19.9
Panama	2001	0.575	0.616	0.273	0.488	0.658	28.4
	2008	0.528	0.518	0.229	0.410	0.553	24.9
	2011	0.528	0.520	0.228	0.404	0.543	25.0
	2014	0.509	0.470	0.212	0.386	0.531	24.3
	2016	0.513	0.475	0.215	0.390	0.532	24.1
	2017	0.508	0.480	0.212	0.382	0.523	24.8
Paraguay	2002	0.584	0.648	0.259	0.439	0.584	24.7
	2008	0.516	0.564	0.224	0.377	0.494	21.1
	2012	0.489	0.438	0.192	0.344	0.472	23.4
	2014	0.522	0.542	0.219	0.372	0.493	21.5
	2016	0.497	0.501	0.207	0.356	0.473	21.4
	2017	0.503	0.500	0.202	0.341	0.447	19.4
Peru	2002	0.544	0.610	0.248	0.422	0.560	24.4
	2008	0.495	0.450	0.201	0.364	0.500	24.7
	2012	0.457	0.383	0.173	0.318	0.445	22.3
	2014	0.446	0.369	0.165	0.303	0.424	21.5
	2016	0.452	0.377	0.169	0.309	0.431	21.4
	2017	0.448	0.368	0.165	0.303	0.422	20.9
Uruguay	2002[d]	0.474	0.393	0.177	0.322	0.448	21.1
	2008	0.453	0.382	0.166	0.295	0.397	18.7
	2012	0.391	0.262	0.122	0.228	0.320	16.5
	2014	0.392	0.271	0.124	0.229	0.319	16.3
	2016	0.391	0.269	0.123	0.227	0.316	16.3
	2017	0.390	0.272	0.123	0.225	0.311	15.8
Venezuela (Bolivarian Republic of)	2002	0.418	0.317	0.140	0.253	0.355	13.7
	2008	0.379	0.248	0.114	0.212	0.298	13.9
	2012	0.384	0.260	0.118	0.218	0.308	15.3
	2014	0.378	0.242	0.112	0.210	0.300	14.8

Source: Economic Commission for Latin America and the Caribbean (ECLAC), on the basis of Household Survey Data Bank (BADEHOG).

[a] Calculation based on the distribution of per capita personal income throughout the country.

[b] Includes persons with no income.

[c] To reduce the effect of extreme values, the Theil and Atkinson indices exclude values close to zero and the three highest per capita incomes.

[d] Urban total.

[e] From 2016 onward, data from the National Household Survey (PNAD-Continua) are not comparable with those of previous years.

[f] Data prior to 2010 are not comparable with those of later years.

[g] Estimates based on the 2016 statistical model for MCS-ENIGH continuity, prepared by the National Institute of Statistics and Geography (INEGI) to mitigate the lack of comparability between the 2016 survey and the 2008–2014 series.

Figure I.A1.1

Latin America (15 countries): share of wages in GDP (at market prices), from early 1970s to latest year with information available[a]

(Percentages)

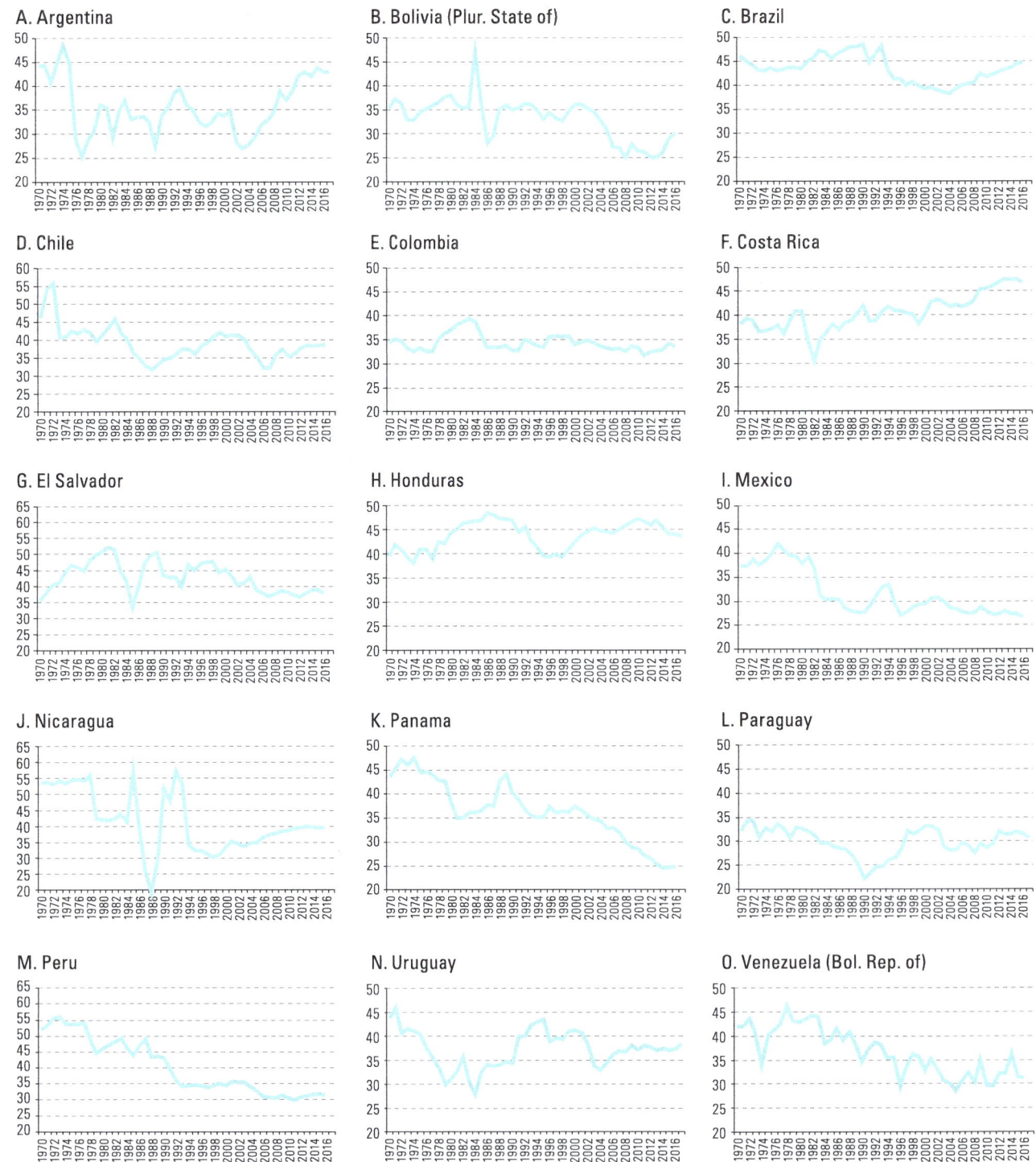

Source: Economic Commission for Latin America and the Caribbean (ECLAC), on the basis of official information from the countries
[a] The latest year with information available is 2016 for most countries; the Bolivarian Republic of Venezuela and Brazil are exceptions.

Table I.A1.2
Latin America (17 countries): shares of wages and estimated labour income in GDP at market prices[a]
(Percentages)

Country	Year	Wage share of GDP	Labour income share of GDP (estimation 1)	Labour income share of GDP (estimation 2)
Argentina	2003	27.0	36.1	30.9
	2016	42.8	56.6	50.7
Bolivia (Plurinational State of)	2002	35.2	81.4	48.7
	2015	28.8	63.9	44.4
Brazil	2002	38.9	58.2	47.5
	2015	44.6	63.2	53.0
Chile	2003	40.0	57.4	47.6
	2015	38.4	50.8	43.7
Colombia	2002	33.7	64.0	45.2
	2015	33.5	65.4	45.3
Costa Rica	2002	43.2	60.5	51.9
	2015	47.5	61.1	54.3
Dominican Republic	2007	34.6	61.7	49.3
	2013	35.0	63.7	49.5
Ecuador	2008	31.0	50.8	41.7
	2015	38.5	62.5	49.1
El Salvador	2005	38.9	64.1	47.9
	2016	37.8	58.5	47.1
Honduras	2004	44.7	78.2	58.4
	2015	44.0	73.2	59.6
Mexico	2004	28.4	41.0	35.6
	2016	26.6	37.1	33.1
Nicaragua	2006	36.5	64.0	49.2
	2014	39.7	66.3	51.5
Panama	2002	35.2	52.3	40.2
	2016	24.8	36.7	28.6
Paraguay	2004	28.0	56.7	41.0
	2016	31.4	52.1	41.4
Peru	2002	35.5	71.1	45.7
	2016	31.5	59.4	41.3
Uruguay	2004	32.6	45.1	40.0
	2016	37.2	51.2	44.8
Venezuela (Bolivarian Republic of)	2002	33.0	49.0	40.9
	2014	38.4	52.8	47.5

Source: Economic Commission for Latin America and the Caribbean (ECLAC), on the basis of CEPALSTAT, Household Survey Data Bank (BADEHOG) and official information from the countries.

[a] In estimation 1 of the mixed income of non-wage-earning workers, the average wage is used as a comparison criterion; and in estimation 2 the comparison is made using different average wages, according to personal characteristics and sector of economic activity.

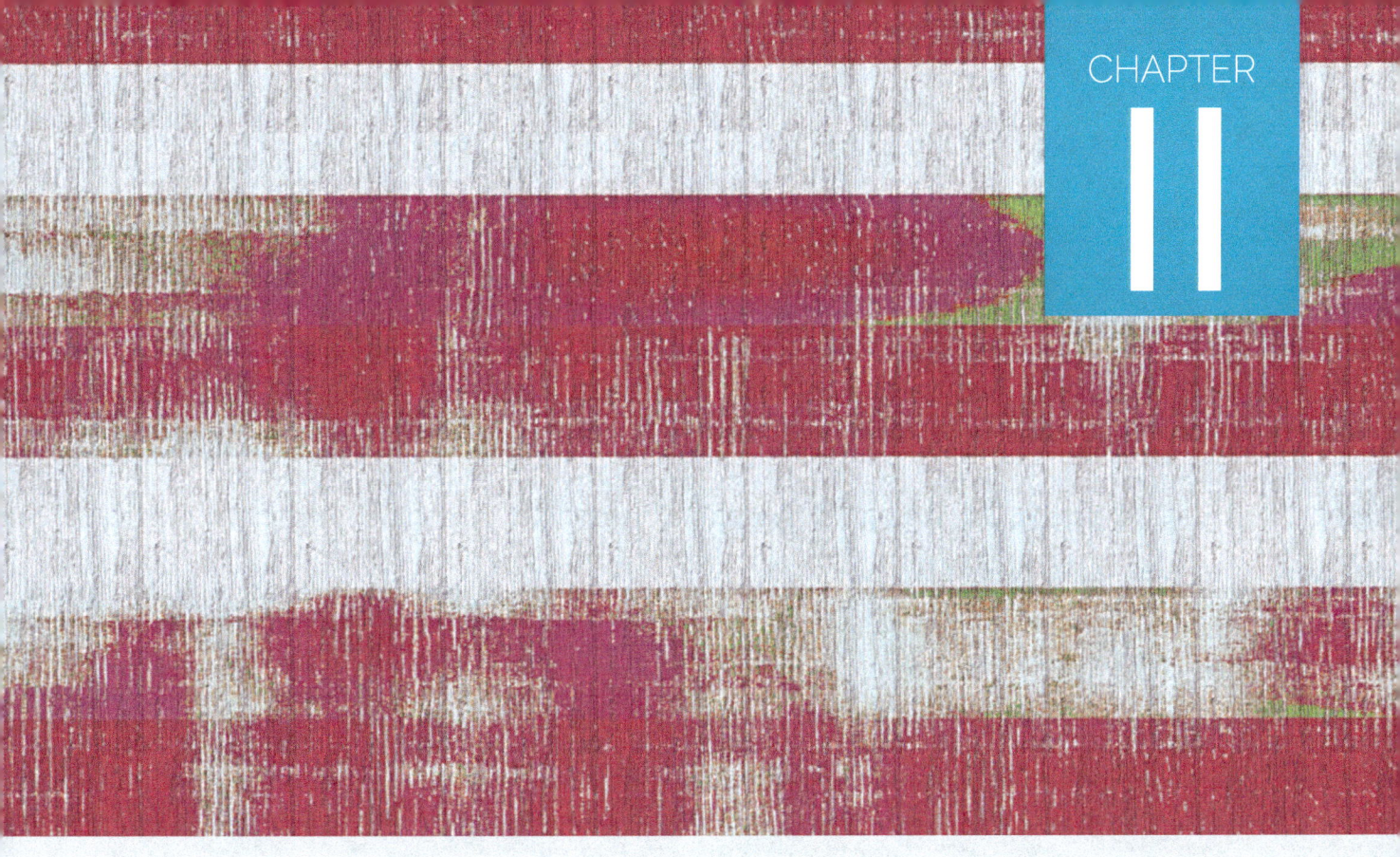

Poverty in Latin America: long-term trends and recent developments

Introduction

This chapter offers an updated review of the magnitude and trends of poverty in Latin America and the factors relating to these. Section A analyses recent developments in poverty and extreme poverty at the regional level, and their trends since 2002, on the basis of comparable measurements estimated by ECLAC using the methodology described in box II.1.[1] This section also examines levels and recent variations in poverty in the countries of the region and compares these with variations in the official estimates of each country.

Section B examines some of the factors relating to poverty trends. In particular, it analyses the effects of changes in average household income and its distribution, and changes in the various income sources of poor households. On this basis, it then analyses each country's probability of achieving the poverty reduction targets proposed in the Sustainable Development Goals.

Lastly, section C describes the incidence of poverty in different population groups, by area of residence, ethnicity, sex, age and educational level. It also looks at the relationship between monetary poverty and other dimensions that complement the analysis, such as access to basic water and sanitation services.

A.   Developments in income poverty

The number of people living in poverty and extreme poverty in Latin America continued to rise in 2017. Although the poverty rate held steady with respect to the previous year, the extreme poverty rate is the highest for at least 10 years. Despite the adverse situation in the region overall, poverty indicators did not rise in most countries.

In 2017, the number of poor in Latin America reached 184 million, equivalent to 30.2% of the population, while the number of extremely poor stood at 62 million, or 10.2% of the population (see figure II.1).

The results presented testify to a standstill in poverty rates and a deterioration in extreme poverty figures since 2015. According to ECLAC estimates, between 2002 and 2014 poverty and extreme poverty both fell considerably in the region: the poverty rate from 44.5% to 27.8%, and the extreme poverty rate from 11.2% to 7.8%, with the steepest fall occurring in the first half of that period. However, in 2015 and again in 2016 both rates rose, representing a setback that was especially severe in the case of extreme poverty. The figures for 2017 show a further rise, albeit a small one, in extreme poverty, while the overall poverty figure shows no variation from 2016.[2]

ECLAC projects a slight rise of 1.3 GDP points in the region's economic growth in 2018, which could help to ease poverty down to 29.6%.[3] This would take the number living in poverty down to around 2 million. In turn, the extreme poverty rate will likely remain at the same level as in 2017, which would push up the numbers living in this situation by around 1 million.

---

[1]   The poverty figures estimated by ECLAC are calculated in order to increase comparability for analytical purposes. Their objectives and uses differ from those of national figures, and they are in no way intended to substitute national figures in describing poverty levels and trends in each country.

[2]   These figures differ from those reported in *Social Panorama of Latin America, 2017*, owing to an overall review of the country estimates following the issue of that publication.

[3]   See [online] https://www.cepal.org/en/pressreleases/economic-activity-latin-america-and-caribbean-will-expand-13-2018-and-18-2019.

Box II.1

Income poverty measurement employed by the Economic Commission for Latin America and the Caribbean (ECLAC)

The poverty and extreme poverty figures presented in this chapter are calculated by ECLAC on the basis of a common methodology, which is intended to provide a regional perspective that is as comparable as possible, within the heterogeneity of the measurement tools and compilation procedures of each country's own data.

Unlike the context in which the first ECLAC poverty estimates were produced, today the countries' national poverty measurements are performed by national statistical offices or other public departments, and in most cases have the status of official data. A range of procedures and assumptions are adopted for these measurements, which gives them the specificity necessary for use in the national context, but limits their comparability between countries.

The data used to build poverty lines come from surveys that measure household expenditure —either income and expenditure surveys or surveys on household living conditions— from the mid-2000s to the mid-2010s.

In turn, the methodology used in this chapter presents certain innovations with respect to ECLAC (1991), on which the poverty measurements published until 2015 were based. As shown in the table below, there are differences at several stages of the process, although the overall procedure remains the same.

Comparison between methodologies used in ECLAC (1991) and ECLAC (2018)

	1991	2018
Information source	- Household budget surveys carried out in the 1980s in 10 countries - Energy intake recommendations in FAO/WHO/UNU (1985)	- Household budget surveys carried out between the mid-2000s and the mid-2010s in 18 countries - Energy intake recommendations in FAO/WHO/UNU (2001)
Reference population	- First rolling quintile that attains the average energy intake	First rolling quintile that meets two conditions: - Presents less than 10% of critical deficiencies - Has a median income equivalent to or above the poverty line (iteration).
Basket of staple foods	- Selected on the basis of observed consumption patterns - With nutritional adjustments - Without consumption outside the household	- Selected on the basis of observed consumption patterns - With nutritional adjustments - With consumption outside the household
Orshansky coefficient	- Single value for all countries (2.0 and 1.75) - From 2007, variable value based on price trends but not price structure	- Country-specific values, based on price structure and trends
Updating of poverty lines	- Various criteria - From 2007, consumer price index (CPI) of foods in the basket of staple foods and CPI for non-food products	- CPI of foods in the basket of staple foods and CPI for non-food products
Total household income	- With correction for non-response - Adjusted to national accounts	- Revised income aggregates to ensure consistency with international recommendations - Application of upper limit to imputed rent - With correction for non-response - Without adjustment to national accounts

Source: Economic Commission for Latin America and the Caribbean (ECLAC), *Medición de la pobreza por ingresos: actualización metodológica y resultados* (LC/PUB.2018/22-P), Santiago, December 2018; Food and Agriculture Organization of the United Nations/World Health Organization/United Nations University (FAO/OMS/UNU), *Human Vitamin and Mineral Requirements*, Bangkok, 2001 and *Energy and protein requirements. Report of a Joint FAO/WHO/UNU Expert Consultation*, 1985 [online] http://apps.who.int/iris/handle/10665/39527.

Figure II.1
Latin America (18 countries): poverty and extreme poverty rates and persons living in poverty and extreme poverty, 2002–2018[a]
(Percentages and millions of persons)

A. Percentages

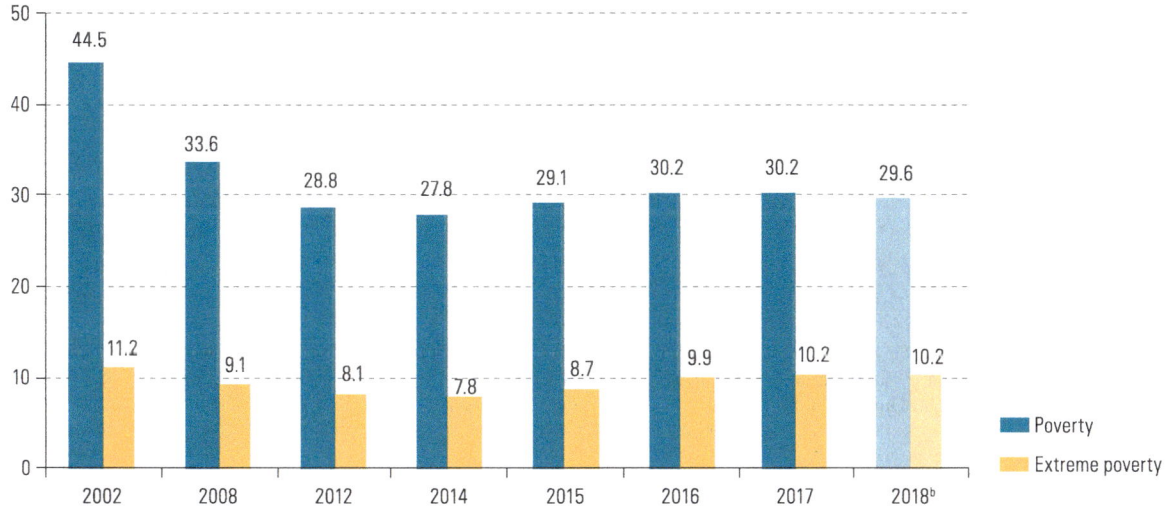

B. Millions of persons

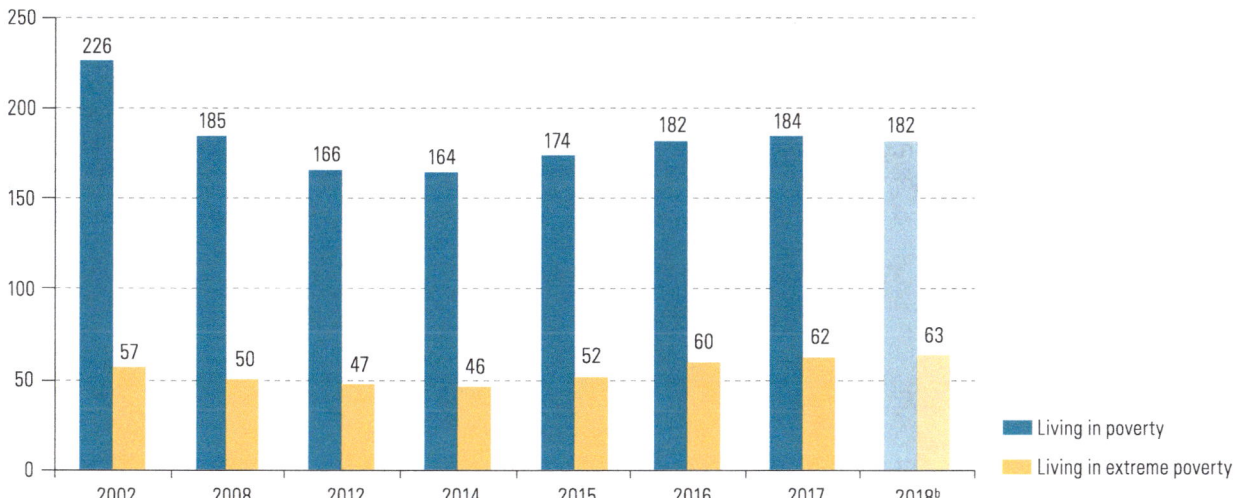

Source: Economic Commission for Latin America and the Caribbean (ECLAC), on the basis of Household Survey Data Bank (BADEHOG).
[a] Weighted average for the following countries: Argentina, Bolivarian Republic of Venezuela, Brazil, Chile, Colombia, Costa Rica, Dominican Republic, Ecuador, El Salvador, Guatemala, Honduras, Mexico, Nicaragua, Panama, Paraguay, Peru, Plurinational State of Bolivia and Uruguay.
[b] The figure for 2018 is a projection.

The change in the number of people living in poverty reflects the combined variations in the poverty rate and in the population. Between 2002 and 2008 and again between 2008 and 2014, the poverty rate fell far enough to offset population growth, which led to a reduction in the absolute number of people living in poverty in both these periods. Between 2014 and 2017, the rise in the poverty rate and growth in the population reinforced each other, so that the absolute number of people living in poverty rose more than the poverty rate (see figure II.2).

Figure II.2
Latin America
(18 countries): effect of
variations in population
and in poverty rates
on the total number of
people living in poverty,
2002–2017[a]
(Percentages)

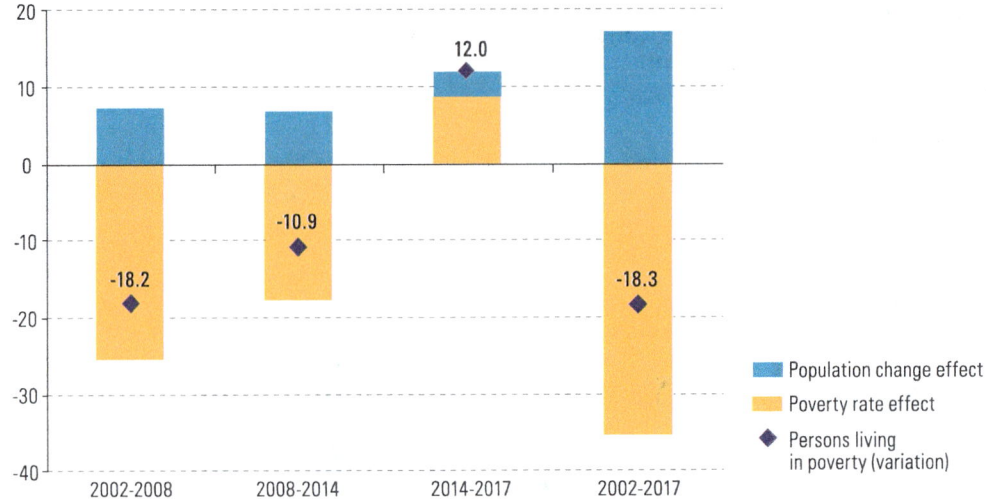

Source: Economic Commission for Latin America and the Caribbean (ECLAC), on the basis of Household Survey Data Bank (BADEHOG).
[a] Weighted average for the following countries: Argentina, Bolivarian Republic of Venezuela, Brazil, Chile, Colombia, Costa Rica,
Dominican Republic, Ecuador, El Salvador, Guatemala, Honduras, Mexico, Nicaragua, Panama, Paraguay, Peru, Plurinational State
of Bolivia and Uruguay.

As occurs with other variables, the Latin American countries show marked differences in levels of poverty and extreme poverty. Only two countries —Chile and Uruguay— have a poverty rate below 15%. Seven countries have a poverty rate between 15% and 25%, and another six have poverty rates of over 25%. There is also a direct relationship between poverty and extreme poverty rates. The countries where poverty is lowest also have the lowest rates of extreme poverty: Argentina, Chile, Costa Rica and Uruguay have extreme poverty rates under 5%; Brazil, the Dominican Republic, Ecuador, El Salvador, Panama, Paraguay and Peru have extreme poverty rates of between 5% and 10%, while in the other countries these rates exceed 10% (see table II.1).

Table II.1
Latin America
(15 countries): classification
of countries by poverty
and extreme poverty
rates, 2017[a]

		Poverty			
		Below 15%	**Between 15% and 25%**	**Between 25% and 35%**	**Over 35%**
Extreme poverty	Below 5%	Chile Uruguay	Argentina Costa Rica		
	Between 5% and 10%		Brazil Ecuador Panama Paraguay Peru	Dominican Republic	El Salvador
	Between 10% and 15%			Colombia	Mexico
	Over 15%				Bolivia (Plurinational State of) Honduras

Source: Economic Commission for Latin America and the Caribbean (ECLAC), on the basis of Household Survey Data Bank (BADEHOG).
[a] The surveys correspond to 2017, except in the Dominican Republic, Honduras and Mexico (2016 in all three cases).

Between 2016 and 2017, poverty rates fell by more than a percentage point in 5 of the 12 countries with information available: in Argentina, Colombia, Costa Rica, El Salvador and Paraguay. Chile also saw poverty decrease, in this case between 2015 and 2017. The official estimates available for these countries corroborate the trends described, although the estimates are larger in Argentina and El Salvador, smaller in Costa Rica and similar in the other countries (see table II.2, figure II.3 and annex table II.A1.2).

Table II.2
Latin America
(15 countries): poverty
and extreme poverty
rates according to
ECLAC estimates and
official national figures,
2015, 2016 and 2017[a]
(Percentages)

	ECLAC estimates							
	Extreme poverty				Poverty			
	2015	2016	2017	Variation 2016–2017	2015	2016	2017	Variation 2016–2017
Argentina[b]	...	2.9	2.8	-0.1	...	21.5	18.7	-2.8
Bolivia (Plurinational State of)	14.7	16.7	16.4	-0.3	35.0	35.3	35.2	-0.1
Brazil[c]	4.0	5.1	5.5	0.4	18.8	19.5	19.9	0.4
Chile	1.8	...	1.4	-0.4[d]	13.7	...	10.7	-3.0[d]
Colombia	11.3	12.0	10.9	-1.1	30.6	30.9	29.8	-1.1
Costa Rica	4.6	4.2	3.3	-0.9	17.4	16.5	15.1	-1.4
Dominican Republic[e]	9.2	8.4	...	...	29.7	27.4	...	...
Ecuador	6.3	6.6	6.2	-0.4	22.9	23.3	22.8	-0.5
El Salvador	10.4	10.7	8.3	-2.4	42.6	40.5	37.8	-2.7
Honduras	19.0	18.8	...	...	55.2	53.2	...	...
Mexico	...	11.7	...	...	...	43.7	...	...
Panama	8.0	8.5	7.6	-0.9	17.9	17.0	16.7	-0.3
Paraguay	7.3	7.9	6.0	-1.9	23.4	24.0	21.6	-2.4
Peru	5.4	5.2	5.0	-0.2	19.0	19.1	18.9	-0.2
Uruguay	0.2	0.2	0.1	-0.1	4.2	3.5	2.7	-0.8

	Official estimates by the countries							
	Extreme poverty				Poverty			
	2015	2016	2017	Variation 2016–2017	2015	2016	2017	Variation 2016–2017
Argentina[b]	...	6.1	4.8	-1.3	...	30.3	25.7	-4.6
Bolivia (Plurinational State of)	16.8	18.3	17.1	-1.2	38.6	39.5	36.4	-3.1
Chile	3.5	...	2.3	-1.2[d]	11.7	...	8.6	-3.1[d]
Colombia	7.9	8.5	7.4	-1.1	27.8	28.0	26.9	-1.1
Costa Rica[f]	7.2	6.3	5.7	-0.6	21.7	20.5	20.0	-0.5
Dominican Republic[e]	6.3	4.5	3.8	-0.7	30.8	28.6	25.5	-3.1
Ecuador	8.5	8.7	7.9	-0.8	23.3	22.9	21.5	-1.4
El Salvador[f]	8.1	7.9	6.2	-1.7	34.9	32.7	29.2	-3.5
Honduras[f]	44.7	42.5	...	...	68.7	65.7	...	...
Mexico[g]	...	17.5	...	...	...	50.6	...	...
Nicaragua	...	6.9	...	...	...	24.9	...	...
Panama	10.2	9.9	9.8	-0.1	23	22.1	20.7	-1.4
Paraguay	5.4	5.7	4.4	-1.3	26.6	28.9	26.4	-2.5
Peru	4.1	3.8	2.8	-1.0	21.8	20.7	21.7	1.0
Uruguay	0.3	0.2	0.1	-0.1	9.7	9.4	7.9	-1.5

Source: Economic Commission for Latin America and the Caribbean (ECLAC), on the basis of Household Survey Data Bank (BADEHOG) and official figures on poverty and extreme poverty.

[a] Countries for which ECLAC poverty estimates are available for 2015 onward.

[b] ECLAC estimates refer to the fourth quarter of each year. The official estimates refer to the second quarter of each year.

[c] The figures from 2015 onward correspond to the continuous national household survey (PNAD Contínua) and are not comparable with those of earlier years.

[d] Refers to the variation between 2015 and 2017.

[e] The ECLAC figures for the Dominican Republic are based on the national labour force survey and refer to September of each year. The official annual estimates from 2016 onward are based on the continuous national labour force survey.

[f] The official estimates refer to households.

[g] In Mexico, the official poverty measurement is multidimensional. For greater comparability, therefore, the estimates published by the National Council for the Evaluation of Social Development Policy (CONEVAL) are used as an unofficial national reference, namely "population below the minimum welfare threshold", which is taken as a measure of "extreme poverty", and "population below the welfare threshold", which serves as a proxy for "total poverty".

Figure II.3
Latin America (11 countries): variation in the poverty and extreme poverty rates according to ECLAC figures and official national figures, 2016–2017[a]
(Percentage points)

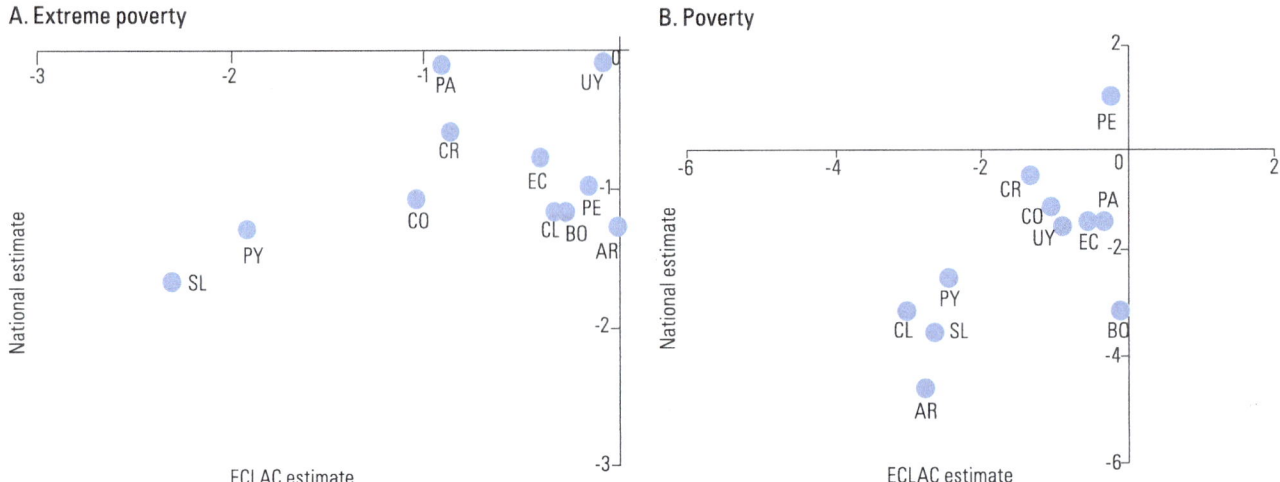

A. Extreme poverty

B. Poverty

Source: Economic Commission for Latin America and the Caribbean (ECLAC), on the basis of Household Survey Data Bank (BADEHOG) and official figures on poverty and extreme poverty.

In the other countries, the poverty rate came down slightly, by less than a percentage point, according to ECLAC estimates. This is the case of Ecuador, Panama, Peru, the Plurinational State of Bolivia and Uruguay. Among the countries with data available to 2017, only Brazil showed a slight rise in poverty. As for the previous group of countries, the official poverty estimates coincide in the direction of variation, although in general they report larger poverty reductions in Ecuador, Panama, the Plurinational State of Bolivia and Uruguay. Peru is the only case in which the direction of the two estimates differs, with the official estimates showing an increase in poverty.[4]

Because the poverty figures calculated by ECLAC and the countries' official figures have different emphases, different criteria are employed in their calculation. The ECLAC figures aim to reflect the situation in the region in the most comparable manner possible, while the national figures seek to best capture the realities of each country. This leads to normal methodological differences in the many decisions that are made in the process of building poverty lines (the way the goods in staple food and non-food baskets are selected, the prices used to allocate value to these goods or the deflators used to update poverty lines, among many other factors), as well as in the definition of household income, the treatment of non-responses or the inclusion of imputed rent for the use of owner-occupied dwellings. Despite these differences, the short- and medium-term variations in the two measurements are consistent, which testifies to the validity of each as a suitable tool for the proposed objectives.

Although it is good news that poverty and extreme poverty decreased in several of the region's countries in 2017, the pace of the decline is slower than in previous periods in most of them. If the variation in poverty from 2015 until the most recent year available (2016 in some countries) is compared with the variation between 2008 and 2012 and between 2012 and 2015,[5] it is evident that the reduction in extreme poverty since 2015

---

4   The official estimates of Peru and the ECLAC estimates differ owing, among other factors, to a discrepancy in the indicator on household resources, as Peru measures consumption and ECLAC calculates income.
5   ECLAC (2018a) gives a more detailed analysis of the variation in poverty since 2002.

exceeds the falls seen since 2008 only in Costa Rica, El Salvador and Paraguay. Mexico also saw a rapid fall in the recent period, but no variation in that immediately preceding. In another nine countries, extreme poverty fell less than in one of the two earlier periods, and in two countries, extreme poverty rose between 2015 and 2017, in contrast to previous periods (see figure II.4).

Figure II.4
Latin America (15 countries): annual variation in poverty and extreme poverty rates by country, 2012–2017[a]
(Percentages)

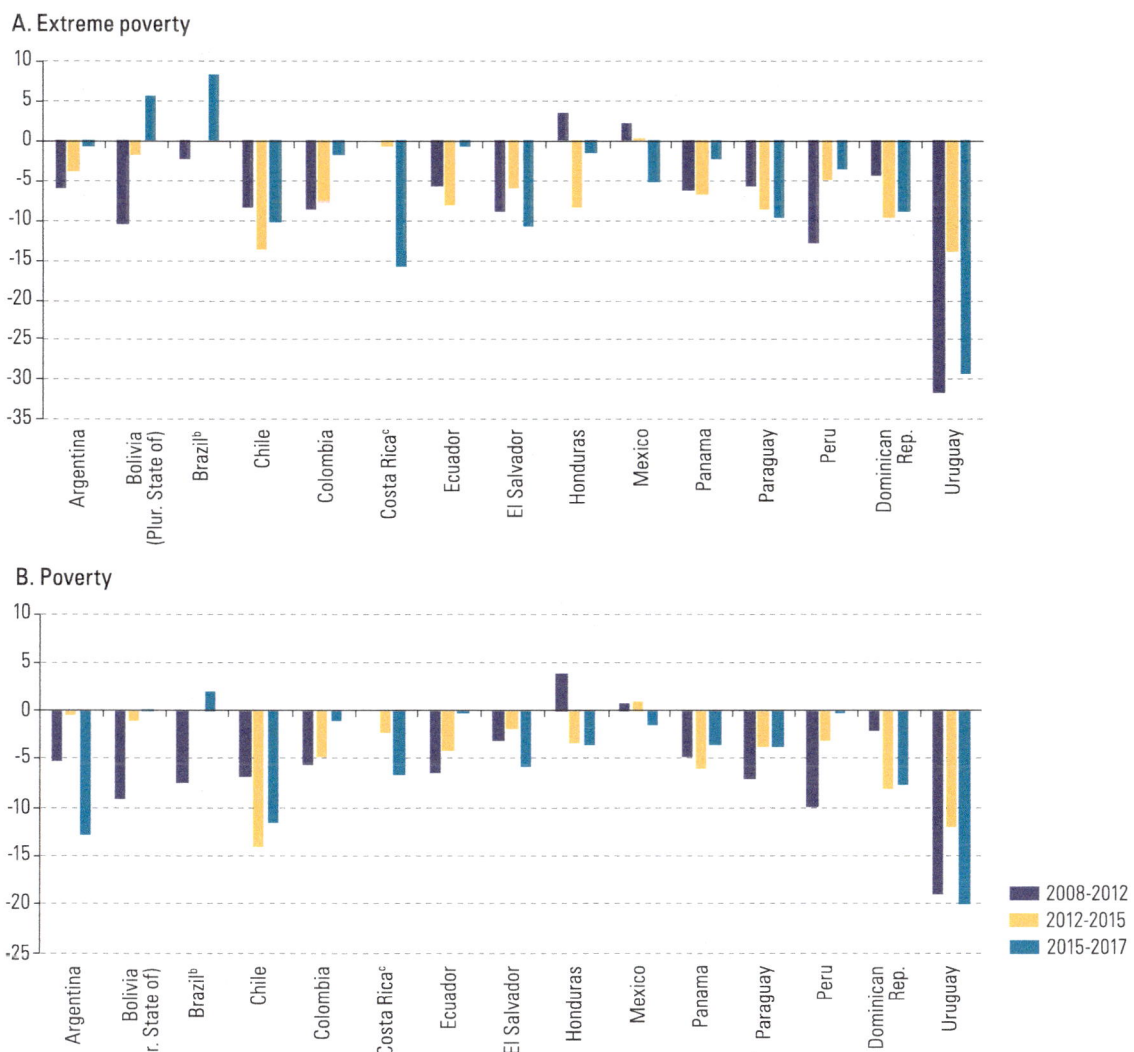

A. Extreme poverty

B. Poverty

2008-2012
2012-2015
2015-2017

Source: Economic Commission for Latin America and the Caribbean (ECLAC), on the basis of Household Survey Data Bank (BADEHOG).

[a] The surveys correspond to the years mentioned in each subperiod, except in the cases of Argentina (2008, 2012, 2016 and 2017), Brazil (2008, 2012, 2016 and 2017), Chile (2009, 2011, 2015 and 2017), the Dominican Republic (2008, 2012, 2015 and 2016), El Salvador (2009, 2013, 2015 and 2017), Honduras (2009, 2013, 2015 and 2016), Mexico (2008, 2012, 2014 and 2016) and Panama (2008, 2011, 2015 and 2017).

[b] The figures for 2016 and 2017 in Brazil are not comparable with those for previous years.

[c] The figures for 2008 in Costa Rica are not comparable with those for 2010 onward.

In the case of poverty, the scenario is a little more positive, in that the variation since 2015 was more favourable than that of the previous period in six countries (Argentina, Costa Rica, El Salvador, Honduras, Mexico and Uruguay). However, in nine countries the poverty reduction since 2015 was weaker than in previous periods, including in three countries where poverty rates stood still and one in which they rose.

B. Factors related to the recent poverty variations

Among the countries that achieved the greatest reduction in poverty in the period 2012–2017, in Chile, the Dominican Republic and El Salvador, labour earnings were the source of income that rose the most in the poorest households, while in Costa Rica, Panama and Uruguay, transfers received by poor households were at least as important as labour income. This corroborates the importance of endowing those living in poverty with greater resources and of bolstering labour income in combination with transfers and stronger social protection systems.

1. Level and distribution of household income

The behaviour of the poverty rate in a given period is directly related to two factors: the change in average household income and the change in how income is distributed among households. If average income rises (in real terms) and distribution remains unchanged, the level of poverty declines. The poverty rate should also fall if average household income remains unchanged, but income inequality decreases.

In practice, changes in poverty levels can be broken down into two groups: the effect of variations in average income (also known as "growth effect") and the "distribution effect" (see box II.2). It is important to analyse the impact of both these elements in the period 2012–2017, when poverty reduction slowed. This also complements similar analyses carried out in the previous edition of *Social Panorama*, which encompassed the periods 2002–2008 and 2008–2016 (ECLAC, 2018a). Changes in the poverty rate over shorter periods (for example, the last year) tend to be too small for this methodology to yield significant results.

Between 2012 and 2017, average income variation was the dominant effect in the countries in which poverty fell the fastest (5% or more per year), where it accounted for over two thirds of the total decline in poverty. This group includes Chile, the Dominican Republic, Panama and Uruguay. In turn, the distribution effect was stronger in countries where poverty declined more slowly. This was the case in Colombia, Ecuador, El Salvador, Honduras and Peru. Argentina and Costa Rica were exceptions within this second group of countries, since their moderate falls in poverty were due almost exclusively to improvements in average household income (see figure II.5).

This result confirms that the redistributive factor has become more important as poverty reduction has slowed in the region. Between 2002 and 2008, when poverty fell considerably in most of the countries, the rise in average household income predominated in almost all cases (ECLAC, 2018a). Although the redistributive factor has not had such a large impact as the rise in average income, its contribution has nevertheless been essential for strengthening poverty reduction and for avoiding backsliding.

Box II.2

Effect of changes in income distribution and levels on households living in poverty

According to the traditional methodology for measuring poverty, based on income insufficiency, a country's poverty rate at a given moment is determined by three elements: the poverty line; average income; and the structure of the income distribution. Hence, if the poverty line is kept constant in real terms, changes in the poverty indicator can be analysed from the perspective of variations in average income and in income distribution.

According to Datt and Ravallion (1992), a poverty indicator can be calculated using the initial-period income distribution and the average income level of the end period. The difference between this indicator and the initial-period poverty rate can be interpreted as a growth effect. It is also possible to calculate the poverty rate that corresponds to the average income of the initial period, but with an income distribution similar to that of the final period. The difference between this indicator and the initial poverty rate is the distribution effect. Both effects can also be calculated by exchanging the initial and end periods.

In formal terms, if $H(yt,dt)$ is the poverty indicator for period t, determined by average income (yt) and the shape of the distribution (dt), the growth and distribution effects can be decomposed as follows:

$$H(y_2,d_2) - H(y_1,d_1) = \underbrace{[H(y_2,d_1) - H(y_1,d_1)]}_{\text{Growth effect}} + \underbrace{[H(y_1,d_2) - H(y_1,d_1)]}_{\text{Distribution effect}} + R$$

In this decomposition, the strength of each effect depends on the base year used in the comparison (initial or final year), and it produces an unexplained residual. Both obstacles can be overcome by averaging the calculated effects using each of the two base years respectively (Kakwani,1997), which is the procedure used to perform the calculations in this chapter.

The link between growth, distributive change and poverty can be used to simulate the trajectory of poverty rates in the future. For this, the methodology used generates a new income distribution (y^*) applying specific growth rates (β) and distributive change (α) to per capita household income (y) in each country, captured in household surveys, by means of the following equations:

If $y \geq \mu$: $y^* = (1+\beta)[(1-\alpha)y_1 + \alpha\mu]$

If $y < \mu$: $y^* = (1+\beta)[\theta y_1]$,

where θ is calculated such that $\mu^* = (1+\beta)\mu$. (where μ represents the average income distribution)

In other words, the methodology is to increase (or decrease) below-average incomes at a fixed rate, and reduce (or increase) higher-than-average incomes at a rate proportional to the distance between each value and the mean.

Source: Economic Commission for Latin America and the Caribbean (ECLAC), on the basis of G. Datt and M. Ravallion, "Growth and redistribution components of changes in poverty measures", *Journal of Development Economics*, vol. 38, No. 2, Amsterdam, Elsevier, 1992, and N. Kakwani, "On measuring growth and inequality components of changes in poverty with application to Thailand", *Discussion Paper*, Sydney, University of New South Wales, 1997.

Figure II.5
Latin America (14 countries): annual variation in poverty rate and growth and distribution effects, 2012–2017[a]
(Percentages)

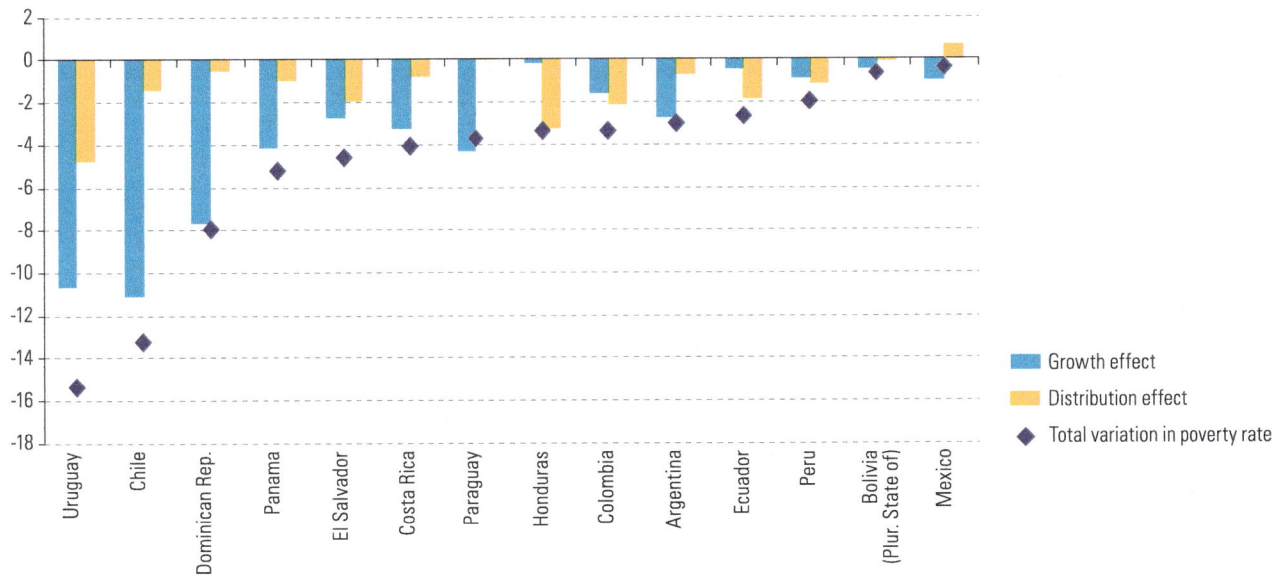

Source: Economic Commission for Latin America and the Caribbean (ECLAC), on the basis of Household Survey Data Bank (BADEHOG).
[a] Countries in order of the annual variation in the poverty rate. The data refer to 2012 and 2017, except in the cases of Chile, El Salvador and Honduras, where the initial year is 2011, and the Dominican Republic, Honduras and Mexico, where the final year is 2016.

2. Trends in the income sources of households living in poverty

The behaviour of poverty levels is determined by the rise or fall in the income of households at the lower end of the distribution. For this analysis, and in the absence of longitudinal surveys that would serve to identify changes in the income sources of the same households, the variations between 2012 and 2017 are studied for the same proportion of households (those whose per capita income at the start of the period was below the poverty line). Thus, if poor households represented 20% of the total in 2012, for 2017 the poorest 20% of households by income are selected, regardless of whether the households in that range are living in poverty or not. This analysis is approximate and is used here in the same way as in similar studies internationally researching this type of phenomena on the basis of non-longitudinal surveys.[6]

Income comes from three sources: (a) labour income; (b) income from pensions and transfers; and (c) other income (which includes income from the ownership of assets and imputed rent in the case of owner-occupied dwellings). Labour income is the compensation obtained for work as a wage-earning or independent worker. Transfers may come from the State, from civil society organizations or from other households. The total income from each source may rise or fall depending on the number of recipients of income from that source in each household and on the average amount they each receive.

Between 2012 and 2017, a distinction may be drawn between countries where poverty fell heavily (by 5% per year or more) and those where the decline was more moderate (less than 5% per year). In the countries in the first group (Chile, the Dominican Republic, Panama and Uruguay), where average household income growth predominated, two

---

[6] This analysis does not include information from countries with variations of less than 1% per year in the poverty rate (Mexico and the Plurinational State of Bolivia), since these do not yield statistically reliable estimates using the factors analysed.

scenarios may be identified. In Chile and the Dominican Republic, the rise in the income of poor households was due essentially to the increase in labour income, particularly in average income per recipient. The number of recipients of labour income also grew in both countries, but accounted for only a sixth of the total variation in income from that source in Chile and a quarter in the Dominican Republic.

A different situation is observed in Panama and Uruguay, where the largest source of income gain for the poorest households was the rise in pensions and transfers, followed by labour income. In both countries, the increase in transfers reflected a rise in the average amount transferred, which offset a slight fall in the number of recipients (see figure II.6 and table II.3).

Figure II.6

Latin America (10 countries): annual variation in total per capita income among poor households by income source, and annual variation in the poverty rate, 2012–2017[a]

(Percentages)

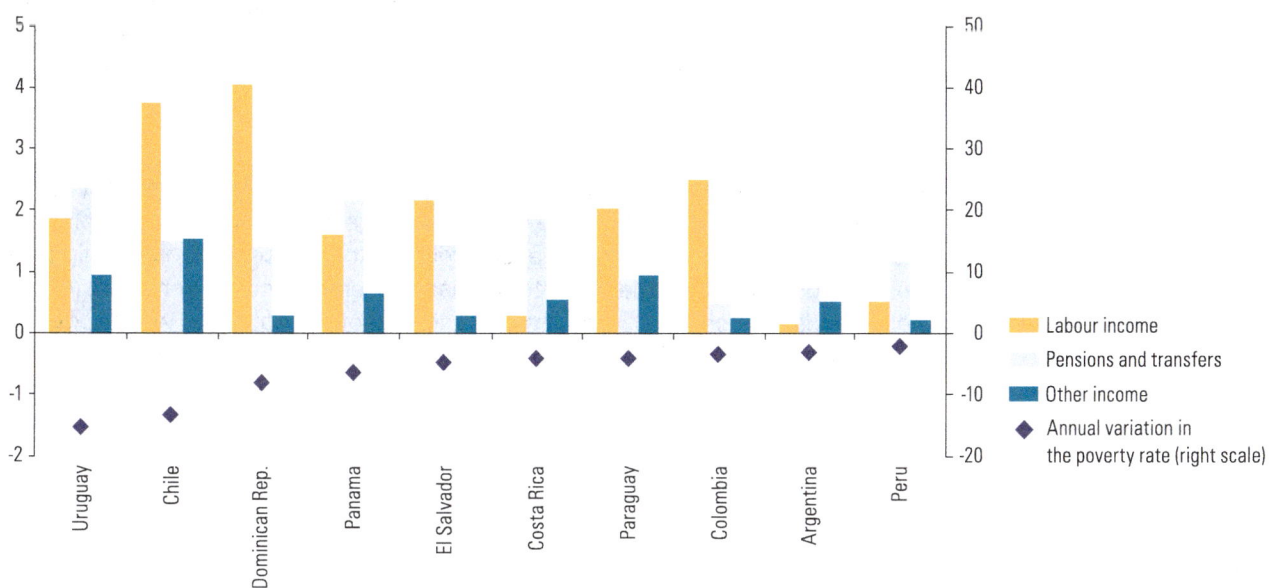

Source: Economic Commission for Latin America and the Caribbean (ECLAC), on the basis of Household Survey Data Bank (BADEHOG).
[a] Countries in order of the annual variation in the poverty rate. Data refer to 2012 and 2017, except in the cases of Chile (2011, 2017), the Dominican Republic (2012, 2016) and Panama (2011, 2017).

	Total income	Labour income	Labour income by recipient	Recipients of labour income	Transfers	Transfers by recipient	Recipients of transfers
Argentina	1.4	0.2	-1.5	1.8	4.3	0.3	4.1
Chile	6.8	6.3	5.0	1.2	7.6	6.7	0.8
Colombia	3.2	3.3	3.0	0.3	3.8	1.4	2.4
Costa Rica	2.6	0.5	-0.2	0.6	7.4	0.8	6.5
Dominican Republic	5.7	5.8	4.1	1.6	7.5	5.4	1.8
Ecuador	1.9	2.0	1.1	0.9	3.0	-4.8	8.2
El Salvador	3.9	3.0	2.5	0.4	8.0	11.6	-3.2
Honduras	3.2	6.8	4.7	2.0	-5.8	0.8	-6.6
Panama	4.1	3.6	2.6	1.0	5.3	5.6	-0.3
Paraguay	3.8	3.1	4.7	-1.5	4.8	5.8	0.0
Peru	1.9	0.7	0.7	0.0	5.6	-5.8	12.1
Uruguay	5.1	4.1	2.8	1.2	6.0	7.2	-1.1

Table II.3
Latin America (12 countries): annual variation in total income, in income by source, in income by recipient and in the number of recipients, among poor households, 2012–2017[a]
(Percentages)

Source: Economic Commission for Latin America and the Caribbean (ECLAC), on the basis of Household Survey Data Bank (BADEHOG).
[a] Data refer to 2012 and 2017, except in the cases of Chile (2011, 2017), the Dominican Republic (2012, 2016), Honduras (2013, 2016) and Panama (2011, 2017).

The countries where poverty rates fell moderately show more uneven patterns, not only in terms of the prevalence of the average income and distribution effects, but also in the way in which the different income sources varied. In Colombia, Ecuador, El Salvador, Honduras and Paraguay, the rise in the income of poor households came mainly from the labour market, in particular from a gain in the average income received by workers. In several of these countries, employment rates edged up among poor households, and in Paraguay the number of labour income earners in fact declined.

In Argentina, Costa Rica and Peru, pensions and transfers were the main source of gains in the income of households living in poverty. In these three countries, the rise was due more to an increase in the number of recipients than in the average amount received, which actually fell in Peru in the period under review.

The "other income" component contributed significantly to the rise in the income of poor households in Chile, Paraguay and Uruguay. This was because of the increase in income from imputed rent, a source which does not reflect income actually received, but the in-kind benefit accruing to households which own the dwelling in which they reside. This rise in the value allocated to dwellings may be the result of a similar phenomenon in the housing rental market, as well as an increase in the sale-purchase price of new and used housing stock. While this point warrants further analysis, it would exceed the scope of this chapter.

Table II.4 classifies, in a summarized manner, the countries by predominant factor in poverty reduction in 2012–2017. In the countries where poverty fell most steeply, this was mainly attributable to the growth effect, relating to the rise in labour earnings in poor households (three countries) and to the rise in average income from transfers to poor households (one country). Conversely, in several of the countries where poverty fell less markedly, the distribution effect was predominant, and the increase in the income of poor households came mainly from labour income in five countries and from transfers in three.

Table II.4
Latin America (12 countries): classification of countries by factors associated with poverty reduction, 2012–2017[a]

Poverty rate (annualized variation)	Share in poverty rate variation	Predominant source of variation in the income of poor households			
		Labour income		Transfers	
		Predominant factor in the variation		Predominant factor in the variation	
		Average income	Recipients	Average income	Recipients
Down by 5% or more	Larger share of growth effect	Chile, Dominican Republic, Panama		Uruguay	
	Larger share of distribution effect				
Down by less than 5%	Larger share of growth effect	Paraguay			Argentina, Costa Rica
	Larger share of distribution effect	Colombia, Ecuador, Honduras, El Salvador			Peru

Source: Economic Commission for Latin America and the Caribbean (ECLAC), on the basis of Household Survey Data Bank (BADEHOG).

The analysis of the variations in the sources of income of poor households may also be applied to the more recent period. Between 2015 and 2017, six countries show an annual reduction of 3% or more in poverty rates. In Chile, El Salvador, Panama and Paraguay, over half of the rise in poor households' income came from labour income, while in Costa Rica and Uruguay increases in contributory and non-contributory transfers predominated. In some countries, especially Chile, Costa Rica and Paraguay, "other income" accounted for a large part of the rise in poor households' income, mainly through imputed rent. In the case of Ecuador, income from pensions and transfers kept poverty from rising between 2015 and 2017 (see figure II.7).

Figure II.7

Latin America (9 countries): contribution of each income source to the growth in total income among poor households and annual variation in the poverty rate, 2015–2017[a]
(Percentages)

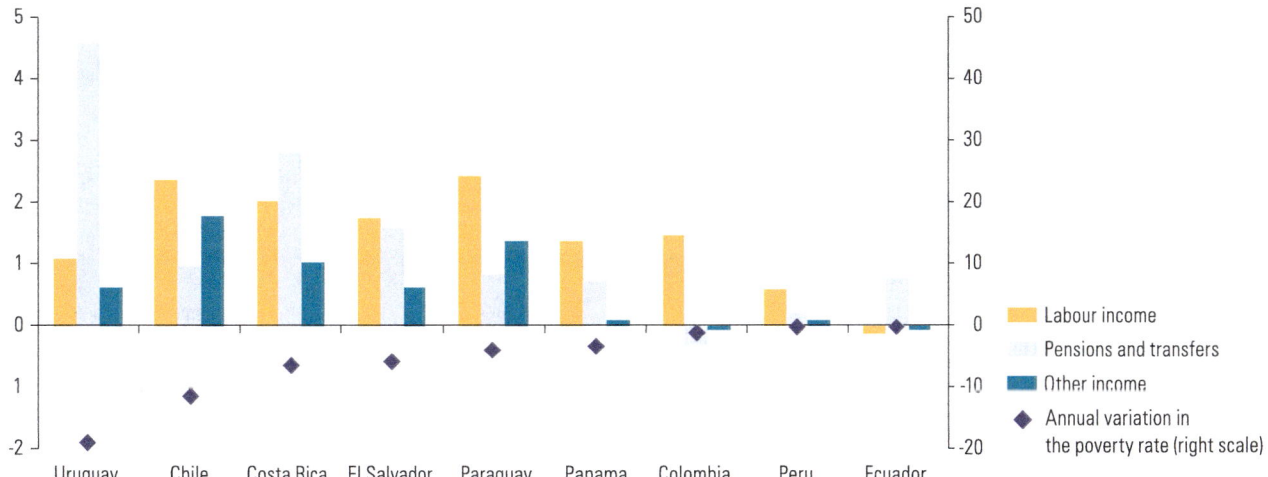

Source: Economic Commission for Latin America and the Caribbean (ECLAC), on the basis of Household Survey Data Bank (BADEHOG).
[a] Countries in order of the annual variation in the poverty rate. Includes countries with significant variations in income and comparable data available for recent years.

Labour income rose in poor households in eight countries, driven by a combination of higher income per recipient (wages or independent workers' earnings) and a larger proportion of the population employed. Income from transfers in poor households rose in almost all the countries. Costa Rica, El Salvador, Paraguay and Uruguay, several of which showed the largest gains in this source, reported increases both in average income per recipient and in coverage. In the other countries, the outcome resulted from a rise in one factor combined with a fall in the other (see figure II.8).

Figure II.8

Latin America (9 countries): annual variation in income by source, in income per recipient and in the percentage of recipients, poor households, 2015–2017[a]
(Percentages)

A. Labour income

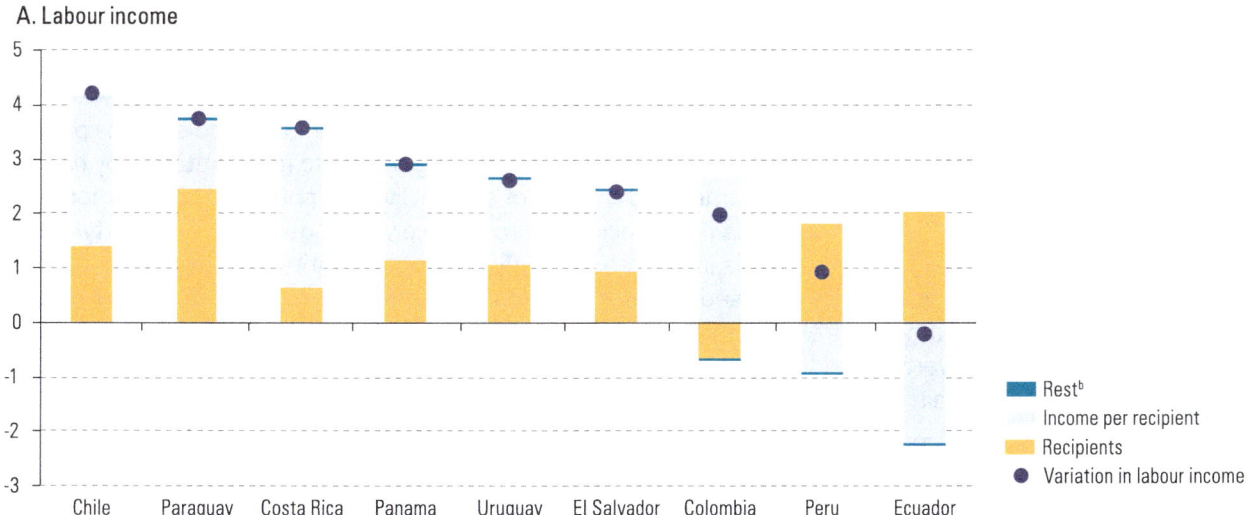

Figure II.8 (concluded)

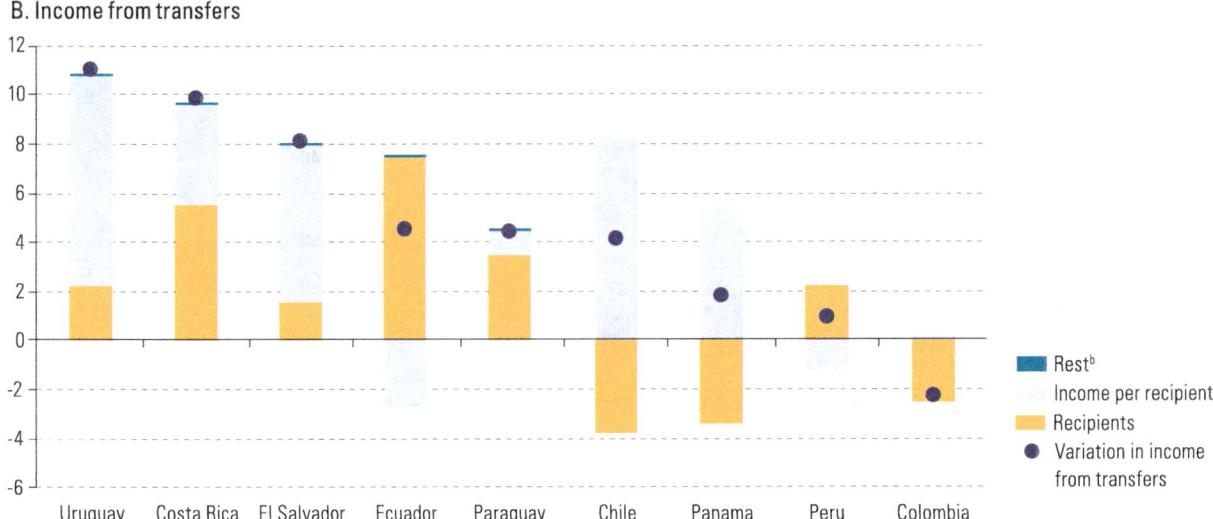

B. Income from transfers

Source: Economic Commission for Latin America and the Caribbean (ECLAC), on the basis of Household Survey Data Bank (BADEHOG).
a Countries in order of annual variation in income by source: A. labour income; B. income from transfers. Includes countries with significant variations in income and comparable data available for recent years.
b The component denominated "Rest" corresponds to the variation in income that is not explained by variations in the number of receipts or in average income.

3. Possibility of achieving the Sustainable Development Goal of no poverty

The direct relationship between shifts in poverty rates, median income growth and distributive changes gives an indication of how poverty rates could evolve in the future under different scenarios in which the last two variables change. Within this framework, it is possible to analyse different combinations of inequality reduction and average income growth that could produce a particular poverty rate, and then assess whether those conditions are in line with the trends observed in recent years.

It is particularly important to analyse the prospects for reducing poverty in the context of the Sustainable Development Goals. Goal 1 is to end poverty in all its forms everywhere and sets targets for achieving that. Target 1.1 is to eradicate extreme poverty for all people everywhere by 2030. The extreme poverty threshold for the target, measured as income per person below the international poverty line, is too low for the countries of the region, so it is considered more appropriate to use the extreme poverty line based on the cost of a basic food basket.[7] Target 1.2 is to reduce at least by half the proportion of men, women and children of all ages living in poverty in all its dimensions by 2030. Although this target includes a multidimensional definition of poverty, which goes beyond shortfalls in income, it clearly defines a quantitative outcome and a time horizon that can be used to assess the prospects for reducing total monetary poverty (and not just extreme poverty). Since the target does not specify from which point poverty should be halved, the analysis takes 2015 as its base year, which is when the Goals were adopted worldwide.

The target of eradicating extreme poverty is particularly difficult to simulate, owing to the results sensitivity to the particular characteristics of household surveys when

---

[7]   The international poverty line corresponds to a daily value of US$ 1.90, based on 2011 purchasing power parity. For reference purposes, of the 15 countries analysed in this section, the incidence of extreme poverty was below 3% in 8 of them in 2016 (according to figures from the World Bank, see "Poverty" [online] https://data.worldbank.org/topic/poverty).

capturing low income. The surveys generally contain observations on households with incomes close to zero, which, in addition to households that have scarce resources, also include those who did not respond to income questions or misreported extremely low values. Given that the income declared in the survey is scaled up under the simulation, the presence of observations with income equal or very close to zero can affect the results significantly. Therefore, in practical terms, a scenario is simulated where the extreme poverty rate is 3%.[8]

The challenge of reducing extreme poverty to 3% differs from country to country. As a target set independently of each country's extreme poverty level, the amount of growth needed and the extent to which inequality must be reduced will depend on the starting point. On the one hand, three countries in the region (Argentina, Chile and Uruguay) already have extreme poverty levels below 3%, and Costa Rica and Peru would need less than 1.5% growth per year, without distributive change. On the other hand, countries with high extreme poverty rates, such as Colombia and Honduras, would need income growth of 6% per year or more, if there were no significant distributional changes (see figure II.9).

Figure II.9
Latin America (14 countries): annual income growth rate needed to reduce extreme poverty to 3% by 2030, under different scenarios of distributive change[a]
(Percentages)

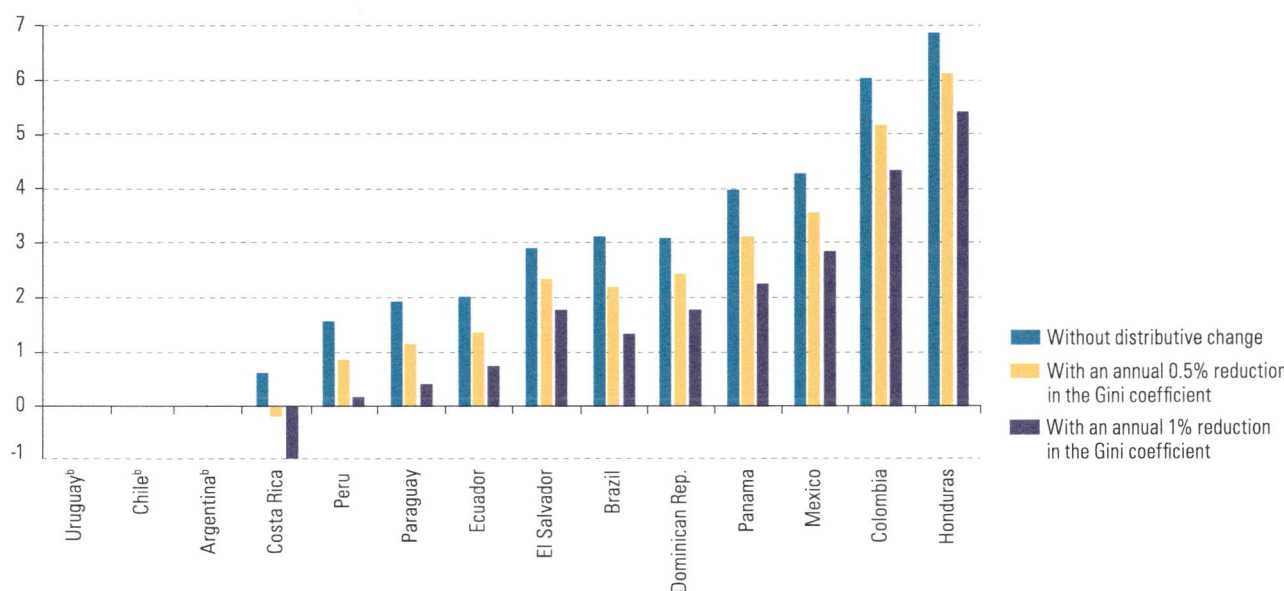

Source: Economic Commission for Latin America and the Caribbean (ECLAC), on the basis of Household Survey Data Bank (BADEHOG).
[a] Countries in order of the annual growth rate of income needed to reduce poverty without distributive change. Countries with information available for 2016 or 2017.
[b] Zero growth rate indicates that the target has already been reached or can be fully achieved by reducing inequality.

These types of simulations clearly show that reducing inequality is key to combating extreme poverty. For example, in Costa Rica, the extreme poverty rate was only 1.2 percentage points above the 3% target in 2017; however, achieving it would require annual average income growth in the order of 0.6% per year for 13 years. The proportional increase in low-income households' revenue equates to a very modest boost to their purchasing power, meaning that it would take a long time for them to obtain the resources needed to lift themselves out of extreme poverty. Distributive improvements

---

[8] This does not mean that an extreme poverty rate of 3% is synonymous with eradication, rather that, given the characteristics of the methodology used, it is not useful to simulate a lower incidence.

help to push up average income which benefits poor households more, by cutting the time needed to achieve the target or easing the pressure on average income growth.

To reduce total poverty by half by 2030 in the countries of the region —with the exception of Uruguay—, average income must grow by between 1.2% and 3.7% per year, assuming that income distribution does not change over this period. Countries with higher initial poverty rates need the greatest growth, since they have further to go to achieve the target, as do countries where income distribution is particularly inequitable. Under a scenario where inequality is reduced by an amount equivalent to a fall in the Gini coefficient of 1% per year, only Chile would achieve the target without needing an increase in average income, while the others would require about 1 percentage point less income growth than they would under a scenario where there is no distributive change (see figure II.10).

Figure II.10
Latin America (14 countries): annual income growth rate needed to reduce extreme poverty by half by 2030, under different scenarios of distributive change[a]
(Percentages)

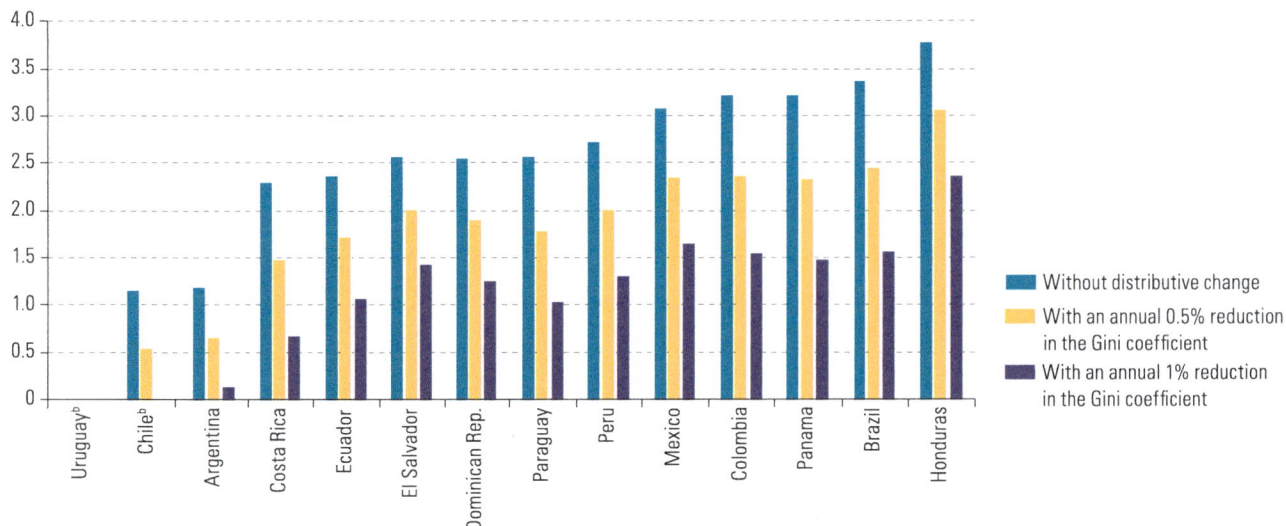

Source: Economic Commission for Latin America and the Caribbean (ECLAC), on the basis of the Household Survey Data Bank (BADEHOG).
[a] Countries in order of the annual growth rate of income needed to reduce poverty without distributive change. Countries with information available for 2016 or 2017.
[b] Zero growth rate indicates that the target has already been reached or can be fully achieved by reducing inequality.

Over a period of about a decade (from 2008 to 2017 in most countries), 10 of 14 countries of the region saw increases in average household incomes and less inequality, factors which helped to cut poverty rates. The other four countries saw either a fall in average income with a reduction in inequality or an increase in average income with worsening distribution (see figure II.11).

If income growth and inequality reduction continue to follow trajectories similar to those described, 10 countries could reduce extreme poverty to 3% and 12 countries could halve poverty by 2030.[9] However, these targets cannot be achieved immediately and only three countries would meet both targets by 2025. Most countries' past performance would allow them to meet the targets one or two years before 2030 (see figure II.12).

---

[9]   These results would be different if the international extreme poverty line were used. Of the four countries that would not meet the extreme poverty target based on the cost of a basic food basket, already less than 3% of the population were living below the international extreme poverty line in El Salvador and Mexico by 2016, while the target was exceeded by less than 4 percentage points in Colombia (according to figures from the World Bank, see "Poverty" [online] https://data.worldbank.org/topic/poverty).

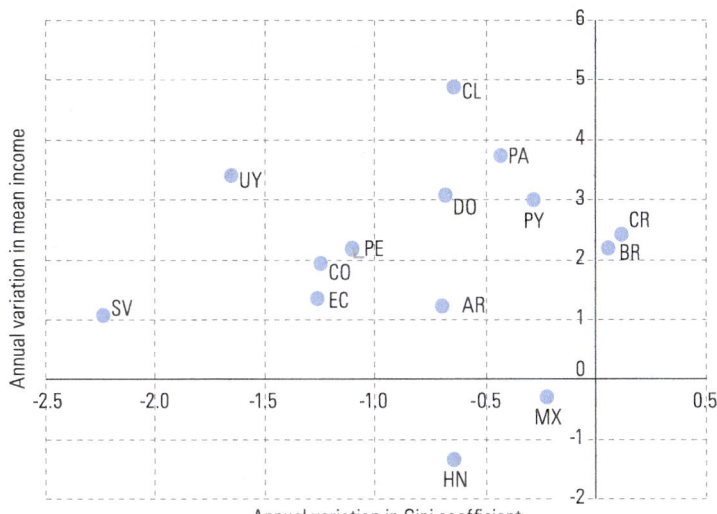

Figure II.11
Latin America
(14 countries): annual
variation in mean income
and Gini coefficient,
2008–2017[a]
(Percentages)

Source: Economic Commission for Latin America and the Caribbean (ECLAC), on the basis of the Household Survey Data Bank
(BADEHOG).
[a] Corresponds to changes between 2008 and 2017, except in Chile, El Salvador and Honduras, where the initial year is 2009, and in
the Dominican Republic, Honduras and Mexico, where the final year is 2016. Corresponds to changes between 2008 and 2015 in
Brazil, and between 2010 and 2017 in Costa Rica, owing to the household surveys' lack of comparability with those of the years
before or after that period.

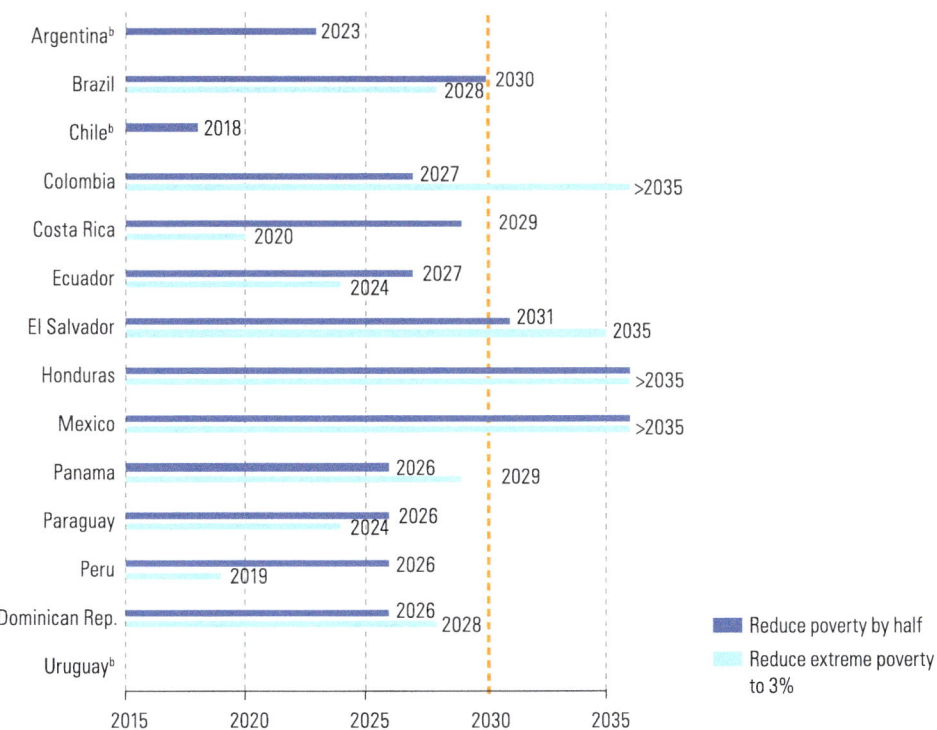

Figure II.12
Latin America
(14 countries): year in
which poverty reduction
targets would be
reached, if income
growth and inequality
reduction trends
continue to follow their
current trajectories[a]

Source: Economic Commission for Latin America and the Caribbean (ECLAC), on the basis of the Household Survey Data Bank
(BADEHOG).
[a] Countries with information available for 2016 or 2017.
[b] The absence of a horizontal bar signifies that the target has been achieved.

These results offer two different perspectives. On the one hand, it is encouraging that the changes in income distribution and levels needed to meet poverty reduction targets are consistent with the regional trajectory of the last decade, assuming past performance is an indicator of feasibility. However, it is also a wake-up call to strengthen social protection systems, because some countries of the region will not meet the targets and because several countries have performed better over the last decade than over the last three years.

C. Other socioeconomic characteristics associated with poverty and extreme poverty

Poverty and extreme poverty do not affect the different demographic and social groups equally. The incidence of poverty is greater among people living in rural areas; children, adolescents and young people; indigenous peoples; working-age women; people with lower levels of educational attainment; and those whose basic needs are not met. While some of these gaps have narrowed since 2012, others have widened.

Poverty and extreme poverty affect the population of Latin America differently depending on where they live. Poverty and extreme poverty rates among people living in rural areas remain well above those of urban areas. In 2017, 46.4% of the inhabitants of rural areas were living in poverty, while 20.4% were living in extreme poverty. In the same year, poverty in urban areas stood at 26.3%, while extreme poverty was 7.8%. Between 2012 and 2014, poverty and extreme poverty rates fell slightly in rural areas, while remaining unchanged in urban areas. Between 2014 and 2016, poverty rates stagnated in rural areas and rose by almost two percentage points in urban areas, while extreme poverty increased in both regions (see figure II.13).

Figure II.13
Latin America (18 countries):[a] poverty and extreme poverty rates by geographical area, 2012–2017
(Percentages)

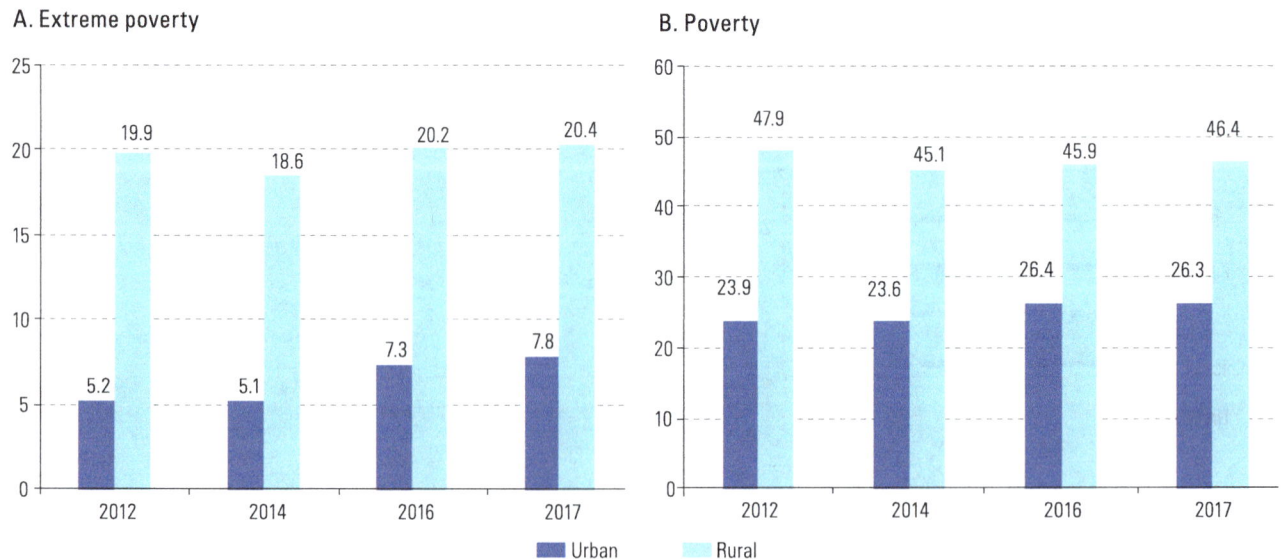

A. Extreme poverty

B. Poverty

Urban   Rural

Source: Economic Commission for Latin America and the Caribbean (ECLAC), on the basis of the Household Survey Data Bank (BADEHOG).
[a] Weighted average for the following countries: Argentina, the Bolivarian Republic of Venezuela, Brazil, Chile, Colombia, Costa Rica, the Dominican Republic, Ecuador, El Salvador, Guatemala, Honduras, Mexico, Nicaragua, Panama, Paraguay, Peru, the Plurinational State of Bolivia and Uruguay.

As with well-being indicators, there are differences in the incidence of poverty and extreme poverty in the countries of the region linked to peoples' race and ethnicity. In 2017, on average, in the nine countries where household surveys allow for the identification of indigenous peoples, the incidence of poverty among those who self-identified as indigenous was 23 percentage points higher than among the non-indigenous, non-Afrodescendent population.[10] Between 2012 and 2017, the gap between the two groups narrowed, as poverty rates fell from 53.1% to 51.0% among indigenous peoples and rose from 26.5% to 27.8% among non-indigenous, non-Afrodescendent population (see figure II.14).

Figure II.14
Latin America (9 countries): poverty and extreme poverty rates by ethnicity and race, 2012–2017[a]
(Percentages)

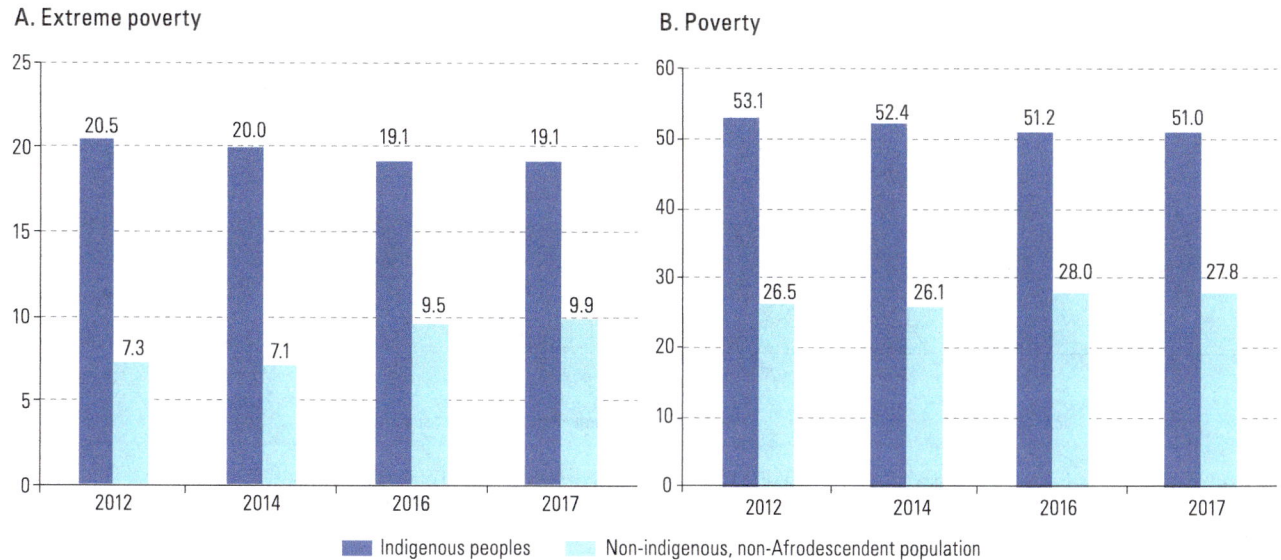

A. Extreme poverty

B. Poverty

Indigenous peoples   Non-indigenous, non-Afrodescendent population

Source: Economic Commission for Latin America and the Caribbean (ECLAC), on the basis of data from the Household Survey Data Bank (BADEHOG).
[a] Weighted average for the following countries: Brazil, Chile, Ecuador, Guatemala, Mexico, Panama, Peru, Plurinational State of Bolivia and Uruguay.

Even when poverty is measured at the level of households, gender differences are a significant factor behind inequality in the incidence of poverty and extreme poverty.[11] Women are more likely to live in poverty or extreme poverty than men. In 2017, the poverty rate among women was 30.7%, while it was 29.7% among men. The ratio between female and male poverty rates in the 20–59 age group, known as the femininity index of poverty, was 1.13, a figure similar to that of extreme poverty (1.16).

---

[10] When analysing poverty based on ethnicity and race, a distinction needs to be made between indigenous peoples and the Afrodescendent populations, as they have different characteristics and follow different trajectories. Specific figures for the Afrodescendent population are not given in this section because two factors particularly affected the calculation of weighted averages, namely the fact that most household surveys in the region do not provide information on this population group and the high percentage of Afrodescendants in Brazil, the most populous country in the region.

[11] To identify people living in poverty, the sum of the income of all members of the household is taken into account, not the income received individually by each person or the percentage of income used by each member of the household. Therefore, the link between living in poverty and individual characteristics is not direct, but depends on the particularities of the households of which people are members. However, even with this methodological limitation, it is clear that poverty disproportionately affects people with particular characteristics (such as sex, age or employment status, among other traits explored in this section).

The femininity index of poverty has remained relatively constant between 2012 and 2017, with values between 1.13 and 1.14.[12] In the case of extreme poverty, the index has been equally stable, with a slight increase between 2014 and 2016, in parallel with the increase in the extreme poverty rate recorded in that period, before falling in 2017 and returning to a level similar to that of 2012 (see figure II.15).

Figure II.15
Latin America (18 countries): poverty and extreme poverty rates by sex and femininity index of poverty and extreme poverty, 2012–2017[a]
(Percentages)

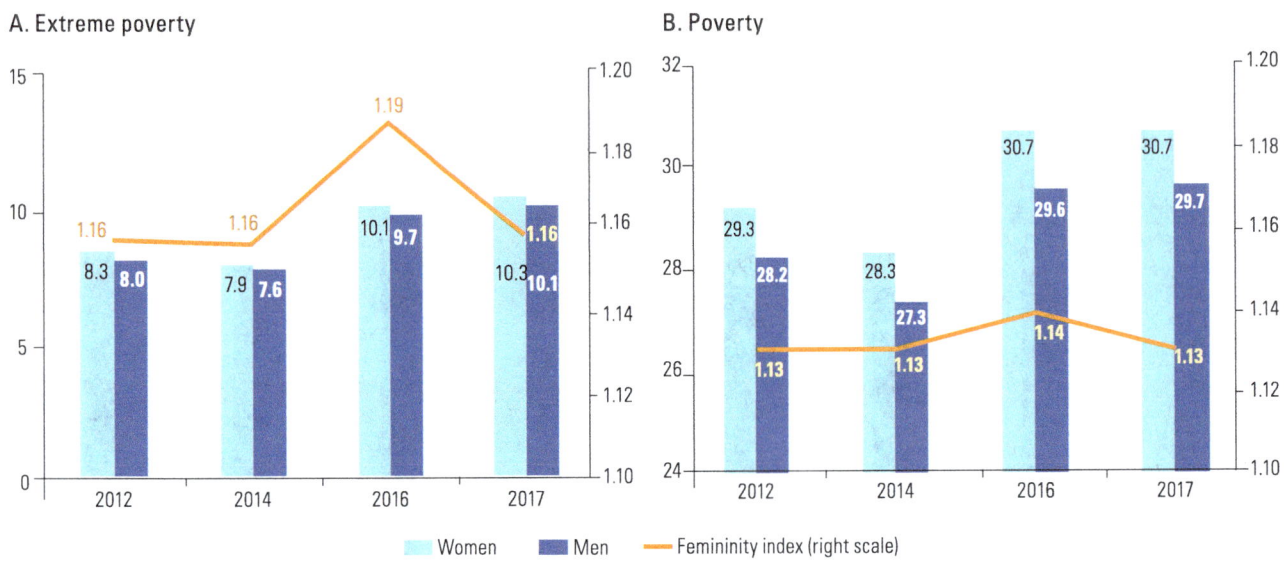

A. Extreme poverty   B. Poverty

Women   Men   —— Femininity index (right scale)

Source: Economic Commission for Latin America and the Caribbean (ECLAC), on the basis of Household Survey Data Bank (BADEHOG).
[a] Weighted average for the following countries: Argentina, the Bolivarian Republic of Venezuela, Brazil, Chile, Colombia, Costa Rica, the Dominican Republic, Ecuador, El Salvador, Guatemala, Honduras, Mexico, Nicaragua, Panama, Paraguay, Peru, the Plurinational State of Bolivia and Uruguay.

Another widespread feature is that the lower the age group, the higher the incidence of poverty. In 2017, the poverty rate was 46% among children and adolescents up to the age of 14 years and 32.5% among those aged between 15 and 24 years, while for persons aged 55 or over it did not exceed 18%. Extreme poverty followed a similar trend, with an incidence of 17.3% among children aged under 14 and less than 6% among persons aged 55 or over (see figure II.16).

Between 2012 and 2017, the poverty gaps between the age groups widened. Among children and adolescents up to the age of 14, the poverty rate increased by almost 3 percentage points, while poverty among those aged over 65 fell by 2 percentage points, owing, among other things, to the expansion of non-contributory pension systems in the region (ECLAC, 2018a). Thus, the ratio between children and young people living in poverty and older people in the same situation rose from 2.5 to 3.0, and in the case of extreme poverty the ratio jumped from 2.6 to 3.7.

---

[12] The femininity index of poverty is calculated as the ratio between the poverty rate of women of working age (20-59 years) and the poverty rate of men of the same age group. It is useful because it demonstrates the extent to which women are either overrepresented or underrepresented among the total population living in poverty.

Figure II.16
Latin America (18 countries): poverty and extreme poverty rates by age group, 2012–2017[a]
(Percentages)

A. Extreme poverty

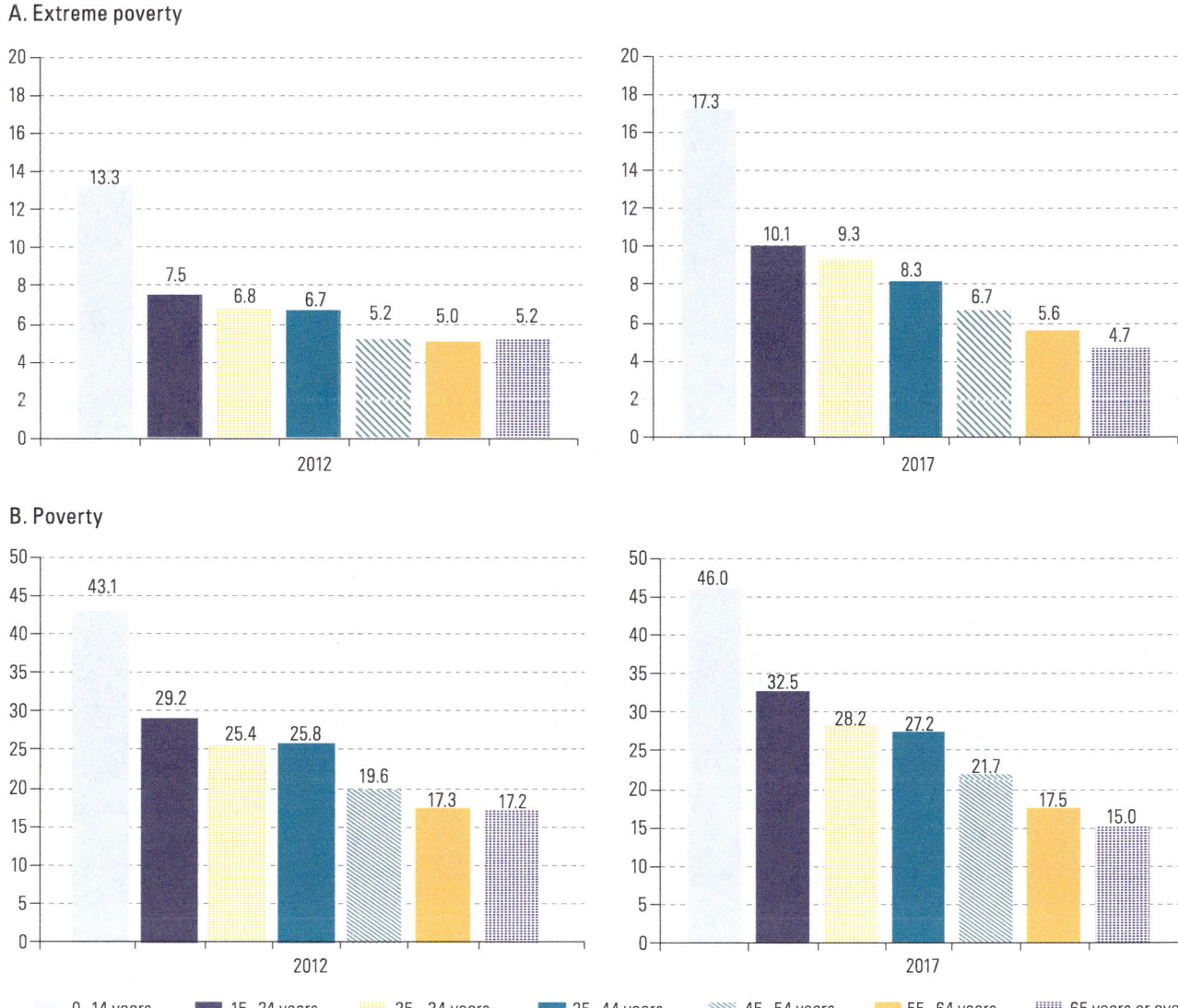

B. Poverty

| 0–14 years | 15–24 years | 25–34 years | 35–44 years | 45–54 years | 55–64 years | 65 years or over |

Source: Economic Commission for Latin America and the Caribbean (ECLAC), on the basis of Household Survey Data Bank (BADEHOG).
[a] Weighted average for the following countries: Argentina, the Bolivarian Republic of Venezuela, Brazil, Chile, Colombia, Costa Rica, the Dominican Republic, Ecuador, El Salvador, Guatemala, Honduras, Mexico, Nicaragua, Panama, Paraguay, Peru, the Plurinational State of Bolivia and Uruguay.

In line with the high incidence of poverty among children, adolescents and young people, the structure of households also has a significant effect on poverty and extreme poverty rates. The incidence of poverty is three times lower among single-person households and couple households without children than in two-parent households with children, single-parent households and extended households. Between 2012 and 2017, the incidence did not vary significantly from one group to another, so the gaps remained constant.

There are greater differences in incidence of extreme poverty among different household structures. In 2017, the incidence among couple households without children was around 3.7%, while it was 5.4% among single-person households. The highest incidence of extreme poverty was found in single-parent households (12%). Single-parent households, two-parent households with children and extended households were more affected by the higher extreme poverty rates seen in 2016 and 2017 (see figure II.17).

Figure II.17
Latin America (18 countries): poverty and extreme poverty rates by type of household, 2012–2017[a]
(Percentages)

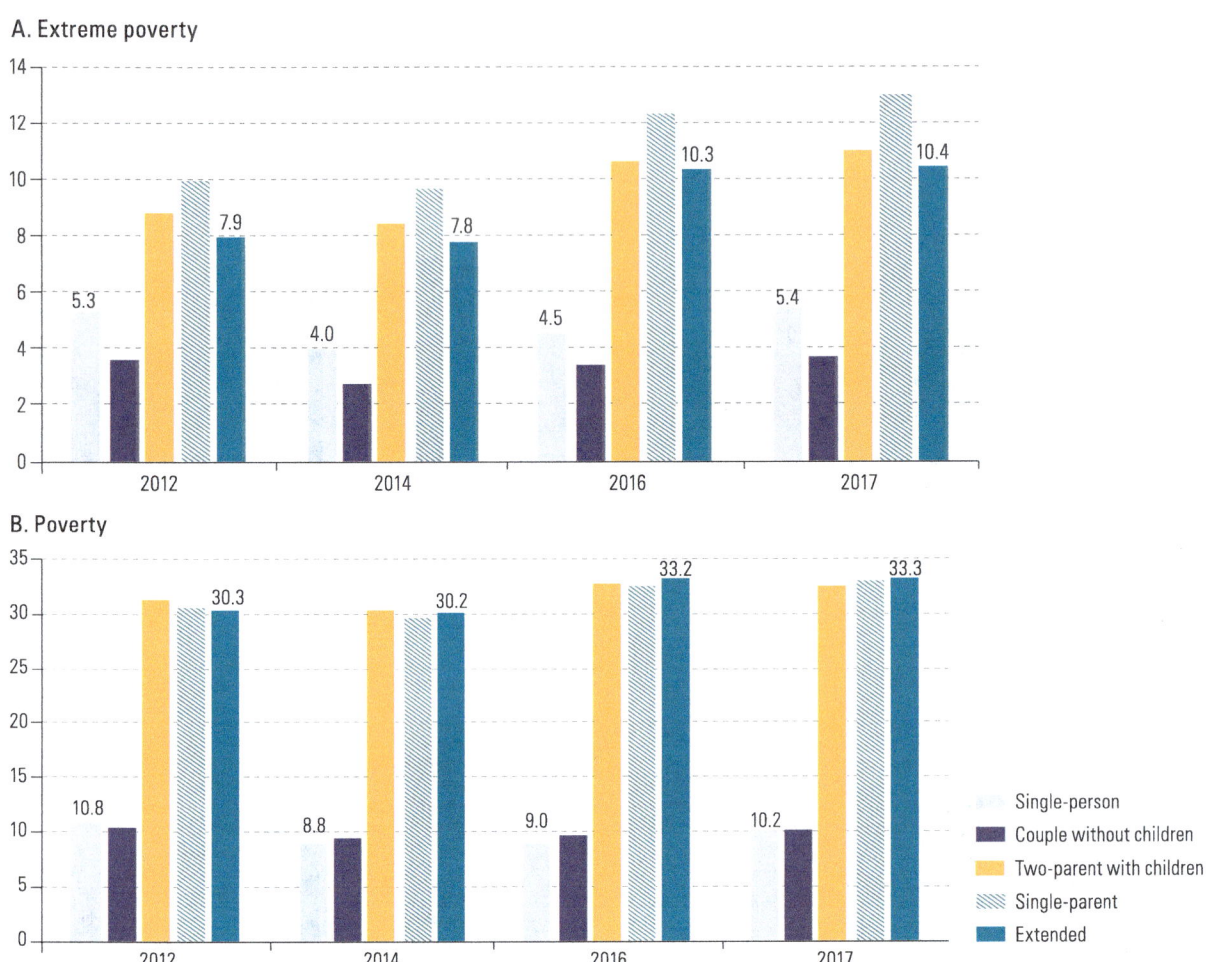

A. Extreme poverty

B. Poverty

Single-person
Couple without children
Two-parent with children
Single-parent
Extended

Source: Economic Commission for Latin America and the Caribbean (ECLAC), on the basis of Household Survey Data Bank (BADEHOG).
[a] Weighted average for the following countries: Argentina, the Bolivarian Republic of Venezuela, Brazil, Chile, Colombia, Costa Rica, the Dominican Republic, Ecuador, El Salvador, Guatemala, Honduras, Mexico, Nicaragua, Panama, Paraguay, Peru, the Plurinational State of Bolivia and Uruguay.

The level of education attained by individuals is another factor linked to poverty levels, since the poverty rate is lower among people who have progressed the furthest through the education system. In 2017, the incidence of poverty among those who did not complete basic education (0 to 5 years of study) was more than five times higher than among people with education up to the tertiary level (13 years or more). The gap is greater for those living in extreme poverty, since the rate among less educated people was almost seven times higher than among the most educated. Between 2002 and 2017, while the incidence of extreme poverty and poverty increased, the gaps between the most and least educated tended to narrow (see figure II.18).

Figure II.18
Latin America (18 countries): poverty and extreme poverty rates by years of education, 2012–2017[a]
(Percentages)

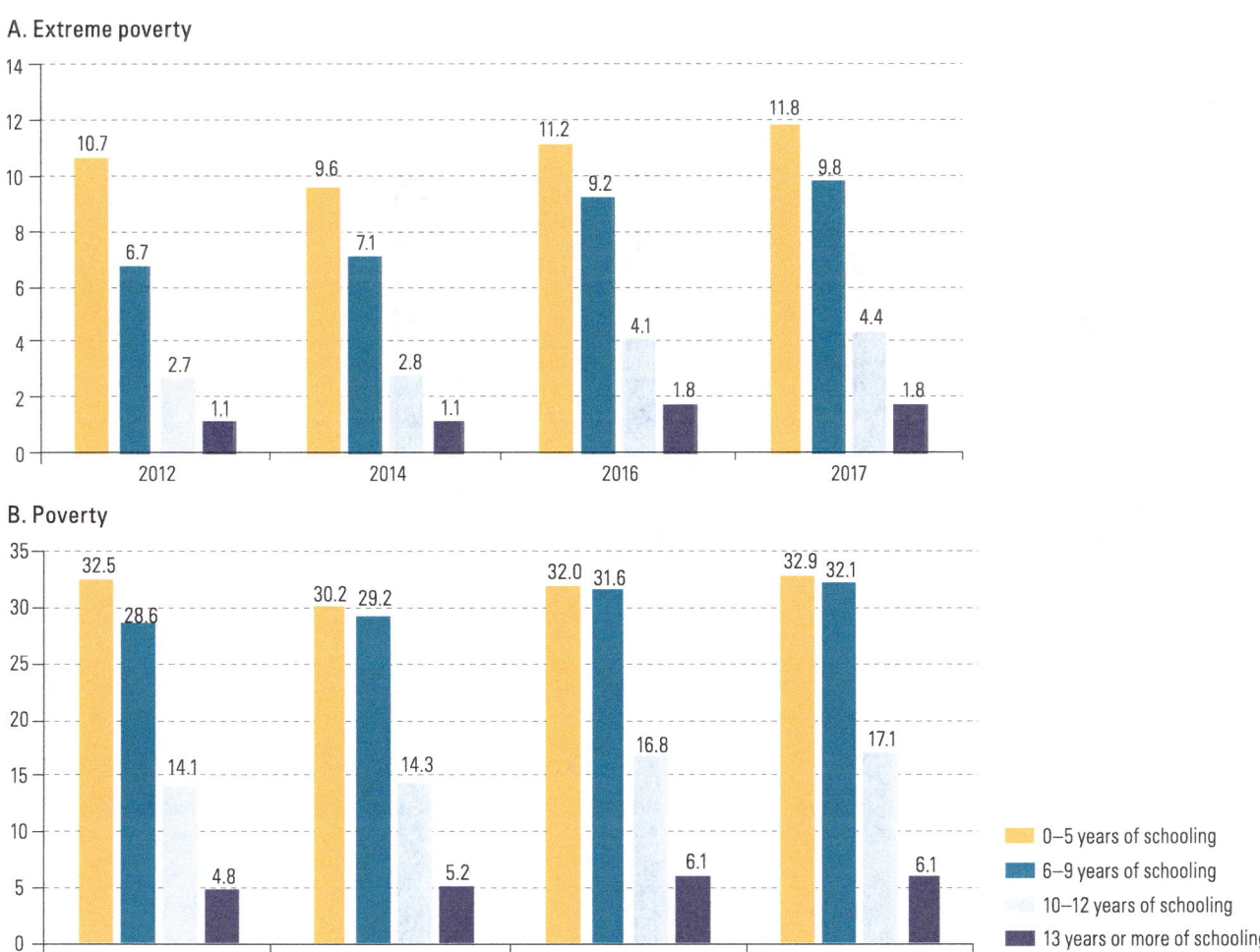

A. Extreme poverty

B. Poverty

0–5 years of schooling
6–9 years of schooling
10–12 years of schooling
13 years or more of schooling

Source: Economic Commission for Latin America and the Caribbean (ECLAC), on the basis of Household Survey Data Bank (BADEHOG).
[a] Weighted average for the following countries: Argentina, the Bolivarian Republic of Venezuela, Brazil, Chile, Colombia, Costa Rica, the Dominican Republic, Ecuador, El Salvador, Guatemala, Honduras, Mexico, Nicaragua, Panama, Paraguay, Peru, the Plurinational State of Bolivia and Uruguay.

The poverty rate among unemployed persons significantly exceeds that of employed and inactive persons. In 2017, the incidence of poverty among the unemployed was double that of employed persons (41.9% compared to 20.9%). Employment status has an even greater impact on the incidence of extreme poverty, where the rate among unemployed persons in 2017 was more than triple that of employed persons. Between 2012 and 2017, the gap between the two groups tended to widen, since poverty and extreme poverty rates rocketed among the unemployed. Poverty rates among inactive persons remained relatively stable over the period, at around 29%, while extreme poverty rates showed a clear upward trend (see figure II.19).[13]

---

[13] The status of people aged 15 or over who are classified as not economically active imply varying degrees of vulnerability to poverty (such as women engaged in unpaid domestic and care work, young students or retired adults). The broad heterogeneity of this group means that the average incidence of poverty is higher than that of the employed, but lower than that of the unemployed.

Figure II.19
Latin America (18 countries): people aged 15 years or older living in poverty and extreme poverty by employment status, 2012–2017[a]
(Percentages)

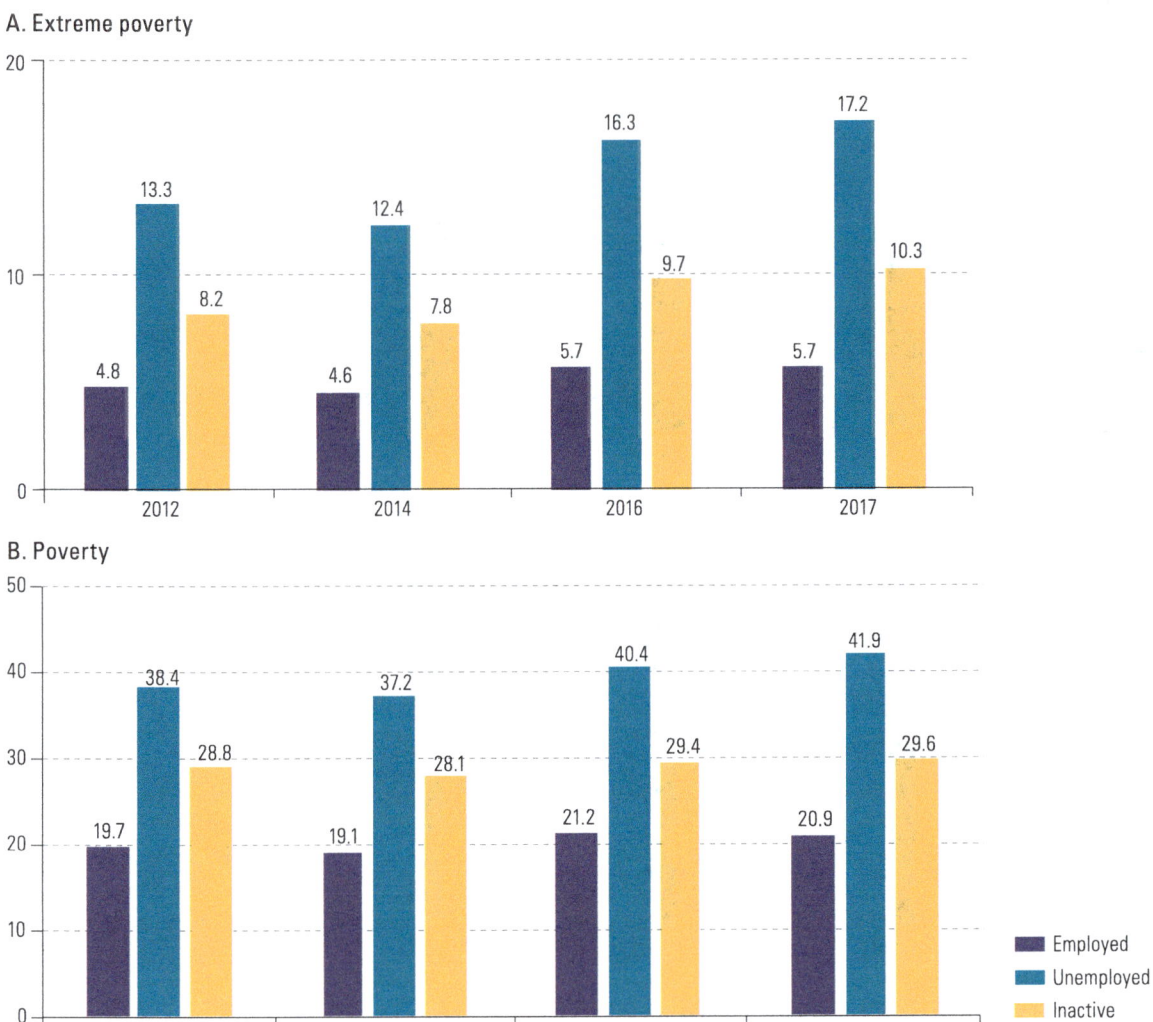

A. Extreme poverty

B. Poverty

Source: Economic Commission for Latin America and the Caribbean (ECLAC), on the basis of Household Survey Data Bank (BADEHOG).
[a] Weighted average for the following countries: Argentina, the Bolivarian Republic of Venezuela, Brazil, Chile, Colombia, Costa Rica, the Dominican Republic, Ecuador, El Salvador, Guatemala, Honduras, Mexico, Nicaragua, Panama, Paraguay, Peru, the Plurinational State of Bolivia and Uruguay.

The link between employment and poverty is evident not only with regard to labour market participation, but also the type of participation of employed persons. In 2017, the poverty rate among people employed in low-productivity jobs was triple that of high-productivity employees. That gap remained stable between 2012 and 2017. With regard to the extreme poverty rate, among people employed in low-productivity jobs, the incidence ranged from 8.5% in 2012 to 9.5% in 2017, more than seven times higher than the extreme poverty rate for high-productivity workers (1.1% in 2012 and 1.8% in 2017) (see figure II.20).

Figure II.20
Latin America (18 countries): people aged 15 years or older living in poverty and extreme poverty by type of labour market participation of employed persons, 2012–2017[a]
(Percentages)

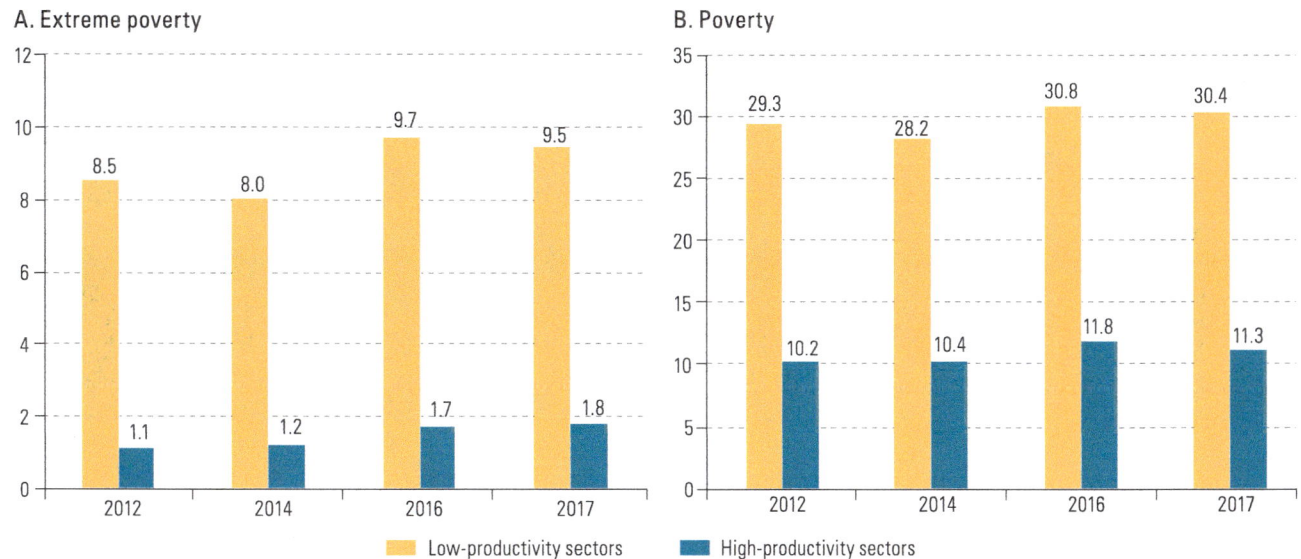

A. Extreme poverty

B. Poverty

Low-productivity sectors　　High-productivity sectors

Source: Economic Commission for Latin America and the Caribbean (ECLAC), on the basis of Household Survey Data Bank (BADEHOG).
[a] Weighted average for the following countries: Argentina, the Bolivarian Republic of Venezuela, Brazil, Chile, Colombia, Costa Rica, the Dominican Republic, Ecuador, El Salvador, Guatemala, Honduras, Mexico, Nicaragua, Panama, Paraguay, Peru, the Plurinational State of Bolivia and Uruguay.

As might be expected, unmet basic needs related to access to basic services have a direct correlation with poverty: the incidence of both is higher among people living in households that do not have access to clean running water and sanitation. For example, in 2012 the incidence of poverty was almost twice as high among people who did not have access to running water, and 1.5 times higher among those who had inadequate access to domestic sanitation services, compared to those who had those needs met.

The gaps are even wider between those whose needs are met and those living in extreme poverty, particularly in the case of inadequate access to drinking water, which was 2.4 times higher for those living in extreme poverty. In both cases, the gap between the groups tended to narrow between 2012 and 2017 (see figures II.21 and II.22).

Figure II.21
Latin America (18 countries): poverty and extreme poverty rates by satisfaction of basic water supply needs, 2012–2017[a]
(Percentages)

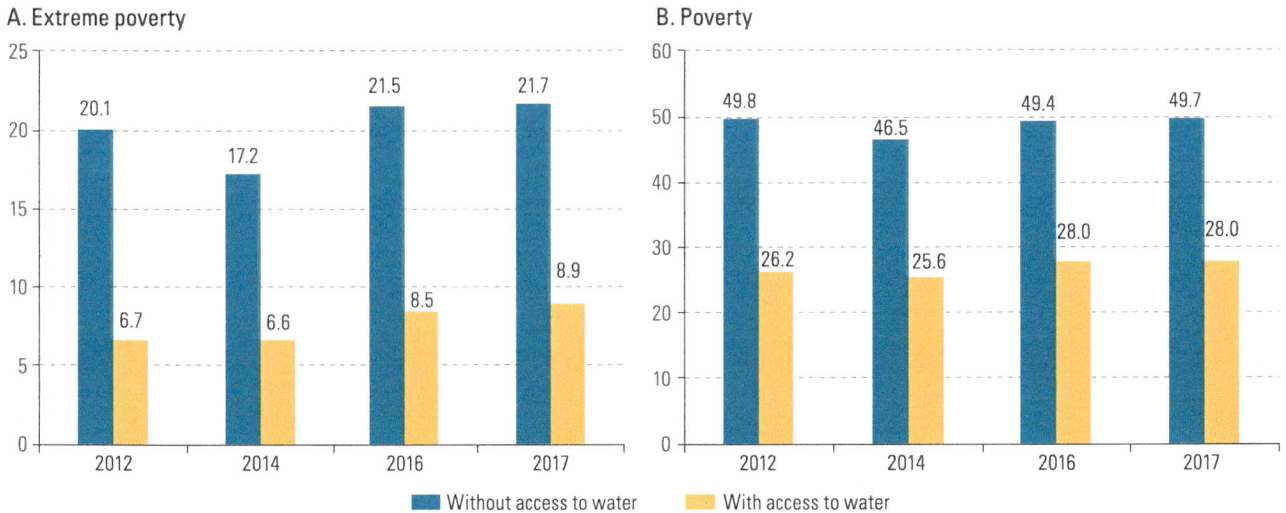

A. Extreme poverty

B. Poverty

Without access to water   With access to water

Source: Economic Commission for Latin America and the Caribbean (ECLAC), on the basis of Household Survey Data Bank (BADEHOG).
[a] Weighted average for the following countries: Argentina, the Bolivarian Republic of Venezuela, Brazil, Chile, Colombia, Costa Rica, the Dominican Republic, Ecuador, El Salvador, Guatemala, Honduras, Mexico, Nicaragua, Panama, Paraguay, Peru, the Plurinational State of Bolivia and Uruguay.

Figure II.22
Latin America (18 countries): poverty and extreme poverty rates by satisfaction of basic sanitation needs, 2012–2017[a]
(Percentages)

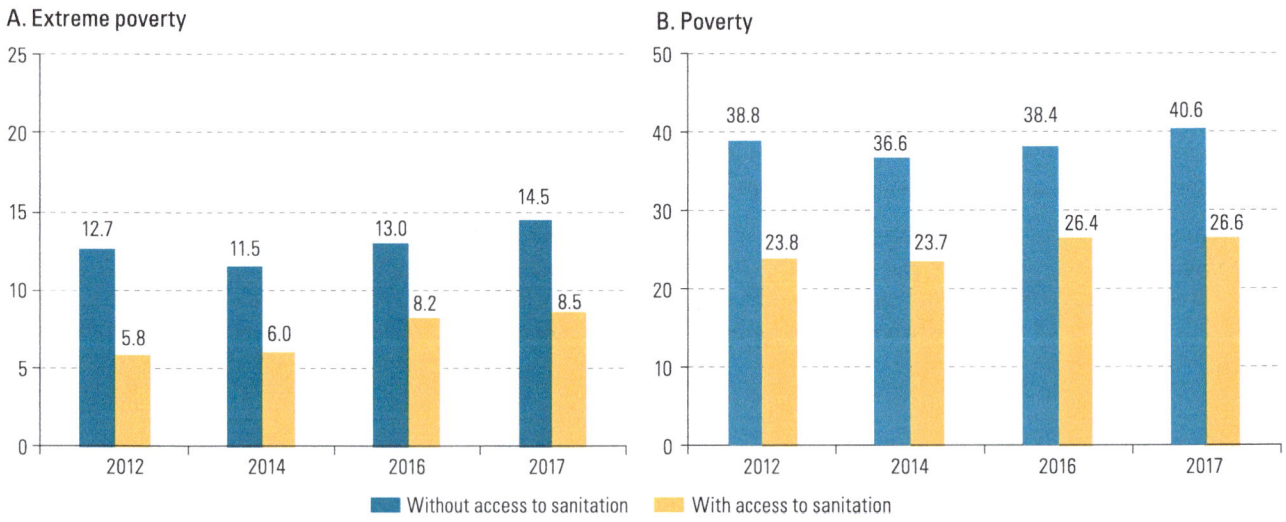

A. Extreme poverty

B. Poverty

Without access to sanitation   With access to sanitation

Source: Economic Commission for Latin America and the Caribbean (ECLAC), on the basis of Household Survey Data Bank (BADEHOG).
[a] Weighted average for the following countries: Argentina, the Bolivarian Republic of Venezuela, Brazil, Chile, Colombia, Costa Rica, the Dominican Republic, Ecuador, El Salvador, Guatemala, Honduras, Mexico, Nicaragua, Panama, Paraguay, Peru, the Plurinational State of Bolivia and Uruguay.

D.   Conclusions

Reducing extreme poverty and poverty rates remains a considerable challenge for Latin American countries, in a context of social, political and economic change. The region is going through a cycle of low economic growth, with GDP growth of 1.3% in 2017 and an estimated GDP growth of 1.1% in 2018. In a context in which the risks of a global slowdown are increasing, Latin America and the Caribbean is expected to post growth of 1.7% in 2019 (ECLAC, 2018d).

Although the region has made great strides over the period between the 2000s and 2015, since then it has experienced setbacks, particularly with regard to extreme poverty rates. The region's poor performance in recent years, coupled with the weak economic cycle, calls for public policies on social protection to be implemented and renewed, particularly with regard to workplace inclusivity and income redistribution measures. Efforts must be redoubled to promote high-quality jobs and the construction and expansion of comprehensive and effective social protection systems, which would enable the most disadvantaged households to accumulate the resources needed to have a decent quality of life.

Achieving the poverty reduction targets set out in the 2030 Agenda for Sustainable Development is still feasible for the vast majority of the region's countries. To this end, economic growth must be accompanied by public policies that help to reduce income inequality, both through labour markets that guarantee good wages and decent working conditions, and through (contributory and non-contributory) pension systems and transfers that ensure an income base for the most vulnerable. Care systems must also be established or strengthened, by fostering the proper provision of public goods and services in that area. When designing and implementing these policies, special attention must be paid to the contexts and reasons that cause poverty to affect children, adolescents, young people, indigenous peoples, Afrodescendants and working-age women disproportionately.

Bibliography

ECLAC (Economic Commission for Latin America and the Caribbean) (2018a), *Social Panorama of Latin America, 2017* (LC/PUB.2018/1-P), Santiago, February.

___(2018b), *Medición de la pobreza por ingresos: actualización metodológica y resultados*, (LC/PUB.2018/22-P), Santiago, December.

___(2018c), *Economic Survey of Latin America and the Caribbean, 2018* (LC/PUB.2018/17-P), Santiago, October.

___(2018d), *Preliminary Overview of the Economies of Latin America and the Caribbean 2018. Briefing paper*, Santiago, December.

___(2010), *Social Panorama of Latin America, 2009* (LC/G.2423-P), Santiago.

___(2009), *Social Panorama of Latin America, 2008* (LC/G.2402-P), Santiago.

___(1990), "Magnitud de la pobreza en América Latina en los años ochenta", *Estudios e Investigaciones*, Santiago, April [online] https://repositorio.cepal.org/handle/11362/33451.

FAO/WHO/UNU (Food and Agriculture Organization of the United Nations/World Health Organization/ United Nations University) (2001), *Human Vitamin and Mineral Requirements*, Bangkok.

___(1985), *Energy and protein requirements. Report of a Joint FAO/WHO/UNU Expert Consultation* [online] http://apps.who.int/iris/bitstream/10665/40157/1/WHO_TRS_724_%28part1%29_spa.pdf.

Annex II.A1

Table II.A1.1
Latin America (18 countries): poverty and extreme poverty indicators, around 2001–2017[a]
(Percentages)

Country	Year	Poverty[b]				Extreme poverty			
		Households	Population			Households	Population		
		Poverty headcount ratio (H)	Poverty headcount ratio (H)	Poverty gap (PG)	Poverty gap squared (FGT2)	Poverty headcount ratio (H)	Poverty headcount ratio (H)	Poverty gap (PG)	Poverty gap squared (FGT2)
Argentina	2003	39.7	50.0	20.5	12.4	8.7	11.2	5.4	3.9
	2008	19.5	27.1	8.6	4.4	3.3	4.3	1.8	1.2
	2012	15.2	21.8	6.5	3.1	2.6	3.3	1.4	0.9
	2014	17.5	24.9	7.2	3.4	3.0	3.3	1.4	1.0
	2016	15.2	21.5	6.4	3.1	2.7	2.9	1.3	0.9
	2017	13.3	18.7	5.5	2.7	2.4	2.8	1.2	0.8
Bolivia (Plurinational State of)	2002	60.0	66.8	37.6	26.4	28.9	34.2	18.7	13.3
	2008	41.5	48.7	22.3	13.7	17.6	22.0	10.0	6.4
	2012	31.5	36.3	16.1	10.0	14.1	16.7	7.8	5.1
	2014	28.8	33.8	14.0	8.2	12.5	14.9	6.5	4.0
	2016	30.4	35.3	15.5	9.6	14.2	16.7	8.1	5.4
	2017	30.6	35.1	15.0	9.1	13.9	16.4	7.5	4.8
Brazil	2002	30.1	37.8	14.4	7.6	4.8	6.2	2.7	1.9
	2008	19.4	25.3	8.9	4.7	3.8	4.3	2.0	1.5
	2012	14.4	18.5	6.6	3.7	3.8	3.9	2.0	1.5
	2014	12.6	16.5	5.5	2.9	3.0	3.3	1.4	1.0
	2016	15.1	19.5	7.2	4.1	4.6	5.1	2.3	1.6
	2017	15.7	19.9	7.5	4.4	5.1	5.5	2.6	1.8
Chile	2003	33.4	40.0	15.3	8.1	4.6	5.6	2.2	1.4
	2009	23.7	29.0	9.6	4.9	3.6	3.8	1.8	1.3
	2011	20.3	25.2	7.9	3.8	2.9	3.2	1.3	0.9
	2013	12.8	16.2	4.8	2.3	1.9	2.0	0.9	0.6
	2015	10.7	13.7	3.9	1.8	1.6	1.8	0.8	0.5
	2017	8.4	10.7	3.0	1.5	1.5	1.4	0.7	0.6
Colombia	2002	46.3	53.8	25.2	15.4	19.8	23.8	10.1	6.0
	2008	37.3	44.6	20.3	12.5	16.8	20.7	9.1	5.7
	2012	29.3	35.5	14.6	8.3	11.8	14.5	5.7	3.3
	2014	25.4	31.1	12.4	6.9	9.9	12.0	4.7	2.7
	2016	25.1	30.9	12.0	6.6	9.9	12.0	4.6	2.7
	2017	24.2	29.8	11.3	6.1	9.0	10.9	4.1	2.4
Costa Rica	2002	25.2	28.0	10.3	5.9	4.9	5.4	2.8	2.2
	2008	17.7	20.1	6.6	3.4	3.5	3.6	1.7	1.2
	2012	15.1	18.6	6.7	3.7	3.9	4.7	2.0	1.3
	2014	14.4	17.5	6.4	3.5	3.7	4.1	1.9	1.2
	2016	13.6	16.5	6.0	3.4	3.7	4.2	1.8	1.2
	2017	12.5	15.1	5.3	2.9	3.0	3.3	1.5	1.0
Dominican Republic	2002	28.0	33.6	13.2	7.3	9.2	11.5	4.1	2.4
	2008	34.2	41.6	16.0	8.2	11.5	15.0	4.4	1.9
	2012	31.8	38.3	14.1	7.1	9.7	12.6	3.6	1.6
	2014	27.0	32.9	11.5	5.6	7.4	9.7	2.8	1.3
	2016	21.8	27.4	9.4	4.5	6.3	8.4	2.5	1.2
Ecuador	2001	48.0	53.5	21.8	11.9	18.0	20.2	6.7	3.6
	2008	28.6	33.9	11.5	5.6	8.3	10.2	3.1	1.5
	2012	22.6	26.1	8.4	3.9	7.1	8.0	2.3	1.1
	2014	18.6	22.9	6.5	2.8	4.1	5.4	1.4	0.6
	2016	19.2	23.3	7.3	3.4	5.2	6.6	2.0	1.0
	2017	18.2	22.8	6.7	3.0	4.7	6.2	1.6	0.7

Table II.A1.1 (concluded)

Country	Year	Poverty[b]				Extreme poverty			
		Households	Population			Households	Population		
		Poverty headcount ratio (H)	Poverty headcount ratio (H)	Poverty gap (PG)	Poverty gap squared (FGT2)	Poverty headcount ratio (H)	Poverty headcount ratio (H)	Poverty gap (PG)	Poverty gap squared (FGT2)
El Salvador	2001	44.2	50.6	23.2	14.1	15.8	19.1	8.0	4.9
	2009	43.0	50.1	20.8	11.4	13.5	17.1	5.5	2.6
	2014	38.0	44.5	16.4	8.1	9.1	11.7	3.3	1.3
	2016	34.1	40.4	14.5	7.1	8.0	10.7	2.8	1.1
	2017	32.1	37.8	12.9	6.0	6.5	8.3	2.2	0.9
Guatemala	2000	46.9	53.6	28.9	19.8	14.4	16.9	8.8	5.9
	2006	34.9	42.7	19.5	11.6	7.7	10.4	3.4	1.7
	2014	43.1	50.5	22.4	13.0	11.8	15.4	5.3	2.7
Honduras	2001	51.3	57.4	26.3	15.3	23.6	27.3	9.5	4.8
	2009	44.8	51.0	21.0	11.2	16.1	19.6	5.7	2.4
	2013	53.1	59.1	25.5	14.2	19.5	22.7	7.0	3.4
	2014	50.0	55.3	22.9	12.3	17.1	19.2	5.5	2.5
	2016	48.3	53.2	22.5	12.6	16.7	18.8	6.4	3.2
Mexico	2002	38.2	46.4	18.1	9.4	7.3	10.4	2.8	1.2
	2008	36.1	43.1	17.2	9.4	9.2	11.8	4.0	2.0
	2012	37.8	44.4	17.6	9.5	10.5	12.9	4.4	2.3
	2014	38.1	45.2	17.6	9.3	10.2	13.0	4.2	2.0
	2016	36.4	43.7	16.2	8.2	9.1	11.7	3.5	1.6
Nicaragua	2001	57.4	65.1	33.0	21.0	29.3	35.8	15.2	9.1
	2009	51.0	58.3	24.8	13.9	18.6	23.1	8.1	4.1
	2014	40.9	46.3	18.7	10.2	16.1	18.3	6.6	3.5
Panama	2001	29.9	36.8	18.5	12.2	14.5	19.2	9.7	6.4
	2008	20.5	26.8	11.5	6.6	8.8	12.8	5.0	2.6
	2011	16.6	23.1	9.3	5.1	6.7	10.5	3.6	1.8
	2014	14.3	19.7	8.1	4.6	5.9	9.2	3.6	1.9
	2016	11.9	17.0	6.8	3.7	5.4	8.5	2.9	1.4
	2017	12.3	16.7	6.5	3.5	5.1	7.6	2.7	1.4
Paraguay	2002	39.9	47.9	22.3	13.6	13.2	17.6	7.2	4.2
	2008	28.1	35.0	13.2	6.9	9.2	12.1	3.8	1.9
	2012	22.6	26.2	10.0	5.2	7.9	9.6	3.2	1.6
	2014	18.5	22.3	8.2	4.2	6.3	7.7	2.4	1.2
	2016	20.5	24.0	8.3	4.0	6.6	7.9	2.3	0.9
	2017	18.4	21.6	6.9	3.1	5.0	6.0	1.5	0.6
Peru	2002	37.4	43.3	18.2	10.2	12.1	14.9	5.6	3.0
	2008	27.5	31.8	12.4	6.6	9.1	10.8	3.6	1.7
	2012	18.5	20.9	7.3	3.6	5.3	6.3	1.9	0.9
	2014	16.7	19.5	6.4	3.1	4.2	5.1	1.5	0.6
	2016	16.5	19.1	6.2	2.9	4.2	5.2	1.4	0.6
	2017	16.3	18.9	6.1	2.8	4.0	5.0	1.4	0.6
Uruguay	2002	13.9	20.7	8.2	4.8	3.3	4.3	2.4	1.8
	2008	8.6	14.2	3.9	1.5	0.6	1.1	0.2	0.1
	2012	3.4	6.1	1.4	0.5	0.2	0.2	0.1	0.0
	2014	2.6	4.5	1.0	0.3	0.2	0.2	0.1	0.0
	2016	2.1	3.5	0.7	0.2	0.1	0.2	0.1	0.0
	2017	1.5	2.7	0.5	0.2	0.1	0.1	0.0	0.0
Venezuela (Bolivarian Republic of)	2002	45.3	51.7	19.9	10.6	6.8	7.2	3.5	2.6
	2008	20.8	24.7	7.6	3.6	4.5	4.7	1.6	1.0
	2012	17.6	20.9	6.7	3.4	4.6	5.1	1.9	1.3
	2014	24.0	28.3	9.3	4.6	10.3	12.0	3.7	2.0

Source: Economic Commission for Latin America and the Caribbean (ECLAC), on the basis of Household Survey Data Bank (BADEHOG).

[a] H = headcount ratio; PG = poverty gap; FGT2 = Foster, Greer and Thorbecke squared poverty gap index.

[b] Includes individuals and households living in extreme poverty.

Table II.A1.2
Latin America (18 countries): official poverty and extreme poverty rates by geographical area, latest two years available
(Percentages of the total population)

Country	Year	Poverty			Extreme poverty		
		National	Urban	Rural	National	Urban	Rural
Argentina	2016	...	30.3	...	...	6.1	...
	2017	...	25.7	...	...	4.8	...
Bolivia (Plurinational State of)	2016	39.5	31.6	56.9	18.3	10.0	36.6
	2017	36.4	28.2	55.1	17.1	9.3	34.6
Brazil[a]	2013	15.1	...	...	5.5	...	...
	2014	13.3	...	...	4.2	...	...
Chile	2015	11.7	10.2	22.1	3.5	3.0	7.0
	2017	8.6	7.4	16.5	2.3	2.0	4.4
Colombia	2016	28.0	24.9	38.6	8.5	5.6	18.1
	2017	26.9	24.2	36.0	7.4	5.0	15.4
Costa Rica[b]	2016	20.5	18.6	25.7	6.3	5.1	9.8
	2017	20.0	18.5	24.1	5.7	4.8	7.9
Dominican Republic[c]	2016	28.6	27.7	32.0	4.5	3.9	6.9
	2017	25.5	24.5	29.6	3.8	3.3	5.5
Ecuador	2016	22.9	15.7	38.2	8.7	4.5	17.6
	2017	21.5	13.2	39.3	7.9	3.3	17.9
El Salvador[b]	2016	32.7	29.9	37.5	7.9	6.4	10.4
	2017	29.2	27.4	32.1	6.2	5.3	7.7
Guatemala	2011	53.7	35.0	71.4	13.3	5.1	21.1
	2014	59.3	...	...	23.4	...	...
Honduras[b]	2015	63.8	63.0	64.8	40.0	29.5	53.6
	2016	60.9	59.4	62.9	38.4	27.7	52.4
Mexico[d]	2014	53.2	...	...	20.6	...	...
	2016	50.6	...	...	17.5	...	...
Nicaragua	2014	29.6	14.8	50.1	8.3	2.4	16.3
	2015	...	...	...	...	...	...
	2016	24.9	...	...	6.9	...	...
Panama	2016	22.1	11.1	45.2	9.9	2.8	24.8
	2017	20.7	11.0	41.4	9.8	2.8	24.6
Paraguay	2016	28.9	21.9	39.7	5.7	1.6	12.2
	2017	26.4	20.3	36.2	4.4	1.6	9.0
Peru	2016	20.7	13.9	43.8	3.8	0.9	13.2
	2017	21.7	15.1	44.4	3.8	1.2	12.8
Uruguay	2016	9.4	9.80	2.7	0.2	0.2	...
	2017	7.9	8.40	1.9	0.1	0.2	...
Venezuela (Bolivarian Republic of)	2014	32.6	...	...	9.5	...	...
	2015	33.1	...	...	9.3	...	...

Source: Economic Commission for Latin America and the Caribbean (ECLAC), on the basis of official information.
[a] There is no official measure of poverty in Brazil. Data correspond to estimates made by the Institute of Applied Economic Research (IPEA).
[b] Percentages of total households.
[c] Official figures on the basis of the continuous national labour force survey.
[d] In Mexico, the official poverty measurement is multidimensional. For greater comparability, therefore, the estimates published by the National Council for the Evaluation of Social Development Policy (CONEVAL) are used as an unofficial national reference, namely "population below the minimum welfare threshold", which is taken as a measure of "extreme poverty", and "population below the welfare threshold", which serves as a proxy for "total poverty".

Social spending and the labour market: recent trends and public policies

Introduction

As reported by the Economic Commission for Latin America and the Caribbean (ECLAC) in *The Inefficiency of Inequality* (ECLAC, 2018a, p. 69),[1] "growth in the region's economies tailed off following the rebound from the international financial crisis in 2010 and 2011. The average growth rate of 2.3% recorded between 2012 and 2017 was lower than the 3.8% the region posted between 2000 and 2008, and well below that achieved in other parts of the world such as South-East Asia (5.3%), North Africa (3.1%) and the largest European emerging economies (2.8%) during the same period" (ECLAC, 2018a, p. 69). ECLAC also noted that "although economic slowdown was largely due to external factors, the intensity with which these affected the region's internal dynamics was also shaped by domestic considerations, some of which augmented the exogenous impact while others attenuated it. The domestic considerations are determined by individual national structures and institutional frameworks, including such elements as a country's production pattern, tax structure, environmental regulations, governance of natural resources, labour institutions, education and health policies, care system, level of openness, financial deregulation and economic policy goals" (ECLAC, 2018a, p. 69). This highlights the interconnectedness of the different dimensions of sustainable development and the virtuous circle between social development, environmental sustainability and economic growth.

Global economic growth is projected to come in at about 3.2% for 2018, with commodity prices rising. GDP growth in Latin America and the Caribbean is estimated at 1.2% (ECLAC, 2018b). In the labour market, the urban unemployment rate held steady at 9.3% after rising by 2.4 percentage points between 2014 and 2017. However, the absolute number of unemployed increased to 22.9 million in urban areas (240,000 more than in 2017 and 7.1 million more than in 2014), and the composition of employment by occupational category has been deteriorating again: while wage employment has risen by 1.3%, own-account work, which is usually of lower quality, has risen by 3.0% (ECLAC, 2018b).

In addition to a propitious external and domestic context and policies that serve the requirements of sustainable development, adequate financial resources are needed to implement those policies and achieve the results aspired to. This chapter analyses the financing situation of the region's social policies. The first part reviews the trend of central government public spending on the various social policies, both in the region as a whole and in its subregions. This exercise is based on the Classification of the Functions of Government (COFOG), which establishes the following categories: (i) environmental protection, (ii) housing and community amenities, (iii) health, (iv) recreation, culture and religion, (v) education and (vi) social protection. The second part analyses the resources available to implement labour market policies in six of the region's countries and includes a description of the types of programmes that currently exist, comparing them with those of member countries of the Organization for Economic Cooperation and Development (OECD).

A. The trend of public and social spending in 2000–2017

Social spending has made significant headway in the region, but the growth trend has faltered in recent years, major public policy financing challenges persist and spending levels are still far lower than in developed countries. There are very large variations between individual countries: whereas annual social policy expenditure per capita in the wealthiest countries averages over US$ 2,000 in dollars at 2010 prices, it averages less than US$ 220 per person per year in those that have higher poverty levels and, consequently, face greater financial challenges in attaining the goals of the 2030 Agenda for Sustainable Development.

---

[1] Position paper presented at the thirty-seventh session of ECLAC, held in Havana in May 2018.

As detailed in *Social Panorama of Latin America, 2016*, the volume of resources that countries allocate to social policy funding can be analysed by the different levels of government or by institutional coverage. Central government coverage is vast and complex. As indicated in the International Monetary Fund (IMF) *Government Finance Statistics Manual 2001* and *Government Finance Statistics Manual 2014* (IMF, 2001 and 2014), it comprises a core group of ministries and secretariats along with administrative units that act under the authority of the central government, even though they may have their own autonomous legal authority. Total public sector coverage[2] is even more complex, as it involves a combination of different types of institutional coverage, and figures for the various countries are not comparable: some only have data on the functional classification for central government, others for general government, others for the non-financial public sector or the public sector. This point is particularly important in the case of federal countries, where subnational governments are responsible for much social spending (ECLAC, 2007b, p. 94).

For comparability purposes, this section presents data on social spending by central government in the years between 2000 and 2016, along with projections for 2017. In specific cases where information is available, the analysis is extended to 2017 and supplemented by wider institutional coverage (see box III.1).

Along with information from Latin American countries, this edition of *Social Panorama of Latin America* contains a special section with data from five English-speaking Caribbean countries: Bahamas, Barbados, Guyana, Jamaica and Trinidad and Tobago.

Box III.1
Information on public social spending

This edition of *Social Panorama of Latin America* reports information on social spending based on a new series spanning the years 2000–2017. The data are drawn from an updated public expenditure database covering 20 Latin American and 6 Caribbean countries. The database has been constructed using the methodology described in the International Monetary Fund *Government Finance Statistics Manual 2014* (IMF, 2014), which allows public expenditure on specific functions or policy areas to be analysed over time and across different countries.

The main changes from the data in previous editions of *Social Panorama of Latin America* that arise from the adoption of this latest iteration of the internationally accepted methodology are:

· Accounting adjustments to reduce discrepancies between the economic classification and the functional classification.

· A review of the consolidation of subnational governments' public spending, especially in decentralized countries.

Another factor explaining the differences between the figures presented in this edition of the *Social Panorama* and previous editions is the updating of the GDP series for the countries of the region.

---

2 As the same document specifies, "a country's public sector is analysed by subsector or type of institutional coverage: (i) central government, which comprises the ministries, secretariats and public institutions exercising authority over the entire territory of the country; (ii) general government, which includes central government and subnational governments (first territorial subdivision and local governments); (iii) the non-financial public sector, which consists of general government and non-financial public corporations; and (iv) the public sector, which comprises the non-financial public sector plus financial public corporations" (ECLAC, 2017b, p. 94).

Box III.1 (concluded)

In this 2018 edition, the analysis is carried out only at the central government level in each country on the basis of the indicators highlighted in the 2016 edition (ECLAC, 2017b). It is important to note that the total social spending effort of the region's governments is not necessarily captured by central government figures. In federal countries or countries with a high level of decentralization in particular, subnational government expenditures can be considerable. In addition, social security institutions in several countries, such as the Ecuadorian Social Security Institute (IESS) in Ecuador and the Social Security Bank in Uruguay, do not come within the central government purview. To maintain consistency with the averages published over time in other ECLAC documents, however, it is convenient to show regional trends at the central government level.

The figures can be consulted in both the CEPALSTAT database and the ECLAC Social Investment Portal in Latin America and the Caribbean.

Latin America and the Caribbean (26 countries): availability of public spending information by functional classification, institutional coverage and years

Country	Central government	Other coverage available		
		General government	Non-financial public sector	Public sector
Latin America				
Argentina	1993–2017		Yes	
Bolivia (Plurinational State of)	1990–2016[a]	Yes		
Brazil	1997–2017	Yes		
Chile	1990–2017			
Colombia	1990–2017	Yes		
Costa Rica	1993–2017			Yes
Cuba	2002–2016			
Dominican Republic	1990–2017			
Ecuador	1990–2017			
El Salvador	2000–2017		Yes	
Guatemala	1995–2017			
Haiti	2012–2015			
Honduras	2000–2016			
Mexico	1999–2017		Yes	
Nicaragua	2000–2017			
Panama	2000–2017			
Paraguay	2003–2017			
Peru		1999–2017		
Uruguay	1990–2017			
Venezuela (Bolivarian Republic of)	1997–2014			
The Caribbean				
Bahamas	2000–2017			
Barbados	1991–2015			
Guyana	2008–2016			
Jamaica	2003–2017			
Saint Kitts and Nevis	2009–2016			
Trinidad and Tobago	2001–2017			

Source: Economic Commission for Latin America and the Caribbean (ECLAC), CEPALSTAT [online database] http://estadisticas.cepal.org/cepalstat/portada.html?idioma=english; Social Investment Portal in Latin America and the Caribbean [online] https://observatoriosocial.cepal.org/inversion/en; *Social Panorama of Latin America, 2016* (LC/PUB.2017/12-P), Santiago, 2017; International Monetary Fund (IMF), *Government Finance Statistics Manual 2014*, Washington, D.C., 2014.
[a] Central administration.

Source: Economic Commission for Latin America and the Caribbean (ECLAC), CEPALSTAT [online database] http://estadisticas.cepal.org/cepalstat/portada.html?idioma=english; Social Investment Portal in Latin America and the Caribbean [online] https://observatoriosocial.cepal.org/inversion/en; *Social Panorama of Latin America, 2016* (LC/PUB.2017/12-P), Santiago, 2017; International Monetary Fund (IMF), *Government Finance Statistics Manual 2014*, Washington, D.C., 2014.

1.   The evolution of social spending in the region

In 2016, as a simple average, central government social spending in 17 Latin American countries[3] was 11.2% of GDP (see figure III.1), a small increase on the previous year and the highest level since 2000. Estimates from the available data indicate that the average was unchanged in 2017. Comparing the results with total central government public spending shows that the share of social spending was 51.4% in 2016, again as a simple average for 17 countries. This proportion represented continuity from the previous year and was among the highest figures for the fiscal priority of social policies since 2000.

Figure III.1
Latin America (17 countries): central government social spending, 2000–2016 and projections for 2017[a]
(Percentages of GDP and of total public spending)

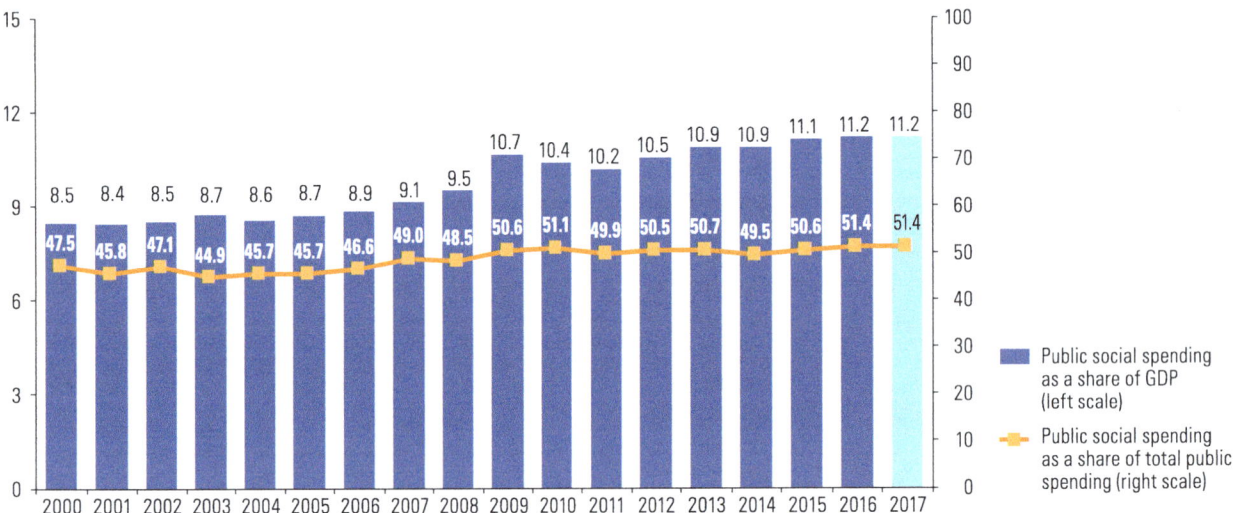

Source: Economic Commission for Latin America and the Caribbean (ECLAC), on the basis of official data from the countries.
[a] The averages are arithmetic means of the values for 17 countries of Latin America: Argentina, Brazil, Chile, Colombia, Costa Rica, the Dominican Republic, Ecuador, El Salvador, Guatemala, Honduras, Mexico, Nicaragua, Panama, Paraguay, Peru, the Plurinational State of Bolivia and Uruguay. The data for Peru and the Plurinational State of Bolivia are general government figures.

As the chart shows, projections for the evolution of central government social spending in Latin America for 2017 indicate average growth rates similar to those of regional GDP and central government public spending generally. While this does not mean resources are adequate for policy implementation, it does show that the priority given to social issues is being maintained.

In the case of the English-speaking Caribbean (see figure III.2), the average 2016 social expenditure of the central governments of five countries (Bahamas, Barbados, Guyana, Jamaica and Trinidad and Tobago), at 11.6% of GDP, was higher than the average for the Latin American countries. The average data for the last three years show that central government social spending has fluctuated in line with economic growth in these countries. Total public expenditure has grown positively since 2012; in 2016, however, public social expenditure averaged only 38% of total public expenditure and

---

[3]   No information is included for the Bolivarian Republic of Venezuela, Cuba or Haiti because they do not have up-to-date figures for the whole series.

was on a declining trend. This means that these Caribbean countries have allocated a smaller proportion of central government public resources to social issues than the Latin American countries, and public spending on other priorities grew by more than social spending.

Figure III.2
The Caribbean (5 countries): central government social spending, 2008–2016[a]
(Percentages of GDP and of total public spending)

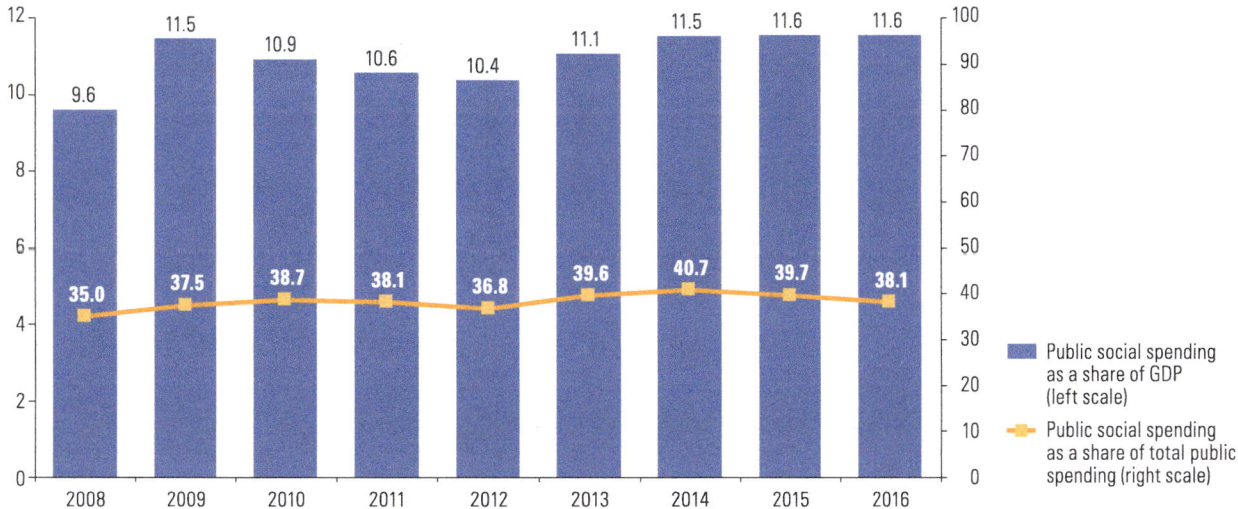

Source: Economic Commission for Latin America and the Caribbean (ECLAC), on the basis of official data from the countries.
[a] The averages are arithmetic means of the values for five Caribbean countries: the Bahamas, Barbados, Guyana, Jamaica and Trinidad and Tobago.

Analysing the relative weight of central government social spending in 2016 in the different countries and subregions of Latin America (see figure III.3) reveals that, while the nine South American countries considered allocate an average of 12.8% of GDP to social policies, the average for the six countries of Central America, The Dominican Republic and Mexico is 9.3% of GDP. Only two countries in the first group spend less than 10% of GDP (Ecuador and Paraguay), while the four countries of the Southern Cone (Argentina, Brazil, Chile and Uruguay) spend between 14.3% and 16.1% of GDP. In the second group of countries, Costa Rica spends almost as much as the South American average (12.3% of GDP), followed by Nicaragua (10.6% of GDP), while none of the other countries spends as much as 10% of GDP. These differences are even more of a concern because the countries devoting smaller proportions of resources to social welfare are the very ones with lower levels of wealth and higher levels of poverty and vulnerability, as well as greater deficiencies in a number of areas of social development.[4]

The average for the five Caribbean countries is 11.6%, with values ranging from 7.6% of GDP in the Bahamas to 16.6% of GDP in Trinidad and Tobago.

---

4   See chapter IV.

Figure III.3
Latin America and the Caribbean (22 countries): central government social spending, by country and subregion, 2016ª
(Percentages of GDP)

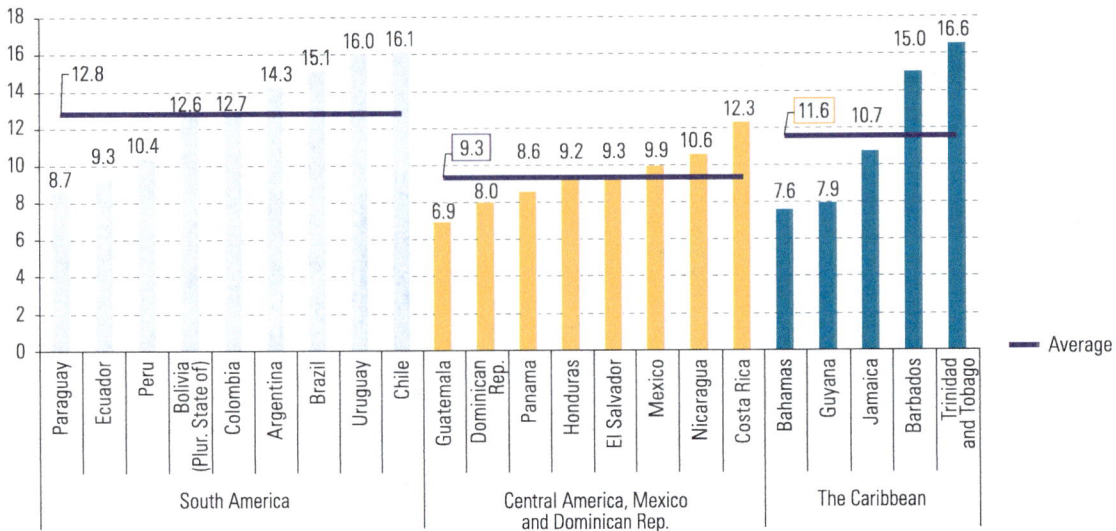

Source: Economic Commission for Latin America and the Caribbean (ECLAC), on the basis of official data from the countries.
ª The Barbados data are for 2015. The data on Peru and the Plurinational State of Bolivia are for general government. The Uruguay data do not include figures for the Social Security Bank.

2.   Per capita social spending

Average per capita central government social spending in the Latin American countries almost doubled between 2002 and 2016 in constant 2010 dollars (see figure III.4). A first point that stands out is the constant increase in such expenditure in the current century, starting in 2002, when it reached its lowest level in the whole period. In 2016, the average was US$ 894 per person, but with a high degree of heterogeneity between subregions and countries. While the average for South America was US$ 1,175 per capita, that for the group formed by the countries of Central America, The Dominican Republic and Mexico was only US$ 579. It is interesting to note that while there was a decline in South America at the beginning of the century (caused by reductions in Argentina, Ecuador and Uruguay), the average trend in the region has been upward over the years (see figure III.4).

When the specific situation of the countries in 2016 is analysed, Chile and Uruguay lead the way as those allocating the most resources to social policies in per capita terms (US$ 2,387 and US$ 2,251, respectively), followed by Brazil, Argentina and Costa Rica (which spend US$ 1,631, US$ 1,469 and US$ 1,176, respectively). Colombia, Cuba, Panama and Mexico make up a third group of countries, with spending of between US$ 945 and US$ 990, followed by Peru and the Dominican Republic with US$ 646 and US$ 552, respectively. Ecuador and Paraguay come next with less than US $500 per person (US$ 472 and US$ 450, respectively), followed by El Salvador and the Plurinational State of Bolivia with about US$ 310, and lastly Guatemala, Nicaragua and Honduras with less than US$ 220 each. Haiti had just US$ 39 per capita to spend on social policies in 2015 (see annex III.A1).[5]

---

[5]   In the cases of Cuba and Haiti, only data from the end of the period are analysed. They are not included in the full series because data for some years are missing.

Figure III.4
Latin America (17 countries): per capita central government social spending, by subregion, 2000–2016[a]
(Dollars at constant 2010 prices)

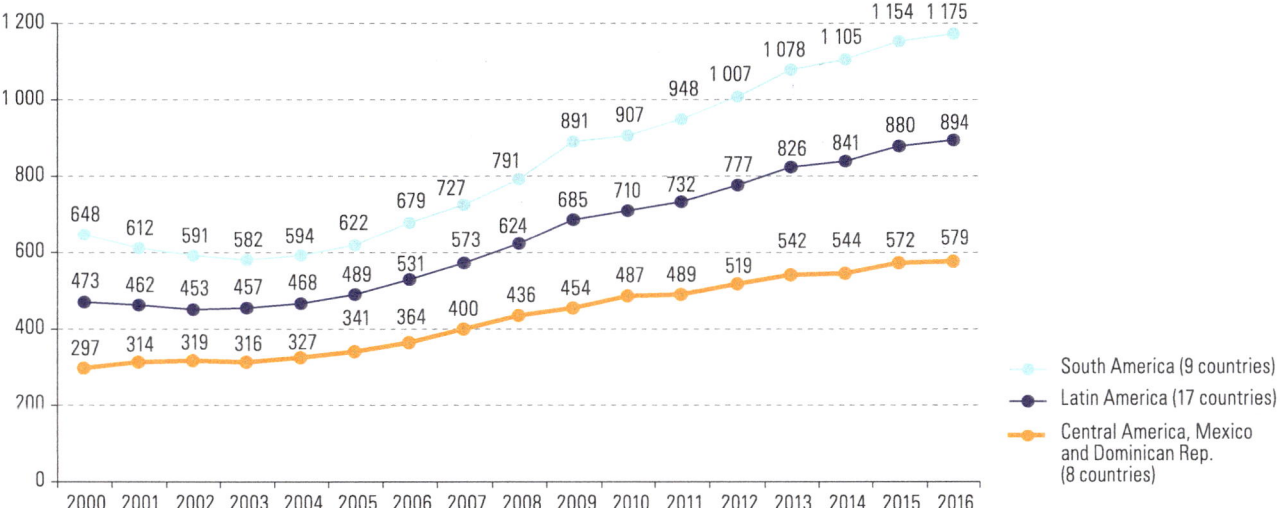

Source: Economic Commission for Latin America and the Caribbean (ECLAC), on the basis of official data from the countries.
[a] The averages are arithmetic means of the values for the countries. The 17 countries included are: Argentina, Brazil, Chile, Colombia, Costa Rica, the Dominican Republic, Ecuador, El Salvador, Guatemala, Honduras, Mexico, Nicaragua, Panama, Paraguay, Peru, the Plurinational State of Bolivia and Uruguay.

As indicated in previous editions of *Social Panorama of Latin America* (2015 and 2016), the region is still a long way behind OECD and the European Union in terms of the availability of resources for social spending, in both absolute and relative terms. At the same time, the detailed data reveal once again that the Latin American countries where the greatest efforts are required to combat poverty and which are most in need of services to guarantee social rights and achieve the social goals of the 2030 Agenda for Sustainable Development (in areas such as health, education, social protection and access to drinking water, electricity and sanitation) have the fewest resources, both in absolute terms and as a proportion of their GDP.

3. Social spending in the region by function

At the central government level, analysis of the evolution of expenditure by social function shows that social protection, education and health remain the most significant functions in terms of the funding allocated. On average, these functions accounted for 4.1%, 3.9% and 2.2% of GDP, respectively, in the Latin American countries in 2016 (see figure III.5). The resources allocated to these functions are also those that grew most between the early years of the century and 2016 in percentage points of GDP: the shares allocated to social protection and health increased by 0.7 percentage points of GDP and the share going on education by 1.1 percentage points of GDP. Although the amounts are smaller, the housing and community amenities function almost doubled its proportion of GDP over the period analysed.

The distribution by functions described here is heavily influenced by what happens in the nine South American countries analysed, where social protection and education expenditures averaged 6.1% of GDP and 3.6% of GDP, respectively, in 2016. In the group made up of Central America, The Dominican Republic and Mexico, social protection accounted for an average of around 2% of GDP, while the amount allocated to education was higher, at 4.3% of GDP. These subregions allocate resources equivalent to 2.4% and 1.9% of GDP, respectively, to the health function.

The group formed by Central America, The Dominican Republic and Mexico allocates on average twice as much funding as a share of GDP to housing and community amenities as the countries of South America, a situation that has remained fairly stable over the years.

Figure III.5
Latin America and the Caribbean (22 countries): central government social spending, by function, 2000–2016[a]
(Percentages of GDP)

A. Latin America (17 countries)

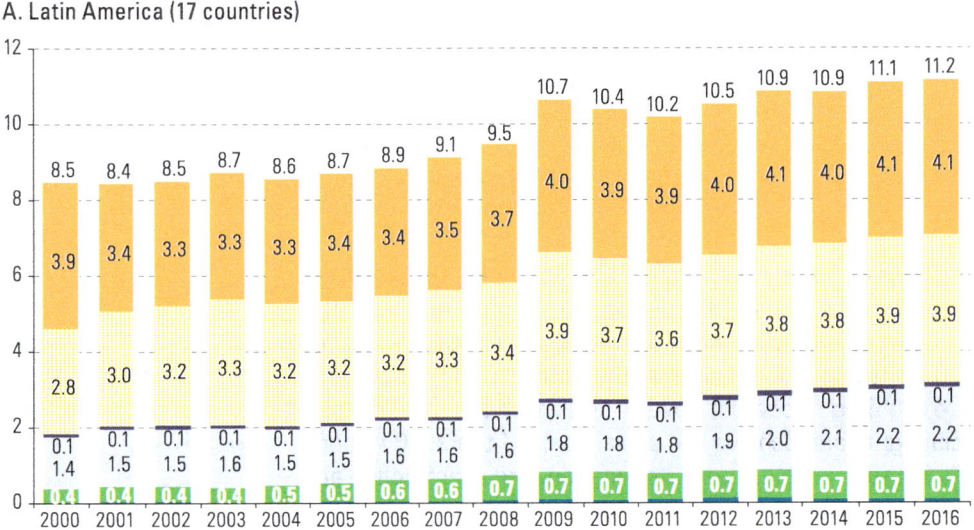

B. South America (9 countries)

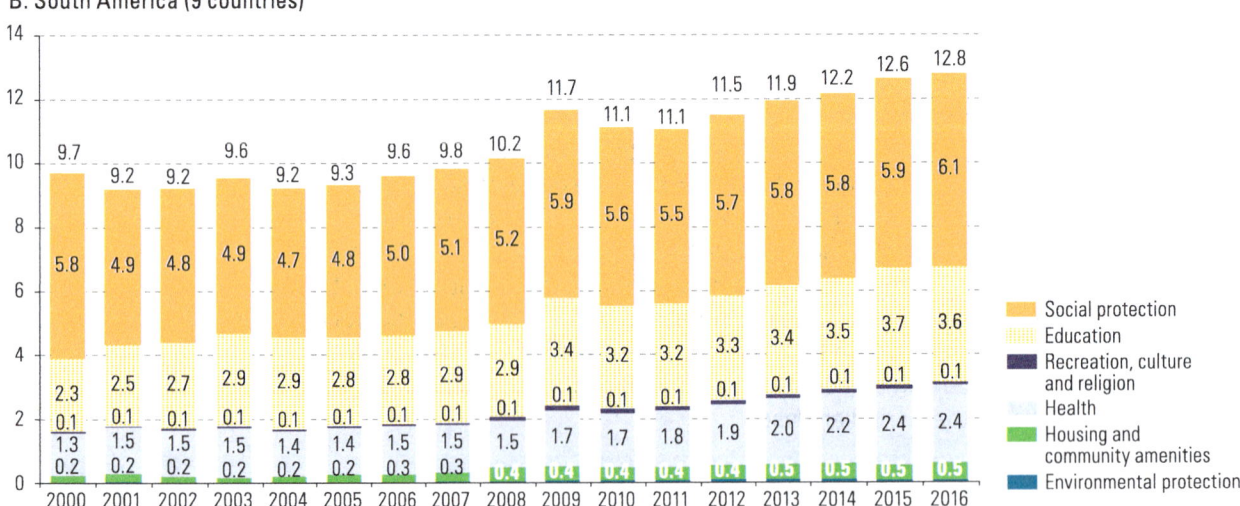

Figure III.5 (concluded)

C. Central America, the Dominican Republic and Mexico (8 countries)

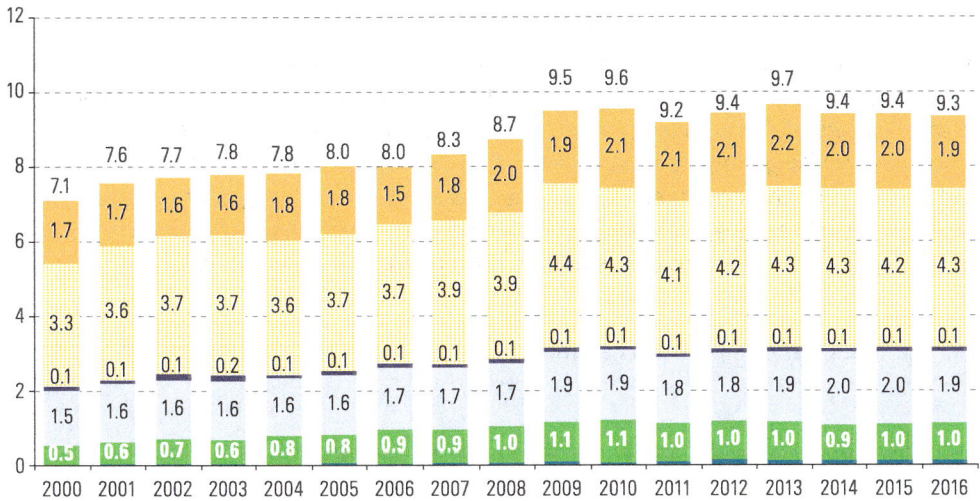

D. The Caribbean (5 countries)

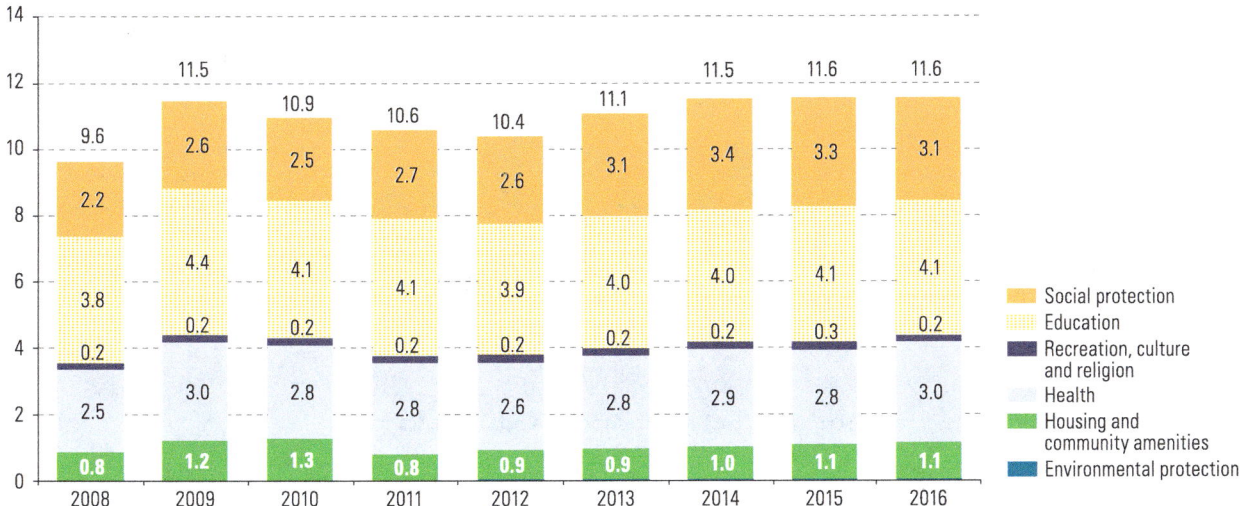

Source: Economic Commission for Latin America and the Caribbean (ECLAC), on the basis of official data from the countries.

ª The averages for Latin America (figure A) are arithmetic means of the values for 17 countries, which are divided into two groups (figures B and C): nine in South America (Argentina, Brazil, Chile, Colombia, Ecuador, Paraguay, Peru, the Plurinational State of Bolivia and Uruguay) and eight in the group formed by Central America (Costa Rica, El Salvador, Guatemala, Honduras, Nicaragua and Panama), the Dominican Republic and Mexico. In the case of the Caribbean (figure D), five countries are included (Bahamas, Barbados, Guyana, Jamaica and Trinidad and Tobago).

In the case of the five English-speaking Caribbean countries analysed, social expenditure data show that the education function is the one that accounts for the most resources (ranging from 3.8% of GDP in 2008 to 4.1% of GDP in 2016), followed by social protection, with values of between 2.2% and 3.4% of GDP in the last decade, and health, which presents an upward trend that has taken it to 3.0% of GDP. The housing and community amenities function, for its part, represents an average of between 0.8% and 1.3% of GDP in this group of countries.

4. The distribution of functional social spending in the countries

Analysing the distribution across central government social spending functions in each of the countries in the region gives an idea of the priorities and commitments expressed in each through the allocation of public resources. Data from the latest years analysed show that, while greater resources are being allotted to social protection, education and health in all the countries (see figure III.6 and annex III.A1), there are also large variations, such as the greater share commanded by the housing and community amenities function in some cases and by recreation, culture and religion in Haiti.

Figure III.6
Latin America and the Caribbean (24 countries): distribution of central government social spending by function, 2016
(Percentages)

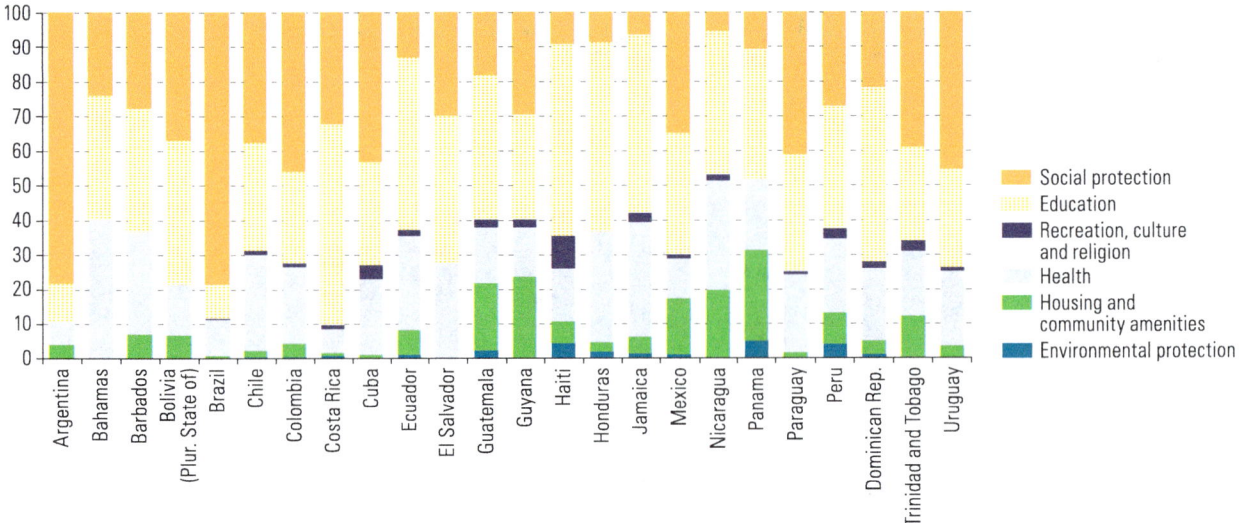

Source: Economic Commission for Latin America and the Caribbean (ECLAC), on the basis of official data from the countries.

It is important to note that the data presented here relate only to central government coverage and that the amounts may change significantly if broader coverage, such as general government or the non-financial public sector, is taken. This is particularly relevant in the case of countries that have federal structures or subnational governments with high levels of autonomy, such as Argentina, Brazil, Colombia and Mexico.

The situation with each function in the different countries is briefly described below.

(a) Social protection

Resources spent on social protection policies include disbursements for services and transfers to individuals and families relating to illness and disability, old age, survivors,[6] families and children, unemployment, housing and social exclusion, in both the contributory and non-contributory social protection systems. This function encompasses policies and programmes designed to cover risks that may affect the whole population (related

---

[6]   Spending associated with survivors is social protection in the form of cash and in-kind benefits for the survivors of deceased persons (such as the spouse, ex-spouse, children, grandchildren, parents and other relatives).

to natural disasters, sickness, old age and unemployment), as well as those aimed at facilitating inclusion and protecting against the consequences of poverty and inequality (such as conditional cash transfer programmes and social pensions).

On average, the 24 countries of Latin America and the Caribbean for which information is available for 2016 at the central government level allocated resources equivalent to 3.7% of GDP to the social protection function that year. Argentina and Brazil are the countries that allocated the most resources to this function (more than 11.2% and 11.9% of GDP, respectively). Uruguay ranked third, with just under 8% of GDP, but consolidating central government data with those on contributory pensions administered by the Social Security Bank (BPS) reveals a significantly higher level of spending on social protection (13.3% of GDP). At the other extreme, Haiti, Honduras, Jamaica, Nicaragua and Panama allocated the least resources (less than 1% of GDP).

In turn, analysing the resources allocated to social protection in relation to total central government social spending shows that Argentina and Brazil are the countries devoting the largest proportions to this function, with a strong emphasis on spending associated with old age, which accounts for more than half of social protection spending. Consistently with what was indicated in the previous paragraph, Uruguay is also among the countries that most prioritize this function within social spending.

Other countries that are notable for the large share of this function in total social spending are Chile, Colombia, Cuba, Mexico, Paraguay, the Plurinational State of Bolivia and Trinidad and Tobago, with proportions of around 40%. Meanwhile, Haiti, Honduras, Jamaica, Nicaragua and Panama are among the countries allocating the smallest proportions of social spending to this function (10% or less).

(b) Education

The education function includes all disbursements to fund policies for the different levels of education, from preschool to tertiary, including ancillary services and education-related research and development.

As indicated above, this is the second-largest social function in the region in terms of central government resources if the average of the 17 Latin American countries for which the full data series is available is considered, but it is the largest if the average of the 24 countries analysed in 2016 is taken (3.9% of GDP). At the central government level, Costa Rica stands out as the country that allocates the largest share of its GDP to education (over 7%), followed by Jamaica, Barbados, the Plurinational State of Bolivia, Chile, Honduras, Ecuador and Uruguay (all with around 5% of GDP).

Although in volume terms the resources do not necessarily cover the needs of each country, these data show that several countries in the region spend a proportion of GDP that is in line with the recommendations of the Education 2030 Framework for Action: allocating at least 4% to 6% of gross domestic product (GDP) or at least 15% to 20% of public expenditure to education (UNESCO, 2015).

A review of the distribution of social expenditure by function in each country shows that in 13 of the 24 countries analysed this is the function to which the greatest resources are allocated, and that in two others it shares the top place with health or social protection. This distribution, while not necessarily reflecting the quality of educational outcomes, shows the preponderance of resources commanded by education policies among social functions.

The country that allocates the largest proportion of social expenditure to this function is Costa Rica (58%), followed by Haiti and Honduras (55% in each case), Jamaica (51%), the Dominican Republic (50%) and Ecuador (49%). In the opposite situation, and consistently with the weight of the social protection function at the central government level, Brazil and Argentina are the countries that allocate the smallest proportions to this function.[7]

(c) Health

Health expenditure includes disbursements for services provided to individuals and groups under both preventive and curative programmes at the different levels of care.

Central government health funding averages 2.4 % of GDP in the 24 countries analysed. Considering that the target for the region in the *Sustainable Health Agenda for the Americas 2018–2030*[8] is to "achieve a level of public expenditure in health of at least 6% of GDP" (PAHO/WHO, 2017, p. 35, target 4.1), which is the funding necessary to move towards universal health care,[9] the scale of the extra effort required to achieve this target by 2030 can be appreciated. When expenditure by each country's central government is considered, it transpires that none is on course to achieve this target. The countries with the largest outlays relative to GDP are Chile and Barbados (4% of GDP), followed by Jamaica, Uruguay, Trinidad and Tobago, Nicaragua, Cuba and the Bahamas (all with more than 3% of GDP).

The Bahamas allocates a particularly large proportion of central government social spending to health, compared to the other social functions; proportionally, it is the country that commits the most resources (40%). Other countries that allocate more than 30% to this function are Jamaica (33%) and Honduras and Nicaragua (32% in each case). Further behind are Barbados (29%), Chile and El Salvador (28%) and Ecuador (27%).

At the other extreme, the countries in the region that allocate the smallest shares of central government social spending to health policies are Argentina, Costa Rica and Brazil, all with 10% or less, followed by Mexico and Guyana, with less than 15%.

Notwithstanding all this, the scale of funding for social protection in some of these countries and the resources that come into the picture when broader institutional coverage is considered, as in the case of education-related expenditures, introduce new elements into the analysis of these data. First, the institutions involved in contributory social protection are often joint providers and insurers of some health services, which requires more in-depth analysis. Second, it is necessary to consider the supplementary contributions of other agencies and levels of government in this area, particularly in countries that have autonomous state and subnational governments, such as Argentina, Brazil, Mexico and Colombia.

(d) Housing and community amenities

Public expenditure on housing and community amenities includes State resources for urbanization (including both the administration of urbanization matters and slum clearance related to housebuilding, the construction and refurbishment of housing for the general public or people with special needs, and the purchase of land needed for housebuilding), community development, the water supply and street lighting.

The Latin American and Caribbean countries spend an average of 0.8% of GDP on this function. Panama, Nicaragua, Trinidad and Tobago and Guyana allocate particularly

---

[7]   The situation is more nuanced when broader institutional coverage is considered, such as that of general government, encompassing the subnational governments which finance much of the education system in these two countries; however, the proportion of social spending allocated to the social protection function still exceeds what is spent on other functions by a substantial margin in both cases.

[8]   Prepared following a decision taken at the 55th Directing Council of the Pan American Health Organization (PAHO) in 2016.

[9]   See target 4 of the *Sustainable Health Agenda for the Americas 2018–2030* (PAHO/WHO, 2017, p. 35).

substantial resources (2.3%, 2.1%, 2.0% and 1.9% of GDP, respectively). In keeping with this, when the resources allocated to housing are analysed in relation to the whole range of social functions, Panama is the country that allocates the largest proportion of central government expenditure to this function (26%). Guyana comes second (24%), followed by Guatemala and Nicaragua (20% each). It should be noted that 18 of the 24 countries analysed allocate less than 10% of total central government social spending to this function, including 13 that allocate less than 5% to it.

(e) Recreation, culture and religion

Financing for recreation, culture and religion includes resources allocated to leisure (sports and cultural activities, radio and television) and religious services.

This function represented 0.15% of GDP at the regional level in 2016, equivalent to two thirds of the level agreed at the tenth Ibero-American Conference on Culture, held in Valparaiso (Chile) in July 2007, where the ministers and high authorities of culture proposed "progressively allocating a minimum of 1% of each State's general budget to the promotion of culture" (ECLAC/OEI, 2014, p. 311). Although their central governments are far from fulfilling this commitment, Cuba, Haiti and Trinidad and Tobago lead the way as the countries that allocate the most resources (0.62%, 0.51% and 0.48% of GDP, respectively). In seven countries, central government public expenditure information makes no mention of funding for this function.

(f) Environmental protection

As part of the social functions, environmental protection includes spending on waste and wastewater management, pollution reduction, biodiversity and landscape protection, and research related to environmental protection.

At the central government level, expenditure on this appears to be the lowest of any social function (0.1% of GDP in 2016). Panama and Peru allocate resources equivalent to four times this average (0.43% of GDP), followed by Haiti (0.24%), Honduras (0.19%), Guatemala (0.16%) and Jamaica (0.15%).

However, these values may vary when broader institutional coverage is considered, including subnational levels of government, given their role in waste management, and public wastewater treatment companies. This is reflected in the importance of the work done to consolidate these outlays in the satellite accounts for this area, which provide a fuller picture of the resources allocated and the actions taken by different actors within the framework of the countries' environmental protection policies.[10]

B.   Public spending on labour market policies

Average public spending on labour market policies in six countries of the region was 0.45% of GDP in 2016. There is a marked heterogeneity between the policies of the Latin American countries analysed, in terms of both level and structure: while Uruguay concentrates on protecting the income of unemployed workers, the other countries (Argentina, Chile, Colombia, Costa Rica and Mexico) prioritize training programmes, direct job creation, employment incentives or start-up incentives. The high rates of informality and job churn that characterize Latin American labour markets, in addition to the challenges posed by technological change in terms of job creation and destruction and the reconfiguration of sectors and jobs, mean there is a need to strengthen labour market policies, especially those aimed at protecting the incomes of unemployed workers.

---

[10]   See, for example, ECLAC (2014 and 2018d) and ECLAC/MMA (2015).

In the light of the structural challenges involved in creating inclusive labour markets in Latin America and the Caribbean (see chapter IV) and of recent debates about the future of work (ECLAC, 2017a; Novick, 2018) and the potential impact of the fourth industrial revolution on society in general and the labour market in particular, it has become even more important to analyse the characteristics of the public policies being implemented by the countries of the region in the area of employment. A central aspect of this analysis concerns the public financing of these policies, i.e. how much governments invest in them, the aim being to evaluate their scope and effectiveness and contribute to decision-making about ways of extending them or altering their design and implementation mechanisms, if necessary.

The structural inequalities characterizing labour markets and the large shortfall of decent work in the region make it necessary to adopt a number of active and passive policies so that "no one is left behind" on the path to development, as set out in the 2030 Agenda for Sustainable Development.[11] In addition, available estimates of the impact of the new wave of technological changes in the region indicate a net loss of jobs ranging from 3.38 million by 2030, representing between 1% and 2% of total employment (OECD/CAF/ECLAC, 2016), to 14 million by 2055 (Manyika and others, 2017). According to Weller (2017), the effect of technological transformations is likely to be not so much the complete destruction of jobs as changes in working methods, the configuration of jobs and the way tasks are performed. The current technological revolution is also taking place in a demographic context characterized by the rapid ageing of the Latin American population. In this regard, Acemoglu and Restrepo (2018) advance the hypothesis that it is the shortage of workers aged between 26 and 55 that leads companies to invest more in robots. Thus, differences in the demographic structures of three industrialized countries (the United States, Germany and Japan) would explain the differences in their levels of automation (investment in robots).

This section is divided into four parts. The first describes the different categorizations of programmes and policies in the employment sphere, a necessary step towards quantifying them; the second describes the programmes and policies of six countries in the region (Argentina, Chile, Colombia, Costa Rica, Mexico and Uruguay); the third quantifies expenditure in the six countries considered; and, lastly, the fourth deals with the need to evaluate these countries' programmes.[12]

1. Quantifying public spending on labour market policies: a typology for analysis

Governments have three types of tools at their disposal to influence the labour market: (i) employment policies, which seek to influence economic growth and in turn have an impact on the level and composition of employment; (ii) labour policies, understood as the rules governing relations between employers and employees, i.e. working conditions; and (iii) labour market policies, which operate directly in the labour market to prevent unemployment and replace income lost in the event that it occurs (Weller, 2004) and to improve the conditions under which the most disadvantaged groups participate. The present section will deal with this last type of tool.

There are different classifications for analysing public interventions in the labour market. A joint publication of the Inter-American Development Bank (IDB) and the

---

[11] With respect to the Sustainable Development Goals (SDGs), this section can be used as an input for following up and reviewing the targets related to decent work, which in addition to five targets of Goal 8 (8.3, 8.5, 8.6, 8.7 and 8.8) include nine other targets, from Goal 1 (1.3 and 1.4), Goal 4 (4.3 and 4.4), Goal 5 (5.4) and Goal 10 (10.1, 10.2, 10.3 and 10.4). These include targets related to social protection for workers.

[12] The six countries were selected because they had budget execution information available for these programmes.

International Labour Organization (ILO) offers a typology of public employment and income policies and programmes in Latin America (ILO/IDB, 1998). The proposed typology consists of six categories: (i) legal incentives for job creation, (ii) public job-search assistance services, (iii) vocational training, (iv) public employment programmes, (v) income support and (vi) unemployment insurance.

The Statistical Office of the European Union (Eurostat) uses a classification to quantify public expenditure on labour market policies that was created in 2001 and revised in 2013, grouping together the different government interventions aimed at people experiencing difficulties in the labour market (Eurostat, 2013). This classification currently contains eight categories of public interventions: (i) labour market services, (ii) training, (iii) employment incentives, (iv) sheltered and supported employment, (v) direct job creation, (vi) start-up incentives, (vii) out-of-work income maintenance and support and (viii) early retirement. According to this classification, public interventions may be services provided to job-seekers, training measures or support for the unemployed. This classification is also used by OECD.

Taking as its starting point the traditional division of passive and active labour market policies, ILO (2016) presents the following classification of active policies for Latin American countries: (i) training, (ii) public employment services, (iii) employment subsidies, (iv) support for self-employment and microenterprise and (v) labour market services.[13] Table III.1 offers a summary of the classifications described.

	International Labour Organization (ILO) and Inter-American Development Bank (IDB) (1998)	Statistical Office of the European Union (Eurostat) (2013) Organization for Economic Cooperation and Development (OECD)	International Labour Organization (ILO) (2016)
Active policies	- Public job-search assistance services - Vocational training - Legal incentives for job creation - Income support - Public employment programmes	- Labour market services - Training - Employment incentives - Sheltered and supported employment - Direct job creation - Start-up incentives	- Public employment services and administration - Training - Employment incentives - Sheltered and supported employment and rehabilitation - Public employment programmes - Start-up incentives
Passive policies	- Unemployment insurance	- Out-of-work income maintenance and support - Early retirement	

Table III.1
Existing classifications of labour market policies

Source: Economic Commission for Latin America and the Caribbean (ECLAC), on the basis of International Labour Organization/Inter-American Development Bank (ILO/IDB), *Programas de empleo e ingresos en América Latina y el Caribe*, Lima, 1998; Eurostat, *Labour Market Policy Statistics: Methodology 2013*, Luxembourg, 2013; International Labour Organization (ILO), *What Works: Active Labour Market Policies in Latin America and the Caribbean*, Geneva, 2016.

For its part, ECLAC (2016a) proposes a typology of labour and productive inclusion programmes organized around two main pillars: labour supply-side support and demand-side support. Labour intermediation services can help to link supply and demand.[14] Labour supply-side support includes those types of interventions that promote technical and vocational training, together with remedial primary and secondary education. Programmes aimed at increasing labour demand-side support, meanwhile, consist of the following actions: (i) support for self-employment, (ii) direct job creation and (iii) indirect job creation.

---

[13] For the OECD countries, the classification includes: (i) training, (ii) direct job creation, (iii) employment incentives, (iv) start-up incentives, (v) public employment services and administration and (vi) sheltered and supported employment and rehabilitation (ILO, 2016, p. 59).

[14] See, in particular, diagram III.1 in ECLAC (2016a).

Both Cecchini and Martínez (2011) and the World Bank (2012) emphasize the relationship between labour market and labour policies and social protection. The former identify labour regulation (which includes labour legislation and inspection, collective bargaining and minimum wages, among other tools) as one of the three pillars of social protection, along with non-contributory social protection (conditional and unconditional cash transfer programmes, social assistance, emergency jobs, social services provision and access) and contributory social protection (contributory pensions, health insurance, unemployment insurance and leave) (Cecchini and Martínez, 2011).

The typology proposed by the World Bank (2012) for social protection and labour programmes also has three major components, the third of which groups labour market programmes, broken down into active and passive programmes. The three components are: (i) the social safety net (non-contributory), (ii) social insurance (contributory) and (iii) labour market programmes: active programmes (training, labour intermediation services and wage subsidies) and passive programmes (unemployment insurance and early retirement incentives).

The proposal for quantifying spending on public sector labour market policies presented in this section reflects the progress made with the classifications described above. To make it as complete as possible, the Eurostat (2013) classification was opted for. However, it is important to note that the other functions and instruments of the region's ministries of labour not included in the classification are not disregarded: labour inspection and regulation, prevention and eradication of child labour, and occupational health and safety, among others.

2. Public policies for the labour market in six countries of the region

Once the limits of the analysis and the classification that would be used to quantify expenditure on public labour market policies had been established, the procedure used was to map the programmes operating in six countries of the region (Argentina, Chile, Colombia, Costa Rica, Mexico and Uruguay) using the ECLAC Database of non-contributory social protection programmes in Latin America and the Caribbean, in particular the module on labour and productive inclusion programmes (see box III.2). Following programme mapping, each country's official information on budget execution by programme was considered. The Classification of the Functions of Government (COFOG),[15] which is the classification usually employed to compile social expenditure information, is not helpful for analysing labour market and labour policies because these are found in three different functions of this classification (economic affairs, education and social protection) and are closely grouped, which precludes analysis of the way policies are being implemented.[16]

---

[15]   See United Nations (2001).
[16]   The same applies to estimates of public expenditure by population group (public expenditure on children, for example), for which COFOG cannot be used and an analysis by budget programme must be opted for (see Tromben and Podestà, 2018).

Box III.2
Database of labour and productive inclusion programmes

The database of labour and productive inclusion programmes is one of three modules of the Database of non-contributory social protection programmes in Latin America and the Caribbean, which was created using official data provided by the countries in response to the mandate conferred on ECLAC at the Regional Conference on Social Development in Latin America and the Caribbean, held in Lima in November 2015. The other two modules concern conditional cash transfer programmes and social pensions.

The database provides information on social programmes in the region aimed at people living in conditions of extreme poverty, poverty or vulnerability. In particular, the database of labour and productive inclusion programmes provides information on both the characteristics of these programmes (e.g., target population, targeting methods, legal framework, responsible and implementing agencies and sources of financing) and quantitative expenditure, budget and coverage data. In addition, bibliographical references are provided with a view to giving a fuller picture of programme outcomes.

Labour and productive inclusion programmes are classified under different areas of action, depending on whether their main function is labour supply-side support (interventions that support technical and vocational training and remedial primary and secondary education), labour demand-side support (support for self-employment, direct job creation and indirect job creation) or labour intermediation.

Although the database is an important step forward in terms of disseminating knowledge about labour and productive inclusion programmes and is systematically updated, it does need to be strengthened, especially as regards the availability of official expenditure and budget data.

Source: Economic Commission for Latin America and the Caribbean (ECLAC), Database of non-contributory social protection programmes in Latin America and the Caribbean [online] https://dds.cepal.org/bpsnc/home.

Table III.2 shows the eight categories of public interventions analysed for this section, accompanied by a description of each and their relationship to COFOG.[17] It is important to note that some programmes could be classified under more than one intervention because they often seek to cover several objectives at once. On this point, ILO (2016, p. 36) states that "importantly, active labour market policies (ALMP) in Latin America and the Caribbean are rarely defined under a clear-cut category. This means, for instance, that training schemes could be included in public works programmes. Data on public spending by type of intervention should therefore not be interpreted as being strictly mutually exclusive."

---

[17]   It is important to note that this analysis has been carried out in response to a request made to ECLAC by the participants in the international seminar/workshop on the progress made and future challenges for social expenditure measurement in Latin America, held in Quito in July 2016, with regard to spending on labour affairs and how to integrate this into social spending. See [online] https://www.cepal.org/es/eventos/seminario-taller-internacional-avances-desafios-la-medicion-gasto-social-america-latina.

Table III.2
Categories and definitions for quantifying public spending on labour market policies

Category	Name of intervention	Description	Relationship with the Classification of the Functions of Government (COFOG)
1	Labour intermediation services	Services provided by public agencies that are related to job-seeking and advice	70412 – General labour affairs (Economic affairs)
2	Training	Measures to improve employability through training	70950 – Education not definable by level
3	Employment incentives	Measures that facilitate the hiring of unemployed persons (or other types of persons) or that help ensure continuity in employment for persons at risk of losing their jobs	70412 - General labour affairs (Economic affairs)
4	Sheltered and supported employment	Measures to promote the integration of persons with disabilities into the labour market through sheltered employment	70412 - General labour affairs (Economic affairs)
5	Direct job creation	Measures that create additional jobs, usually for the benefit of the community	Programmes will be classified by the function (objective) they fulfil
6	Start-up incentives	Measures that promote start-ups by encouraging the unemployed to set up their own businesses or become self-employed	Programmes will be classified by the function (objective) they fulfil
7	Out-of-work income maintenance and support	Monetary support to compensate people for the loss of their wage	7105 – Unemployment (Social protection)
8	Early retirement	Monetary support facilitating early retirement for people close to retirement age who have little prospect of finding a job	7105 – Unemployment (Social protection)

Source: Economic Commission for Latin America and the Caribbean (ECLAC).

Each of the eight categories of programmes through which labour market policies are implemented in the six countries studied will now be briefly described.

Labour intermediation services or programmes are usually organized into two broad areas: first, face-to-face intermediation services that come under local governments and, second, an online system developed or financed by the countries' ministries of labour. This is the case with Costa Rica, which in 2009 implemented the National System of Employment Intermediation, Guidance and Information (SIOIE) with the aim of improving interaction between the public employment service, the vocational training system and start-up programmes. Costa Rica currently has more than 40 employment offices run by municipalities[18] and has had the Busco Empleo online portal since 2009. It is also the case with Chile, where many municipalities have Municipal Labour Information Offices (OMIL)[19] and where the National Employment Exchange (BNE), a free online tool that lets workers seek new job opportunities in the public and private sectors, has been operating since 2009; enrolling in the BNE is a condition for entitlement to unemployment insurance and training programmes. Argentina operates by the same logic: enrolment in some employment office[20] belonging to the Employment Services Network provides access to job-seeking support, guidance and advice and to guidance on employment programmes (Bertranou, 2013; Helbig, Mazzola and García, 2016). In Mexico, lastly, the National Employment Service (SNE) operates on a decentralized basis through a network of 167 employment offices and 36 service modules distributed throughout the country, although they are coordinated and financed by the central authorities, in particular the Secretariat of Labour and Social Security. The Job Matching Services subprogramme of the Employment Support Programme is organized into three major components: (i) job matching with a view to placement; (ii) job matching with a view to placement abroad; (iii) supplementary assistance mechanisms.

The efforts made in recent years in all the above-mentioned countries to modernize labour intermediation services (in particular by creating online tools) are indisputable. These efforts have made it possible to serve more people, but the most vulnerable will

---

[18] Costa Rica is organized geographically into 7 provinces and 82 cantons.

[19] These offices are run by municipal authorities but are technically and financially dependent on the central government via the National Training and Employment Service (SENCE), which in turn is part of the Ministry of Labour and Social Security.

[20] According to official data from the Ministry of Production and Labour, there are 630 municipal employment offices.

always need more personalized support, so that existing local government systems must continue to be maintained to ensure that no one is left behind.[21]

The six countries under consideration have more than 40 training programmes, and spending on these is estimated to have averaged 0.15% of GDP in 2016. Their main objective is to improve people's employability. Some are targeted at women, unemployed people, persons with disabilities, indigenous persons or young people without any experience, among others, while others are aimed at the general population. The programmes are sometimes accompanied by income support, an example being the Training and Employment Insurance Programme in Argentina. A predominant feature of training programmes is that they focus on short-term courses designed for participants to acquire fairly basic skills (ILO, 2016). Although training programmes have existed for many decades, training systems underwent major organizational changes in the 1990s, with the appearance of new providers, prompting a new role for the State as an organizer, regulator and supervisor of training provision, and in some cases as a provider. As noted in Llisterri and others (2014), three training systems currently coexist in the countries of the region: (i) the traditional institutional model, in which the State maintains its virtual monopoly position in training provision (Colombia and Costa Rica);[22] (ii) the regulatory and enabling State model, in which the regulatory function is separated from the provision of the training service (Argentina, Chile and Uruguay); and (iii) the mixed model, which combines characteristics of the first two (Mexico). Weller and Gontero (2016) analyse the persistent weaknesses of training systems in Latin America and highlight aspects associated with the supply of training that prevent adequate levels of coverage and quality from being achieved.

Employment incentive programmes, by definition, aim to facilitate the employment of unemployed people. What is observed in the six countries under consideration is that these measures are aimed at population groups facing particular barriers to participation in the labour market, such as young people and women. The most commonly used incentive arrangements are part-payment of employees' wages for a stipulated time and tax discounts.

Sheltered and supported employment programmes aim to integrate persons with disabilities into the labour market. The Convention on the Rights of Persons with Disabilities, which entered into force in 2008 and has been ratified by all Latin American countries, asserts that "States Parties recognize the right of persons with disabilities to work, on an equal basis with others; this includes the right to the opportunity to gain a living by work freely chosen or accepted in a labour market and work environment that is open, inclusive and accessible to persons with disabilities" (United Nations, 2007, p. 16, art. 27). The Ibero-American Social Security Organization (OISS, 2012) notes that all countries in Latin America have specific laws protecting persons with disabilities which contain provisions designed to promote their inclusion in society and in the workplace. In fact, many countries have recently amended their laws to bring them into line with the Convention on the Rights of Persons with Disabilities. There are 11 such programmes in the countries under consideration, but there are also labour intermediation programmes (for example, in Argentina, Chile and Uruguay) and training programmes (Argentina) aimed at persons with disabilities. The programmes the countries have developed in recent years reflect the spirit of article 1 of the Convention, with its stated

---

[21]　See International Labour Organization (ILO), "Notas sobre Servicios Públicos de Empleo" [online] https://www.ilo.org/santiago/publicaciones/servicios-publicos-empleo/lang--es/index.htm.

[22]　In Colombia, the National Training Service (SENA) is an autonomous public agency that is 90% financed from payroll contributions. The programmes considered in the present study include eight run by SENA. In Costa Rica, the National Training Institute (INA) is an autonomous public agency that is 96% financed from payroll contributions. The present study did not consider any INA programme because it was not possible to isolate programmes targeted on the unemployed; however, INA spent 2.9% of GDP on training operations in 2016, with a total of 302,400 enrolments.

purpose of promoting respect for the inherent dignity of all persons with disabilities, and accordingly seek to incorporate them into the labour market.

Something else that is important to note, even though it does not come into the measurement of spending on sheltered employment measures, are mandatory quota laws reserving jobs for persons with disabilities, whether in the public administration or the private sector. Among the countries considered, such quotas exist in Argentina, Chile, Costa Rica and Uruguay. In Argentina, Law No. 25698 (enacted in 2003) sets a quota of 4% for the public sector and private companies operating public service concessions. In Chile, Law No. 21015 (enacted recently, in 2017) reserves 1% of jobs for persons with disabilities in State agencies and private companies with 100 or more workers. In Costa Rica, Law No. 8862 (enacted in 2010) reserves 5% of jobs in government agencies. In Uruguay, likewise, Law No. 18844 (enacted in 2010) reserves 4% of jobs in public bodies. While the enactment of these laws represents indisputable progress towards the full inclusion of persons with disabilities in the labour market, enforcement is another necessary step towards the desired inclusion.

All the countries studied have direct job creation programmes. These programmes are usually designed for the most vulnerable and, in Colombia, for displaced persons.[23] In Argentina, the Social Income with Work Programme, in operation since 2009, aims to promote economic development and social inclusion by generating new jobs on the basis of organized and community work. In 2016, the programme provided work for 140,000 people at a cost of 0.13% of GDP. Chile has two programmes, the Emergency Employment Programme of the National Forestry Corporation (CONAF) and the Community Investment Programme of the Ministry of Labour and Social Security, which are activated when the demand for labour contracts.[24] These programmes averaged 25,923 jobs per month between them in 2016, with the largest being the Community Investment Programme, at a cost of 0.08% of GDP. In Colombia, there are currently two direct job creation programmes: Temporary Employment, run by the Administrative Department for Social Prosperity, and the National Programme of Territorial Technical Assistance of the Ministry of Labour. In the case of Costa Rica, the two categories of the National Employment Programme (indigenous and community work) provided financial support to an average of 8,100 people in 2016, at an annual cost of 0.13% of GDP. In Mexico, the Temporary Employment Program (PET) supported 13.3% of underemployed and unemployed people below the official minimum welfare line in 2016. The 281,144 temporary jobs generated benefited the same number of people aged 16 and over whose income or wealth had been reduced as a result of adverse economic and social situations. In Uruguay, lastly, the Uruguay Trabaja, Social Cooperatives and Primera Experiencia Laboral programmes generate employment for around 10,000 people each year. In the case of Uruguay Trabaja, there are quotas for persons of African descent (8% of places), persons with disabilities (4% of places) and transsexual persons (2% of places).

Start-up incentive programmes aimed at unemployed or vulnerable people or social production programmes are present in all the countries under consideration. In general, they aim to encourage small-scale entrepreneurship. Like training programmes, they are numerous, with an average of seven per country. As analysed in ECLAC (2016a), start-up incentive programmes tend to be effective only for a minority of workers and translate into better results when these are highly educated (Farné, 2009). Some programmes provide seed capital (Yo Emprendo Semilla in Chile) and others include

---

[23]   Law No. 1448 of 2011 created the National System of Care and Comprehensive Redress for Victims, whose purpose is to provide comprehensive redress to victims of Colombia's internal armed conflict.

[24]   The Contingency Programme against Unemployment, created under Law No. 20128 on Fiscal Responsibility of 2008, is activated in two eventualities: (i) when the quarterly national unemployment rate exceeds its average for the previous five years or is 10% or above, and (ii) when there is an unemployment rate of 10% or above in one or more regions or in particular provinces.

support services for the development of business plans (De la Idea al Proyecto in Argentina; Yo Trabajo: Apoyo a tu Plan Laboral in Chile; Mi Negocio in Colombia). Several programmes with a gender perspective were also found: the Fund for the Promotion of Women's Productive and Organizational Activities (FOMUJERES) in Costa Rica and the Support Programme for the Productivity of Women Entrepreneurs (PROMETE) and National Programme for the Financing of Microentrepreneurs and Rural Women (PRONAFIM) in Mexico.

Out-of-work income maintenance and support programmes exist in five of the six countries considered in this analysis (the exception is Costa Rica). As Velásquez (2016a and 2016b) states, without adequate protection mechanisms, unemployment can leave the family of a laid-off worker in a highly vulnerable situation. However, although there are various mechanisms in several countries of the region, only six have unemployment insurance.[25] Even in these cases, furthermore, a significant percentage of workers do not benefit from the system because they work in informal conditions.[26] This is the largest component of public spending on labour market policies in Uruguay, where it accounted for 0.52% of GDP in 2016, as opposed to just 0.06% of GDP in Colombia and 0.01% of GDP in Chile. It is important to note that only public unemployment insurance systems are considered in this analysis, leaving private insurance systems out of consideration, even if they are compulsory. In Chile, a private unemployment insurance scheme has existed since 2002, operating as an individual capitalization system with a small unfunded component financed by the State. Workers and employers are required by law to contribute to this unemployment insurance. In the present quantification exercise only the public component was considered, i.e. the contribution of the Chilean State to the Solidarity Unemployment Fund and the unemployment benefits that still exist for employees who were hired before the unemployment insurance scheme began. If private spending were considered in the case of Chile, this category would be worth 0.4% of GDP. Lastly, it should be noted that the effectiveness of unemployment protection is enhanced if it is combined with active policies, such as training and labour intermediation policies.

3. Public spending on labour market policies in six countries of Latin America

Figure III.7 shows the number of programmes through which current labour market policies are implemented by country, in accordance with the proposed classification. A total of 151 programmes were analysed in the six countries considered. The institutional coverage of the programmes is confined to central government; this is particularly relevant when analysing cases such as those of Argentina and Mexico, which are countries with a federal structure, meaning that there may be other programmes financed and executed by subnational governments that are not considered in this study.

Chile comes out as the country with the largest number of programmes, this being explained mainly by the number of training programmes (15) and start-up incentive programmes (9).

---

[25] According to the study published by Velásquez (2016c), there are four types of instruments for protecting income in the event of unemployment: (i) severance pay, (ii) unemployment saving accounts, (iii) unemployment insurance and (iv) unemployment benefits. While severance pay exists in almost all the countries, nine countries in the region (Argentina, the Bolivarian Republic of Venezuela, Brazil, Chile, Colombia, Costa Rica, Ecuador, Panama and Peru) have individual unemployment saving accounts, six have unemployment insurance systems (Argentina, the Bolivarian Republic of Venezuela, Brazil, Chile, Ecuador and Uruguay) and just two have unemployment benefits (Chile and Mexico).

[26] This is demonstrated by the small number of beneficiaries of unemployment insurance: according to a study by ILO (2014), 23.6% of all unemployed in Chile, 21.3% in Uruguay and 14.3% in Argentina received unemployment insurance income in 2011.

Figure III.7
Latin America (6 countries): labour market policy programmes, by intervention type, 2016
(Numbers)

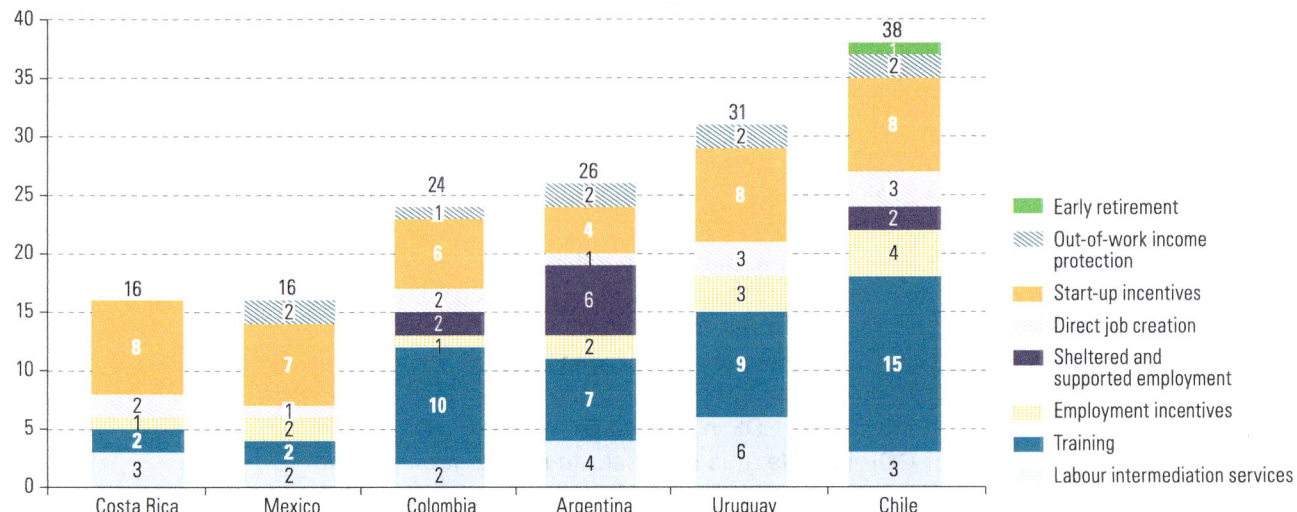

Source: Economic Commission for Latin America and the Caribbean (ECLAC), Database of non-contributory social protection programmes in Latin America and the Caribbean [online] https://dds.cepal.org/bpsnc/home; official data from the countries.

Labour market programmes and public policies for each of the countries studied are mapped out in annex III.A2. The number of programmes in a country does not necessarily bear a relation to their coverage or the resources allocated. In fact, programmes are often fairly small (in terms of the resources allocated) and targeted on a specific population (women, young people, persons with disabilities, indigenous persons, displaced persons or older people). The existence of a large number of programmes may have negative implications for policy efficiency: it may be inefficient for one service to have to manage several programmes or for different services (ministries) to offer similar programmes. It is therefore important for countries to have analyses that map and quantify a sectoral policy, irrespective of the ministry responsible, for the purpose of decision-making about possible changes in programme design and in management and implementation mechanisms.

The information about public expenditure on these programmes by country (see figure III.8) brings to light a variety of situations when it comes to the level, structure and trends of expenditure. While in five countries expenditure on labour market policies shows an upward trend between 2012 and 2016, Mexico is an exception: since 2015, the country's government has implemented fiscal adjustment measures and cut spending on budget programmes not deemed of high priority.[27] Consequently, public spending on labour market policies in Mexico fell from 0.91% of GDP in 2012 to 0.35% of GDP in 2016.

With regard to the structure of public expenditure on labour market programmes in each of the countries, these estimates show that Argentina focuses its fiscal effort on training and direct job creation, Colombia on training and Uruguay on income protection in the event of unemployment, while Chile and Mexico are the two countries with the most diversified structures. In Chile, the three main measures are training, direct job creation and employment incentives, while in Mexico they are start-up incentives, direct job creation and employment incentives.

---

[27]   Since 2010, the National Council for the Evaluation of Social Development Policy (CONEVAL) has published a document titled *Consideraciones para el proceso presupuestario* which provides performance evaluations of social programmes and actions (high-, medium- and low-priority programmes) with a view to progressing with results-based budgeting. The Secretariat of Finance and Public Credit takes up these evaluations and incorporates them into the General Economic Policy Criteria for the Revenue Bill and Draft Expenditure Budget for each fiscal year to determine which budget programme will be affected by fiscal austerity.

Figure III.8
Latin America (6 countries): public spending on labour market policies, by intervention category, 2012–2016
(Percentages of GDP)

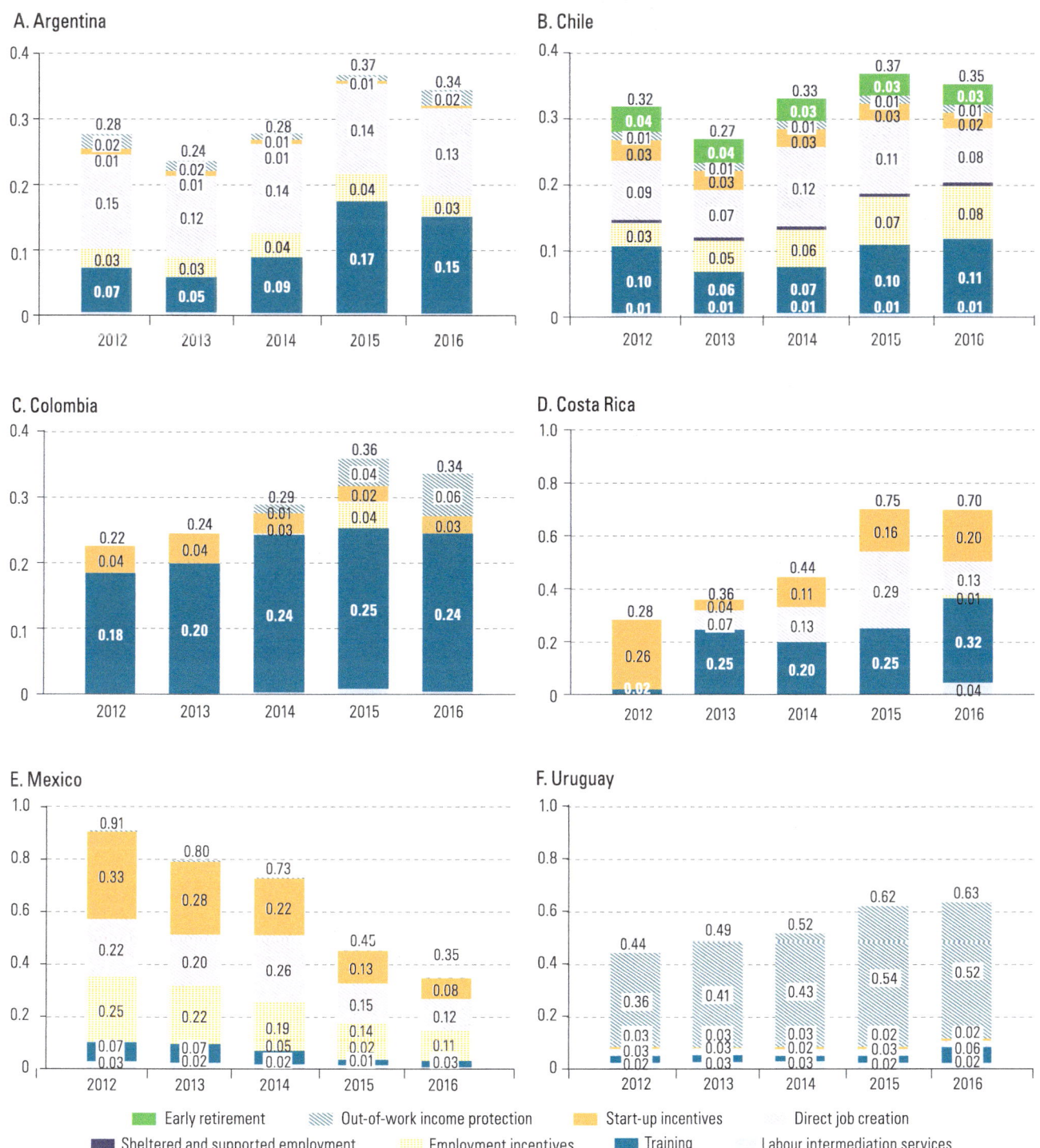

A. Argentina
B. Chile
C. Colombia
D. Costa Rica
E. Mexico
F. Uruguay

Early retirement   Out-of-work income protection   Start-up incentives   Direct job creation
Sheltered and supported employment   Employment incentives   Training   Labour intermediation services

Source: Economic Commission for Latin America and the Caribbean (ECLAC), on the basis of official data from the countries.

Expenditure is also heterogeneous. It is striking that, as percentages of GDP, Costa Rica and Uruguay spend twice as much as the other four countries studied. This heterogeneity is found not only in the six Latin American countries considered in this analysis, but also in the OECD countries (see figure III.9A). While Japan and the United States make up the group of countries that invest least in labour market policies (less than 0.3% of GDP), spending in France and Denmark exceeds 3% of GDP.

Figure III.9
Latin America (6 countries) and Organization for Economic Cooperation and Development (OECD) (32 countries): public spending on labour market policies, 2016

A. Total public spending on labour market policies
(percentages of GDP)

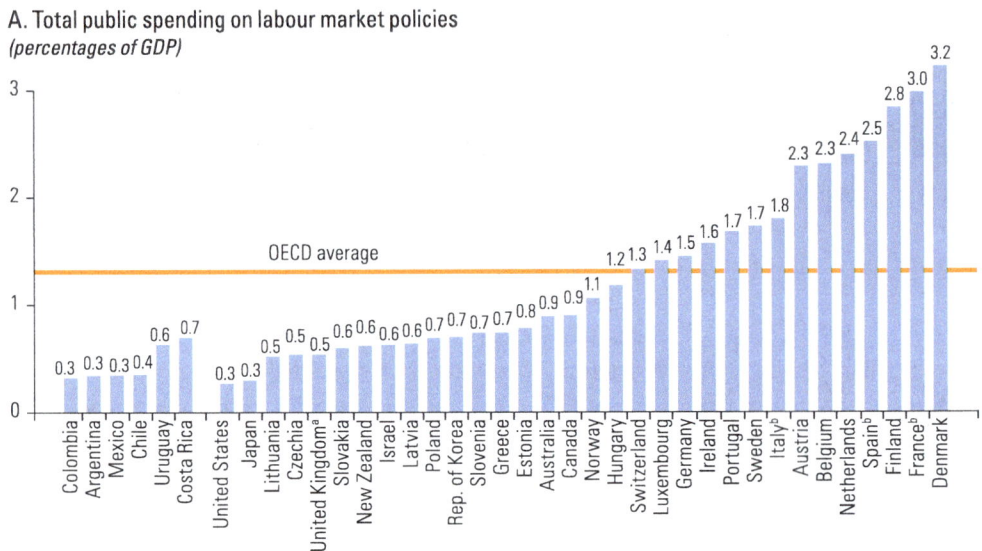

B. Composition of spending on labour market policies, by intervention category
(percentages)

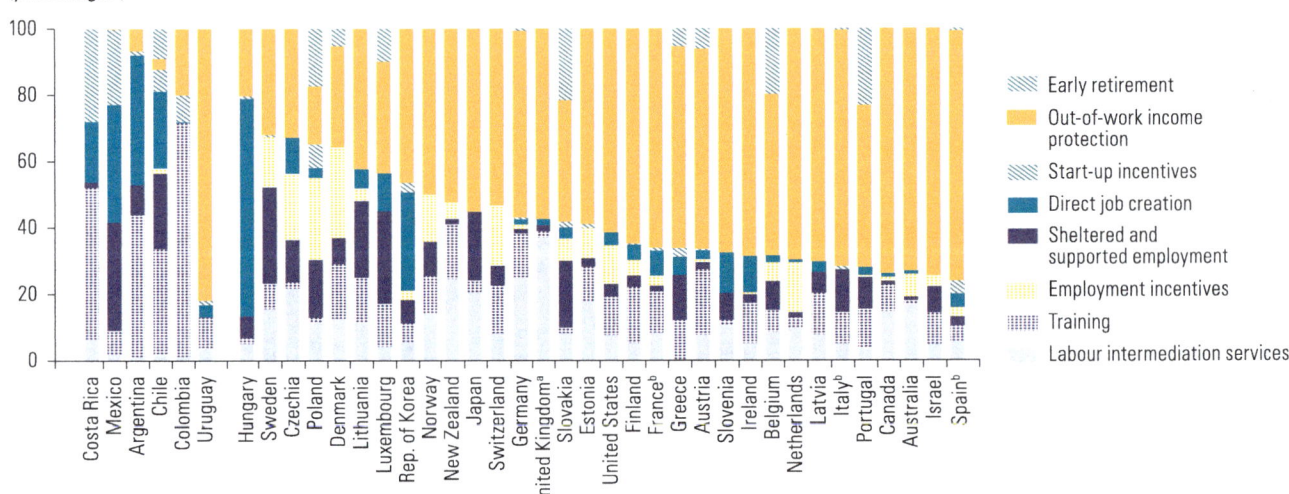

Legend:
- Early retirement
- Out-of-work income protection
- Start-up incentives
- Direct job creation
- Sheltered and supported employment
- Employment incentives
- Training
- Labour intermediation services

Source: Economic Commission for Latin America and the Caribbean (ECLAC), on the basis of official data from the countries and Organization for Economic Cooperation and Development (OECD).

Note: In figure B, the countries are ranked in ascending order by the proportion of total labour market policy spending going on passive policies (unemployment and early retirement).

[a] Data for 2010.
[b] Data for 2015.

The composition of labour market policy expenditure in the OECD countries (see figure III.9B) also shows a degree of heterogeneity. On the one hand, there is a very diverse group of countries that invest significantly in employment incentive and sheltered employment programmes, such as Sweden, Lithuania, Luxembourg and Japan. On the other hand, the United Kingdom and Germany give high priority to labour intermediation services. Lastly, all OECD countries except Hungary have passive policies (out-of-work income protection and early retirement programmes) that account for more than 20% of total spending on labour market policies. This last finding reinforces the idea that progress needs to be made in the region towards strengthening and expanding the coverage of labour market policies and programmes, especially with regard to unemployment protection, as a fundamental part of integrated social protection systems. To this end, it is also necessary to develop policies to improve the structuring of the labour market, including the formalization of employment and production units, a trend that was present in the region between 2002 and 2014 (ECLAC, 2018c).

Analysing the average level of public spending on labour market policies yields a figure of 0.45% of GDP in the six Latin American countries in 2016, while the OECD countries (using data for 28 countries) spent three times that percentage, with an average of 1.31% of GDP that same year.[28] The great difference between the countries of the region selected and those of OECD is in their out-of-work income maintenance and support programmes: whereas in the six countries of Latin America this intervention category averages barely 0.1% of GDP, the figure rises to 0.72% of GDP in the OECD countries. There, more than half of all labour market policy expenditure goes on passive policies, including out-of-work income protection and early retirement programmes. This difference is explained, first, by the fact that only six Latin American countries (including three of those included in this analysis) have unemployment insurance; second, by the high degree of informality that characterizes the labour markets of the region's countries, which means that a large proportion of workers do not have protection covering part of their income if they lose their jobs, even if there is a public system in place to cover that risk in their country. Two other differences that stand out when the six Latin American countries are compared with the OECD countries are, first, the greater spending by the former on start-up incentive policies, which also reflects the larger share of own-account work in Latin America, and, second, the greater importance of labour intermediation services in the OECD countries, which can be considered an indicator of more structured labour institutions.

4.   The need for programme evaluation

The large number of programmes in operation and the scale of the resources committed to them mean there is a need for systematic and at least reasonably regular evaluation. Evaluations are periodic assessments of a planned, ongoing or completed project, programme or policy (Gertler and others, 2017). Programme evaluations can be of various types: impact evaluations (aimed at ascertaining whether the objective pursued is achieved by the programme); cost-effectiveness evaluations (aimed at determining the cost of the programme in relation to the objective achieved); and evaluations of programme processes (aimed at finding out whether programme management processes are efficient). The purpose of any impact evaluation is to quantify the extent to which an intervention has achieved certain outcomes of interest. Impact is the difference between the person's situation after the intervention and what it would have been if they had not participated in the programme. To estimate this counterfactual result, the situation of people exposed to the intervention (treated individuals) is compared with

---

[28]   The differences between average public spending on labour market policies in Latin America (6 countries) and OECD (28 countries) could be greater if more countries in Latin America and the Caribbean were included in the analysis.

the situation of a group of people who have similar characteristics to those treated but did not participate in the programme (the control group). This type of assessment makes extensive use of econometrics, in particular random assessment techniques.[29]

This type of evaluation has been carried out in the region since the 1980s. As Martínez (2015) puts it in an overview of the subject, the region has a quite diverse track record in evaluating social programmes. In fact, one of the evaluations that is often cited in the literature and that has played an important role in the dissemination of this instrument was the one conducted by the International Food Policy Research Institute (IFPRI) to evaluate the Education, Health and Food Programme (PROGRESA) in Mexico (Skoufias, 2006).

A total of 147 evaluations are recorded for the 151 programmes analysed in this chapter. Some programmes have been evaluated several times, while 82 have never been evaluated at all (see diagram III.1). The countries with the most evaluations are Chile and Mexico, which is not surprising, since the evaluation systems of both countries are institutionalized. In Chile, the Budget Department of the Ministry of Finance implemented a pilot programme of government programme evaluations in 1997. Since 2003, the Ministry of Finance and the national Congress have agreed each year on the programmes to be evaluated during the year as part of the budget bill approval process (see Budget Directorate, 2015). In the case of Mexico, the National Council for the Evaluation of Social Development Policy (CONEVAL), an autonomous public body, is responsible for carrying out social programme evaluations. The legal underpinnings of this institution's work are strong: CONEVAL was created in 2004 by the Social Development Act and in 2014 a constitutional reform was carried out that designated the Council as the institution responsible for carrying out evaluations of social development policy programmes (paragraph c of article 26).

Diagram III.1
Latin America
(6 countries): impact
evaluations of
labour market policy
programmes, 2002–2018

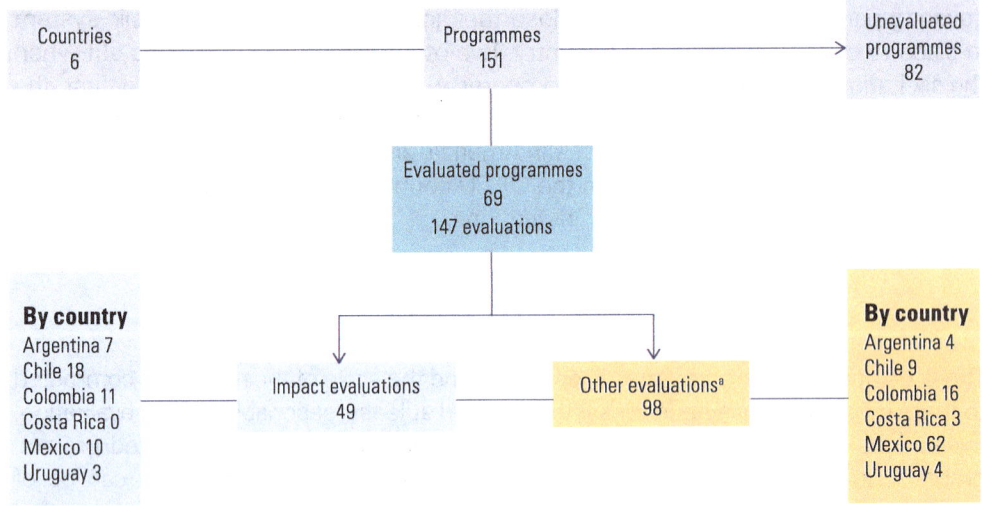

Source: Economic Commission for Latin America and the Caribbean (ECLAC), on the basis of official data from the countries.
[a] Other evaluations may deal with cost-effectiveness or processes.

---

[29] There are numerous manuals and courses on how to conduct impact assessments prepared and run by international bodies such as the United Nations Development Programme (UNDP), the World Bank and the Inter-American Development Bank (IDB) and by academic centres such as the Abdul Latif Jameel Poverty Action Lab (J-PAL), founded in 2003 at the Department of Economics of the Massachusetts Institute of Technology (MIT), which today constitutes a network of 53 universities around the world. The most recent publications include Khandker, Koolwal and Samad (2010) and Duflo and Banerjee (2011).

A breakdown by evaluation type shows that 49 of the 147 evaluations are impact evaluations, while 98 are of some other type. The country with the most impact evaluations is Chile, with 18, most of them relating to training programmes and start-up incentives.

C.   Conclusions

As has been seen in this chapter, central government social spending is at one of its highest levels since the century began in both the Latin American and Caribbean countries. Similarly, average per capita spending in 2017 was at its highest in 18 years, having doubled in real dollar terms since the early 2000s. There has clearly been a stabilizing trend in the level of priority and commitment assigned by the region's countries to social policies. However, these countries' expenditure is still far below the amounts appropriated for these purposes by developed countries or committed to at intergovernmental forums by the countries of Latin America and the Caribbean themselves in areas such as health, education and culture. The situation thus needs to be kept under constant review, taking into consideration the role of financing as a vehicle and medium of implementation for the policies required to achieve the targets of the 2030 Agenda for Sustainable Development, which are demanding and are due to be reached in just 11 years' time.

These averages mask a high degree of heterogeneity, however. While the central governments of Argentina, Brazil, Chile and Uruguay, in Latin America, and Barbados and Trinidad and Tobago, in the Caribbean, allocate more than 14% of GDP to social policy financing, the central governments of most of the countries in the Central American Integration System (SICA) (the Dominican Republic, El Salvador, Guatemala, Honduras and Panama), two of the South American countries (Ecuador and Paraguay) and two of the Caribbean countries (Bahamas and Guyana) spend less than 10% of GDP on these functions. This distribution highlights the fact that the very Latin American countries that will struggle most to achieve the social goals of the 2030 Agenda for Sustainable Development are the ones that allocate the least resources to policies in this area, both in relative terms and in amounts per person.

The distribution of central government resources among the various social functions has been stable in the region's countries, with social protection and education accounting for the largest proportions, followed at a considerable distance by the health function. This is not surprising, considering the large and growing commitments the countries have made to their social security systems, coupled to a lesser extent with anti-poverty policies and non-contributory social protection. Once again, as discussed in section A, this average distribution conceals a number of different realities. While the social protection function is very prominent in the countries with the greatest social investment (particularly Argentina, Brazil and Uruguay), the proportions allocated to education and health are considerably more uniform across the region's countries. On the other hand, countries with expenditure equal to or below the regional average allocate proportionally more to functions other than those already mentioned, such as housing and community amenities in the cases of Guatemala, Guyana, Mexico, Nicaragua and Panama and recreation, culture and religion in the case of Haiti.

It should be recalled that the data presented in part A of the chapter focus on central government coverage and that amounts can vary significantly if broader coverage is considered, such as non-financial public sector or general government coverage. This is particularly relevant in the case of countries that have autonomous or federal subnational governments.

Part B of the chapter presented a quantification of public expenditure on labour market policies, yielding some insights into its structure and recent evolution in six countries of the region (Argentina, Chile, Colombia, Costa Rica, Mexico and Uruguay). This exercise is similar to one carried out by ILO and IDB (1998) for seven countries in the region with data for 1995.[30] The main finding of the estimates presented in this chapter is that average public expenditure on labour market policies in these countries was 0.45% of GDP in 2016. Also striking is how much both the level and the composition of this expenditure vary between the six countries and how much they differ from the OECD countries, owing to the important role played in the latter by the system of income protection for unemployed workers. This is associated both with the characteristics of the social protection system there and with the higher level of labour market formality compared to the Latin American countries. Thus, once again, the labour informality characterizing the region emerges as a factor that limits the development capacity, coverage and impact of social protection systems. However, while further progress is needed in the formalization of employment, it is essential to strengthen and expand the coverage of labour market policies and programmes as a constituent part of integrated social protection systems in Latin America, especially those related to unemployment protection.

There are various possible ways in which labour market policies can improve the quality of the match between labour supply and demand through an efficient and inclusive public labour intermediation service; ensure that workers' skills are increased and updated through training; directly or indirectly promote the creation of productive jobs through direct job creation programmes and hiring subsidies; promote the labour market integration of individuals and groups facing greater barriers to access, such as low-skilled workers, women, young people, indigenous and Afrodescendent persons and persons with disabilities; and lastly, promote entrepreneurship. As ECLAC has argued, active and passive labour market policies are also a constituent part of social protection systems and play an important role in guaranteeing the fulfilment of rights and improving levels of well-being for workers and their families.

Bibliography

Acemoglu, D. and P. Restrepo (2018), "Demographics and automation", *NBER Working Paper*, No. 24421, Cambridge, National Bureau of Economic Research (NBER), March.

Bertranou, F. (2013), "Employment policy implementation mechanisms in Argentina", *Working Paper*, No. 3, Buenos Aires, International Labour Organization (ILO).

Budget Directorate (2015), "Evaluación ex-post: conceptos y metodologías", Santiago, June [online] http://www.dipres.gob.cl/598/articles-135135_doc_pdf.pdf.

Cecchini, S. and R. Martínez (2011), *Inclusive social protection in Latin America: a comprehensive, rights-based approach*, ECLAC Books, No. 111 (LC/G.2488-P), Santiago, Economic Commission for Latin America and the Caribbean (ECLAC), March.

Duflo, E. and A. Banerjee (2012), *Poor Economics: A Radical Rethinking of The Way to Fight Global Poverty*, New York, PublicAffairs.

ECLAC (Economic Commission for Latin America and the Caribbean) (2018a), *The Inefficiency of Inequality* (LC/SES.37/3-P), Santiago, May.

_____(2018b), *Economic Survey of Latin America and the Caribbean, 2018* (LC/PUB.2018/17-P), Santiago, October.

_____(2018c), *Social Panorama of Latin America, 2017* (LC/PUB.2018/1-P), Santiago, February.

_____(2018d), *Estimación del gasto en protección ambiental en Costa Rica* (LC/TS.2018/14), Santiago, February.

---

[30] In that study, public expenditure on active labour market policies in each of the seven countries was estimated at 2.09% of GDP in Brazil, 1.33% of GDP in Costa Rica, 0.87% of GDP in Peru, 0.71% of GDP in Jamaica, 0.61% of GDP in Mexico, 0.25% of GDP in Argentina and 0.05% of GDP in Chile.

___(2017a), *Linkages between the social and production spheres: gaps, pillars and challenges* (LC/CDS.2/3), Santiago, October.

___(2017b), *Social Panorama of Latin America, 2016* (LC/PUB.2017/12-P), Santiago, August.

___(2016a), *Social Panorama of Latin America, 2015* (LC/G.2691-P), Santiago, October.

___(2016b), *Preliminary Overview of the Economies of Latin America and the Caribbean, 2016* (LC/G.2698-P), Santiago, December.

___(2016c), *The social inequality matrix in Latin America* (LC/G.2690(MDS.1/2)), Santiago, October.

___(2014), "El gasto en protección ambiental en América Latina y el Caribe: bases conceptuales y experiencia regional", *Project Documents* (LC/W.634), Santiago.

ECLAC/MMA (Economic Commission for Latin America and the Caribbean/Ministry of the Environment of Chile) (2015), *Estimación del gasto público en protección ambiental en Chile* (LC/W.655), Santiago.

ECLAC/OEI (Economic Commission for Latin America and the Caribbean/Organization of Ibero-American States for Education, Science and Culture) (2014), *Cultura y desarrollo económico en Iberoamérica*, E. Espíndola (coord.), Madrid.

Eurostat (2013), *Labour Market Policy Statistics: Methodology 2013*, Luxembourg.

___(2001), *Labour Market Policy Expenditure and Participants: Data 1998*, Luxembourg.

Farné, S. (2009), "Políticas activas del mercado de trabajo en Colombia, México y Perú", *Macroeconomics of Development series*, No. 96 (LC/L.3118-P), Santiago, Economic Commission for Latin America and the Caribbean (ECLAC), November.

Gertler, P. and others (2017), *Impact Evaluation in Practice: Second Edition*, Washington, D.C., World Bank/Inter-American Development Bank (IDB).

Helbig, D., R. Mazzola and M. García (2016), "Servicios públicos de empleo en Argentina como pilar de apoyo a la política de empleo", *Documento de Trabajo*, No. 13, Buenos Aires, International Labour Organization (ILO), January.

ILO (International Labour Organization) (2016), *What Works: Active Labour Market Policies in Latin America and the Caribbean*, Geneva.

___(2014), *Trabajo decente y juventud en América Latina 2013: políticas para la acción*, Lima, February.

ILO/IDB (International Labour Organization/Inter-American Development Bank) (1998), *Programas de empleo e ingresos en América Latina y el Caribe*, Lima.

IMF (International Monetary Fund) (2014), *Government Finance Statistics Manual 2014*, Washington, D.C.

___(2001), *Government Finance Statistics Manual 2001*, Washington, D.C.

Isgut, A. and J. Weller (eds.) (2016), *Protection and training: institutions for improving workforce integration in Latin America and Asia*, ECLAC Books, No. 140 (LC/G.2687-P), Santiago, Economic Commission for Latin America and the Caribbean (ECLAC), October.

Llisterri, J. and others (2014), "Educación técnica y formación profesional en América Latina: el reto de la productividad", *Políticas Públicas y Transformación Productiva series*, No. 13/2014, Caracas, Development Bank of Latin America (CAF).

Khandker, S., G. Koolwal and H. Samad (2010), *Handbook on Impact Evaluation: Quantitative Methods and Practices*, Washington, D.C., World Bank.

Manyika, J. and others (2017), *A Future that Works: Automation, Employment, and Productivity*, New York, McKinsey Global Institute, January.

Martínez, R. (2015), "Monitoring and evaluation of social protection policies and programmes", *Towards universal social protection: Latin American pathways and policy tools*, ECLAC Books, No. 136 (LC/G.2644-P), S. Cecchini and others (eds.), Santiago, Economic Commission for Latin America and the Caribbean (ECLAC), July.

Novik, M. (2018), "El mundo del trabajo: cambios y desafíos en materia de inclusión", *Social Policy series*, No. 228 (LC/TS.2018/2), Santiago, Economic Commission for Latin America and the Caribbean (ECLAC), January.

OECD/CAF/ECLAC (Organization for Economic Cooperation and Development/Development Bank of Latin America/Economic Commission for Latin America and the Caribbean) (2016), *Latin American Economic Outlook 2017: Youth, Skills and Entrepreneurship* (LC/G.2689), Santiago, October.

OISS (Ibero-American Social Security Organization) (2012), *Medidas para la promoción del empleo de personas con discapacidad en Iberoamérica*, Madrid.

PAHO/WHO (Pan American Health Organization/World Health Organization) (2017), *Sustainable Health Agenda for the Americas 2018-2030: A Call to Action for Health and Well-Being in the Region*, Washington, D.C., September.

___(2014), "Resolution CD53.R14: strategy for universal access to health and universal health coverage", Washington, D.C., October [online] http://iris.paho.org/xmlui/bitstream/handle/123456789/7652/CD53-R14-s.pdf.

Skoufias, E. (2006), "PROGRESA y sus efectos sobre el bienestar de las familias rurales en México", *Informe de Investigación*, No. 39, Washington, D.C., International Food Policy Research Institute (IFPRI).

Tromben, V. and A. Podestá (2018), "Las prestaciones familiares públicas en América Latina", *Project Documents* (LC.TS.2018/97), Santiago, Economic Commission for Latin America and the Caribbean (ECLAC), November.

UNESCO (United Nations Educational, Scientific and Cultural Organization) (2015), *Education 2030. Incheon Declaration and Framework for Action: Towards Inclusive and Equitable Quality Education and Lifelong Learning for All*, Paris.

United Nations (2007), *Convention on the Rights of Persons with Disabilities* (A/RES/61/106), New York, January.

___(2001), "Classifications of expenditure according to purpose", *Statistical Papers: Series M*, No. 84, New York.

Velásquez, M. (2017), "Labour market regulation and social protection: institutional challenges", *Institutional frameworks for social policy in Latin America and the Caribbean*, ECLAC Books, No. 146 (LC/PUB.2017/14-P), R. Martínez (ed.), Santiago, Economic Commission for Latin America and the Caribbean (ECLAC), October.

___(2016a), "Regulación del mercado de trabajo y protección social en países de América Latina", *Social Policy series*, No. 218 (LC/L.4244), Santiago, Economic Commission for Latin America and the Caribbean (ECLAC), November.

___(2016b), "Los desafíos de la protección contra el desempleo: opciones para Colombia y la República Dominicana", *Macroeconomics of Development series*, No. 179 (LC/L.4253), Santiago, Economic Commission for Latin America and the Caribbean (ECLAC), December.

___(2016c), "An analysis of unemployment protection in Latin America", *Protection and training: institutions for improving workforce integration in Latin America and Asia*, ECLAC Books, No. 140 (LC/G.2687-P), A. Isgut and J. Weller (eds.), Santiago, Economic Commission for Latin America and the Caribbean (ECLAC), October.

Weller, J. (2017), "Las transformaciones tecnológicas y su impacto en los mercados laborales", *Macroeconomics of Development series*, No. 190 (LC/TS.2017/76), Santiago, Economic Commission for Latin America and the Caribbean (ECLAC), September.

___(2004) (comp.), *En búsqueda de efectividad, eficiencia y equidad: las políticas del mercado de trabajo de trabajo y los instrumentos de su evaluación*, Santiago, Economic Commission for Latin America and the Caribbean (ECLAC)/LOM Ediciones.

Weller, J. and S. Gontero (2016), "Creating effective, efficient and inclusive national systems of technical and vocational education and training in Latin America", *Protection and training: institutions for improving workforce integration in Latin America and Asia*, ECLAC Books, No. 140 (LC/G.2687-P), A. Isgut and J. Weller (eds.), Santiago, Economic Commission for Latin America and the Caribbean (ECLAC), October.

World Bank (2012), "Resilience, equity, and opportunity: The World Bank's social protection strategy 2012-2022", *Board Report*, No. 73235, Washington, D.C.

Annex III.A1

Table III.A1.1
Latin America and the Caribbean (24 countries): central government social spending, 2016
(Percentages of GDP, dollars at 2010 prices and percentages)

Country	Social spending (percentages of GDP)	Social spending (constant 2010 dollars per capita)	Distribution of social spending by function (percentages)						
			Environmental protection[a]	Housing and community amenities	Health	Recreation, culture and religion	Education	Social protection	Total
Argentina	14.3	1 469	0.43	3.8	6.4	0.00	11.1	78.3	100
Bahamas	7.6	2 056	0.00	0.4	39.9	0.00	35.8	23.9	100
Barbados[b]	15.0	2 437	0.00	7.3	29.5	0.00	35.5	27.7	100
Bolivia (Plurinational State of)	12.6	310	0.00	6.8	14.8	0.00	41.4	37.0	100
Brazil	15.1	1 631	0.37	0.4	10.6	0.15	10.1	78.4	100
Chile	16.1	2 387	0.55	1.9	27.8	1.20	30.9	37.7	100
Colombia	12.7	945	0.54	4.1	22.1	1.07	26.3	46.0	100
Costa Rica	12.3	1 176	0.96	0.8	6.9	1.26	57.9	32.2	100
Cuba	14.6	951	0.00	1.3	21.7	4.26	29.4	43.4	100
Dominican Republic	8.0	552	1.10	4.0	20.8	1.99	50.3	21.8	100
Ecuador	9.3	482	1.04	7.2	27.4	1.78	49.5	13.1	100
El Salvador	9.3	316	0.00	0.0	27.7	0.00	42.6	29.7	100
Guatemala	6.9	220	2.26	19.6	16.0	2.39	41.5	18.2	100
Guyana	7.9	298	0.00	23.6	14.3	2.32	30.1	29.6	100
Haiti[b]	5.3	39	4.58	6.1	15.4	9.54	55.1	9.2	100
Honduras	9.2	201	2.06	2.7	32.1	0.00	54.7	8.5	100
Jamaica	10.7	516	1.39	5.0	33.2	2.61	51.5	6.4	100
Mexico	9.9	990	1.28	16.1	11.5	1.17	35.2	34.8	100
Nicaragua	10.6	207	0.00	19.6	31.7	1.94	41.5	5.2	100
Panama	8.6	969	4.96	26.5	20.4	0.00	37.4	10.7	100
Paraguay	8.7	450	0.00	1.7	22.6	0.64	33.9	41.1	100
Peru[c]	10.4	646	4.12	9.0	21.6	2.95	35.0	27.2	100
Trinidad and Tobago	16.6	2 605	0.00	12.3	18.7	2.88	27.1	39.0	100
Uruguay[d]	16.0	2 251	0.26	3.4	21.4	1.12	28.5	45.3	100

Source: Economic Commission for Latin America and the Caribbean (ECLAC), on the basis of official data from the countries.

[a] Environmental protection data may not match the estimates in environmental satellite accounts.

[b] The Barbados and Haiti data are for 2015.

[c] Coverage is general government in the case of Peru.

[d] The Uruguay data do not include disbursements by the Social Security Bank.

Annex III.A2

Diagram III.A2.1
Argentina: labour market programmes, 2016

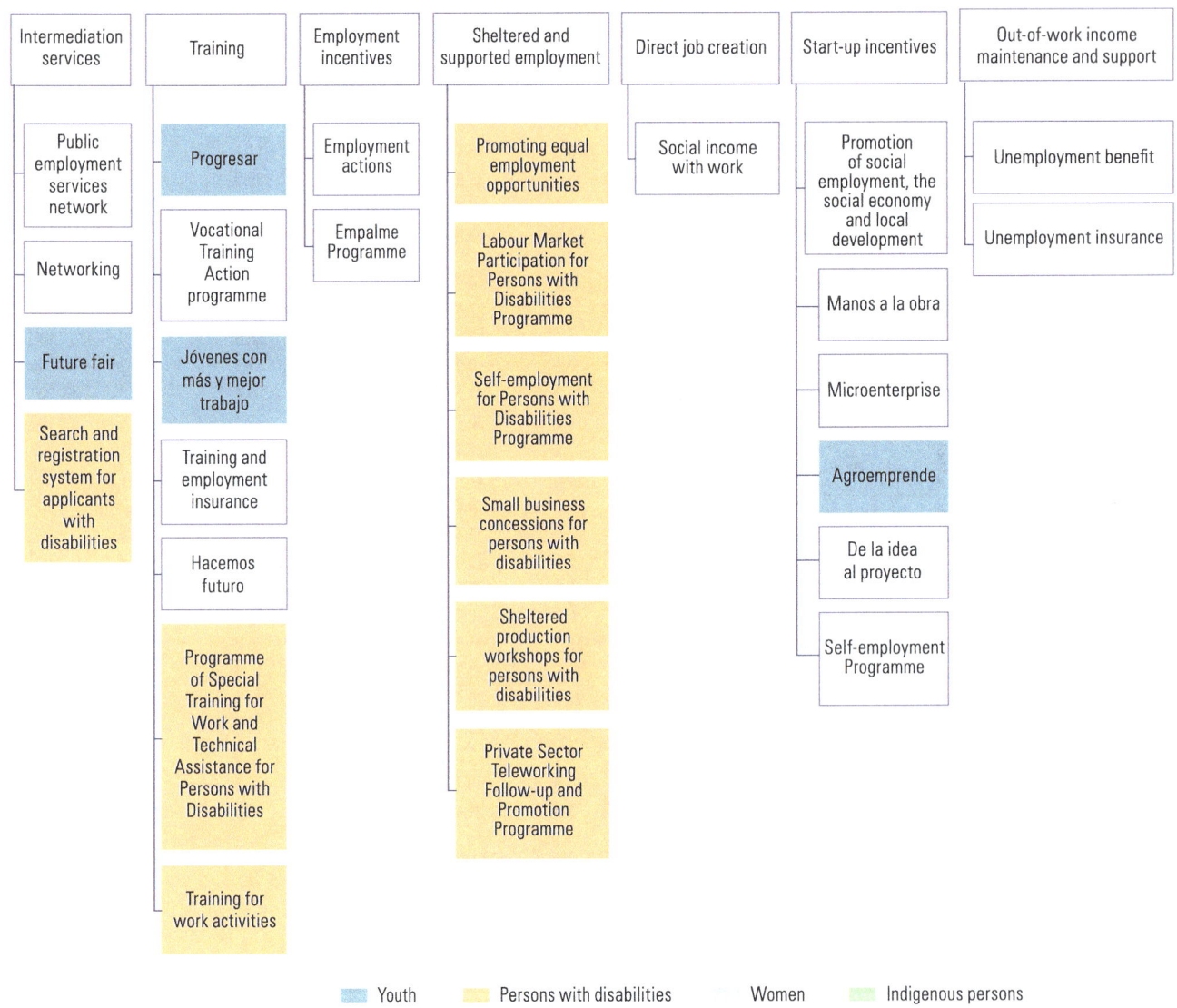

Source: Economic Commission for Latin America and the Caribbean (ECLAC), on the basis of official data from the country.

Diagram III.A2.2
Chile: labour market programmes, 2016

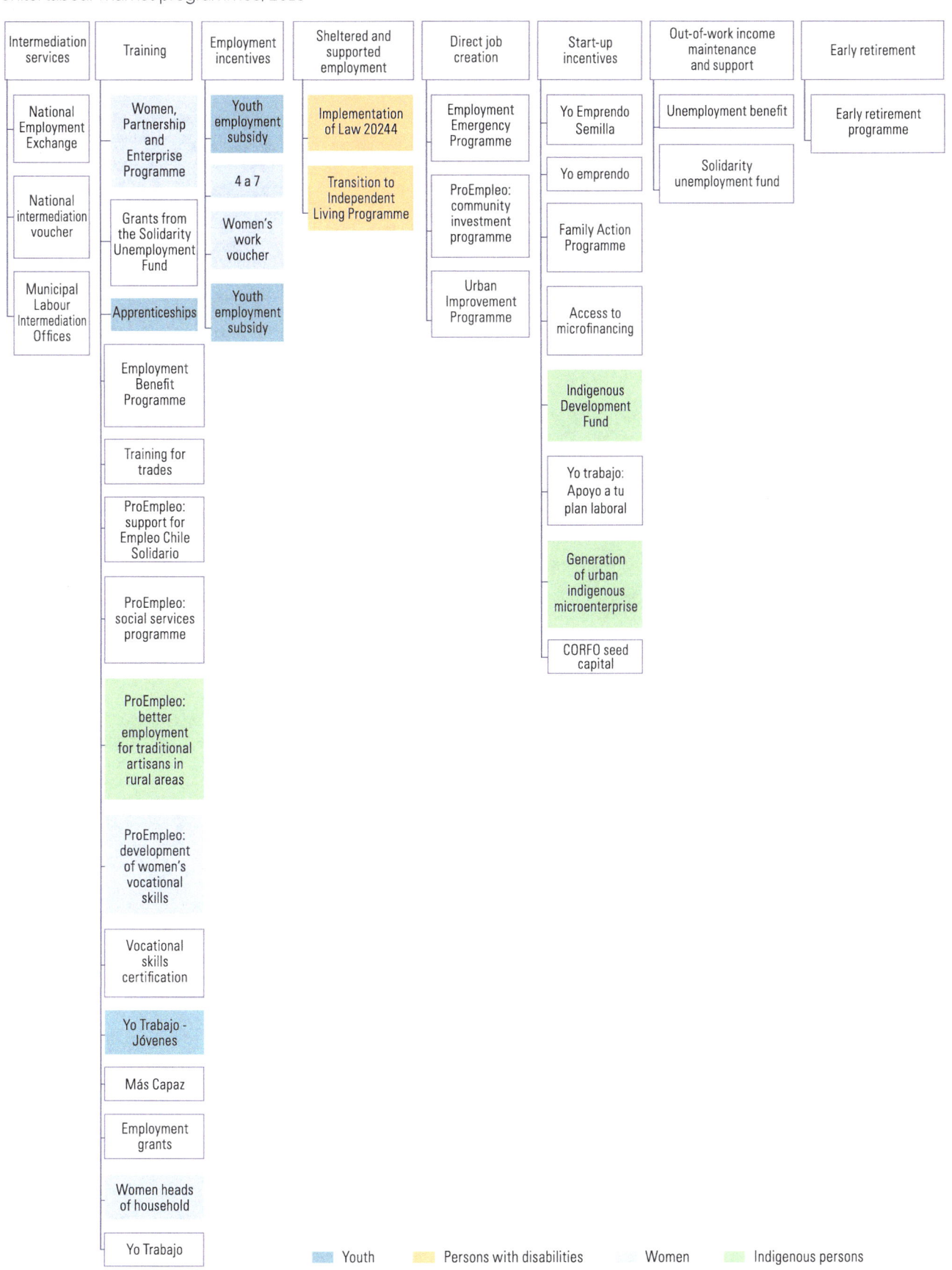

Source: Economic Commission for Latin America and the Caribbean (ECLAC), on the basis of official data from the country.

Diagram III.A2.3
Colombia: labour market programmes, 2016

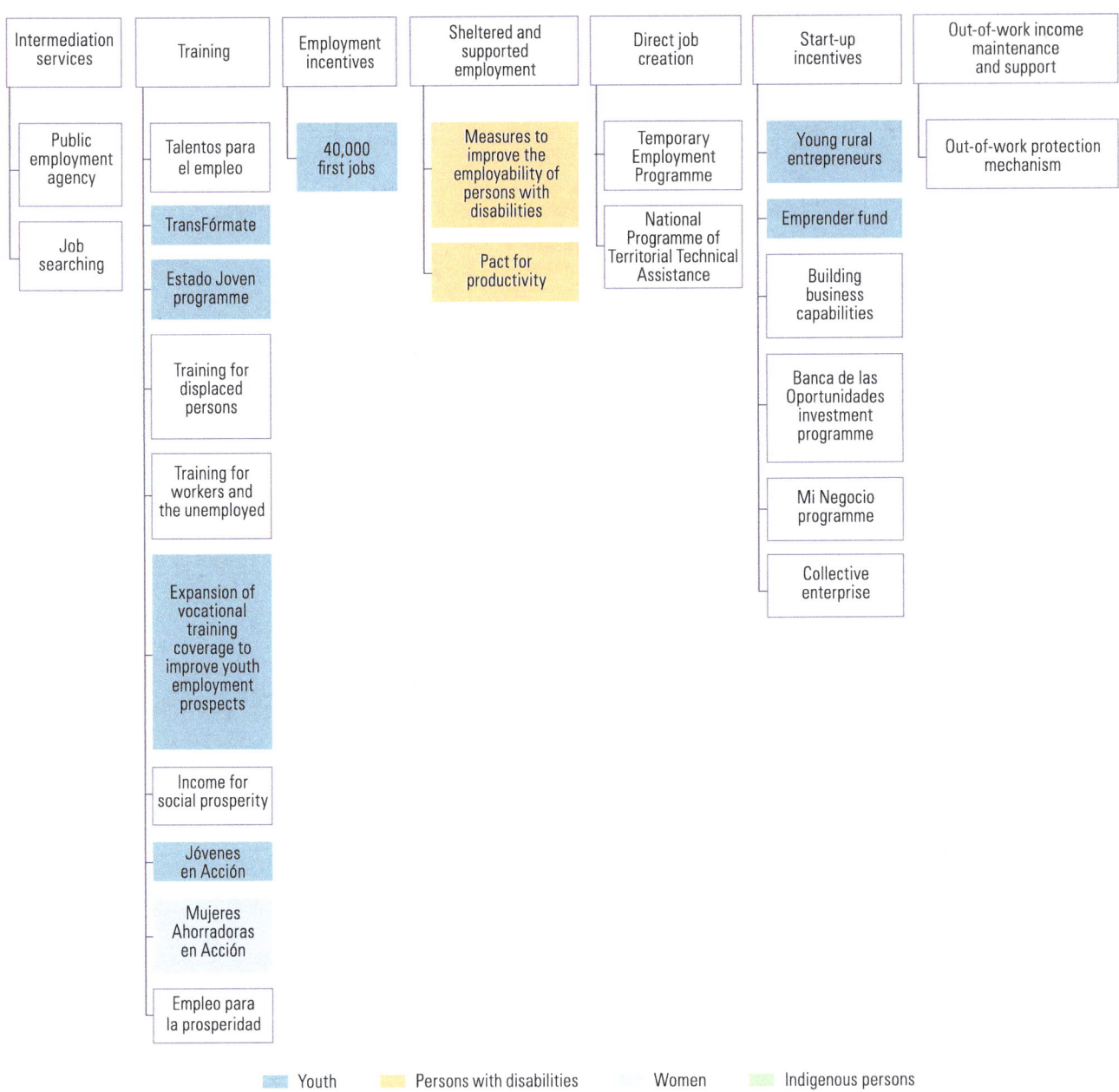

Source: Economic Commission for Latin America and the Caribbean (ECLAC), on the basis of official data from the country.

Diagram III.A2.4
Costa Rica: labour market programmes, 2016

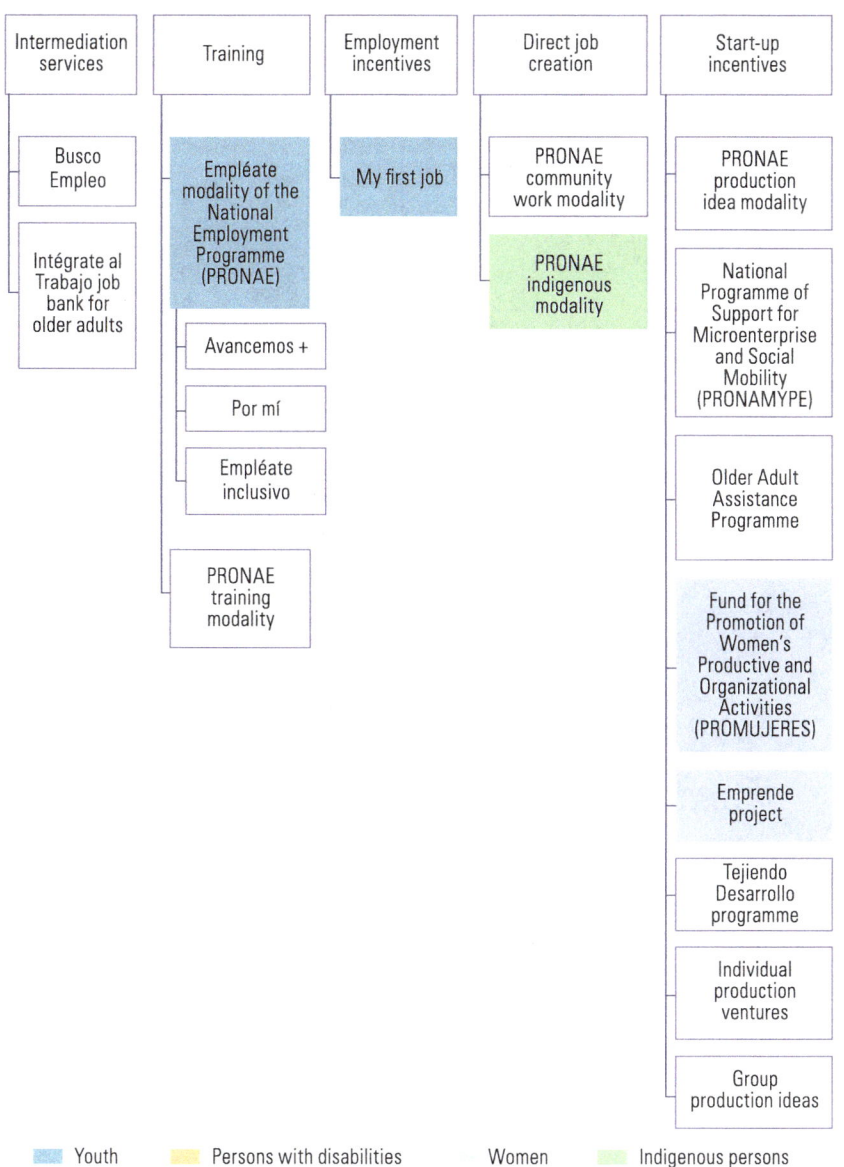

Source: Economic Commission for Latin America and the Caribbean (ECLAC), on the basis of official data from the country.

Diagram III.A2.5
Mexico: labour market programmes, 2016

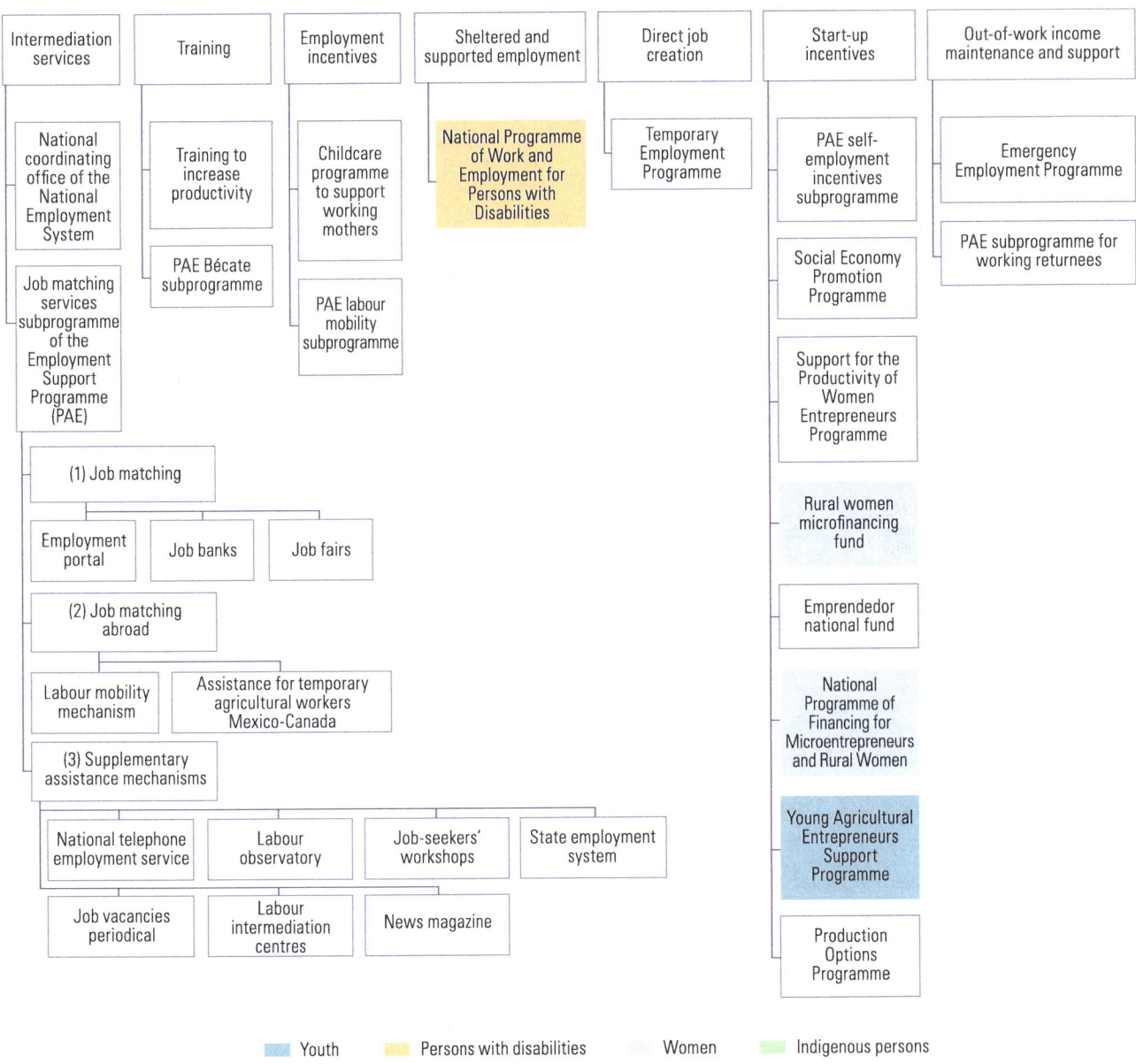

Source: Economic Commission for Latin America and the Caribbean (ECLAC), on the basis of official data from the country.

Diagram III.A2.6
Uruguay: labour market programmes, 2016

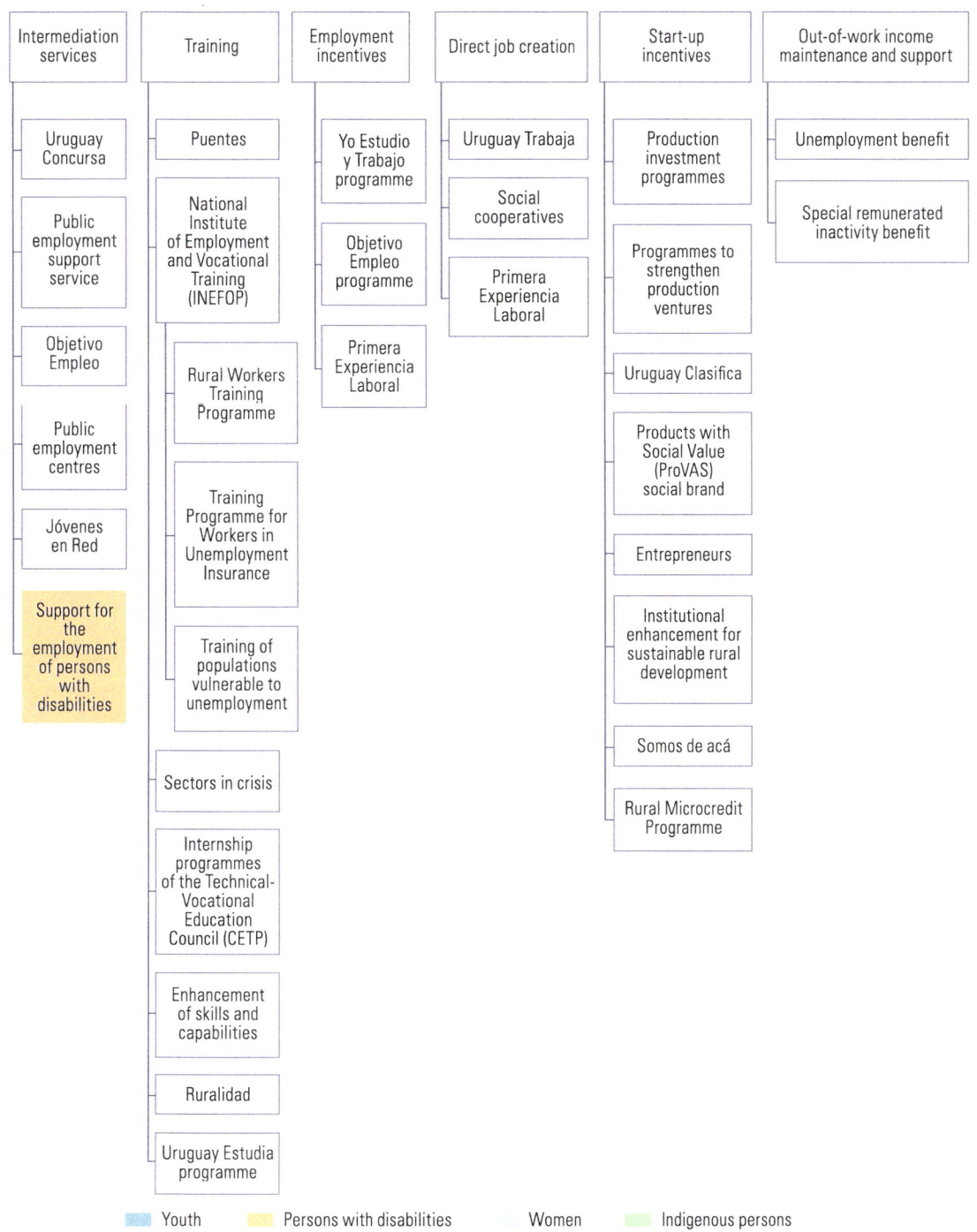

Intermediation services	Training	Employment incentives	Direct job creation	Start-up incentives	Out-of-work income maintenance and support

Intermediation services
- Uruguay Concursa
- Public employment support service
- Objetivo Empleo
- Public employment centres
- Jóvenes en Red
- Support for the employment of persons with disabilities

Training
- Puentes
- National Institute of Employment and Vocational Training (INEFOP)
  - Rural Workers Training Programme
  - Training Programme for Workers in Unemployment Insurance
  - Training of populations vulnerable to unemployment
- Sectors in crisis
- Internship programmes of the Technical-Vocational Education Council (CETP)
- Enhancement of skills and capabilities
- Ruralidad
- Uruguay Estudia programme

Employment incentives
- Yo Estudio y Trabajo programme
- Objetivo Empleo programme
- Primera Experiencia Laboral

Direct job creation
- Uruguay Trabaja
- Social cooperatives
- Primera Experiencia Laboral

Start-up incentives
- Production investment programmes
- Programmes to strengthen production ventures
- Uruguay Clasifica
- Products with Social Value (ProVAS) social brand
- Entrepreneurs
- Institutional enhancement for sustainable rural development
- Somos de acá
- Rural Microcredit Programme

Out-of-work income maintenance and support
- Unemployment benefit
- Special remunerated inactivity benefit

Legend: Youth · Persons with disabilities · Women · Indigenous persons

Source: Economic Commission for Latin America and the Caribbean (ECLAC), on the basis of official data from the country.

Structural challenges of inclusion and the labour market

A. Changes in the socioeconomic context and inclusion challenges

Stalled progress on poverty reduction, in conjunction with emerging dynamics associated with the technological revolution and demographic changes, compounded by more frequent disasters and other factors, raise uncertainty levels and put sustainable development processes in Latin America and the Caribbean under threat. To turn a risk scenario into one of opportunities, it is important to analyse the dynamics of social and labour inclusion, and to identify the persisting areas of structural deficit. Promoting universal policies that are sensitive to differences in the social and labour domains will be crucial for contributing to the inclusion of all people, well-being and sustainable development, with no one left behind.

The Latin America and the Caribbean region is confronting a complex social and economic situation, in which structural challenges and disparities persist and compound one another. These include discouraging trends in poverty and inequality (as shown in chapters I and II) and a number of emerging dynamics that include far-reaching transformations in the world of work and in demographic processes, more frequent disasters and the transition towards an environmentally sustainable economy (ECLAC, 2018a, 2018b and 2018c). The current context involves great uncertainty and combines both structural and circumstantial features that could further accentuate the region's historical inequality (Bárcena, 2015). The gathering pace of the technological revolution and changes in international production patterns heighten instability and introduce new risks. Disruptive technologies and their combinations trigger changes that have major repercussions in the world of work.

In recent decades, globalization has strengthened the interconnections that exist between economic agents in different sectors and countries. This has affected labour markets, since many jobs have been converted or displaced, with asymmetric effects for the less mobile factors of production, such as labour. Moreover, the Latin American countries have joined global production chains in relatively low value added segments, which implies poor-quality jobs, precarious employment, less training provided by firms and low wages. It also poses new challenges for gender equality because women are more heavily concentrated in firms located in the lower segments of outsourcing networks (ECLAC, 2017a).

These risks overlay labour markets that are characterized by high levels of precariousness and informality, and they generate major problems for social protection and labour regulation (Novick, 2018). The unknown consequences of impending changes in the world of work will be compounded by other emerging challenges. In particular, rapid population aging, with the consequent increase in the proportion of older people and reduction in that of children (ECLAC, 2018a), marks a turning point in the debate on inclusion, in terms of requirements throughout the life cycle (ECLAC, 2017a).[1] It is increasingly important to take advantage of the demographic bonus to invest in incorporating children, adolescents and young people fully into development, with adults who, more and more, have the skills and resources needed to attain well-being, while guaranteeing rights in the various stages of the life cycle. Compounding these changes, the panorama of migratory dynamics is becoming increasingly complex and heterogeneous in the region's individual countries. Intraregional flows are increasing, and immigrants from within the region itself outnumber those from elsewhere. Motivations for migration are varied and include the search for greater employment and economic opportunities, family reunification, disasters and, more recently, violence (Maldonado, Martínez and Martínez, 2018).

In short, the current situation poses several challenges; and it calls into question the conditions for continuing to progress towards the major goal of eradicating poverty in

---

[1]   It is estimated that, by around 2036, the region will have more people aged 60 years or older than children and adolescents under 15. This trend is set to persist and will continue to intensify until 2080 (ECLAC, 2018a, p. 24).

all its forms and ensuring that no one is left behind, as proclaimed in the 2030 Agenda for Sustainable Development. This Agenda reflects the aspiration to achieve a new development model, and it adopts an interrelated approach to the social, economic and environmental dimensions of sustainable development. At the regional level, a rights approach and an in-depth view of the structural axes of the social inequality matrix proposed by ECLAC (2016a and 2016d), which, in addition to income inequalities, include gender, ethnic and racial, and territorial inequalities and those related to the life cycle, show that sustainable development cannot be achieved without ensuring the rights of all people. Along with this, and under the same approach, the emergence of indigenous peoples as active social and political actors on public agendas, and the existence of human rights standards for these peoples, pose the challenge of also ensuring collective rights —in other words, equal enjoyment of individual human rights and, at the same time, the right to be collectively different.

Analysing the dynamics of inclusion in its various manifestations is relevant for identifying areas that persist as structural deficits in access to social services and fundamental rights, and also in the labour market, to draw attention and respond to the unfolding changes, and thus turn a risk scenario to one of opportunities. This chapter deals with social and labour inclusion, and argues that both must occur simultaneously. To achieve this objective, the advances and constraints that households face in overcoming social exclusion and vulnerability are highlighted as two persistent phenomena that have potential for amplification in the region, given the emerging risks identified. In particular, there is a need to address the inequalities faced by various groups in accessing social and labour inclusion mechanisms, which requires the implementation of policies which, while seeking to guarantee universal rights in these areas, are formulated in a way that is sensitive to differences.

B. Social and labour inclusion in Latin America

This section reviews some of the key dimensions of the dynamics of social and labour inclusion in the region, identifying gaps in access to rights and social services, and to decent work.

1. Social inclusion

In recent decades, the region has made great progress in various areas of social inclusion, such as the right to education, health care and access to basic infrastructure (water, sanitation, electricity and the Internet). Nonetheless, glaring inequalities persist both in the coverage of the services that uphold these rights and in their quality, which is insufficient and segmented. Strengthening policies that increase coverage and access to education (at the various levels) and to health and infrastructure, while enhancing the quality with which these services are supplied, needs to be an active public policy in the region's countries, if they are to make headway on social inclusion.

(a) Education: a crucial link for labour inclusion

Improving access to quality education is at once a key pillar of social inclusion and a crucial link for labour inclusion and increased productivity. Progress in this area is associated with poverty reduction, better health indicators, upward social mobility and more wide-ranging possibilities for exercising citizenship. Additional years of schooling improve job opportunities and enable fuller participation in democratic societies. The region has made very significant progress in the last 15 years (especially during the 2000 decade), particularly in terms of access to primary and secondary education (see figures IV.1, IV.2 and IV.3).

Figure IV.1
Latin America
(18 countries): young
people aged 15–29
with complete primary,
secondary and tertiary
education, by age group,
2002–2016[a]
(Percentages)

Source: Economic Commission for Latin America and the Caribbean (ECLAC), on the basis of Household Survey Data Bank (BADEHOG).
[a] Simple averages.

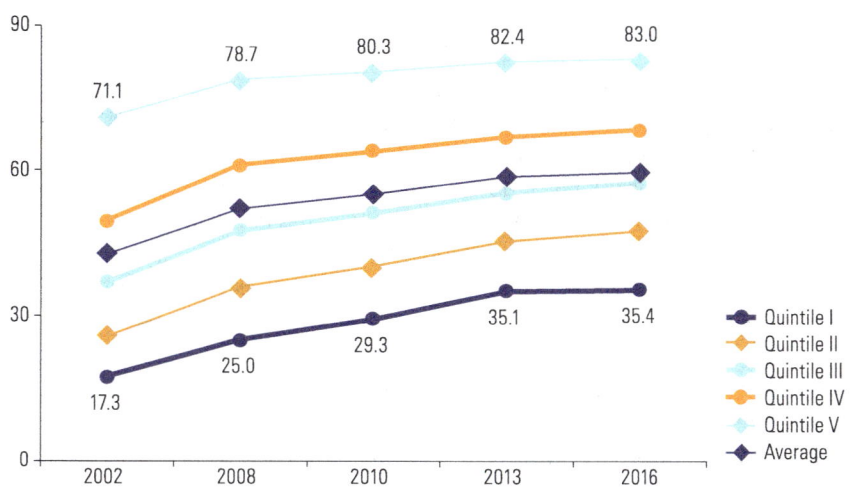

Figure IV.2
Latin America
(18 countries): young
people aged 20–24 years
with complete secondary
education, by income
quintile, 2002–2016[a]
(Percentages)

Source: Economic Commission for Latin America and the Caribbean (ECLAC), on the basis of household surveys from the respective countries.
[a] Simple averages.

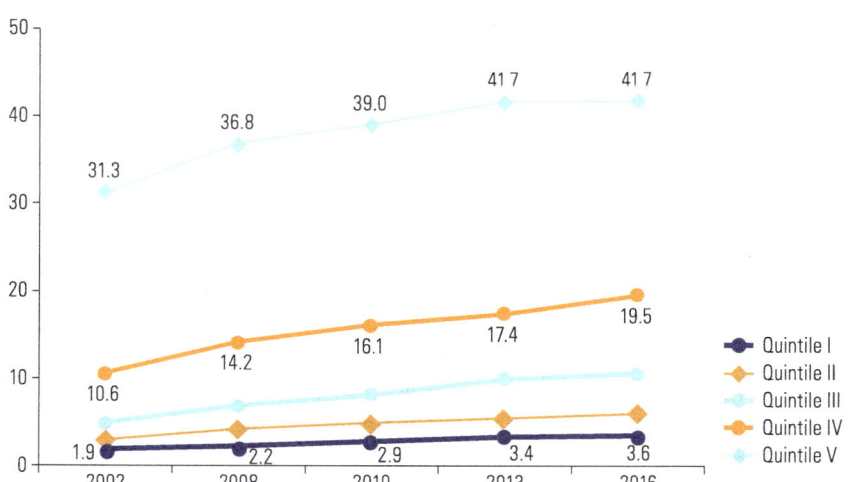

Figure IV.3
Latin America
(18 countries): young
people aged 25–29
with complete tertiary
education (four years
of study), by income
quintile, 2002–2016[a]
(Percentages)

Source: Economic Commission for Latin America and the Caribbean (ECLAC), on the basis of household surveys from the respective countries.
[a] Simple averages.

In terms of educational attainment, however, progress has varied within and between countries, especially at the secondary and higher levels (see annex table IV.A1.1). While in some countries, such as Chile and Peru, over 80% of the 20–24-year-old population had completed their secondary education in 2016, in others, such as Guatemala and Honduras, the proportion was below 40%. As an average across all countries, there is a 48 percentage-point gap between young people who complete high school in the highest income quintile and those who do so in the lowest quintile. Higher education remains reserved for a small proportion of the population (see figures IV.1 and IV.3). Progress at this level of education has been concentrated exclusively in the highest-income group: on average, in 2016, while more than 40% of 25–29-year-olds in the highest income quintile had completed at least four years of tertiary education, only 3.6% of those in the lowest quintile had attained that level.

In the Caribbean countries, the coverage of primary and secondary education has expanded considerably and is now practically universal. In contrast, access to higher education is very sparse, with just 15% of students making the transition from secondary to tertiary. Only 30% of students who are eligible to take the Caribbean Secondary Education Certificate (CSEC) exams actually do so; and of these only about 65% pass in all areas. Even more worrying is the fact that pass rates in the mathematics and science tests have declined in recent years (ECLAC, 2018f).

There is a large core of young people who are excluded from the education system, particularly those belonging to the lowest-income sectors (see table IV.A1.1 of the annex) and those living in remote areas. In addition, the indigenous and Afrodescendent populations suffer multiple inequalities as a result of historical discrimination and exclusion processes. Although the educational inclusion rates among indigenous and Afrodescendent youth have increased in recent decades, inequalities persist. The former lag mainly in terms of completing secondary education and in access to higher education, while the latter face problems of access and permanency at the higher level (ECLAC, 2017a, 2017b and 2017c; Del Popolo, 2018). These inequalities are compounded by gender and territorial disparities, even in countries that can boast greater achievements (see box IV.1). Education plays a crucial role in overcoming this situation, by helping to uphold the rights of indigenous and Afrodescendent people, narrowing gaps in access to mechanisms that are crucial for overcoming poverty (such as decent work), and by helping to recognize them and reduce the inequalities that affect them.

In this setting, discussions on interculturality and self-education have an important role to play. While individual States have made efforts to promote bilingual intercultural education, the supply of such services is less than the minimum recommended and below the levels provided to other sectors of the population. There are also problems of geographical access, poor infrastructure, absence of culturally appropriate education policies, and a lack of mechanisms for effective community participation in teaching and learning projects and processes (Del Popolo, 2018). A new paradigm is currently emerging that seeks to mainstream interculturality throughout educational systems as a whole, with the aim of dissipating asymmetric relationships and positions in society, with actions targeting both indigenous and Afrodescendent populations, as well as people who belong to neither of those groups (Corbetta and others, 2018). This requires official systems to be able to "decolonize" educational contents, by taking account of the history, values and knowledge of indigenous and Afrodescendent cultures. While some progress has been made at the primary and secondary levels, there is still much to be done in higher education institutions. As a result, the indigenous peoples themselves have launched initiatives in the region, such as the Kawsay Intercultural University of Indigenous Peoples in the Plurinational State of Bolivia or the University of the Autonomous Regions of the Nicaraguan Caribbean Coast (URACCAN). At least nine Latin American countries have some form of intercultural or indigenous university, which offers a framework of experiences to advance indigenous peoples' right to education and, at the same time, help build pluricultural societies (Del Popolo, 2018). These include a policy in Brazil to reserve quotas for Afrodescendent and indigenous students in universities and public technical education institutes, and also on a number of postgraduate programmes at private universities. The latter also offer scholarships for Afrodescendent and indigenous students. This affirmative action policy has had significant results in terms of attendance at higher education by 18–24-year-olds of African descent (black and mixed race). According to data from the Brazilian Geography and Statistical Institute (IBGE), the proportion of this group entering higher education rose from 16.7% to 45.5% between 2004 and 2014, thereby outpacing the increase among whites, despite the persistence of ethno-racial inequalities (ECLAC, 2017b).

Box IV.1
Ethnic and territorial inequalities in education: Chile and indigenous peoples

Chile is one of the Latin American countries that has achieved most in expanding coverage at all levels of education, including among indigenous children and youth. Nonetheless, ethnic gaps compounded by territorial disparities persist, and the situation among indigenous peoples varies greatly. The latest nationwide population and housing census, conducted in 2017, shows that 20% of indigenous youth aged 20 to 29 had not completed secondary education, compared to 16% of their non-indigenous peers. The failure by indigenous youth to complete high school is most prevalent in the regions that encompass the ancestral lands of the Mapuche people, namely Los Lagos (with the highest non-completion rate of 26%), Araucanía, Los Ríos, Bío-Bío and, to a lesser extent, Magallanes. Moreover, these regions also display the largest ethnic gaps (up to 8 percentage points in Araucanía).

Chile: persons aged 20–29 years with incomplete secondary education, by ethnicity and region, 2017 census
(Percentages)

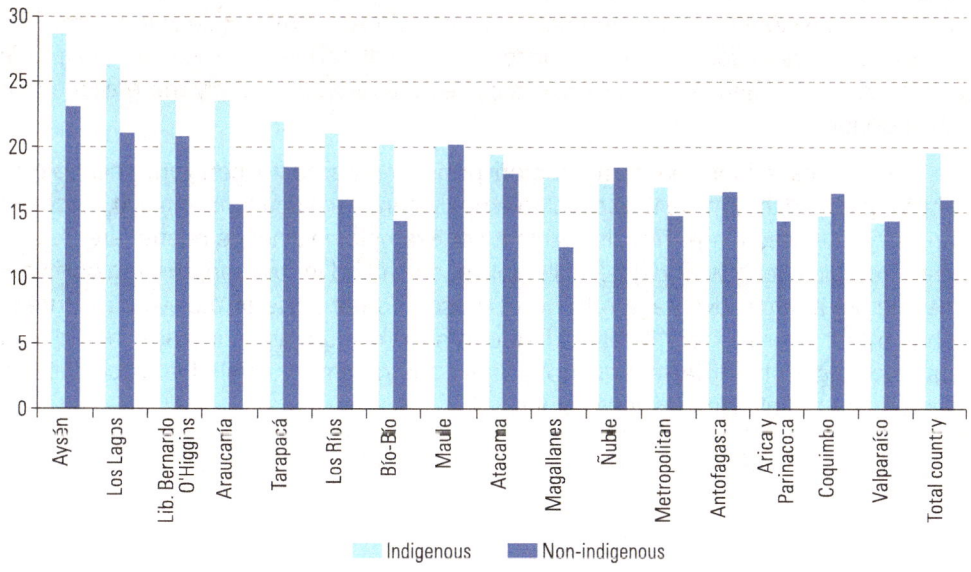

The Tarapacá region, in the north, is also one of those with the highest percentages of indigenous youth who did not finish high school, most of whom belong to the Aymara people. Nonetheless, the ethnic gaps in this region are smaller than the national average. The regions of Antofagasta and Arica and Parinacota (which include territories belonging to the Aymara, Quechua and Lican Antai peoples) and also Valparaíso (which includes Easter Island of the Rapa Nui people) display the lowest figures without ethnic gaps. These results provide important inputs for targeting educational actions, which should be designed with the specific needs of each indigenous group in mind, and fulfil the rights standards established in the Indigenous and Tribal Peoples Convention, 1989 (No. 169) of the International Organization of Labour (ILO) and in the United Nations Declaration on the Rights of Indigenous Peoples.

Source: Latin American and Caribbean Demographic Centre (CELADE)-Population Division of ECLAC, on the basis of special processing of census microdata using the retrieval of data for small areas by microcomputer program (REDATAM).

Unequal access to quality education is a major obstacle to the dissemination of capacities that are crucial for a country's development (ECLAC, 2018d). These inequalities exist not only as gaps in educational supply, but also in the quality of services, infrastructure, school size and teachers and, lastly, in the learning outcomes attained by the students.

Evaluating and measuring the quality of the education provided over the school trajectory is a complex and controversial issue. The most common way to monitor progress is to use standardized tests that are performed in a comparable way across the region's countries for primary and secondary school students, both nationally and internationally. Although this tool projects a restricted view of what education quality means, it does serve to monitor certain basic skills. In most of the region's countries, family socioeconomic level is the factor that most explains the differences in the learning outcomes evaluated. In this connection, and comparatively, both the Programme of International Student Assessment (PISA)[2] and the Third Regional Comparative and Explanatory Study (TERCE),[3] as well as educational research generally, show that the majority of students of lower socioeconomic and cultural level in Latin American countries do not gain the minimum skills.[4] In contrast, in the most developed countries, the vast majority of students attain the expected basic proficiency level (level 2 or higher in the PISA test), although there are also inequalities in terms of learning outcomes between students from different socioeconomic strata (ECLAC, 2010b, 2016c and 2018d).

Unlike what happens in terms of completing the different school cycles (where women have achieved better than men), there are still marked gender differences in learning outcomes that impair women's training paths. On average, girls perform better in measurements of reading, while boys do better in mathematics and science. These differences later affect their fields of study and employment, since the market mostly rewards the scientific and mathematical fields (ECLAC, 2010a; Rico and Trucco, 2014). These results are affected by (often unconscious) cultural biases in schools and families, which steer girls and boys towards disciplines that are supposedly more aligned with their gender.

These disparities leave the region poorly prepared to confront technological challenges; and they make the school-to-employment transition more difficult, since there are major shortcomings in skills training. For example, in science-related areas, which are strategic (along with digital skills) for research and innovation, the region's young people are at a disadvantage relative to those in other parts of the world. Figure IV.4 shows that over half of 15-year-old students from the eight countries in the region participating in the PISA test did not achieve the minimum level of science skills, the worst result of all participating regions.[5]

---

[2]   Evaluation performed by the Organization for Economic Cooperation and Development (OECD) to measure basic skills among 15-year-old students.

[3]   Evaluation performed by the UNESCO Regional Office for Education in Latin America and the Caribbean (OREALC) in 2013 to measure skills among 3rd and 6th grade students in Latin American and Caribbean countries.

[4]   Since these measurements do not include the family-income variable, an indicator is constructed to represent the socioeconomic and cultural status of the household of the student being evaluated. In the case of the PISA test, this is based on the following variables: international socioeconomic index of occupational status; the highest educational level of the student's parents, converted into years of schooling; the PISA index of family wealth; the PISA index of educational resources; and index used by PISA to measure possessions related to the "classical" culture in the family's home. See Organization for Economic Cooperation and Development (OECD), "PISA index of economic, social and cultural status (ESCS)", Paris, 2003 [online] http://stats.oecd.org/glossary/detail.asp?ID = 5401

[5]   The region also displays relatively poor outcomes in other areas of learning that have been measured by international assessments, such as reading, mathematics, civic education and digital skills.

Figure IV.4
PISA 2015 test: 15-year-old students' attainment levels in science, by region[a]
(Percentages)

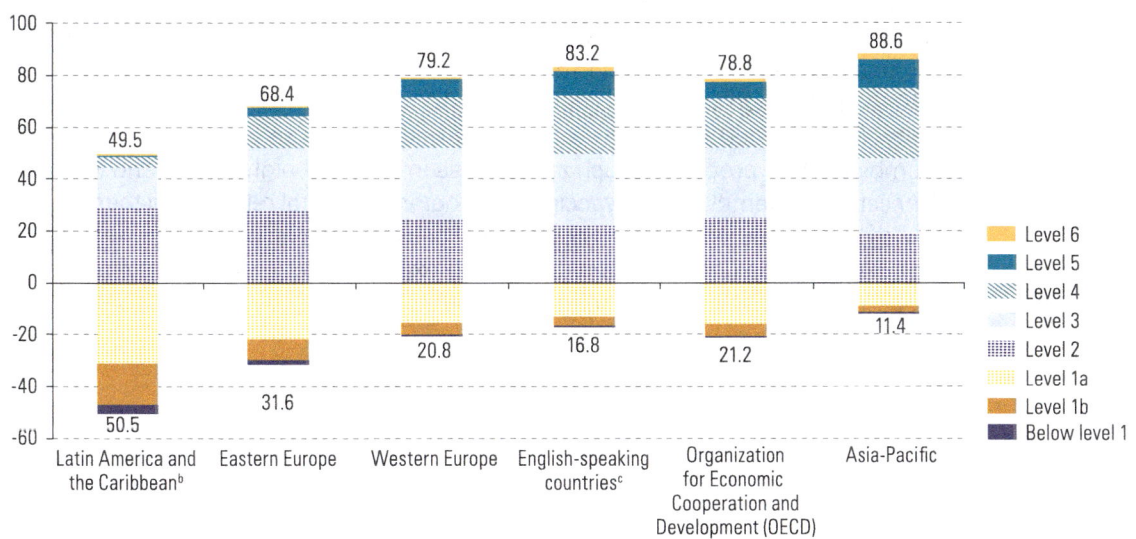

Source: Economic Commission for Latin America and the Caribbean (ECLAC), on the basis of Organization for Economic Cooperation and Development (OECD),
        Programme for International Student Assessment (PISA), 2015.
[a] Students located below level 2 (level 1a, level 1b and below level 1) do not attain the basic expected proficiency level.
[b] Latin America includes eight countries: Brazil, Chile, Colombia, Costa Rica, Dominican Republic, Mexico, Peru and Uruguay.
[c] English-speaking countries include Australia, Canada, New Zealand, the United Kingdom and the United States.

To ensure that the new generations acquire the skills and competencies that the labour market will need, steps must be taken to close access and completion gaps (socioeconomic, gender, ethno-racial and territorial) and improve the quality of education and its relevance, by fostering meaningful life-long learning, and acting collectively to equalize educational opportunities and outcomes. Among other factors, the new global trends that are transforming the world of work are increasing the importance of technical education and not just scientific education. Technical-vocational education and training needs to be increasingly articulated with public policies to support innovation, labour and productive inclusion, and the fostering of entrepreneurship and cooperativism. It is also important for this form of education to be articulated with general and propaedeutic education, particularly at the secondary level. It should complement general education, rather than diverge from it; but it should not replace training in the general skills that are essential for full citizenship in today's societies.

For all of these reasons, ECLAC reiterates that strengthening policies that expand coverage and access to education and tend toward universalization at the different levels should be a central plank of an active public policy to advance social inclusion and eliminate inequalities.

(b) Health: basic condition for the development of capabilities

Progress in upholding the right to health and guaranteeing access to quality services can be expected to have a multiplier effect on people's well-being, since health is a basic condition for developing the human capacities needed to overcome poverty and reduce inequalities. An adequate health status is needed to attend and achieve well at school, work effectively, or care for and feed a family. By enabling people to develop to their full potential, health contributes to sustainable and equitable development (ECLAC, 2018d).

In recent decades, the Latin America and the Caribbean region has achieved major progress in various indicators of health access and outcomes, including a reduction in the infant mortality rate (see figure IV.5). This summary indicator of the population's health status reflects the set of economic and social conditions facing mothers and newborns, along with the sociopolitical context and the characteristics of health systems. Across 31 countries in Latin America and the Caribbean, infant mortality declined by more than 30% on average between 2000 and 2015. Countries that started from lower mortality levels tended to have lower rates of decline. This reduction was the result of a combination of processes such as progress in terms of high-impact and low-cost primary care (for example, mass vaccination programmes, oral rehydration therapy and healthy child check-ups), increased coverage of basic utilities (especially drinking water and sanitation), expansion of antenatal care to expectant mothers, improvements in nutrition, increased schooling among the population (especially among women) and the decline in fertility.

Figure IV.5
Latin America and the Caribbean (31 countries): variation in the infant mortality rate, 2000–2015
(Percentages)

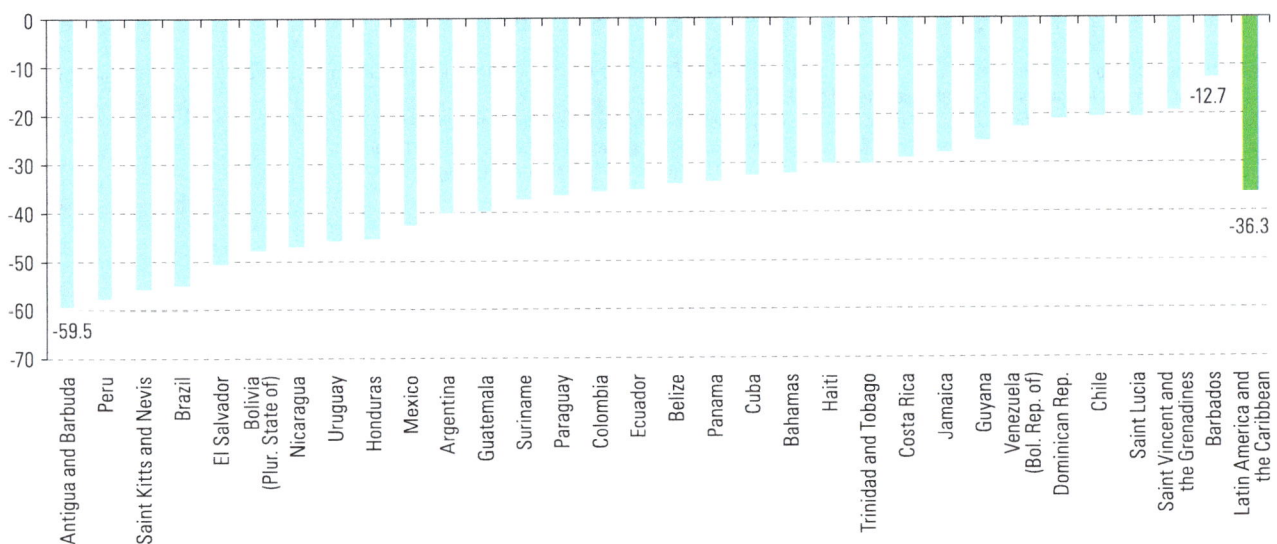

Source: Economic Commission for Latin America and the Caribbean (ECLAC), CEPALSTAT database [online] http://estadisticas.cepal.org/cepalstat/portada.html?idioma=english.
Note: The figure for Latin America and the Caribbean represents the simple average of the gaps in the 31 countries.

As in education, progress in health is uneven and highly segmented according to the main axes of the social inequality matrix. Economic and social contexts have a major influence on the development of diseases, and on their detection and treatment. Poverty, inequality and social exclusion have serious consequences for the population's health. Thus, despite the steep reduction that has occurred, maternal mortality remains high among Afrodescendent and indigenous women, as highlighted in box IV.2.

Box IV.2
Maternal mortality
among Afrodescendent
and indigenous women:
a manifestation of secular
inequalities and violation
of the right to life

One of the most dramatic expressions of inequality to the detriment of ethno-racial groups is the high rate of maternal mortality among Afrodescendent and indigenous women in the region's countries. Although the information is fragmentary, estimates based on a variety of sources corroborate this fact. The census conducted in the Plurinational State of Bolivia in 2012, for example, reported maternal mortality figures of 372.8 per 100,000 live births for the female population at large and 650.5 per 100,000 among indigenous women.

Based on the vital statistics for 2010–2013, Colombia and Ecuador show that Afrodescendent and indigenous maternal mortality rates far exceed those of other women. In Colombia, that period saw an average of 277.7 maternal deaths per 100,000 live births among indigenous women and 152.9 per 100,000 among Afrodescendants, compared to 56.7 per 100,000 live births among other women. In Ecuador, the differential is almost five times for Afrodescendent women and more than twice for indigenous women: 272.5 deaths per 100,000 live births among Afrodescendants and 137.7 among indigenous women, compared to 56.9 per 100,000 live births among other women. Although inequalities in Brazil are less accentuated, in 2011 the maternal mortality rate among Afrodescendants was 1.4 times that of the white population (68.8 maternal deaths per 100,000 live births among Afrodescendent women, compared to 50.6 per 100,000 among white women).

Studies that use a territorial approach show that the highest maternal mortality rates occur among indigenous women in Honduras, Mexico, Guatemala, Peru and Panama, with very worrying figures in the indigenous territories (comarcas). In Panama, there were 52.7 maternal deaths per 100,000 live births in 2015; in the Ngäbe Buglé comarca there were 130.2 maternal deaths, in the Kuna Yala comarca there were 273.2 per 100,000 and in the Emberá comarca there were 515.5 maternal deaths per 100,000 live births.

Medical care during pregnancy, childbirth and postpartum is an area where intercultural health has been widely promoted, based on pioneering experiences in Guatemala and Mexico to incorporate traditional indigenous medicine agents and practices, which are likely to be reflected in broader coverage. Nonetheless, detailed studies are needed on how these health models are implemented in contexts where racism and institutional discrimination, marginalization and material poverty prevail. Intercultural care models are not widespread in all countries and they often diverge widely from the established standards (for example, they limit the role of midwives to a position that is subordinated to the health team). Moreover, several studies and diagnostic assessments, some promoted by the organizations of indigenous and Afrodescendent women themselves, continue to report low service quality, discriminatory practices and a lack of cultural adaptation.

Source: Economic Commission for Latin America and the Caribbean (ECLAC), Draft first regional report on the implementation of the Montevideo Consensus on Population and Development (LC/CRPD.3/3), Santiago, 2018; "Situación de las personas afrodescendientes en América Latina y desafíos de políticas para la garantía de sus derechos", Project Documents (LC/TS.2017/121), Santiago, 2017.

The countries of the region are also experiencing shifts in their epidemiological profile, with marked changes in patterns of morbidity and mortality, characterized by a declining proportion of communicable diseases and an increase in chronic noncommunicable diseases. This poses new and more complex challenges for health policies, particularly in the case of non-communicable diseases. Their increase, in developed and developing countries alike, reflects changes in the age structure, nutritional patterns, modes of consumption, urbanization and sedentary lifestyle —phenomena associated with commodification and globalization.

A key way to reduce inequalities in the health domain is to make progress in universalizing coverage and access to quality services, so that all people can prevent, detect and treat their health problems. Health systems in Latin America are generally organized through public sector services for people living in poverty, social security services for formal workers and private services for those who can afford them (Titelman, Cetrángolo and Acosta, 2015). Few countries have universal health systems that can be accessed independently of employment status, as is the case of Brazil's Unified Health System (SUS).

Although affiliation or contribution to health systems associated with employment has increased, and the socioeconomic gaps have narrowed, there is still a long way to travel before more equitable access levels are attained. Figure IV.6 shows the access to health systems by the employed or wage earners (excluding access through student insurance or unrestricted public health care). Between 2002 and 2016, there was a substantial increase in coverage, especially in the first few deciles. Although this meant a narrowing of the gaps between the deciles, a 37 percentage-point difference still persists between decile 1 and decile 10.

Figure IV.6
Latin America (14 countries): affiliation or contribution to health systems by employed persons aged 15 and over, by income deciles, national totals, 2002–2016[a][b]
(Percentages)

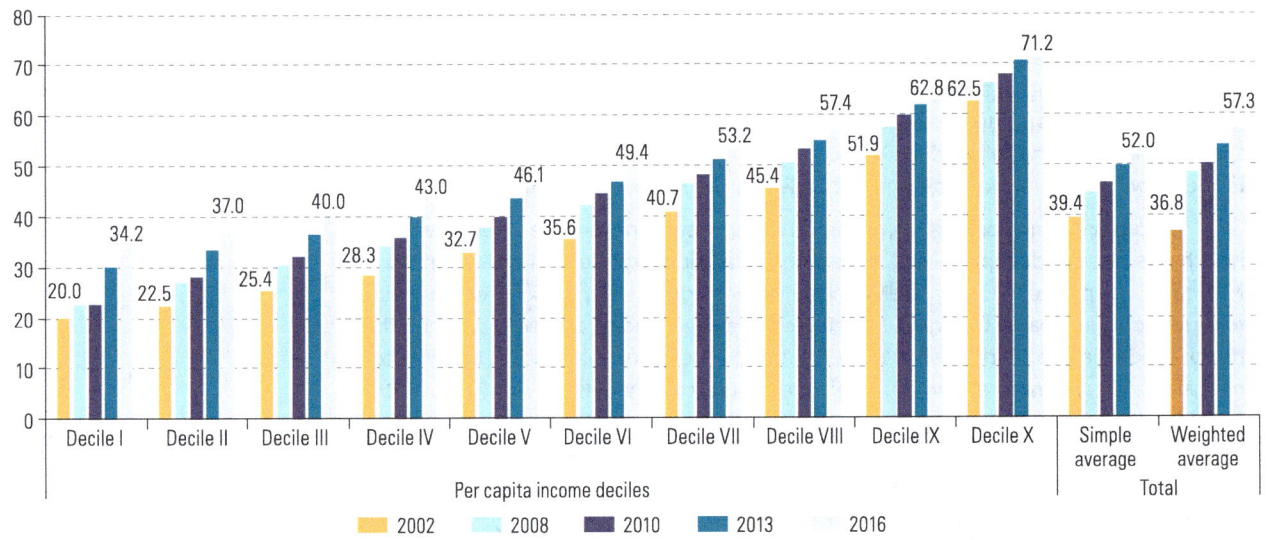

Source: Economic Commission for Latin America and the Caribbean (ECLAC), on the basis of Household Survey Data Bank (BADEHOG).

[a] In Argentina, the figures represent wage earners aged 15 or older. The data for Mexico in 2016 are not strictly comparable to those of previous years owing to changes in the wording of some of the questions on social security access. Further details of these changes, their effects on the estimation of social security coverage (health and pensions) and procedures to adjust the estimation, are provided in CONEVAL (2017).

[b] Simple average of the countries by deciles. The countries included are: Argentina (urban areas), Chile, Colombia, Costa Rica, Ecuador, El Salvador, Guatemala, Honduras, Mexico, Nicaragua, Paraguay, Peru, Plurinational State of Bolivia and Uruguay (urban areas).

The fact that benefits and coverage remain highly segmented in the region, as shown by the large differences in the quality of services accessed by different population groups, is worrying and acts as an obstacle to progress on equality.

(c) Infrastructure: guarantee the well-being and inclusion of people

Access to basic infrastructure has improved continuously in the region, and its coverage has expanded into increasingly remote areas. Access to drinking water and sanitation services is essential to enable the population to enjoy good health and prevent diseases, and also to maintain a healthy environment. The coverage of these services has improved significantly, especially in the rural areas of various countries, thanks to the efforts made. In 2002–2016, the proportion of individuals with access to adequate sources of drinking water rose in 17 Latin American countries by an average of 2.8 percentage points in urban areas and 11 percentage points in rural zones (see figure IV.7). The greatest strides were made in Brazil, Peru and the Plurinational State of Bolivia, where the coverage of drinking water sources in rural areas increased by 27, 24 and 22 percentage points, respectively. Access to adequate sources of sanitation in rural areas also increased by more than 22 points on average in the same period (see figure IV.8). The greatest advances were made in rural areas of the Plurinational State of Bolivia, where coverage increased by 48 percentage points, and in Ecuador, Chile and Mexico, which recorded increases of over 35 points.

A. Urban zones

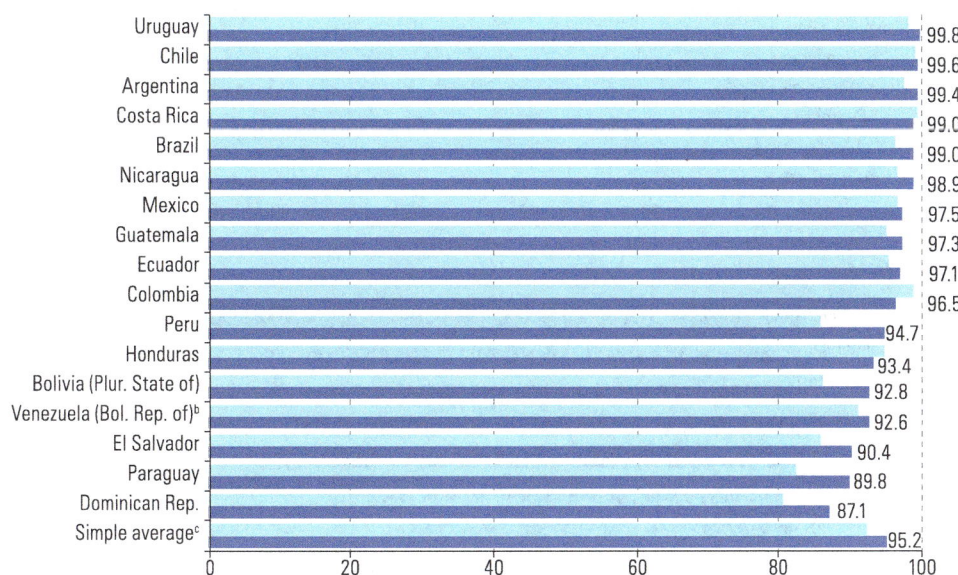

B. Rural zones

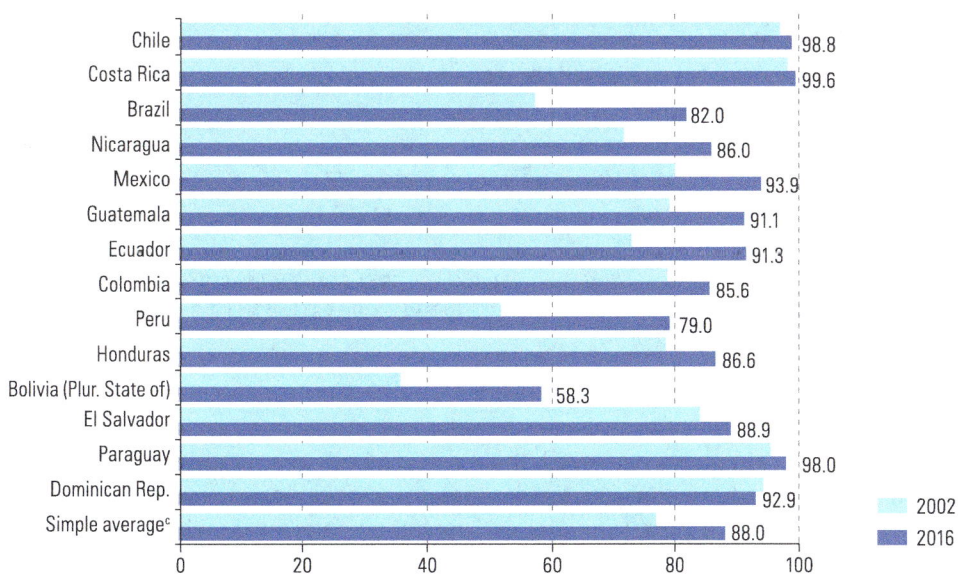

Figure IV.7
Latin America (17 countries): persons with access to adequate sources of drinking water, by geographical area, 2002–2016[a]
(Percentages)

Source: Economic Commission for Latin America and the Caribbean (ECLAC), on the basis of Household Survey Data Bank (BADEHOG).
[a] Information available for: Argentina, Chile and Paraguay (2003); Colombia (1999); Costa Rica (2004); Dominican Republic (2005); Ecuador, El Salvador and Nicaragua (2001); Guatemala (2000); Honduras (2007). The countries are listed according to the level of access in urban areas in the last available year.
[b] National total.
[c] Does not include Argentina, the Bolivarian Republic of Venezuela, or Uruguay.

Figure IV.8
Latin America
(17 countries): persons
with access to adequate
sources of sanitation,
by geographical area,
2002–2016[a]
(Percentages)

A. Urban areas

B. Rural areas

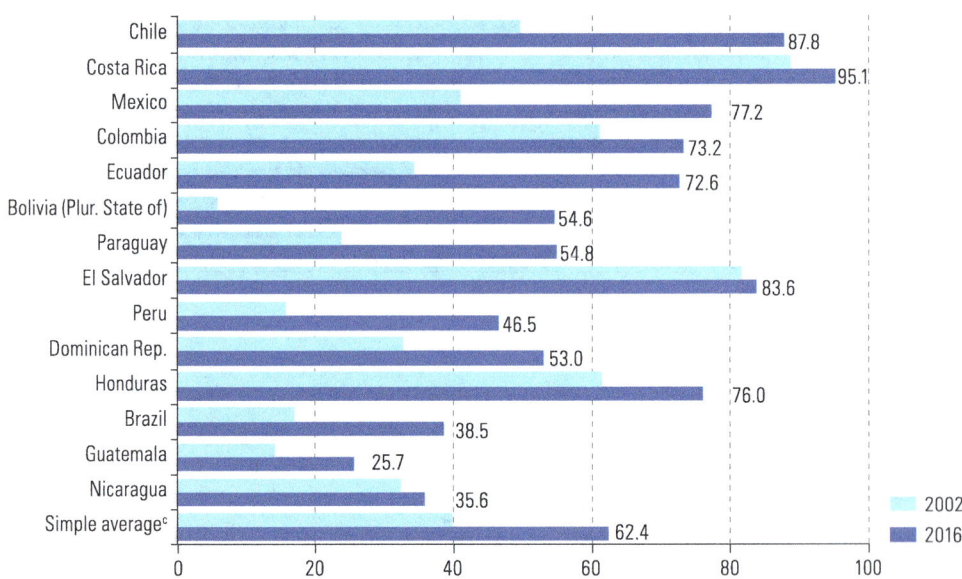

Source: Economic Commission for Latin America and the Caribbean (ECLAC), on the basis of Household Survey Data Bank (BADEHOG).
[a] Information available for: Argentina, Chile and Paraguay (2003); Colombia (1999); Costa Rica (2004); Dominican Republic (2005); Ecuador, El Salvador and Nicaragua (2001); Guatemala (2000); Honduras (2007). The countries are listed according to the level of access in urban areas in the last available year.
[b] National total.
[c] Does not include Argentina, the Bolivarian Republic of Venezuela, or Uruguay

Although the gaps have narrowed, there are still both quantitative and qualitative disparities in access between geographical areas and socioeconomic levels. In terms of the latter, there is inequality in water and sanitation services, in which households of lower socioeconomic status, often receive these services through solutions that do not ensure the same quality as higher-income households (for example, they have a latrine or septic tank instead of a household connection to a sewerage network). Water services are also unstable or intermittent, as the facilities in question are more vulnerable to disasters or weather events and there is less control over quality. This has serious consequences for personal health, especially among the youngest (ECLAC, 2018d).

The 2030 Agenda imposes new, more ambitious and complex challenges in this area, by adopting a more comprehensive and demanding approach in its application to services. It not only requires the coverage of water and sanitation services to be increased, but also that services are adequate and equitable. There are additional considerations on service quality and environmental impact, since the Agenda includes wastewater treatment and the need for provision to be more efficient (reducing losses or controlling excessive consumption).[6] Lastly, the Sustainable Development Goals include securing water sources (surface or underground) to enhance ecosystem protection (Ferro, 2017). This implies higher costs and requires policies to adopt more efficient strategies in the provision of these services.

Access to more advanced services, such as digital infrastructure, is increasingly essential for social inclusion, given the rapid technological transformations and their penetration into the different areas of people's lives. The increasingly widespread dissemination of technologies changes activities and processes in the economic, social, cultural and political spheres. The potential benefits of these innovations are enormous for sustainable development. Some new technologies represent a great opportunity for development and social welfare, aside from productivity increases. Biotechnology, nanotechnology and digital technologies (including big data analytics) can improve access to health services and their quality, nutrition, the availability of information and access to education. The use of big data analytics in the management of social policies opens up opportunities to reach the population more effectively, increase transparency in the use of resources and react in a timely manner to emergencies and disasters, among other benefits.

In Latin America, technological change is occurring against backdrops of historical and persistent inequality, which structures the various fields of action and life experiences. The spread of new technologies has been accompanied by digital gaps that exacerbate pre-existing inequalities in access to information and knowledge. This hinders the social integration of part of the population and restricts its capacity to develop basic skills (such as searching for, selecting, analysing, sharing and collaborating with information in a digital environment) for full participation in today's societies.

The first step that needs to be taken is to ensure equal conditions of access to equipment and technological infrastructure, particularly in terms of connectivity, for people who are unable to gain access through the market. The deployment of mobile broadband networks that emerged in the last decade has enhanced connectivity and fostered very widespread use of digital technologies; but universal inclusion is still a distant goal (ECLAC, 2016c). The connectivity level among households in urban areas is, on average, six times higher than in rural areas, with wide variations across countries (see figures IV.9A and IV.9B). Guatemala and the Plurinational State of Bolivia are among several countries with very precarious access to connectivity in the outlying areas of the cities, where less than 5% of the rural population has Internet access from home. Mobile connectivity plays an important role in Internet access for households in the rural areas of Chile, Ecuador, El Salvador and Peru.

---

[6]   In particular, Sustainable Development Goal target 6.b, to support and strengthen the participation of local communities in improving water and sanitation management, is of particular interest to indigenous peoples, since it relates to the State's duty of consultation to guarantee free, prior and informed consent to any decision that affects them, including their lands, territories and natural resources.

Figure IV.9
Latin America (13 countries): proportion of the total population with Internet access at home and mobile Internet, by geographical area, around 2016
(Percentages)

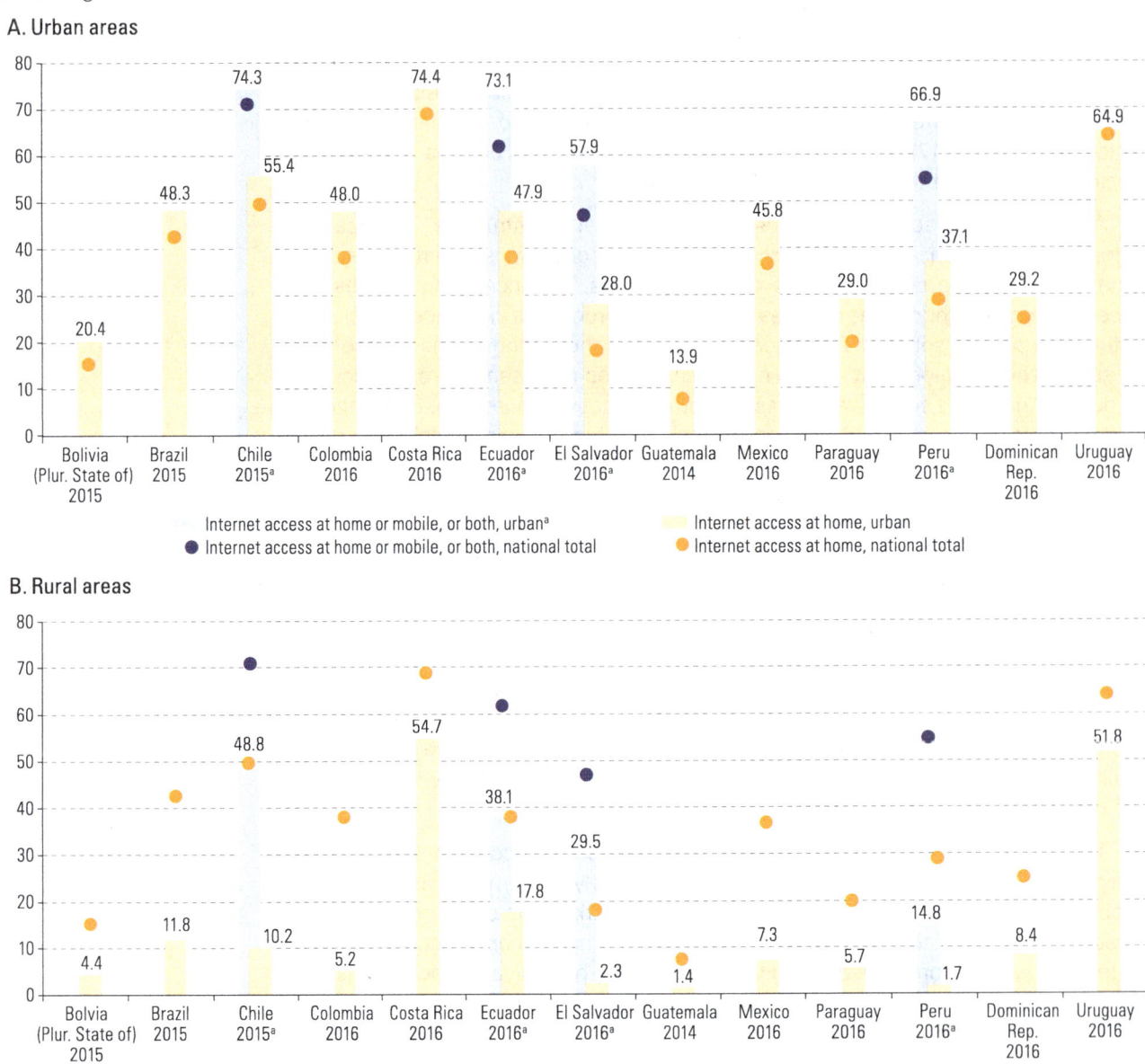

A. Urban areas

Internet access at home or mobile, or both, urban[a]
● Internet access at home or mobile, or both, national total
Internet access at home, urban
● Internet access at home, national total

B. Rural areas

Internet access either at home or mobile, or both, rural[a]
● Internet access either at home or mobile, or both, national total
Internet access at home, rural
● Internet access at home, national total

Source: Economic Commission for Latin America and the Caribbean (ECLAC), on the basis of Household Survey Data Bank (BADEHOG).
[a] Includes access through mobile devices (wireless Internet, smartphones, tablets and others).

Guaranteeing access to technologies is a necessary condition, but it is far from sufficient for the technologies in question to have a significant impact on the lives of individuals and communities. Technological changes give rise to additional sources of differentiation in terms of the ability to understand the effects on people's daily lives and decisions. This involves not only differences in access to technology in personal activities, but also understanding the impact of not knowing how to protect personal data and privacy, for example, or how to identify sources of reliable and high-quality information to make decisions that affect personal trajectories, such as those related to job opportunities, health or political representation.

2.   Labour inclusion and labour market

Labour markets in Latin America display high levels of informality and wide disparities in job quality, access to social protection and labour income. A large proportion of such income is lower than the legal minimum and less than what is needed to achieve adequate levels of well-being, which means that a large number of employed people must work long hours. The challenges are even greater for women and young people making the transition from education to the labour market. Labour market institutions play a key role in promoting better employment conditions and access to decent work.

(a) Employment and unemployment rates

Employment has increased in most of the region's countries in the last two decades, with job growth between 2002 and 2014 associated with a reduction in unemployment and greater female participation in the labour market. Levels of formalization and average labour income also increased (ECLAC, 2018a). In 2014–2016, however, the trend has been less favourable, and unemployment has risen on average, as occurred in the countries of the Southern Cone (Argentina, Brazil, Chile, Paraguay and Uruguay), as well as in Ecuador and the Plurinational State of Bolivia. In Central America and the Dominican Republic, on the other hand, the trends were positive in those years despite the complexity of the regional and international scenarios. The greater buoyancy of these economies had a positive impact on the labour market, and the average unemployment rate eased from 6.1% to 5.7% between 2015 and 2016 (ECLAC, 2017d). The Caribbean countries also moved against the regional trend, with the average unemployment rate falling from 15.2% to 11.2% between 2015 and 2016 (ECLAC, 2018d).

During 2017 and in early 2018, the regional labour market showed signs of recovery. There were slight improvements in the creation of wage employment (up 0.3% in 2017); the employment rate stabilized relative to the previous period; and, although the urban unemployment rate rose from 8.9% to 9.3% on average in 2017, this was less than the previous year's increase of 1.6 percentage points (ECLAC, 2018e). Despite the stronger momentum, the demand for labour remains weak, so self-employment is tending to grow (2.5%) faster than wage-earning jobs. This has major consequences for the quality of employment, because own-account work normally involves conditions of informality, low income and the absence of protection and access to other benefits.

(b) Lack of protection in employment

High rates of informality are a key feature of labour markets in Latin America and the Caribbean. This situation is explained, firstly, by the region's high degree of structural heterogeneity, where a large proportion of employment is created in the low-productivity segment, which does not have the economic conditions to assume the costs of formalization. This is compounded by non-observance of labour standards in sectors of high or medium productivity, which results in at least as large a proportion of informal employment within otherwise formal enterprises (Weller, 2017).

Informality usually implies the absence of protection normally associated with formal employment in terms of social security coverage for health care; affiliation (contribution) to contributory pension systems; defined working hours; insurance against unemployment, workplace accidents and diseases; and maternity protection. In 2002–2015, significant advances were made in the coverage of pension systems, a central indicator of protected labour market participation (ECLAC, 2018a). This progress was largely due to the drop in unemployment, the rise in the proportion of wage earners in total employment and the increase in formalization rates.[7] In some countries, efforts to encourage self-employed workers to affiliate voluntarily to pension systems strengthened these trends, as did policies aimed at extending social protection and formalization. Actions tending to formalize work in domestic service included "tax simplification measures… measures to strengthen labour administration and labour inspection, and increased training, credit and technical assistance for companies and informal workers" (ECLAC, 2016d, p. 36). Nonetheless, major challenges persist in terms of the proportion of employed persons who are not affiliated to pension systems or who do not make contributions to them.

Figure IV.10 shows that, on average, 52% of employed persons are in this least protected situation, while just 48% are affiliated to, or pay into, a pension system. This proportion is much lower in the lowest income quintiles, especially among women; and only workers in the highest quintile attain an average coverage rate close to 65%. On average, in the countries of Latin America there are no gender differences between the proportion of employed persons who are affiliated or who contribute to pension systems. Nonetheless, the proportion of unprotected women in the first four income quintiles is higher than that of men, especially in the first two quintiles, where the proportions of women and men who contribute or are affiliated to a pension system are 16.3% and 22.1%, respectively (in the first quintile), and 27.1% and 34.8% (in the second).

Figure IV.10
Latin America (18 countries): employed persons who are affiliated or contribute to pension systems relative to the total number of employed persons aged 15 or over, by income quintile and gender, around 2002 and 2016[a][b][c]
(Percentages)

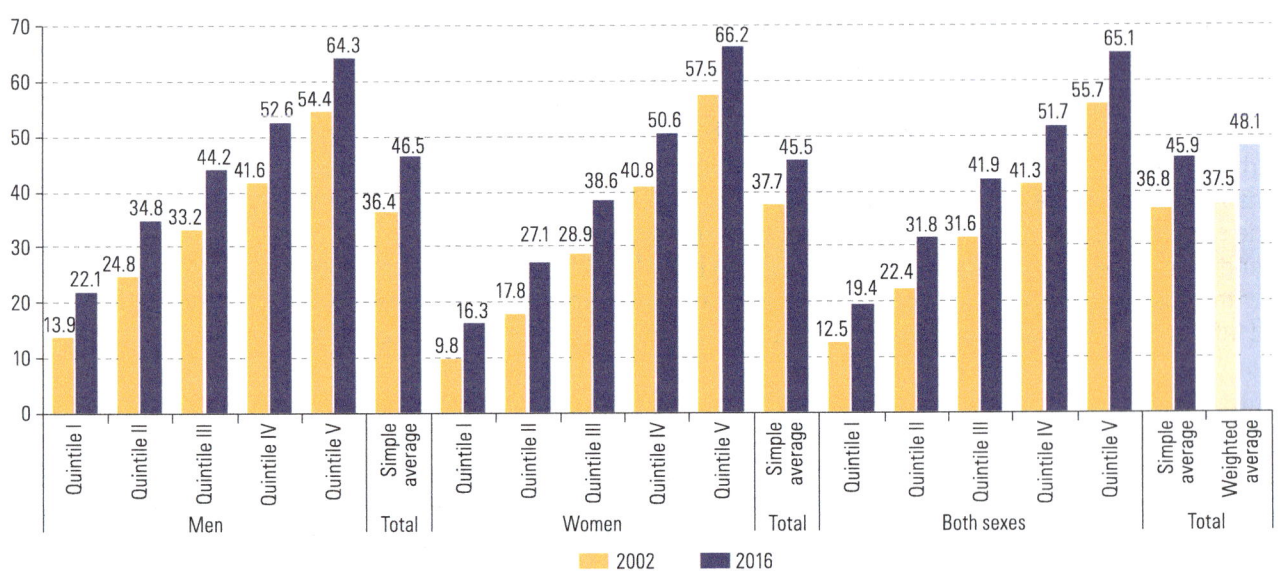

Source: Economic Commission for Latin America and the Caribbean (ECLAC), on the basis of Household Survey Data Bank (BADEHOG).
[a] Simple averages by quintile. The countries included are: Argentina (urban areas), Bolivarian Republic of Venezuela, Brazil, Chile, Colombia, Costa Rica, Dominican Republic, Ecuador, El Salvador, Guatemala, Honduras, Mexico, Nicaragua, Panama, Paraguay, Peru, Plurinational State of Bolivia and Uruguay (urban areas).
[b] Worker affiliation to pension systems is recorded in Colombia (1999), Ecuador, El Salvador, Guatemala, Paraguay (2003), the Dominican Republic, Peru and the Plurinational State of Bolivia. In the remaining countries, the indicator used corresponds to the contribution paid into pension systems or to comparable measurements. The data for Mexico for 2016 are not strictly comparable with those of previous years owing to changes in the wording of some of the questions on social security access. Further details of these changes, their effects on the estimation of social security coverage (health and pensions) and procedures to adjust the estimation are provided in CONEVAL (2017).
[c] In Argentina, the Bolivarian Republic of Venezuela, the Dominican Republic and Guatemala, the figures refer to wage earners.

---

[7]   A large proportion of wage earners do not have formal work contracts. According to the ECLAC publication *Social Panorama of Latin America, 2015*, 42.8% of wage earners were in this situation around 2013. According to *2016 Labour Overview of Latin America and the Caribbean* (ILO, 2016), that proportion is likely to have persisted at least until 2015.

Inequalities in modes of employment are reflected in people's capacity to develop more protected and stable career paths, and also affect their opportunities for well-being in the final stage of the life cycle, due to their different capacities to contribute to pension systems. The region has high levels of employment among older people, who are beyond the legal retirement age. This is primarily due to the weakness of social protection systems and the absence of other sources of income, particularly pensions, which forces them to continue working in old age (ECLAC/ILO, 2018).

Another form of less protected labour market participation is unskilled self-employment. Own-account work is a very important source of employment and income generation in the region's labour markets (Weller and Gontero, 2017). This is a heterogeneous occupational category, but with tendencies towards precariousness, since it is usually concentrated in low-productivity sectors with little access to social benefits (especially to contributory social protection). Those systems were originally designed for workers in an employment relationship, thus excluding those who work on their own account. Changes in the world of work, associated with the technological revolution, could further increase the proportion of self-employment. Many countries in the region have taken steps to recognize the importance of providing this occupational category with access to social and job security to enable them to hedge against risks they may face throughout the life cycle (ECLAC, 2016d; Weller and Gontero, 2017).

Unskilled self-employed workers represent one third of all employment in the region's countries on average. In the countries shown in figure IV.11, the average share of self-employment decreased from 36.5% to 32.7% between 2002 and 2016. Nonetheless, the proportion rises to an average of over 60% employed persons in the first income quintile. In, Guatemala, Honduras, Panama, Paraguay, Peru and the Plurinational State of Bolivia they account for over 80% of the employed population in the first income quintile.

Figure IV.11
Latin America (18 countries): unskilled self-employed workers aged 15 or over, in the highest and lowest income quintiles, around 2016 and averages for 2002 and 2016[a]
(Percentages)

Source: Economic Commission for Latin America and the Caribbean (ECLAC), on the basis of Household Survey Data Bank (BADEHOG).
[a] Simple averages.

Other important dimensions of the inequality matrix, such as ethno-racial status and the situations faced by migrants, generate circles of labour market exclusion and aggravate differences by socioeconomic level (see box IV.3). In the case of indigenous peoples, the indicators generally used to analyse labour market participation reflect conventional parameters of work in market-oriented societies, but they are not necessarily relevant to understanding the economy, well-being and population dynamics of these peoples. Moreover, the Indigenous and Tribal Peoples Convention, 1989 (No. 169), of the International Labour Organization (ILO), establishes that the traditional activities related to the subsistence economy of the peoples concerned shall be recognized as important factors in the maintenance of their culture and their economic self-reliance and development; and steps should be taken to ensure that these activities are strengthened and promoted, whenever appropriate. Nonetheless, although the self-employment is associated with traditional services and activities, the large proportion of indigenous population occupied in this category (far exceeding that of the rest of the population) indicates that indigenous persons engaged in the labour market enjoy less protection. The largest gaps in this regard are found in Brazil, Panama, Peru and the Plurinational State of Bolivia (see figure IV.12). Yet, both traditional and modern forms coexist in the indigenous economies, which are integrated into complex and diverse production and marketing structures. The challenge is therefore to move towards indigenous economic governance (Gros and Foyer, 2010).

Figure IV.12
Latin America (8 countries): unskilled self-employed, aged 15 or over, by ethnicity, around 2016
(Percentages)

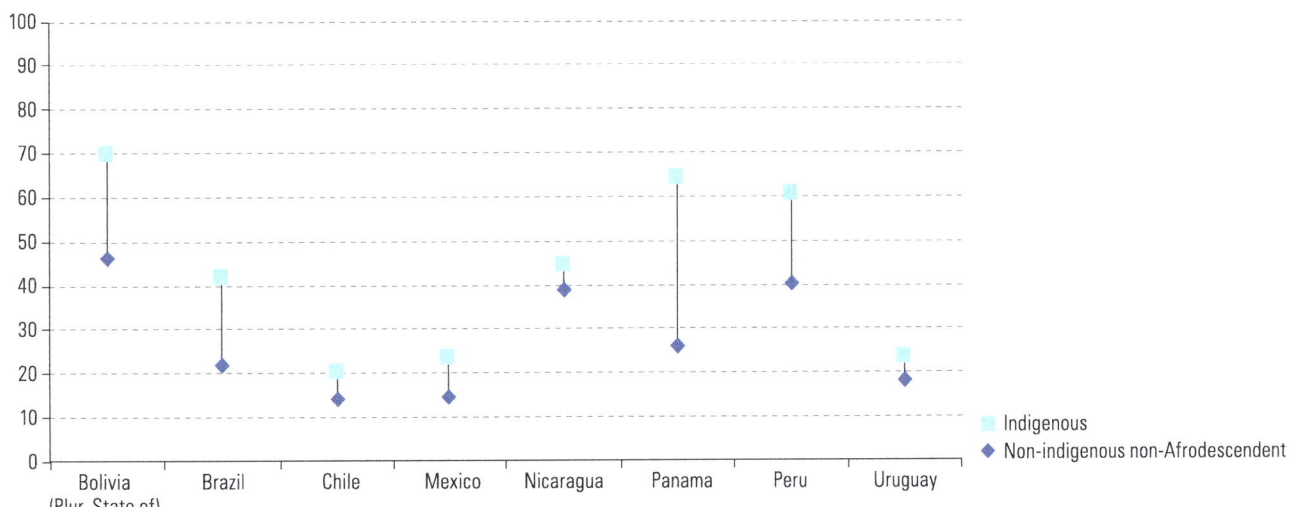

Source: Economic Commission for Latin America and the Caribbean (ECLAC), on the basis of Household Survey Data Bank (BADEHOG).

Box IV.3
Challenges of labour inclusion for immigrants in Latin America

One of the inclusion challenges in Latin America and the Caribbean is how to integrate the immigrant population in the destination countries. Social, labour, migration and social protection policies play a key role in achieving this objective. In the current situation, high levels of employment among migrant workers coexist with multiple inclusion gaps relative to the local population, which are manifested in unequal access to the formal labour market and in affiliation to health and pension systems. This is backdropped by changing migratory patterns: immigration in the region is no longer mostly from other parts of the world but has become intraregional; and new flows have been created and intensified in corridors leading to Argentina, Brazil, Chile, Costa Rica, the Dominican Republic, Mexico, Peru and Uruguay.

From a rights-based approach, one of the main challenges facing the inclusion of the migrant population in the region is to confront their irregular status, labour informality and worse working conditions. Although there is a demand for labour in the receiving countries, the regulatory and institutional frameworks and public policies for immigrants are usually insufficiently developed and are not always consistent with international instruments and the complexity of the phenomenon. For example, difficulties in obtaining work permits are one of the barriers to accessing the formal labour market and the associated social protection system; so coordination between labour and migratory policies is essential to avoid making it harder to obtain employment contracts, and to prevent job loss implying loss of the migrant's residence permit.

Box IV.3 (concluded)

Addressing this challenge firstly requires recognition that, in the absence of adequate policies, migratory status can interact with the other axes of the social inequality matrix (social class, gender, race and ethnicity, life cycle and territory); it can also worsen the risks of exclusion and widen gaps. In particular, as migratory status raises a basic question of belonging for the States involved, as well as access to labour markets and social protection systems, it is essential to underscore the social exclusion risks faced by the migrant population in the destination countries.

The sociodemographic profile of immigration in the region displays a majority of people of working age, whose education levels are, with some exceptions, at least as high as those of the local population. At the same time, there is heterogeneity in terms of gender composition; and the predominance of men or women varies across countries. Immigration in Latin America has a clear labour orientation, as confirmed by indicators of the working-age population, economically active population (EAP), employment rate and unemployment (see table A1.2 of the annex). According to the World Population Prospects database of the United Nations Department of Economic and Social Affairs (DESA), in 2015 only a minority of countries in the region had labour inclusion policies aimed at reducing access barriers and discrimination against the migrant population in the labour market. This is worrying, especially considering the high impact of these problems on the possibilities for migrant workers and their families to integrate into the destination countries. In fact, the migrant share of employment in low-productivity sectors is greater than that of the local population, even though their levels of schooling are, on average, higher. This generates problems of overqualification, increased informality, lower income and limits on access to social protection systems among migrant workers and their families.

Latin America (6 countries): overqualification among employed migrants and local population aged 15 years or older, around 2015
(Percentages)

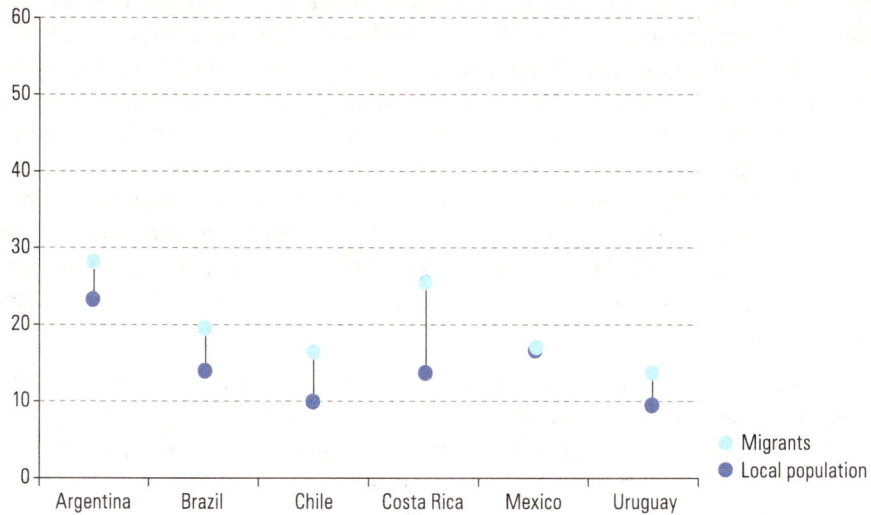

Source: I. Carrasco and J. Suárez, "Migración internacional e inclusión en América Latina: análisis en los países de destino mediante encuestas de hogares", Social Policy series, No. 231 (LC/TS.2018/57), Santiago, Economic Commission for Latin America and the Caribbean (ECLAC), 2018; on the basis of household surveys from the respective countries.
Note: Overqualification is operationally defined as workers with tertiary education who are employed in low-productivity sectors.

Source: Economic Commission for Latin America and the Caribbean (ECLAC), on the basis of D. Acosta, "Regional report on citizenship: the South American and Mexican cases", Comparative Report, No. 2016/01, Florence, European University Institute, 2016; D. Acosta and L. Freier, "Turning the immigration policy paradox upside down? Populist liberalism and discursive gaps in South America", International Migration Review, vol. 49, No. 3, New York, Center for Migration Studies of New York (CMS), 2015; I. Carrasco and J. Suárez, "Migración internacional e inclusión en América Latina: análisis en los países de destino mediante encuestas de hogares", Social Policy series, No. 231 (LC/TS.2018/57), Santiago, Economic Commission for Latin America and the Caribbean (ECLAC), 2018; Economic Commission for Latin America and the Caribbean/International Labour Organization (ECLAC/ILO), "Labour immigration in Latin America", Employment Situation in Latin America and the Caribbean, No. 16 (LC/TS.2017/30), Santiago, 2017; J. Martínez, M. Cano and M. Soffia, "Tendencias y patrones de la migración latinoamericana y caribeña hacia 2010 y desafíos para una agenda regional", Population and Development series, No. 109 (LC/L.3914), Santiago, Economic Commission for Latin America and the Caribbean (ECLAC), 2014; J. Martínez and C. Orrego, "Nuevas tendencias y dinámicas migratorias en América Latina y el Caribe", Population and Development series, No.114 (LC/L.4164), Santiago, Economic Commission for Latin America and the Caribbean (ECLAC), 2016; C. Maldonado, J. Martínez and R. Martínez, "Protección social y migración: una mirada desde las vulnerabilidades a lo largo del ciclo de la migración y de la vida de las personas", Project Documents (LC/TS.2018/62), Santiago, Economic Commission for Latin America and the Caribbean (ECLAC), 2018; International Labour Organization (ILO), "Labour migration in Latin America and the Caribbean: diagnosis, strategy and ILO's work in the region", Technical Report, No. 2016/2, Geneva, 2017; United Nations, Transforming our world: the 2030 Agenda for Sustainable Development (A/RES/70/1), New York, 2015; World Population Policies Database, New York, 2015 [online] https://esa.un.org/poppolicy/about_database.aspx; International Convention on the Protection of the Rights of All Migrant Workers and Members of Their Families (A/RES/45/158), New York, 18 December 1990; and household surveys from the respective countries.

(c) Labour incomes and underemployment

ECLAC has repeatedly stated the importance of work as a pillar enabling people and their families to access income that affords adequate living standards. As the level of income is one of the key elements of the quality of labour market participation, most countries legislate a minimum wage, as a key element of labour institutions, with a view to protecting the purchasing power of workers in the most disadvantaged sectors. This represents a threshold labour income (per hour or by output, depending on each legislation) that cannot be lowered and should guarantee minimum living conditions for the worker and his or her family, considering the socioeconomic context of each country (ECLAC, 2017b).

Minimum wage laws in the region's countries are varied, in terms of level and the regulations governing how the minimum wage is set. Some are national in scope, while others are specific to occupational categories. Although the real minimum wage has risen in some countries in the last decade and a half, in others it has remained at very low levels, sometimes even below the poverty line (ECLAC, 2017b). The proportion of employed persons whose labour income is lower than the minimum established by each country indicates how labour market participation is insufficient to guarantee adequate living standards. On average, around 40% of the working population of Latin American countries is in this situation.[8]

Figure IV.13 shows age and gender inequalities in relation to this indicator. In terms of the life cycle, both young people (15–24-year-olds) and persons over 65 are more likely to have labour incomes below the minimum wage (on average, 55.9% and 64.7% of them, respectively). Labour income is higher during productive adult life, especially among employed 25–44-year-olds, where, for the average of the countries, the proportion of people receiving income below the minimum wage drops to 34.6%. Throughout the life cycle, women also display a higher rate of low-income labour market participation. The information contained in figure IV.13 shows how the gap widens during the work trajectory to peak in the 45–64 age bracket (on average, the proportion of women in this age group with incomes below the minimum wage is 16 percentage points higher than that of men).

Another sign that part of the employed population does not earn enough income to achieve adequate levels of wellbeing is the existence of significant income underemployment —in other words individuals who have to work very long hours to earn labour incomes above the relative poverty levels in their country. In 2016, around 20% of employed persons, on average, worked longer than 44 hours per week, with equivalent labour incomes below the relative poverty line.[9] This proportion is much higher in rural areas (35%) than in urban zones (16%) (see figure IV.14). Although the gaps have narrowed since the early years of the 2000 decade, the differences remain very large. Moreover, the average number of workers subject to income underemployment in urban areas has increased recently; and no progress was made in rural areas between 2008 and 2016.

[8] Strictly speaking, minimum-wage legislation only applies to employees with an employment contract, so part of the working population (non-wage-earners and informal wage earners or those employed without contracts) is not legally covered by this regime. Nonetheless, it proxies for the proportion of workers who do not earn enough from their work to sustain a decent standard of living. Moreover, the minimum wage usually has a "beacon" effect, since it also serves as a benchmark for the income of the self-employed and part-time workers.

[9] If those employed persons were to work no more than 44 hours per week, their monthly income would be below the country's relative poverty line. Relative poverty is defined as 50% of the median per capita income, without applying equivalence scales.

Figure IV.13
Latin America (18 countries): employed persons aged 15 years or over whose average earnings are below the national minimum wage, by gender and age group, around 2016[a]
(Percentages)

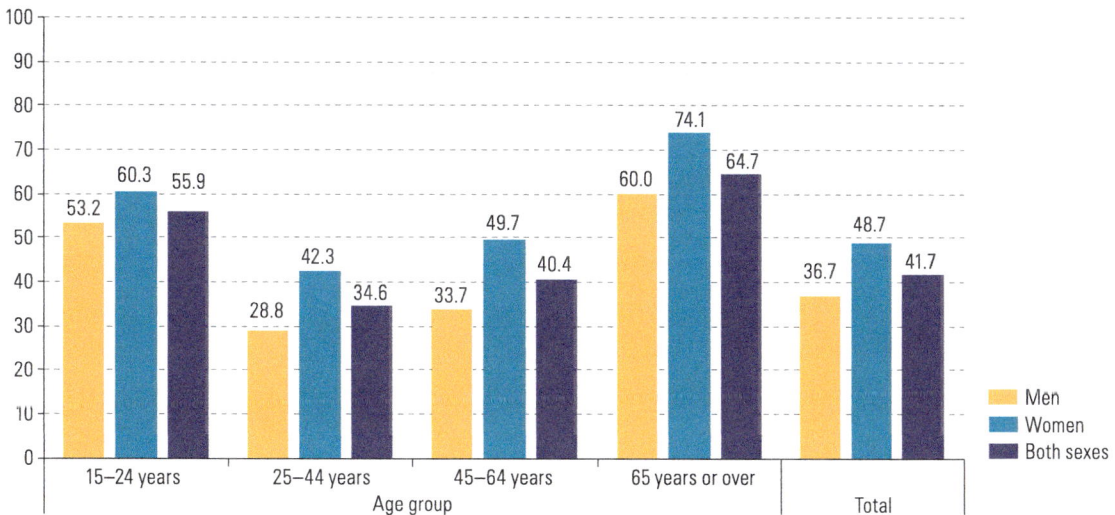

Source: Economic Commission for Latin America and the Caribbean (ECLAC), on the basis of Household Survey Data Bank (BADEHOG).
[a] Simple averages. The countries included are: Argentina (urban areas), Bolivarian Republic of Venezuela, Brazil, Chile, Colombia, Costa Rica, the Dominican Republic, Ecuador, El Salvador, Guatemala, Honduras, Mexico, Nicaragua, Panama, Paraguay, Peru, Plurinational State of Bolivia and Uruguay (urban areas).

Figure IV.14
Latin America (14 countries): employed persons aged 15 years or over with working weeks in excess of 44 hours and equivalent labour income below the relative poverty line, by geographical area, 2002–2016[a]
(Percentages)

Source: Economic Commission for Latin America and the Caribbean (ECLAC), on the basis of Household Survey Data Bank (BADEHOG).
[a] Simple averages. The countries included are: Brazil, Chile, Colombia, Costa Rica, Dominican Republic, Ecuador, El Salvador, Guatemala, Honduras, Mexico, Nicaragua, Paraguay, Peru and Plurinational State of Bolivia.

Gender inequality is also associated with this indicator of low-quality employment. Although the gap between men and women is less pronounced than that between geographical areas, it has widened in the last decade and a half. In the most recent year for which information is available, on average, 26.9% of employed women were in a situation of income underemployment, which returned to its 2002 level (see figure IV.15). Among men, the proportion has also increased in recent years to an average of 19% of those employed with extended working hours. As the increase was less for men than among women, the gender gap widened.

Figure IV.15
Latin America
(18 countries): employed
persons aged 15 years
or older, with a working
week in excess of
44 hours and equivalent
labour income below
the relative poverty line,
by gender, 2002–2016[a]
(Percentages)

Source: Economic Commission for Latin America and the Caribbean (ECLAC), on the basis of Household Survey Data Bank (BADEHOG).
[a] Simple averages. The countries included are: Argentina (urban areas), Bolivarian Republic of Venezuela, Brazil, Chile, Colombia, Costa Rica, Dominican Republic, Ecuador, El Salvador, Guatemala, Honduras, Mexico, Nicaragua, Panama, Paraguay, Peru, Plurinational State of Bolivia and Uruguay (urban areas).

Labour institutions play a key role in improving working conditions and promoting decent work, both in terms of employment opportunities and unemployment protection, and in terms of remuneration, access to social security and observance of rights at work. In this connection, ECLAC recommends strengthening inclusive labour policies in conjunction with those of social security, to encourage formalization, promote social dialogue and strengthen union organization and collective bargaining (ECLAC, 2018a).

(d) Challenges of youth labour integration

The transition from school to the world of work is a fundamental stage in a person's life cycle, emancipation and development of autonomy, which involves particularly difficult processes for young people. Entry into a first job often foreshadows the characteristics of future labour market participation and a career path. Traditionally, these difficulties have been analysed in terms of youth unemployment rates, which are much higher than those of adults, particularly in the case of unemployment while searching for a first job (ECLAC/ILO, 2017). Despite their higher levels of education and skills, young people are the most prone to unemployment, which is particularly acute among young women. The Caribbean countries, in particular, have some of the highest youth unemployment rates in the world, which fuels high rates of youth emigration.

Transformations in the context of the lives of young people in the region have made analysing this phase more complex and less linear than in the past. The diversity of young people's situations and characteristics, along with their environments, produces a diversity of trajectories and irregular transitions, in which the participants frequently move back and forth between the education system and the labour market, or sometimes they are in both at the same time. Some of the factors that affect these transformations are related to education systems, which have significantly expanded their coverage; others are linked to demand from the production sectors, which has become more dynamic and global and requires ongoing training processes. The increase in female labour force participation and changes in family structures have led to the postponement of maternity and paternity, which has also delayed young people's demands for economic autonomy (Trucco and Ullmann, 2015).

An approach to the dynamics of transitions to employment by young people in the region reveals a number of specific characteristics (Gontero and Weller, 2015). First, compared to OECD and other developed countries, young people in the region leave the education system relatively early (between 18 and 19 years old). Moreover, simultaneously combining study and work time is less common than in developed countries. Thirdly, the proportion of young people who are outside the education system but not employed in the labour market increases during adolescence, but starts to decline with age (from 25 years old) among men. In contrast, women remain in this situation of exclusion for longer and in much larger proportions than their peers in OECD countries.

As a result, young people who are neither in education nor employed in the labour market, a situation that evidences major barriers to access and permanency in these key areas of inclusion, are a special focus of attention for the Latin American and Caribbean countries. The average proportion of young people in this situation has remained around 21% since 2008, when it dropped from over 24%, mainly reflecting the fall in the average proportion of young women who were outside both the education system and the labour market (see figure IV.16). Although the average percentage of young women who are neither studying nor employed in the labour market is almost three times the equivalent for young men, the gap narrowed slightly (by 3.9 percentage points) in the period analysed, especially in the 2000 decade.

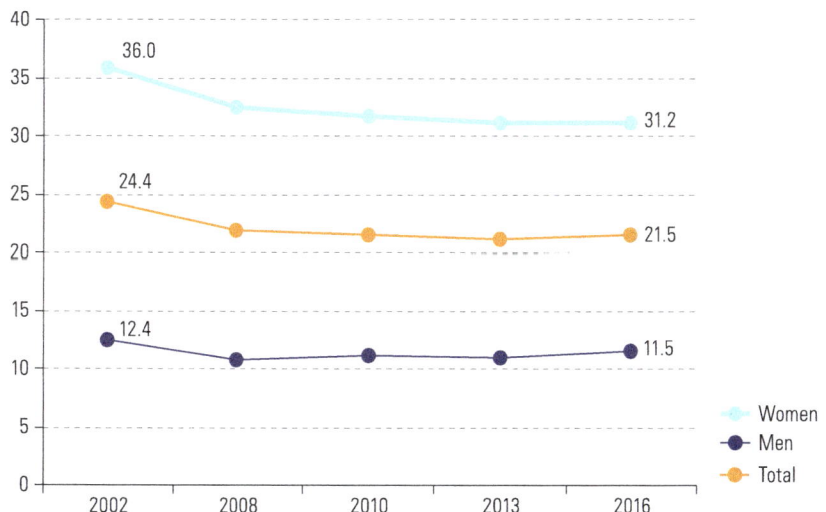

Figure IV.16
Latin America (18 countries): young people aged 15–29 who are in neither education or employment, by gender, 2002–2016[a] *(Percentages)*

Source: Economic Commission for Latin America and the Caribbean (ECLAC), on the basis of Household Survey Data Bank (BADEHOG).
[a] Simple averages. The countries included are: Argentina (urban areas), Bolivarian Republic of Venezuela, Brazil, Chile, Colombia, Costa Rica, Dominican Republic, Ecuador, El Salvador, Guatemala, Honduras, Mexico, Nicaragua, Panama, Paraguay, Peru, Plurinational State of Bolivia and Uruguay urban areas).

The larger proportion of young women who are excluded in Latin America contrasts with the situation in more developed countries, where the probability of exclusion is the same for men and women alike (OECD/ECLAC/CAF, 2016). This gender gap is largely explained by the absence of care policies and systems and a significant change in the gender division of labour in the family, compounded by adolescent pregnancy and the high burden of domestic work and unpaid care performed by women. In particular, the unequal distribution of unpaid work and care between men and women, the failure to recognize its economic value and the barriers that this poses for women's full integration into the labour market and, hence, to obtaining their economic autonomy, reproduce gender inequalities throughout the life cycle (ECLAC, 2016b). In this context, it is crucial to consider how to respond to the need for reconciliation between work, studies and the family and personal life of young people, and to reinforce integrated care policies and systems.

A decisive factor in the transition from school to work is the level of education attained: young people who drop out of primary school, in other words individuals with truncated educational trajectories, are more likely to be out of the labour market as well. Education level is closely associated with the socioeconomic inequalities that characterize the region, which the education system has not succeeded in reversing, despite the progress analysed in section B.1.a. of this chapter. While, on average for Latin America, 41.3% of young people with incomplete primary education were neither studying nor employed in the labour market in 2016, the proportion falls to 20% among young people with incomplete secondary education or with incomplete university education. The proportion of young people who attained a university level of education (at least five years of higher education) and who are in a situation of exclusion is just 14% (see figure IV.17).

Figure IV.17
Latin America
(18 countries): young
people aged 15–29 who
are in neither education
or employment, by
education level and
geographical area,
around 2016[a]
(Percentages)

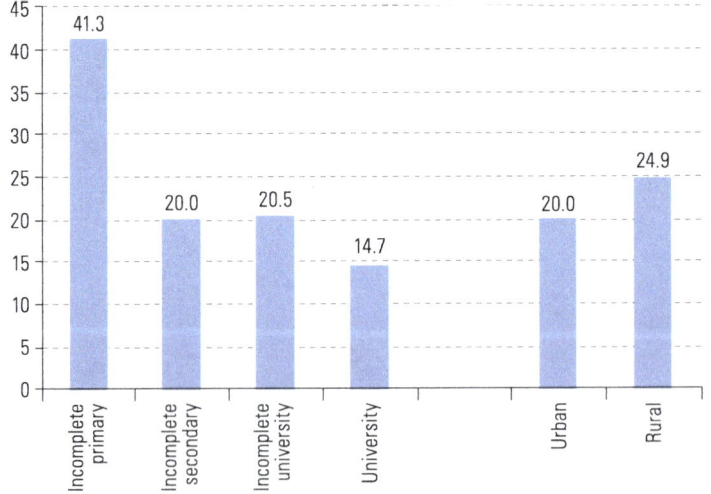

Source: Economic Commission for Latin America and the Caribbean (ECLAC), on the basis of Household Survey Data Bank (BADEHOG).
[a] Simple averages. The countries included are: Argentina (urban areas), Bolivarian Republic of Venezuela, Brazil, Chile, Colombia, Costa Rica, Dominican Republic, Ecuador, El Salvador, Guatemala, Honduras, Mexico, Nicaragua, Panama, Paraguay, Peru, Plurinational State of Bolivia and Uruguay (urban areas).

In rural areas, 25% of young people are neither studying nor employed in the labour market, compared to 20% in urban zones (see figure IV.17). This reflects the lower educational coverage in rural areas, especially post-high school, compounded by the characteristics of the labour markets in those areas, together with fertility patterns and other cultural features that influence the life trajectories of rural youth (ECLAC, 2017b).

The dimensions that determine patterns of social inequality in the region are often linked, interwoven and mutually empowered, thereby generating circles of exclusion among certain population groups. Thus, gender inequality combines with the inequality that affects the Afrodescendent population; and, except in Panama, they affect Afrodescendent young women to a greater extent (see figure IV.18). On average, the proportion of young Afrodescendent women in this situation is 2.6 times that of young people who are neither of African descent nor indigenous. The main reason why young women are not studying or employed in the labour market is that they are doing unpaid domestic work in their homes or otherwise engaged in care work. In fact Afrodescendants are much more likely to be engaged in unpaid domestic chores than non-Afrodescendants (ECLAC, 2017c).

Figure IV.18
Latin America (5 countries): young people aged 15–29 who are in neither education or employment, by ethnicity and gender, around 2016[a]
(Percentages)

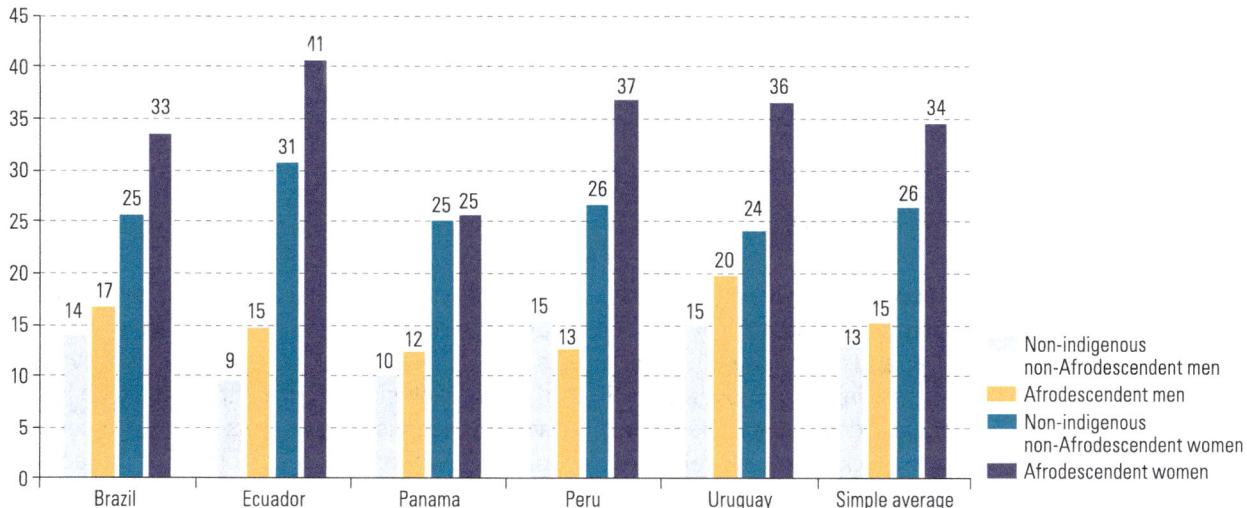

Source: Economic Commission for Latin America and the Caribbean (ECLAC), on the basis of Household Survey Data Bank (BADEHOG).
[a] Simple averages.

C. Universal access to the exercise of rights and the benefits of development: dual social and labour inclusion

To move towards higher levels of inclusion and participation in the benefits of development and in the exercise of rights, progress needs to be made simultaneously on social and labour inclusion. Since 2002, the proportion of households in a situation of dual inclusion (social and labour) has grown steadily, while the percentage subject to dual exclusion has declined. Nonetheless, just one in four Latin American households is in a situation of dual inclusion, and the gaps are greater for the rural population and for households whose head or leader is indigenous or Afrodescendent.

Latin America not only has large sectors of society living in poverty or extreme poverty (see chapter II), also others in a situation of vulnerability, with incomes slightly above the poverty line and working in informal and precarious jobs, without social protection to cope with crises, old age, work-related illnesses and accidents, and other situations such as maternity and paternity (ECLAC, 2016d). Moreover, as discussed above, many still suffer from restricted access to education, health care or basic infrastructure, especially in rural areas.

Social policy needs a universalist orientation that contributes to construction of the welfare state for the entire population (ECLAC, 2016d and 2018d). Accordingly, the institutions responsible for social development policies need to take a broad view, both of the target populations and of the actions required to sustainably promote improvements in their well-being, which must include both the social and labour domains. The authorities responsible for social development in the region's countries are analysing and acting on this issue. Two decades after the launch of monetary transfer programmes to overcome poverty, which seek to raise household incomes and improve the capacities of their members and have had significant results (ECLAC, 2016d), the public policies that have been implemented to achieve inclusive social development also target the labour and productive integration of young people and adults of working age.

In particular, to move towards higher levels of inclusion and sharing in the benefits of development and the exercise of rights, there is a growing consensus on the need to achieve at least basic levels of well-being through universal access to rights and quality social services, and also to decent work opportunities. This invokes the twin challenge of social and labour inclusion.

1.   A measurement exercise

Social inclusion is a multidimensional concept that encompasses the realization of rights, participation in social life, access to education, health and care, as well as basic infrastructure services and housing, and the availability of income. It refers to a process of improving economic, social, cultural and political conditions to enable people to participate fully in society (ECLAC, 2008 and 2009; United Nations, 2016; Levitas and others, 2007). There is thus a continuum that runs from very high levels of exclusion, in which most rights violated, to full inclusion, in which there are high levels of socioeconomic well-being and capacity to exercise rights. This is set in a context where a lack of basic levels of education or health, or living in a home without access to basic utilities, such as water, sanitation and electricity, means the conditions for social inclusion are not fulfilled.

The concept of labour inclusion is linked to that of decent work, as defined by ILO (1999) and incorporated into Goal 8 of the 2030 Agenda for Sustainable Development (Promote sustained, inclusive and sustainable economic growth, full and productive employment and decent work for all). The concept of decent work concerns the promotion of opportunities for men and women to engage in productive and quality work, under conditions of freedom, equity, safety and human dignity. It is a multidimensional concept that blends the quantitative and qualitative dimensions of work. It proposes measures that are aimed not only at creating jobs and reducing unemployment, but also at overcoming forms of work that generate insufficient income for individuals and their families to overcome poverty, or which are based on unhealthy, dangerous, insecure or degrading activities, and thus contribute to the reproduction of poverty, inequality and exclusion. It affirms the need for employment to be associated with social protection and full observance of rights at work, including the rights of representation, association, union organization and collective bargaining (ILO, 1999; Rodgers, 2002; Abramo, 2015; ECLAC, 2016b).

The following exercise of measuring dual social and labour inclusion highlights the following: (i) the ability of States to simultaneously guarantee universal access to rights to social services and basic infrastructure, regardless of income level and other household characteristics; and (ii) participation by people in paid work under dignified conditions, with decent jobs that give them access to social protection and enable them to escape poverty. The analysis of dual inclusion seeks to draw attention to some of the deficits in guaranteeing basic rights that enable people to move towards inclusive social development, emphasizing the interrelationships that exist between access to social services and decent work. This analysis complements that of monetary poverty, presented in chapter II of this edition of *Social Panorama of Latin America*; and it considers the effects of public policy actions in individual countries, aimed at expanding access to basic utilities, education and contributory social protection, for example.

The dual inclusion typology was prepared for the document *Linkages between the social and production spheres: gaps, pillars and challenges*, which was prepared for the second session of the Regional Conference on Social Development of Latin America and the Caribbean, held in Montevideo (ECLAC, 2017a). It is inspired both in the concept of dual inclusion proposed by Martínez and Sánchez-Ancochea (2013), which analyses the dual inclusion process in Costa Rica, understood as the expansion of social services and job creation; and also in making the exercise of dual inclusion operational in Colombia, as described by Angulo and Gómez (2014). This document was very well received by the countries, and Resolution 2 (II) of the Regional Conference on Social Development of Latin America and the Caribbean called for it to be widely disseminated to promote national dialogue on its main recommendations. Box IV.4 describes how the exercise of dual (social and labour) inclusion is actually performed in this chapter, using household survey data. This is a more demanding exercise than that performed for the second session of the aforementioned Regional Conference, especially in the labour dimension.

The two dimensions of the dual inclusion measurement exercise are labour inclusion and social inclusion. Each one classifies households in a situation of inclusion or exclusion, through the indicators comprising it. The indicators that are used characterize households —which are the unit of analysis in keeping with their role as the main unit of intervention of many social development policies— either directly or through properties that characterize some of their members and which are subsequently used to classify the household as a whole.

In terms of social inclusion, a household is considered to be in a situation of inclusion when all of the following conditions are met:

- Education: (i) there is no family member of school age, according to national legislation (usually from 6 to 17 years old), who is not attending school without having completed secondary; (ii) there is no member of school age lagging three or more years behind the school grade corresponding to their age; (iii) there are no members from 18 to 64 years of age with incomplete basic education (primary and lower secondary); (iv) there is no person of 65 years or older without complete primary education.

- Equipment for basic services in the household: (i) the household has electricity; (ii) it has adequate access to sanitation systems (in urban areas it is unacceptable that there is no sewerage connection or that access is outside the household and the property; in rural areas it is unacceptable that there is no type of sewage disposal service (for example, discharge directly into the river); (iii) it has adequate access to drinking water (in urban areas it is unacceptable that the water is drawn from a well or by ferris wheel, or that the water supply is outside the household and the property (for example, public standpipes, truck or other); in rural areas it is unacceptable that the water is obtained from natural sources (rivers, springs), or that it takes at least 15 minutes to reach the water source).

In the labour inclusion dimension, a household is considered included if:

- Labour incomes and contributory pensions per capita (the sum of all of the household's labour income and contributory pensions, divided by the total number of household members) are equal to or greater than the relative poverty line used in the Sustainable Development Goals. (corresponding to 50% of median per capita income).

Box IV.4
Dual inclusion and its social and labour components: measurement methodology

Box IV.4 (concluded)

And, at least one of these conditions is also satisfied:

- All persons of 15 years or older who work are paying into (or are affiliated to) a contributory social security system (pensions or health).

- All economically inactive persons from 60 to 64 years of age and all persons aged 65 or over receive a contributory pension.

By combining these two dimensions (social and labour inclusion), households can be classified into one of four categories: (i) included in both the labour and social dimensions (dual inclusion); (ii) included in the labour dimension, but not in the social dimension (labour inclusion only); (iii) included in the social dimension, but not in the labour dimension (social inclusion only); and (iv) not included in the labour or the social dimension (dual exclusion).

Measuring inclusion via a small number of indicators is not ideal. For example, the concept of social inclusion also refers to access to health care and broader issues of participation in society that are not generally captured in household surveys. Moreover, the concept of labour inclusion also refers to decent work, which ILO defines much more broadly than the indicators used in this exercise.

Source: Economic Commission for Latin America and the Caribbean (ECLAC).

2.   Trends in dual inclusion: progress and gaps

In 2016, just 23.5% of households in Latin America were in a situation of dual inclusion, having achieved both social and labour inclusion simultaneously (see figure IV.19). As a simple average of the region's countries, the proportion of households in a situation of dual inclusion has risen continuously since 2002, while the percentage of households subject to dual exclusion has declined. As a result, the ratio between the percentage of households subject to dual exclusion and those in a situation of dual inclusion has been cut by half: from 3.9 in 2002 to 1.9 in 2016.

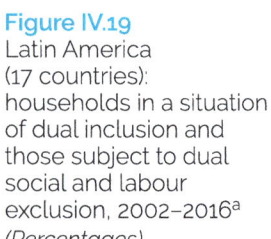

Figure IV.19
Latin America
(17 countries):
households in a situation
of dual inclusion and
those subject to dual
social and labour
exclusion, 2002–2016[a]
(Percentages)

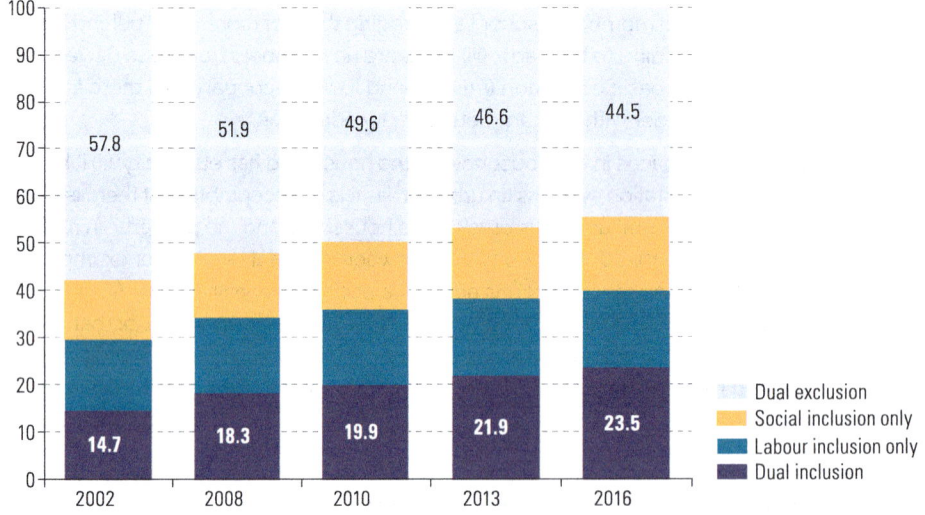

Source: Economic Commission for Latin America and the Caribbean (ECLAC), on the basis of Household Survey Data Bank (BADEHOG).
[a] Simple averages. The countries included are: Argentina (urban areas), Bolivarian Republic of Venezuela, Brazil, Chile, Colombia, Costa Rica, Dominican Republic, Ecuador, El Salvador, Guatemala, Honduras, Mexico, Nicaragua, Paraguay, Peru, Plurinational State of Bolivia and Uruguay (urban areas).

In absolute terms, 46.5 million households (encompassing 132.9 million people) attained dual inclusion levels in 2016, while 60.6 million households (238.5 million people) were in a condition of dual exclusion. The trends of dual inclusion are explained by a continuous increase in social and labour inclusion between 2002 and 2016, although progress in the former has outpaced the latter.

Dual inclusion levels are associated with the relative strength of the welfare state, defined according to the welfare regime typology (ECLAC, 2016b).[10] Countries with the highest levels of dual inclusion are those with a more developed welfare state, followed by those of intermediate development. In countries with a less advanced welfare state (countries with large gaps), dual inclusion levels do not exceed 15%. In all countries of the region, dual inclusion has increased in the last decade and a half (see figure IV.20). The greatest increases between 2002 and 2016 occurred in the Dominican Republic, Colombia, Brazil and Argentina (with variations of close to 15 percentage points).

Figure IV.20
Latin America (17 countries): households in a situation of dual inclusion, by country, around 2002 and 2016
(Percentages)

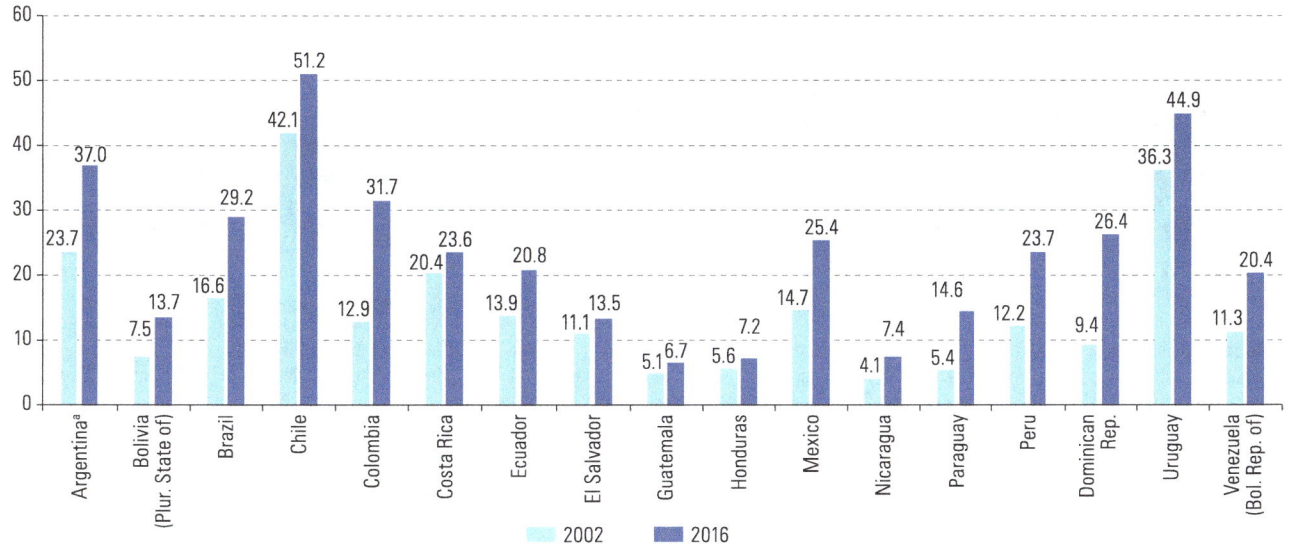

Source: Economic Commission for Latin America and the Caribbean (ECLAC), on the basis of Household Survey Data Bank (BADEHOG).
[a] Urban areas.

Dual inclusion remains a remote prospect for the vast majority of the rural population in Latin American countries (see figure IV.21), owing to the lack of access to basic infrastructure, low education levels and lack of protection at work. Rates of social security affiliation by rural workers in the region are significantly lower than those of their urban peers —partly because of differences in the organization of production and the characteristics of the labour market. For example, wage rates are lower in rural areas, and a number of productive activities performed mainly by women are not counted as employment in official statistics. It is also influenced by the fact that contributory pension systems were designed on the basis of models that excluded rural sectors or those that are highly segmented by type of employment (Rossel, 2012). Nonetheless, the implementation of public policies to provide basic infrastructure in rural areas has resulted in a significant, 12.2 percentage-point, reduction in the proportion of rural households subject to dual exclusion between 2002 and 2016.

---

[10]   This typology was based on factors such as the capacity of the State to provide sustenance and protection to those who receive insufficient or no income; and society's capacity to generate sufficient income in the labour market. Based on this classification, the following groups of countries were formed: (i) countries with moderate gaps: Argentina, Bolivarian Republic of Venezuela, Brazil, Chile, Costa Rica, Panama and Uruguay; (ii) those with modest gaps: Colombia, the Dominican Republic, Ecuador, Mexico and Peru; and (iii) those with severe gaps: El Salvador, Guatemala, Honduras, Nicaragua, Paraguay and Plurinational State of Bolivia (ECLAC, 2016b).

Inequalities are also manifested in other dimensions, such as ethnic or racial ones: households whose heads are indigenous or Afrodescendent have lower levels of dual inclusion and higher levels of dual exclusion than the rest of the population, which reflects the structural gaps in well-being and exercise of rights among these populations, relative to those who are neither indigenous nor of African descent (see figure IV.22).

Figure IV.21
Latin America (16 countries): households in a situation of dual inclusion or dual exclusion (social and labour), by urban and rural area, 2002–2016[a]
(Percentages)

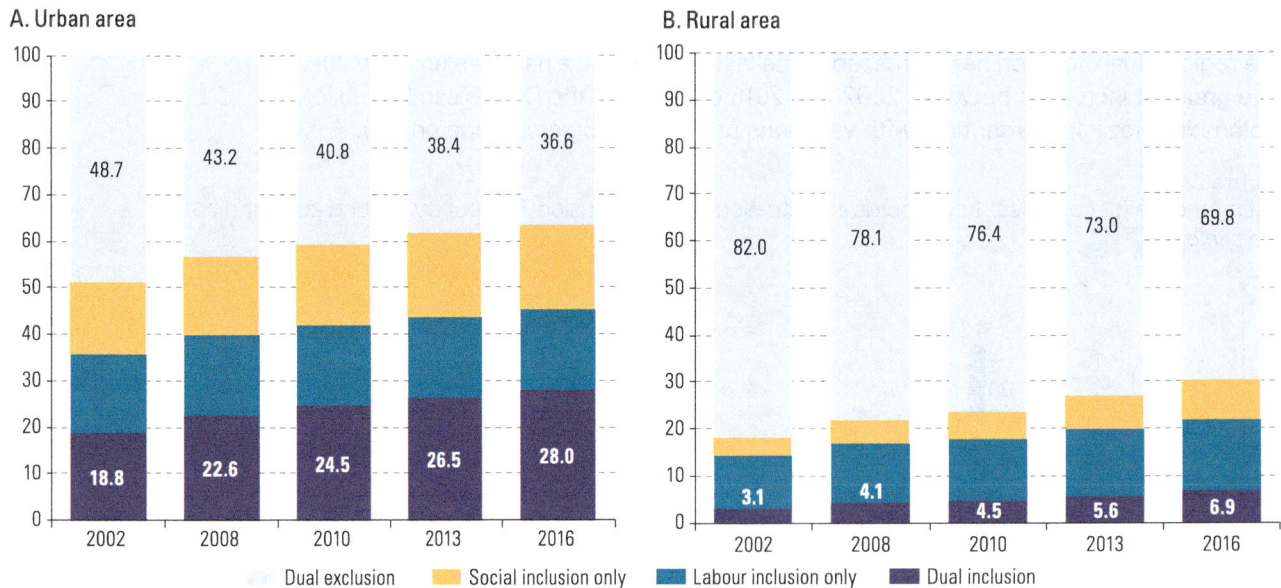

Source: Economic Commission for Latin America and the Caribbean (ECLAC), on the basis of Household Survey Data Bank (BADEHOG).
[a] Simple averages. The countries included are: Argentina (urban areas only), Bolivia (Plurinational State of), Brazil, Chile, Colombia, Costa Rica, Ecuador, El Salvador, Guatemala, Honduras, Mexico, Nicaragua, Paraguay, Peru, Dominican Republic and Uruguay (urban areas only).

Figure IV.22
Latin America: households in a situation of dual inclusion or dual exclusion (social and labour), by ethno-racial status of the head of household, around 2016
(Percentages)

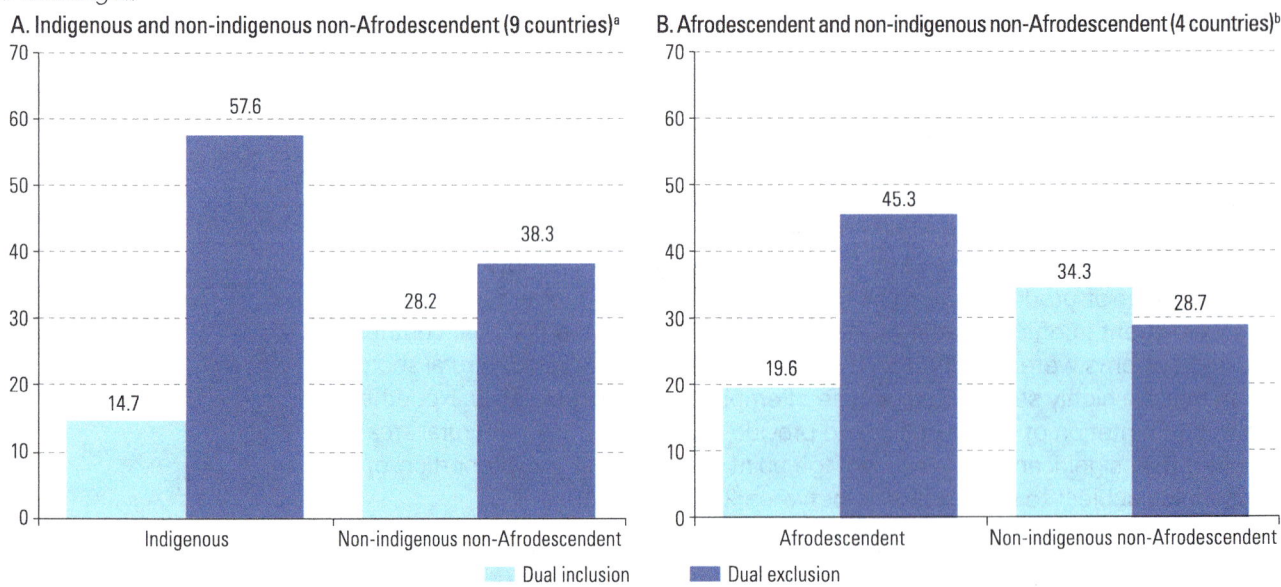

Source: Economic Commission for Latin America and the Caribbean (ECLAC), on the basis of Household Survey Data Bank (BADEHOG).
[a] Simple average, based on information from Bolivia (Plurinational State of), Brazil, Chile, Ecuador, Guatemala, Mexico, Nicaragua, Peru and Uruguay.
[b] Simple average, based on information from Brazil, Ecuador, Peru and Uruguay.

The dimensions of dual exclusion are more accentuated among persons with disabilities (see box IV.5), of whom a very small proportion attain dual inclusion. The scarcity of equal employment opportunities for persons with disabilities is one of the underlying causes of poverty and exclusion for this population group and their families. Accordingly, expanding access to continuing education for persons with disabilities and promoting their full participation in the world of work must be a priority in building more inclusive and tolerant societies.

The concept of disability has evolved greatly in recent decades. It has developed from a biomedical approach, which considers disability as a personal health problem, to a rights-based approach, as proclaimed in the Convention on the Rights of Persons with Disabilities (CRPD). Radically different policy responses emerge from each perspective. The biomedical model calls for actions at the individual level for the provision of medical and rehabilitation services; and those responsible for carrying out this intervention would be health and rehabilitation professionals. In contrast, under a rights perspective, public action should aim to eliminate barriers (both physical and attitudinal) to enable the exercise of rights and full participation by persons with disabilities in all areas, which is a responsibility of society at large.

This change of focus entails changing public policies to address the needs of the population with disabilities, moving from charitable-welfarist policies to those that actively seek to eliminate discrimination and expand inclusion opportunities for persons with disabilities in the different domains of society. The countries of Latin America and the Caribbean have made great strides in this direction, but progress has not been sufficient to close the vast gaps that persist between the populations with and without disabilities in the different dimensions of inclusion.

Box IV.5
Deficits in the social and labour inclusion of persons with disabilities in Latin America

For development to be sustainable, it must include everyone. It is therefore imperative to expand opportunities for persons with disabilities to participate in the various spheres of society, and to develop and contribute with their potentials. The diversity of the population with disabilities also demands differentiated approaches that respond not only to different types and degrees of disability, but also to the specific realities and experiences of persons with disabilities who, owing to their gender, ethno-racial condition, place of residence and age, may experience multiple discriminations that restrict their inclusion possibilities. Fundamentally, moving towards the full inclusion of the population with disabilities requires a cultural shift: towards full appreciation of human diversity.

The constituent elements of social and labour inclusion for the population with disabilities are codified in various international, regional and national instruments. The most relevant for progress in the area of rights to education and decent work for this population at the international level is the Convention on the Rights of Persons with Disabilities. Other instruments include the ILO Discrimination (Employment and Occupation) Convention, 1958 (No. 111) and Vocational Rehabilitation and Employment (Disabled Persons) Convention, 1983 (No. 159). Despite this legal recognition, data on the social and labour inclusion of this population reveal a harsh reality.

As shown in the following figure, a very small proportion of people with disabilities achieves dual inclusion; and, in all countries, the percentage is lower than that of the population without disability. Moreover, in all countries, except Chile, the population with disabilities subject to dual exclusion exceeds 50%. These data display a discouraging scenario of inclusion of the population with disabilities and reflect the huge barriers they face to achieve social and labour inclusion. Furthermore, even among those who are "included", the quality of that inclusion remains in doubt. Accordingly, dual inclusion for the population with disabilities remains an aspiration for the time being.

Box IV.5 (concluded)

Latin America (5 countries): persons in a situation of dual inclusion, social inclusion, labour inclusion and dual exclusion, by disability status, around 2015
(Percentages)

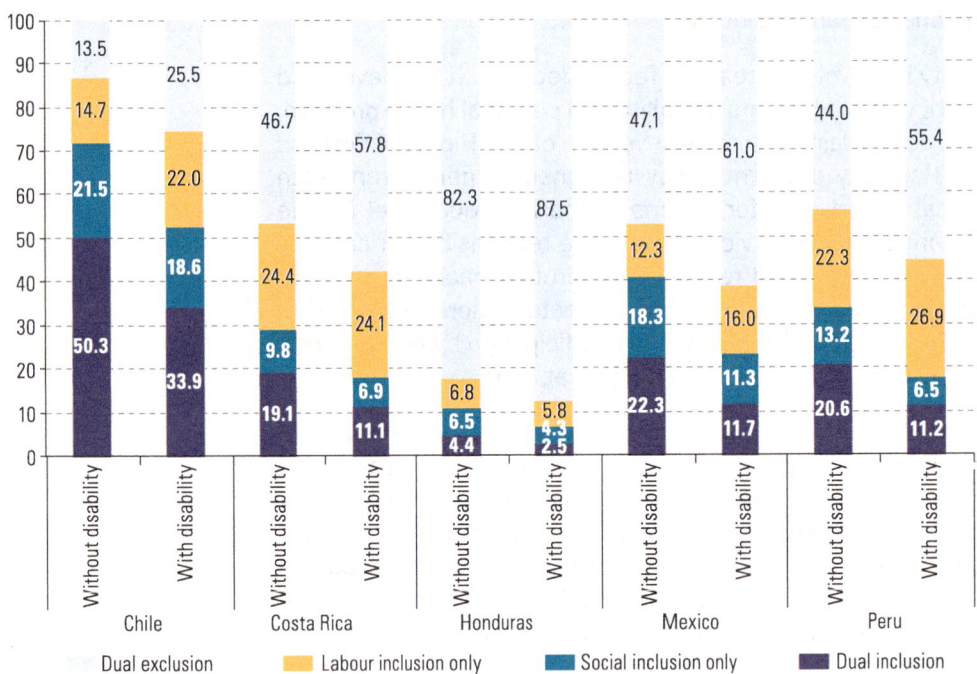

Source: Economic Commission for Latin America and the Caribbean (ECLAC), on the basis of Household Survey Data Bank (BADEHOG).

In the education domain, the exclusion of children, adolescents and young people with disabilities at all levels is not only a serious violation of their rights, but limits their future chances of participating in the labour market and in other spheres of society on equal terms. This exclusion is caused by barriers of various types: accessibility (for example, the physical accessibility of schools and transport); the school context (for example, teacher training, learning materials, adapted curricula), financial and, fundamentally, the attitudes of teachers, and of students and their parents. Expanding access to continuing education for persons with disabilities must be a priority for building more inclusive and tolerant societies.

In the work place, some of the obstacles faced by persons with disabilities operate at the individual level (low technical qualifications and low levels of soft skills) and family (low family expectations and family overprotection); or else they arise from barriers in the environment (interruptions in the chain of accessibility from home to the work place) and those faced in work places (ignorance, lack of experience with disability in work places and a non-inclusive culture). As a result, persons with disabilities experience higher unemployment rates and are more likely to be economically inactive than those without disabilities. If they are working, they are more likely to have low-paying jobs, with limited career prospects. The lack of equal employment opportunities for people with disabilities is one of the causes of poverty and exclusion of this population group and their families.

Source: Economic Commission for Latin America and the Caribbean (ECLAC), *Linkages between the social and production spheres: gaps, pillars and challenges* (LC/CDS.2/3), Santiago, 2017; International Labour Organization (ILO), *Decent work for persons with disabilities: promoting rights in the global development agenda*, Geneva, 2015; I. Zúñiga, "Capacitación para personas con discapacidad", *Project Documents* (LC/W.674), Santiago, Economic Commission for Latin America and the Caribbean (ECLAC), 2015; household surveys from the respective countries.

Lastly, there are also significant gender biases in social and, especially, labour inclusion. Women face major barriers to entering the labour market and obtaining formal jobs, largely due to the unequal distribution of time between men and women, which restricts their possibilities for undertaking paid work; and this is compounded by gender segmentation of occupations and direct discrimination. The analysis performed in this section tends to conceal the differences that exist within households, which are particularly important from a gender perspective. Accordingly, chapter V deals in greater detail with the subject of women's economic autonomy in the face of changes in the labour market.

D.   Summary and conclusions

The situation of inclusion in Latin America and the Caribbean presents a picture of light and shade. On the one hand, despite great progress in social and labour inclusion processes, the region is confronting major challenges, with significant gaps in coverage and quality in the realization of social rights, and also in people's work trajectories. Meeting these challenges becomes central in the current scenario, especially in view of the impending transformations envisioned in the world of work. Social and labour inclusion are central and complementary dimensions of inclusive social development, to guarantee a basic level of well-being for all people; and social policy must foster progress in both areas simultaneously.

The evidence presented in this chapter provides a panorama of light and shade for inclusion in the region. On the one hand, continuous improvements have been made in social inclusion indicators related to access to education, health and basic infrastructure, albeit with significant inequalities in the coverage and quality of the services. These gaps are manifested, for example, in the fact that higher education remains reserved for a minority of the population (the highest income group); a family's social level is what most explains differences in learning outcomes; and marked gender differences persist that undermine women's vocational training trajectories. Inequities between income groups in terms of affiliation or contribution to the pension and health systems also reflect the dynamics of exclusion that persist in the region. The challenges include overcoming segmentation in the quality of the benefits that are delivered through the services received by different population groups, which reflects still partial and uneven inclusion in key mechanisms for exercising rights.

There are also major challenges associated with the quality of labour force participation and the levels of unemployment, low income and high levels of vulnerability that affect a large segment of the population. The prevalence of self-employment, especially in the lower-income population, together with the lack of protection for these workers compared to those with higher incomes, and the proportion of workers who earn less than the minimum wage, or are subject to low-income underemployment, reveal the challenges that exist for labour inclusion. These include the persistence of structural gaps in labour inclusion among the rural population, women, youth, indigenous peoples and persons of African descent.

By simultaneously analysing the capacity of governments to guarantee access to social services and basic infrastructure, and people's participation in paid work under decent conditions, the results evidence substantial progress, but also indicate major challenges. The exercise of measuring dual social and labour inclusion reveals a situation that has been improving in the last decade and a half. Nonetheless, only one in four Latin American households is in a situation of dual inclusion; and the gaps are widening in the rural population and in indigenous- or Afrodescendant-headed households.

In short, the challenges identified in the review of these indicators confirms a panorama that raises issues for a region facing major challenges in ensuring social and labour inclusion for its population and in which deep inequalities persist —especially in the current context and the transformations currently unfolding in the world of work. In terms of access to social services, the region will face additional demands in the health and care sectors, associated with population aging, while it is still consolidating universal opportunities in these dimensions and in access to, and the quality of, education for children, adolescents and young people. In terms of labour inclusion, the improvements made in pension coverage, for example, or the capacity of labour incomes to sustain adequate living standards, are insufficient to close gaps. At the same time, phenomena such as the weakening of typical employment structures and the emergence of new modes of employment are intensifying. These directly affect requirements for training, education and digital inclusion, social protection systems and the quality of workers' labour force participation. A scenario is thus formed in which pre-existing deficits are compounded by emerging tensions, with uncertain results for the population's well-being.

Social and labour inclusion are central and complementary dimensions of inclusive social development, to guarantee a basic level of well-being for all people; and social policy must foster progress in these two areas simultaneously. This is a condition for advancing steadily towards the commitments assumed in the 2030 Agenda for Sustainable Development and, in particular, to fulfil its mandate of leaving no one behind. This chapter has stressed the fundamental need to adopt a universalist approach in public policies, contributing to the construction of welfare states. Within this framework it will be possible to advance towards full inclusion of the entire population, not just those who are in a situation of poverty, while disabling the marks and mechanisms that reproduce the culture of privilege (ECLAC, 2018d). This will require mobilizing specific strategies that are sensitive to differences, to close access gaps that affect certain population groups and recognize the scenario of new and pre-existing risks that have an impact on society as a whole (ECLAC, 2018d).

Governments have a set of public policies to address this twin challenge, which must be tackled in the light of the intertwined gaps that have been identified in terms of the structuring axes of social inequality, lack of decent work and changes in the spheres of technology, economy and employment, demography and the environment. In the case of labour inclusion, there is a wide array of macroeconomic, productive and sectoral policies to encourage the creation of quality jobs and foster decent work (ECLAC, 2016d and 2017a). These include reducing informal economic activity and employment; furthering women's economic autonomy, mechanisms to reconcile work and family life, and the construction of decent work trajectories for young people; policies to increase the minimum wage; unemployment insurance and other employment protection measures, as well as the prevention and eradication of forms of work that violate rights and reproduce poverty (such as child labour). It is also important to develop the capacity to foresee opportunities for creating new jobs and the demands associated with job profiles and worker skills in a scenario of continuous change. Other measures include strengthening the institutional framework of the labour market as discussed in chapter III, along with negotiation processes and the forging of agreements, public employment systems and active and passive labour market policies, among others (ECLAC, 2017a).

The priorities for social inclusion involve continuing to promote universal coverage of education, health care, housing and basic utilities, while also strengthening systems of technical and vocational education, training and skill development on a continuous and enabling basis. This includes developing skills for work, addressing the multiple inequalities that persist in this area and taking special account of the transition towards an environmentally sustainable economy and of the technological transformations that are currently under way (ECLAC, 2017a). The strengthening of universal and integrated systems of social protection (in both the contributory and the non-contributory pillars, in the dimension of labour regulation and care) is doubly linked to social and labour inclusion, insofar as its instruments, which promote access to social services and decent work, need to be articulated with labour and productive inclusion policies. All these elements are fundamental in the new world of change. Implementing universal policies that are sensitive to differences, and take account of income, gender, ethno-racial and territorial inequalities, as well as those related to the life cycle, is crucial for ensuring all people are included in well-being and sustainable development on an equal footing.

Bibliography

Abramo, L. (2015), *Uma década de promoção do trabalho decente no Brasil: uma estratégia de ação baseada no diálogo social*, Geneva, International Labour Organization (ILO), December.

Angulo, R. and N. Gómez (2014), "Inclusión social e inclusión productiva de los beneficiarios del programa Más Familias en Acción: estudio de caso de Colombia", document presented at the regional seminar Articulation between Monetary Transfers and Interventions for Social and Productive Inclusion: Differentiated Strategies in Rural Areas and Urban Areas, Antigua Guatemala, 8-9 June [online] https://dds.cepal.org/redesoc/archivos_recursos/4371/Roberto-Angulo_2014_Colombia.pdf.

Bárcena, A. (2015), "Los desafíos de América Latina y el Caribe en la actual encrucijada del desarrollo", *Revista de Trabajo*, No. 13, Buenos Aires, Ministry of Production and Labour.

CONEVAL (National Council for the Evaluation of Social Development Policy) (2017), "Nota técnica 2: ejercicio de adecuación histórica de la carencia por acceso a la seguridad social 2016 a la serie 2010-2014", Mexico City, August [online] http://www.beta.inegi.org.mx/contenidos/proyectos/investigacion/eash/2016/doc/NT2.pdf.

Corbetta, S. and others (2018), "Educación intercultural bilingüe y enfoque de interculturalidad en los sistemas educativos latinoamericanos: avances y desafíos", *Project Documents* (LC/TS.2018/98), Santiago, Economic Commission for Latin America and the Caribbean (ECLAC), November.

Del Popolo, F. (ed.) (2018), *Los pueblos indígenas en América (Abya Yala): desafíos para la igualdad en la diversidad*, ECLAC Books, No. 151 (LC/PUB.2017/26), Santiago, Economic Commission for Latin America and the Caribbean (ECLAC), January.

ECLAC (Economic Commission for Latin America and the Caribbean) (2018a), *Social Panorama of Latin America, 2017* (LC/PUB.2018/1-P), Santiago, February.

____(2018b), *Towards a regional agenda for inclusive social development: bases and initial proposal* (LC/MDS.2/2), Santiago, September.

____(2018c), *Report of the Second Session of the Regional Conference on Social Development in Latin America and the Caribbean* (LC/CDS.2/4/Rev.1), Santiago, February.

____(2018d), *The inefficiency of inequality* (LC/SES.37/3-P), Santiago, May.

____(2018e), *Economic Survey of Latin America and the Caribbean, 2018* (LC/PUB.2018/17-P), Santiago, October.

____(2018f), *The Caribbean Outlook, 2018* (LC/SES.37/14/Rev.1), Santiago, June.

____(2017a), *Linkages between the social and production spheres: gaps, pillars and challenges* (LC/CDS.2/3), Santiago, October.

____(2017b), *Social Panorama of Latin America, 2016* (LC/PUB.2017/12-P), Santiago, October.

____(2017c), "Situación de las personas afrodescendientes en América Latina y desafíos de políticas para la garantía de sus derechos", *Project Documents* (LC/TS.2017/121), Santiago, December.

____(2017d), *El mercado laboral en la subregión de Centroamérica y la República Dominicana: realidades y retos de la inserción laboral desde una perspectiva de género* (LC/MEX/TS.2017/32), Mexico City, December.

____(2016a), *The social inequality matrix in Latin America* (LC/G.2690(MDS.1/2)), Santiago, October.

____(2016b), *Social Panorama of Latin America, 2015* (LC/G.2691-P), Santiago, October.

____(2016c), *The new digital revolution: from the consumer Internet to the industrial Internet* (LC/L.4029(CMSI.5/4)/Rev.1), Santiago, August.

____(2016d), *Inclusive social development: the next generation of policies for overcoming poverty and reducing inequality in Latin America and the Caribbean* (LC.L/4056/Rev.1), Santiago, January.

____(2014), *Compacts for equality: towards a sustainable future* (LC/G.2586(SES.35/3)), Santiago, April.

____(2012), *Structural change for equality: an integrated approach to development* (LC/G.2524(SES.34/3)), Santiago, July.

____(2010a), *Time for equality: closing gaps, opening trails* (LC/G.2432(SES.33/3)), Santiago, May.

____(2010b), *Social Panorama of Latin America, 2009* (LC/G.2423-P), Santiago, April.

____(2009), *Social Panorama of Latin America, 2008* (LC/G.2402-P), Santiago, March.

____(2008), *Social Panorama of Latin America, 2007* (LC/G.2351-P), Santiago, May.

ECLAC/ILO (Economic Commission for Latin America and the Caribbean/International Labour Organization) (2018), "Labour market participation of older persons: needs and options", *Employment Situation in Latin America and the Caribbean*, No. 18 (LC/TS.2018/39), Santiago, May.

___(2017), "The transition of young people from school to the labour market", *Employment Situation in Latin America and the Caribbean*, No. 17 (LC/TS.2017/86), Santiago, October.

Ferro, G. (2017), "América Latina y el Caribe hacia los Objetivos de Desarrollo Sostenible en agua y saneamiento: reformas recientes de las políticas sectoriales", *Natural Resources and Infrastructure series*, No. 180 (LC/TS.2017/17), Santiago, Economic Commission for Latin America and the Caribbean (ECLAC), April.

Gontero, S. and J. Weller (2015), "¿Estudias o trabajas? El largo camino hacia la independencia de los jóvenes de América Latina", *Macroeconomics of Development series*, No. 169 (LC/L.4103), Santiago, Economic Commission for Latin America and the Caribbean (ECLAC), September.

Gros, C. and J. Foyer (eds.) (2010), ¿Desarrollo con identidad?: gobernanza económica indígena: siete estudios de caso, Lima, French Institute of Andean Studies/Facultad Latinoamericana de Ciencias Sociales/Center for Mexican and Central American Studies (IFEA/FLACSO/CEMCA), June.

ILO (International Labour Organization) (2016), *2016 Labour Overview of Latin America and the Caribbean*, Lima.

___(1999), "Report of the Director-General: decent work", Geneva, June [online] https://www.ilo.org/public/english/standards/relm/ilc/ilc87/rep-i.htm.

Levitas, R. and others (2007), *The multi-dimensional analysis of social exclusion*, Bristol, University of Bristol, January.

Maldonado, C., J. Martínez and R. Martínez (2018), "Protección social y migración: una mirada desde las vulnerabilidades a lo largo del ciclo de la migración y de la vida de las personas", *Project Documents* (LC/TS.2018/62), Santiago, Economic Commission for Latin America and the Caribbean (ECLAC), September.

Martínez, J. and D. Sánchez-Ancochea (2013), *Good Jobs and Social Services: How Costa Rica Achieved the Elusive Double Incorporation*, Basingstoke, Palgrave Macmillan, January.

Novick, M. (2018), "El mundo del trabajo: cambios y desafíos de inclusión", *Social Policy series*, No. 228 (LC/TS.2018/2), Santiago, Economic Commission for Latin America and the Caribbean (ECLAC), January.

OECD/ECLAC/CAF (Organization for Economic Cooperation and Development/Economic Commission for Latin America and the Caribbean/Development Bank of Latin America) (2016), *Latin American Economic Outlook 2017: Youth, Skills and Entrepreneurship* (LC/G.2689), Paris, October.

Rico, M. N. and D. Trucco (2014), "Adolescentes: derecho a la educación y al bienestar futuro", *Social Policy series*, No. 190 (LC/L.3791), Santiago, Economic Commission for Latin America and the Caribbean/United Nations Children's Fund (ECLAC/UNICEF), March.

Rodgers, G. (2002), "El trabajo decente como una meta para la economía global", *CINTERFOR Bulletin*, No. 153, Montevideo, Inter-American Centre for Knowledge Development in Vocational Training/International Labour Organization (CINTERFOR/ILO).

Rossel, C. (2012), "Protección social y pobreza rural en América Latina", document presented at the VII international seminar on Food Security, Rural Poverty and Social Protection in Latin America and the Caribbean, Santiago, 22-23 November [online] http://www.fao.org/3/a-au333s.pdf.

Titelman D., O. Cetrángolo and O. Acosta (2015), "La cobertura universal de salud en los países de América Latina: cómo mejorar los esquemas basados en la solidaridad", *MEDICC Review*, vol. 17, Oakland, MEDICC.

Trucco, D. and H. Ullmann (eds.) (2015), *Youth: realities and challenges for achieving development with equality*, ECLAC Books, No. 137 (LC/G.2647-P), Santiago, Economic Commission for Latin America and the Caribbean (ECLAC), September.

United Nations (2016), *Report on the World Social Situation, 2016. Leaving no one behind: the imperative of inclusive development* (ST/ESA/362), New York.

___(2015), *Transforming our world: the 2030 Agenda for Sustainable Development* (A/RES/70/1), New York, October.

___(1995), *Report of the World Summit for Social Development* (A/CONF.166/9), Copenhagen, April.

___(1969), "Declaration on Social Progress and Development" (A/RES/2542(XXIV)), New York, 11 December [online] http://undocs.org/es/A/RES/2542(XXIV).

____(1966), "International Covenant on Economic, Social and Cultural Rights" (A/RES/2200(XXI)), New York, 16 December [online] https://undocs.org/es/A/RES/2200(XXI).

____(1948), "International Bill of Human Rights" (A/RES/217(III)), Paris, 10 December [online] https://undocs.org/es/A/RES/217(III).

Weller, J. (comp.) (2017), "Empleo en América Latina y el Caribe: textos seleccionados 2006-2017", *Select Pages of ECLAC* (LC/M.2017/4), Santiago, Economic Commission for Latin America and the Caribbean (ECLAC), November.

Weller, J. and S. Gontero (2017), "Consideraciones para aumentar la participación de los trabajadores por cuenta propia en los sistemas contributivos de protección social en América Latina", *Macroeconomics of Development series*, No. 189 (LC/TS.2017/69), Santiago, Economic Commission for Latin America and the Caribbean (ECLAC), August.

Weller, J. and C. Kaldewey (2013), "Empleo, crecimiento sostenible e igualdad", *Macroeconomics of Development series*, No. 145 (LC/L.3743), Santiago, Economic Commission for Latin America and the Caribbean (ECLAC), December.

Annex IV.A1

Table IV.A1.1

Latin America (18 countries): 20–29 year-olds with secondary and four years of tertiary education completed, by age group and highest and lowest income quintiles, around 2016[a]
(Percentages)

	20–24 year-olds with complete secondary education				25–29 year-olds with complete tertiary education (4 years of study)			
	Average	Quintile I	QuintileV	Gap	Average	Quintile I	QuintileV	Gap
Argentina (2016)[b]	66.6	51.9	89.3	37.4	24.1	9.0	48.3	39.3
Bolivia (Plurinational State of) (2015)	70.3	44.3	83.6	39.3	23.2	5.1	42.0	37.0
Brazil (2015)	64.2	38.8	89.4	50.6	15.5	2.3	46.1	43.8
Chile (2015)	86.3	74.5	95.7	21.2	26.1	6.4	57.5	51.1
Colombia (2016)	73.2	45.2	92.7	47.5	17.3	2.3	46.9	44.6
Costa Rica (2016)	58.2	27.4	88.8	61.4	16.3	1.6	43.1	41.5
Dominican Republic (2016)	61.5	42.6	78.4	35.8	9.9	0.8	26.2	25.4
Ecuador (2016)	67.0	47.9	88.9	41.0	14.2	3.9	33.2	29.3
Guatemala (2014)	33.1	9.6	69.4	59.9	18.3	3.2	42.3	39.1
Honduras (2016)	37.7	11.9	67.3	55.5	6.4	1.5	18.7	17.2
Mexico (2016)	53.5	27.2	79.5	52.3	7.6	0.6	25.8	25.3
Nicaragua (2014)	44.2	26.9	72.0	45.1	20.3	2.7	50.9	48.3
Panama (2016)	62.8	24.0	92.1	68.1	14.5	2.8	39.8	37.1
Peru (2016)	82.2	58.6	93.4	34.8	21.2	3.9	52.5	48.5
Paraguay (2016)	61.5	28.1	84.8	56.7	36.0	7.1	64.8	57.7
El Salvador (2016)	40.3	12.7	70.5	57.8	18.1	2.6	38.1	35.5
Uruguay (2016)	36.6	8.7	73.4	64.7	13.5	0.0	35.2	35.2
Venezuela (Bolivarian Republic of) (2014)	72.6	57.8	84.6	26.7	23.2	9.0	39.8	30.8
Latin America	59.5	35.4	83.0	47.5	18.1	3.6	41.7	38.1

Source: Economic Commission for Latin America and the Caribbean (ECLAC), on the basis of Household Survey Data Bank (BADEHOG).
[a] The gap is calculated as the percentage-point difference between quintiles V and I.
[b] The data correspond to urban areas only.

Table IV.A1.2

Latin America (6 countries): economically active population (EAP), working-age population, employment rate and unemployment rate, by gender and migration status, around 2015
(Percentages)

Country	Population	Working-age population			EAP			Employed			Unemployed
		Total	Men	Women	Total	Men	Women	Total	Men	Women	Total
Argentina	Local	64.9	64.9	64.9	60.1	72.5	48.9	56.0	68.2	45.0	7.0
	Long-term migrants	71.0	70.3	71.5	54.0	68.7	42.0	51.3	64.8	40.3	5.2
	Recent migrants	87.0	96.5	78.7	73.7	73.5	74.0	65.2	61.68[a]	68.87[a]	12.3
Brazil	Local	69.2	69.0	69.3	64.8	76.2	54.4	58.6	70.2	48.0	9.6
	Long-term migrants	55.8	59.5	51.3	54.8	67.8	38.8	52.6	65.5	36.8	4.1
	Recent migrants	77.4	78.4	76.1	80.2	91.6	65.1	67.7	84.2	45.83[a]	15.6
Chile	Local	72.1	72.8	71.5	59.8	73.8	48.2	55.6	69.2	44.3	7.1
	Long-term migrants	82.8	79.1	86.2	73.6	83.6	65.3	69.6	79.6	61.4	5.4
	Recent migrants	84.1	83.8	84.4	82.4	93.1	72.2	76.7	87.8	66.2	6.9
Costa Rica	Local	67.3	67.0	67.7	59.1	73.6	45.6	54.1	68.3	40.9	8.5
	Long-term migrants	85.7	86.1	85.4	69.3	85.6	54.9	63.8	80.5	49.1	8.0
	Recent migrants	83.2	86.7	79.5	68.2	80.0	54.8	57.4	69.5	43.75[a]	15.4
Mexico	Local	64.9	64.0	65.8	61.4	79.8	44.7	58.3	75.0	43.1	5.3
	Recent migrants	79.7	84.2	71.7	76.3	91.8	43.8	70.5	84.0	42.1	8.0
Uruguay	Local	65.3	66.5	64.2	65.1	74.5	56.5	60.2	69.8	51.5	7.5
	Long-term migrants	57.2	60.0	54.7	55.9	67.2	46.5	52.1	62.7	43.1	6.9
	Recent migrants	74.4	71.9	76.7	80.0	87.6	73.1	70.0	77.4	63.5	12.4

Source: I. Carrasco and J. Suárez, "Migración internacional e inclusión en América Latina: análisis en los países de destino mediante encuestas de hogares", *Social Policy series*, No. 231 (LC/TS.2018/57), Santiago, Economic Commission for Latin America and the Caribbean (ECLAC), 2018; on the basis of household surveys from the respective countries.
Note: Long-term migration corresponds to migrants who have lived in their country of destination for more than five years; recent migration corresponds to a residence period of five years or less.
[a] The sample size (N) comprises fewer than 40 cases.

Table IV.A1.3
Latin America (17 countries): households in a situation of social inclusion, labour inclusion,
dual exclusion and dual inclusion, by country, around 2016
(Percentages)

Country	Social inclusion	Labour inclusion	Dual exclusion	Dual inclusion
Argentina	60.7	52.7	23.7	37.0
Bolivia (Plurinational State of)[a]	39.7	20.2	53.8	13.7
Brazil[a]	44.3	54.6	30.3	29.2
Chile[a]	71.5	66.4	13.3	51.2
Colombia	40.6	63.9	27.1	31.7
Costa Rica	34.3	47.0	42.3	23.6
Dominican Republic	42.6	47.8	36.0	26.4
Ecuador	41.4	32.4	47.0	20.8
El Salvador	25.3	25.6	62.5	13.5
Guatemala[b]	14.5	16.8	75.5	6.7
Honduras	18.8	15.2	73.3	7.2
Mexico	46.7	37.3	41.4	25.4
Nicaragua[h]	18.0	19.7	69.6	7.4
Paraguay	34.0	21.7	58.9	14.6
Peru	36.7	45.7	41.3	23.7
Uruguay	51.7	75.1	18.1	44.9
Venezuela (Bolivarian Republic of)[b]	43.2	35.2	42.0	20.4
Latin America[c]	39.1	39.8	44.5	23.5

Source: Economic Commission for Latin America and the Caribbean (ECLAC), on the basis of Household Survey Data Bank (BADEHOG).
[a] Data correspond to 2015.
[b] Data correspond to 2014.
[c] Simple average.

Women's economic autonomy in a changing labour market

Introduction

In Latin America and the Caribbean, there are all sorts of structural constraints that limit the full enjoyment of women's rights and progress towards gender equality. Globalization, changing demographic patterns, climate change, economic conditions and inequality in technology access and use within and between countries pose additional challenges. In addition, the appearance, interaction and confluence of a whole number of disruptive technologies have all the features of a new technological revolution. The rapid changes associated with existing and emerging technologies are making themselves felt in a number of dimensions of development, creating opportunities and challenges for societies and economies; in particular, they are giving rise to new scenarios for the world of work.

All-round analysis of the world of work is required, encompassing both the dynamics of work for the market and those of unpaid work done in the home for the benefit of societies, which underpins the functioning of the economy.

These new situations necessitate an analysis of the extent to which technological changes will create new opportunities to improve jobs or will further polarize the world of work. The countries of the region are faced with the challenge of harnessing the transformative potential of the technological revolution, anticipating the effects it will have on productivity, growth, development and equality. This means adapting technologies to each country's structures and development needs, not only as a production policy aimed at improving the integration of the Latin American and Caribbean countries into the global economy, but also as a means of closing structural gaps more rapidly, particularly gender gaps in the labour market.

Without effective intersectoral public policies designed to do away with the sexual division of labour, gender segregation and discrimination in the labour market, gender gaps in technology use and segregation in education and in technical and vocational training, there will be differentiated impacts for men and women in employment access and quality which, far from closing the gaps, are likely to widen them.

The purpose of this chapter of *Social Panorama* is to use statistical information to reveal some of the structural constraints of gender inequality in the world of work. Section A deals with the situation of women in the labour market and warns of the possible effects of technological change on the complex processes of job creation, destruction and transformation, which may have significant impacts on women's work. Section B deals with gender biases in education and technical and vocational training systems and the challenges they face in meeting the demand for new skills. Section C recognizes unpaid domestic and care work as a cornerstone of life in society and its contribution to countries' economies, while emphasizing that closing gaps in the labour market results not only in better opportunities for women, but also in economic growth. Lastly, section D proposes intersectoral public policies to deal with current structural constraints and possible future threats while helping to exploit the opportunities that have been opening up in these new circumstances for progress with decent work for men and women.

A. Risks and challenges for women in the labour market

Trends show that women have a lower rate of participation in employment than men and are more concentrated in vulnerable and low-productivity sectors. The excessive burden of unpaid work, horizontal and vertical segmentation in the labour market and the gender segregation of occupations act as barriers to full inclusion in the labour market under decent working conditions. With the changes in employment and occupations that are in prospect, women run the risk of being excluded from the benefits of the jobs of the future unless the right public policies are implemented.

1.   The current situation: segmentation and gaps

The labour market plays a fundamental role in income distribution and in the recognition and exercise of men's and women's rights (ECLAC, 2016a). The large gaps in women's participation in this market in Latin America and the Caribbean are thus a cause for concern. Although the female participation rate increased by 5.3 percentage points between 1997 and 2007, growth has been moderate since then. It averaged 50.2% in the third quarter of 2017, compared with a male participation rate of 74.4% (see figure V.1).

Figure V.1
Latin America and the Caribbean (weighted average for 24 countries): activity and employment rates, by sex, 2007–2017
(Percentages)

Source: Economic Commission for Latin America and the Caribbean (ECLAC), on the basis of International Labour Organization, *2017 Labour Overview of Latin America and the Caribbean*, Lima, 2017.

Although the female labour force participation rate has increased greatly in recent decades, to the point where it is above the world average (48.5% according to ILO, 2018a), this has not been matched by an increase in time spent by men on unpaid work, owing to social, cultural and demographic factors. The results are, first, that there is a group of women who are unable to participate in the labour market because of family situations, particularly care for dependents (between 12% and 66% of women who are not employed, depending on the country, compared with a figure of less than 6% for men who are outside the labour market because of family situations) (ECLAC, 2016a). Second, total working hours (combined hours spent on paid and unpaid work) are longer for women who do manage to participate in the labour market than they are for men (ECLAC, 2017c).

Low labour market participation is compounded by the fact that many women who do enter the labour market looking for work do not find it or obtain only low-quality jobs. In recent years, the increased participation of women in the labour market, together with a slower rate of job creation, has resulted in an increase in female unemployment, which is still higher than men's. In 2012, average unemployment rates in Latin America and the Caribbean were 7.9% for women and 5.4% for men. By 2017, these rates had risen to 10.4% and 7.6%, respectively, so that the gap between the two was still over 2 percentage points (see figure V.1).

Latin American labour markets are also characterized by marked horizontal segmentation as a result of the great structural heterogeneity and constraints constituting gender inequality, which restricts women's labour market participation and leaves them concentrated in certain sectors of the economy. Figure V.2 shows that as of around 2016, an average of 21.9% of women were working in commerce, a sector that also employed a large percentage of men (17.7%). The Central American countries, most notably Guatemala (36.1%), El Salvador (30.2%), Nicaragua (29.5%) and Honduras (28.2%), had the highest concentrations of women workers in this sector. In contrast, Argentina, Brazil and Uruguay had lower rates of female employment in the commerce sector (16.5%, 17.5% and 18%, respectively). The heavy concentration of women in commerce, domestic service and accommodation and food service activities has been associated with a high incidence of part-time work and relatively low wages (ILO, 2016).

Figure V.2
Latin America (weighted averages of 16 countries): distribution of the employed population by sector of economic activity, around 2016[a][b]
(Percentages)

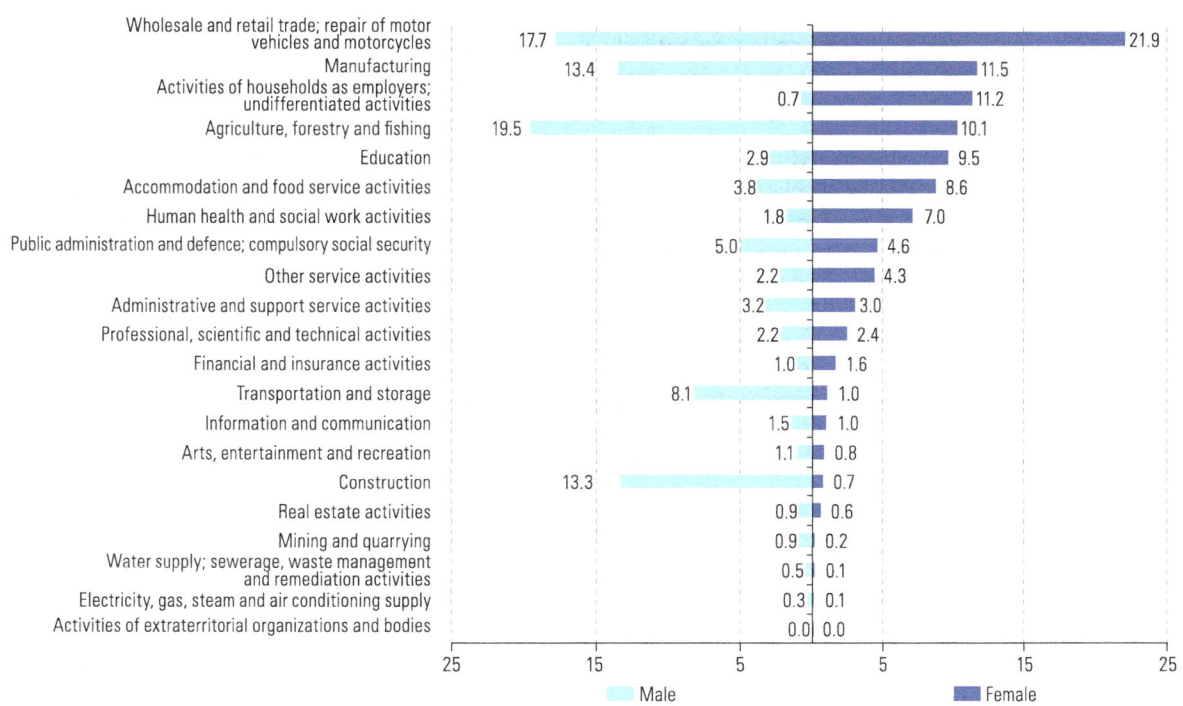

Source: Economic Commission for Latin America and the Caribbean (ECLAC), on the basis of the Household Survey Data Bank (BADEHOG).
[a] Sectors of economic activity have been standardized in accordance with the International Standard Industrial Classification of All Economic Activities (ISIC), Rev. 4.
[b] The data are for 2016 in the cases of Argentina, Colombia, Costa Rica, Ecuador, El Salvador, Honduras, Mexico, Panama, Peru and Uruguay, 2015 in the cases of Brazil, Chile and the Plurinational State of Bolivia and 2014 in the cases of the Bolivarian Republic of Venezuela, Guatemala and Nicaragua.

The second largest sector for female employment in the region is manufacturing, accounting for 11.5% of employed women. In most of the countries, a greater proportion of men than women participate in this sector, the exceptions being Colombia (11.7% of employed women), Guatemala (16.3%), Nicaragua (13.5%), El Salvador (16.7%) and Honduras (19.4%). In the last four countries, the strong presence of female employees in maquiladora firms could explain this characteristic of employment (ECLAC, 2010a). Mexico is another country with strong maquiladora activity owing to the manufacture of textile products in general and the metal industry (INEGI, 2018). Both men (16.9%) and women (16%) have high participation rates in this sector.

In addition, there are some "masculinized" sectors that employ almost no women but large numbers of men in the region. This is the case with construction and transportation, which account for 13.3% and 8.1% of male employment, respectively. An analysis of the structure of the labour market by country shows that whereas no more than 1.6% of women are employed in the construction sector in any country, the figure for men is over 7% in all countries. The countries with the highest percentages of male employment in this sector are Panama and the Plurinational State of Bolivia (both with 15.8%), Argentina (15.4%), Chile (15.3%) and Brazil (15.2%).

The care sector (education, health, social work and domestic employment) is a large source of employment for women.[1] The proportion of women working in care industries in the region is 27.7%, while only 5.4% of men are employed there. The countries with the highest concentrations of women in the paid care sector are Argentina (42.8%), Uruguay (38.4%), Chile (34.9%), Brazil (33.7%), Costa Rica (32.6%) and the Bolivarian Republic of Venezuela (30.5%). The highest rate of male employment in the sector is in Chile, where it is 8.4%.

This overrepresentation of women in the care sector is an extension to the labour market of the role assigned to them as carers, which can be attributed to social assumptions about the existence of an innate aptitude in women for this type of work. For example, certain branches of education, particularly the teaching of the youngest children, are seen as an extension of women's traditional maternal role (ILO, 2016).

The health and social work sector not only employs a large percentage of the region's women but is one of the sectors with large differences in earnings between men and women, reflecting considerable gender segregation in occupations. Uruguay and Argentina have the highest proportions of women participating in this sector, with 14% and 10.9% of female employment, respectively. The Bolivarian Republic of Venezuela, Brazil, Chile, Costa Rica, Honduras and Panama have rates above 5% (between 6.8% and 9%).

While the incomes, job quality and skill levels that characterize women workers in the health and education sectors vary greatly, large segments of these categories are exposed to low wages, long working hours, substandard working conditions, a lack of social protection and, in all likelihood, discriminatory practices. For example, it is common for health workers who provide services to households to receive lower wages, lack adequate training and work very long hours under extreme conditions (ILO, 2018c).

The household sector employs an average of 11.2% of women and is characterized by having the lowest earnings in the economy. Women in this sector are generally engaged in domestic work and paid care, i.e., they are the ones working in domestic service or as caregivers in the homes of sick dependents, children and older adults. The highest proportions are found in Argentina (17.8%), Costa Rica (17.7%), Brazil (14.2%) and Uruguay (13.9%). For there to be good quality care jobs that promote gender equality and benefit all

---

[1]   These figures are based on a broad definition of care that includes all those working in education, health and social services and those providing services in households. Not all occupations in these sectors directly involve caring for children or dependent persons. Although teaching and health care exhibit large differences in the skills required, the services provided (and the potential for them to be replaced by services provided by households) and the pay associated with the different occupations, the present chapter does not examine these differences in detail.

parties involved, transformative public policies are needed to guarantee both decent work for those employed for pay in the care sector and the necessary quality of care for those who need it. Recognition of the work of unpaid carers is also essential (Calderón Magaña, 2013; ECLAC, 2016a; ILO, 2018c).

The agriculture, forestry and fishing sector is a major employer of men and women in several countries of the region. In an analysis by occupational category, there are marked gender differences in the quality of employment. For example, this sector accounts for 27.5% of employed Bolivian men and 28.4% of employed Bolivian women, 27.5% of employed Ecuadorean men and 23% of employed Ecuadorian women, and 30% of employed Peruvian men and 24.7% of employed Peruvian women. In Ecuador, Peru and the Plurinational State of Bolivia, unpaid family work is the most common occupational category for women employed in this sector, accounting for 64%, 44% and 51% of the distribution of female employment, respectively. In the case of men, in none of the three countries does unpaid family work exceed 20% of employment in the sector (the lowest proportion is in Peru, with 9%). The bulk of male employment in this sector is in own-account work in the Plurinational State of Bolivia and Peru (66% and 61% of the distribution, respectively), and in wage work (48% of the distribution) followed by own-account work (37% of those employed in this sector) in Ecuador.

Another manifestation of the patriarchal order in the labour market is occupational gender segregation, evinced by a high concentration of women in professions and trades that require fewer skills and in lower pay for occupations where women are more heavily represented. More than half of women are employed in low-skilled jobs: they are heavily concentrated in occupations such as sales work and other services (29.5%) and unskilled jobs (26%) (see figure V.3). In the case of men, there is greater dispersion across occupational categories. In particular, men are overrepresented in occupations such as plant and machine operators, craft and related workers, and farmers. With regard to income by type of occupation, the average hourly wages of men are higher than those of women in all these activities. The greatest difference is found among service workers, with women having hourly wages 19.8% lower than men's —this being precisely the occupation that accounts for the largest proportion of women in the labour market.

Irrespective of the economic sectors or occupational categories in which women engage in paid employment, they usually work under worse conditions than men, in more vulnerable jobs, without contracts and without access to social benefits (Weller and Roethlisberger, 2011; ECLAC, 2017a).

These more adverse working conditions are due in part to the fact that women tend to work in low-productivity sectors, since there is a significant relationship between the degree of formality of jobs and levels of productivity (ECLAC, 2018a). For example, an average of 51.8% of women in the region are employed in low-productivity sectors, of whom 82.2% are not affiliated with or do not pay into a pension system (see figure V.4). Women's greater tendency to seek shorter working hours or interrupt their careers to reconcile work for the market with care responsibilities (in the absence of adequate care systems or a better distribution of domestic and unpaid care work between men and women in households) leads to disparities in social protection between men and women. Likewise, the overrepresentation of women in informal and insecure work affects their ability to consolidate pension rights in the contributory pension system, threatening their economic autonomy in old age (ILO, 2018a). This is not homogeneous across countries in the region but varies depending on the structure of the labour market (for example, the extent of formalization and wage employment) and labour institutions (legislation, the scale and dynamics of collective bargaining and labour inspection arrangements, among other factors). In Uruguay, for example, 51.9% of women employed in low-productivity sectors do not contribute to social security, while in Nicaragua and Peru the proportion is 99%. Conversely, 88.8% of Latin American workers who contribute to social security are in medium- and high-productivity jobs (ECLAC, 2018a).

Figure V.3

Latin America (weighted averages of 9 countries): distribution of the employed population and wage gaps between women and men, by occupation type and sex, around 2016[a][b][c]
(Percentages)

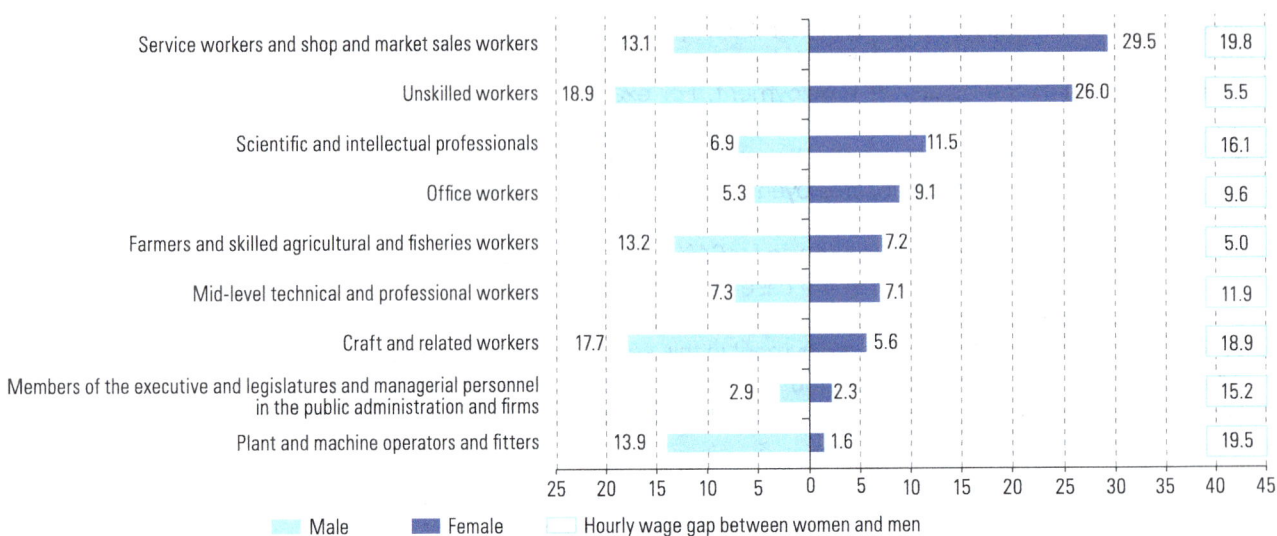

Source: Economic Commission for Latin America and the Caribbean (ECLAC), on the basis of the Household Survey Data Bank (BADEHOG).
[a] The left side of the figure refers to the total employed population of 15 years of age and over. The right side refers to the waged population. The wage gap refers to the difference in labour earnings difference between waged women aged 20–49 working 35 or more hours per week in urban areas and men with the same characteristics.
[b] The data are for 2016 in the cases of Argentina, Costa Rica, Ecuador, El Salvador, Panama, Peru and Uruguay and 2015 for Chile and the Plurinational State of Bolivia.
[c] Occupations were standardized for countries with information organized in accordance with the International Standard Classification of Occupations (ISCO-88).

Figure V.4

Latin America (weighted average for 18 countries): women aged between 15 and 64 employed in low-productivity sectors as a proportion of all those employed, and women affiliated to or paying into pension systems, around 2016[a][b]
(Percentages)

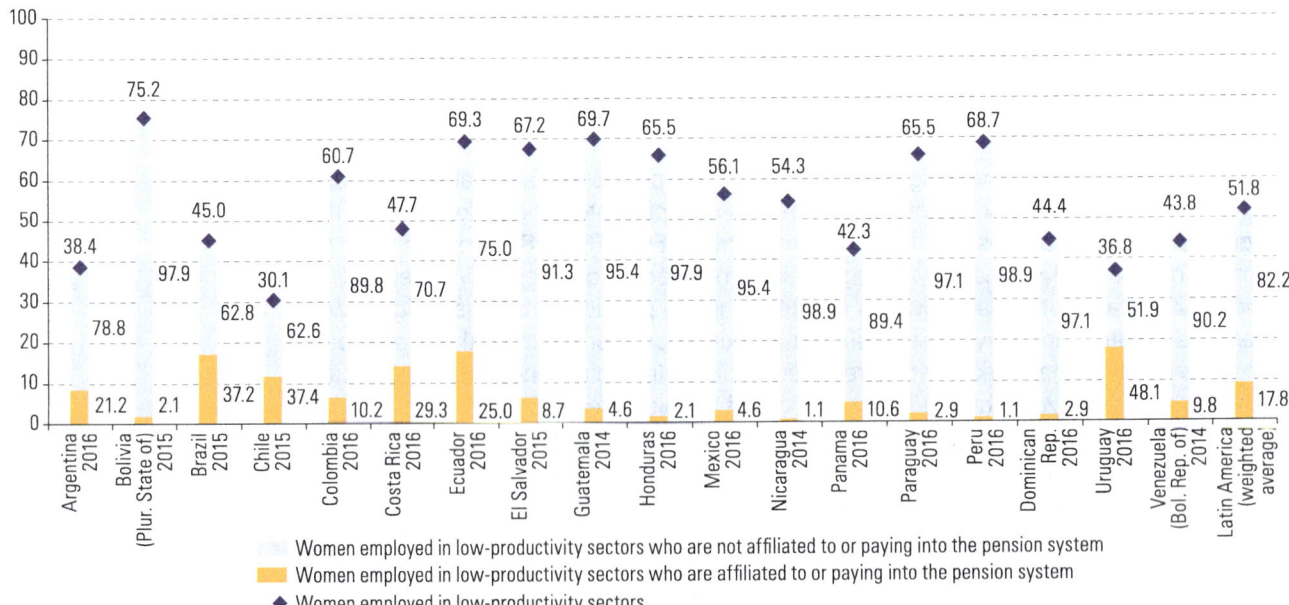

Source: Economic Commission for Latin America and the Caribbean (ECLAC), on the basis of the Household Survey Data Bank (BADEHOG).
[a] Each country's household surveys provide information on affiliation or contributions to a pension system. The countries presenting affiliation data are: the Dominican Republic, Ecuador, Guatemala and the Plurinational State of Bolivia.
[b] The data are for 2016 except in the cases of the Bolivarian Republic of Venezuela, Brazil, Chile, El Salvador, Guatemala, Nicaragua and the Plurinational State of Bolivia. Data are national totals except in the case of Argentina, where they cover 31 conurbations.

Gender inequalities in the labour market are also manifested in vertical segregation, i.e., the difficulties women experience in developing professionally and gaining access to positions with greater decision-making power and better pay. There is a "glass ceiling" of invisible factors such as gender stereotypes and prejudices, unfavourable corporate policies and insufficient experience for managerial positions which have an impact on this situation (ECLAC, 2013). Women tend to be employed at the lower levels of the hierarchical structure, and once in this position they usually remain trapped in the lowest-paying, lowest-ranking or least responsible jobs. These factors make it more difficult for them to move up to managerial positions. Thus, a large proportion of women are excluded from economic decision-making and influence, and this acts as a major obstacle to progress towards gender equality and a greater impetus towards sustainable development (ECLAC, 2016a).

Women's lower participation in employment, concentration in lower-productivity sectors and tendency to hold informal or lower quality jobs are factors that have a significant impact on their ability to generate their own income, limiting their economic autonomy. In addition, the differences in the types of work done by men and women, the production sectors in which they are mainly employed and the time they can spend on paid work have a direct impact on the income gaps between them.

The differences in income between men and women cannot be explained only by the different economic sectors they work in. Given the same level of education and experience, women tend to earn lower wages than men, which reflects persistent discrimination. For example, in the case of urban wage earners between the ages of 20 and 49 who are engaged in paid work for 35 hours or more per week, the average income of women is only 83.9% that of men (ECLAC, 2016a). The greatest gap is in the sector with the highest level of education, which shows that greater investment in educating women does not necessarily bring them closer to men in their earnings prospects (ECLAC, 2016a).

Career breaks to accommodate domestic and care responsibilities, gender prejudices and stereotypes and discriminatory corporate cultures reduce women's opportunities to enter and gain experience in the labour market. This is a key determinant of their medium-term occupational and earnings prospects (ECLAC, 2013) and reduces their ability to adapt to the challenges of technological change.

2. Technological change: opportunities and risks for women

Since inequality in the region is heavily determined by its production structure, the production paradigm shift brought about by the fourth industrial revolution is creating opportunities to close inequality gaps. Technological change is occurring at an exponential rate and its effects have spread throughout the economy and society, transforming entire production, management and governance systems (ECLAC, 2018a). The development of digital technologies has been fundamental in altering economic structures and forms of production and consumption by making it possible to create digital goods and services, add digital value to non-digital products and make use of digital platforms (ECLAC, 2016b).

The dynamics of technological change are giving rise to concerns and uncertainty about the effects on employment and labour relations (ECLAC, 2018a). If they are not approached in a manner calculated to do away with the structural constraints of inequality, these changes will have differentiated gender effects, and women's ability to take advantage of the opportunities offered by technology will be jeopardized. Without the right public policies, women will face new challenges and risks in their prospects of participating in the labour market under decent working conditions and may be excluded from the benefits of the jobs of the future.

The digital technological revolution has disrupted the workplace in various ways. One is the emergence of business models based on digital platforms, with new technologies allowing for more flexible working models but at the same time potentially producing poorer working conditions that, given the characteristics of the labour market, could significantly affect women.[2] Another is industry 4.0, characterized by improvements in the cognitive capacities of robots and machines driven by the development of artificial intelligence technologies, which will have a great impact on the labour market (ECLAC, 2018a). It is still difficult to analyse the consequences for employment in the medium and long term, but it is certain that technological changes will make the current functioning of the labour market obsolete in many dimensions, with far-reaching effects on the dynamics of job destruction and creation, the characteristics of future jobs, the skills required for them and the ways in which work will be organized (Weller, 2017). New technologies will displace many low-skilled routine jobs while requiring human resources with new skills to implement and manage the new jobs.

The technological revolution is not only allowing routine tasks to be automated but is generating deep disruptions in other types of activities owing to the growing cognitive capacities of robots and machines (see box V.1) (ECLAC, 2018a). For this reason, new technologies threaten jobs not only in manufacturing sectors but also in service activities, most particularly a number of roles in which women are strongly represented. It is likely that many jobs for which women represent a high proportion of the workforce will be lost and that women will struggle more to access the new jobs that will be created because they are underrepresented in potentially more dynamic sectors.

Box V.1
The risk of automation in female-dominated sectors

There are numerous studies estimating the effects of automation developments on employment. They include Frey and Osborne (2013), World Bank (2016), OECD/ECLAC/CAF (2016), OECD (2017), Manyika, J. and others (2017) and Cadena and others (2017). Although their quantitative results differ, all point to a significant impact that would alter labour market conditions across multiple sectors or activities. In the light of these analyses, the current situation of women in some sectors and occupations with a greater likelihood of job replacement will now be examined.

Care work

This is the sector accounting for the largest proportion of employed women (27.6%). It comprises: (i) health care and social work, (ii) education and (iii) activities of households as employers and undifferentiated goods- and services-producing activities of households for own use.

In the health sector, women are concentrated in the "mid-level professionals, scientists or technicians" classification, where most work as nurses or health assistants. According to Frey and Osborne (2013), these occupations have a low probability of automation, as they require sound social intelligence skills such as emotional support and empathy. OECD (2017) agrees that the health sector is at low risk of automation, but points out that, since it is a sector that accounts for a large share of female employment, the absolute number of women workers at risk of being displaced is large.

The dynamics in the education sector are similar to those indicated for the health sector, so that the likelihood of teaching or kindergarten work being automated is very low, as long as teaching is understood as a comprehensive process of intellectual, moral and affective integration into society.

In the household activities sector, unskilled female workers make up more than 75% of women employed. This sector employs domestic workers, who are among the lowest-paid in the region and suffer from large social protection deficits.

---

[2]   By business models based on digital platforms are meant those employing Internet-based platforms to provide services to customers in specific tasks through crowdwork (an online services market where providers do not have to be physically present) or work commissioned through applications (the service provider must be physically present).

Box V.1 (concluded)

The relational nature of some of the tasks involved in care work limits the scope for human labour to be replaced by robots or other technologies. Women account for 72.9% of employment in the care sector in the region. In addition, population ageing provides grounds for anticipating greater demand for care services, creating an opportunity to employ more women. However, if the aim is to do away with the discrimination affecting women in the labour market, it is important to properly address the gender gaps that exist in this sector in terms of employment quality. Care work, paid and unpaid, is crucial to the future of work.

Wholesale and retail

A large number of women work in this sector in Latin America (21.9% on average), with most being classified as service workers and shop and market sales workers (71.4% of women in the sector). The concentration of women in these occupations exceeds the regional average in countries such as Argentina (74.5%), Ecuador (83%), El Salvador (85%), the Plurinational State of Bolivia (91.1%) and Uruguay (72.7%).

The sales and services sector includes occupations at high risk of automation. Frey and Osborne (2013) find that a large part of the commerce sector is made up of occupations that are at high risk of automation (47% of jobs). These mainly include occupations such as cashiers and the areas of telesales and telephony services.

Manufacturing

OECD/ECLAC/CAF (2016) estimates a net loss of 3.38 million jobs by 2030 and maintains that these declines will be concentrated in manufacturing. On average, this sector accounts for 11.6% of working women, the majority of whom (53%) are employed in occupations classified as "craft and related workers". This occupation has many routine tasks requiring a low cognitive level, putting it at high risk of rapid automation. Countries such as Colombia, El Salvador, Guatemala, Honduras and Mexico, where large proportions of women are employed in this sector, also have large proportions of women working as craft and related workers (63.4%, 53.4%, 55.1%, 81.8% and 63.7%, respectively).[a]

The studies mentioned highlight the negative correlation between education and the likelihood of an occupation being automated. The high concentration of women in occupations requiring levels of capabilities associated with lower levels of education means that they are vulnerable to automation. Frey and Osborne (2013) also point out that there is a negative correlation between the likelihood of automation and wage levels, something that is particularly risky for women because of their overrepresentation in the working population with lower earnings. However, low wages can reduce the economic incentives (returns) to invest in technically feasible automation processes, which can be very capital-intensive. It is therefore always important to distinguish between the technical feasibility, economic profitability and political and social acceptability of each specific automation process.

The information presented shows a high risk of automation in sectors employing large numbers of women. For this reason, technological changes and production strategies need to be matched by public policies and business and trade union initiatives (including technical education and vocational training, collective bargaining and social dialogue) to prevent women from leaving the labour market en masse or being forced into more vulnerable sectors of the economy. These actions should seek to broaden their access to the new employment opportunities opened up by the technological revolution, especially the most skilled and highest-quality jobs.

Source: Economic Commission for Latin America and the Caribbean (ECLAC), on the basis of the Household Survey Data Bank (BADEHOG); G. Bensusán, W. Eichhorst and J. M. Rodríguez, "Las transformaciones tecnológicas y sus desafíos para el empleo, las relaciones laborales y la identificación de la demanda de cualificaciones", *Project Documents* (LC/TS.2017/111), Santiago, ECLAC and J. Weller, "Las transformaciones tecnológicas y su impacto en los mercados laborales", *Macroeconomics of Development series*, No. 190 (LC/TS.2017/76), Santiago, ECLAC.
[a] Female craft and related workers as a proportion of all women employed in manufacturing.

The new technologies have been accompanied by new types and forms of work that have altered labour relations by establishing more flexible arrangements, with weaker links between employer and worker and a number of non-standard forms of work, including new arrangements for workspaces and working hours (such as intermittent and zero-hour working arrangements) (Novick, 2018).

The task of analysing the effects of technological change on employment opportunities and working conditions generally, and women's in particular, is urgent but largely unaddressed in the Latin American countries. For one thing, greater flexibility in working hours and workspaces could benefit women by allowing them to reconcile work and care time. For another, robotics, by reducing the need for physical strength, can create opportunities for women to work with collaborative robots (cobots) on activities in which their participation is very low, such as construction.

However, these new forms of work organization may increase uncertainty in the distribution of working time and will not improve women's well-being if the cultural forms and allocation of household and care tasks remain unchanged. Moreover, these new models of more flexible work are often more insecure, worse paid and lacking in access to traditional social protection mechanisms, all of which may particularly affect women. This makes it necessary to surmount current divides in the use of advanced digital technologies because of their potential to contribute to greater economic autonomy for women. Progressive structural change requires the participation of men and women, with everyone making the best use of their capacities and skills (ECLAC, 2016a).

B. Gender stereotypes in technical and vocational education and training (TVET)

Gender roles and stereotypes are transmitted through education. From the earliest school years, cultural patterns are reinforced by way of educational curricula and institutional and teaching practices. Over time, marked biases are observed in educational provision and in the preferences of students of one or the other sex for different careers. This has a significant impact on women's opportunities to obtain better-quality jobs. Technological advances and automation in production systems have made productivity dependent on broad, complex and dynamic skills. To respond to the effect these changes will have on employment, the technological revolution will need to be accompanied by a transformation of education and technical and vocational capacity-building from a gender perspective.

1. Technical and vocational education and technological change

One of the challenges for Latin America and the Caribbean is to relate knowledge, skills and the gender perspective to employment, productivity and development. To this end, it is necessary to coordinate the work of institutions and their policies with the people involved in the worlds of education and work, as well as with trade unions, the private sector and civil society organizations. It is therefore essential for education and vocational training provision to change, and this will require a partnership between educational institutions and firms whereby training is integrated into a production logic (Bensusán, Eichhorst and Rodríguez, 2017). Given that a system of continuous, relevant, reliable and appropriate training is required (Novick, 2018), there needs to be a strategy for investing in training programmes tailored to market demands with a financing model that combines public and private investment.

Rapid and unremitting change in the labour market means that a skills training model involving an initial training for a single lifelong qualification is no longer sufficient or effective. Training systems will need to be flexible and ensure continuous renewal of workforce skills over the life cycle. This requires a systemic commitment by governments, workers and businesses to decide when and how to adapt and retrain (ILO, 2018d). Technological changes require the strengthening of education systems, in particular national systems of vocational training. These systems must be inclusive and reflect the demand from businesses, the needs of individuals and the development strategy (Weller and Gontero cited in Bensusán, Eichhorst and Rodríguez, 2017). In addition, they must incorporate measures to deal with labour market segmentation.

Investing in male and female employee skills creates a virtuous circle that benefits both companies and workers. Highly skilled workers are able to transform traditional industries and increase productivity for firms, which in turn can pay higher wages, helping to close income inequality gaps. Promoting women's participation in vocational training that prepares them to make better use of digital technologies will also make it possible to work towards closing gender gaps in earnings resulting from labour market segmentation. It is therefore important that strategies to meet the demand for skills required by production sectors should recognize the factors that prevent women from developing their full innovative potential and participating actively in the technological and digital revolution. To this end, education and vocational training systems will need to be closely aligned with the labour market in order to anticipate the demand for skills, including those required by emerging occupations, and match it to the development of current skills, training opportunities and occupational retraining (ILO, 2018d). In particular, proper institutional coordination is required to enable vocational training systems to increase the participation of men and women in high-quality jobs, improve their pay prospects and eliminate gender segmentation in the labour market.

Although educational attainment has increased in Latin America and the Caribbean, there are problems when it comes to linking secondary and post-secondary education with the requirements of the labour market, the result being fewer employment opportunities for young people and a struggle for employers to find workers with the profiles they need to carry out their production activities (ECLAC, 2017b).[3]

The right mix of technical and vocational skills and capabilities will give both male and female workers better employment prospects in the future by making it easier for them to move between jobs, occupations and sectors (ILO, 2018d). It is important for there to be a gender perspective in the design of skills development strategies and in education system reforms so that women can be provided with training tools that enable them to adapt to change and move into jobs with better employment conditions. Otherwise, the disadvantages they face from being overrepresented in lower-skilled jobs will be exacerbated.

Faced with rapid structural change in the demand for skills, all levels of education will need to make changes that enhance retention and quality as well as the timeliness, relevance and suitability of skills (ILO, 2017). In practical terms, this vision will require coordination and alignment between the world of education and vocational training and production development policies.

---

[3]   See chapter IV for further details of the increase in education levels in Latin America and the Caribbean.

2.   Continuation and transmission of gender biases

Gender stereotypes are transmitted in the educational process from the earliest years and are reinforced over time through biases in the curriculum and teaching practices. Parental expectations also affect girls' self-confidence and decisions about higher education (Stevenson and Baker, 1987; Eccles and others, 1990; Tiedemann, 2000).

According to UNESCO (2016) data for Latin America, whereas in third grade there are no significant performance differences between girls and boys in mathematics, by sixth grade there are very marked differences in favour of boys. Empirical exercises indicate that boys' advantages in mathematics cannot be explained by observable variables, suggesting these differences are caused by cultural practices that permeate classrooms, conveying systematic, implicit and almost imperceptible messages which shape opportunities and expectations about the potential of girls and boys in different disciplines. This, in turn, affects the likelihood of women choosing careers in science, technology, engineering and mathematics (STEM).

Despite the great increase in higher education access in Latin America and the Caribbean (see chapter IV), bringing about changes in the production structure of the region's countries will mean increasing technological capabilities and promoting the training of professionals in STEM subjects. These are precisely the disciplines whose profiles are predicted to offer the best prospects of employment. However, although women outnumber men in tertiary education enrolment rates, they are still less likely to pursue STEM studies. In the region, women make up only 34.6% of graduates in these areas.[4]

Figure V.5
Latin America (12 countries): graduates in science, technology, engineering and mathematics (STEM) subjects, by sex, and graduates in STEM subjects as a proportion of all graduates, both sexes, between 2002 and 2015 [a][b]
(Percentages)

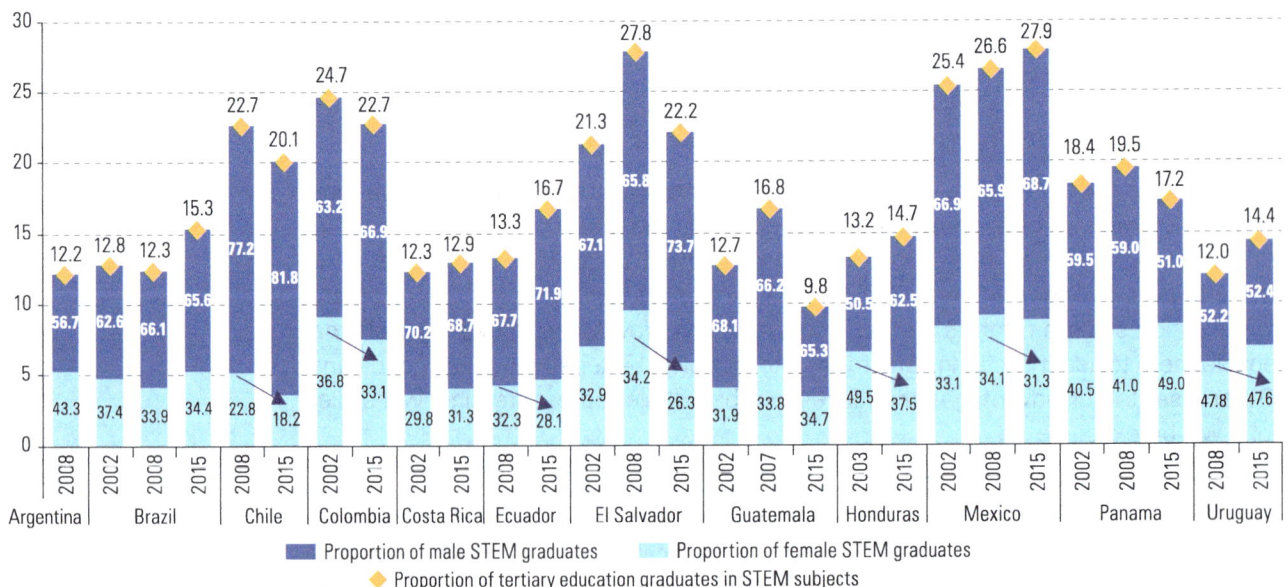

Proportion of male STEM graduates   Proportion of female STEM graduates
Proportion of tertiary education graduates in STEM subjects

Source: Economic Commission for Latin America and the Caribbean (ECLAC), on the basis of United Nations Educational, Scientific and Cultural Organization (UNESCO), "Data for Sustainable Development" [online] https://sdg.uis.unesco.org/.
[a] STEM graduates by sex are calculated as the respective female and male proportions of all those graduating in STEM subjects each year.
[b] Tertiary education graduates in STEM subjects are calculated as a proportion of all tertiary education graduates.

---

4   Simple average for 2015 in 12 countries of the region (except Argentina, whose latest figure is for 2010), on the basis of UNESCO, "Data for Sustainable Development" [online] https://sdg.uis.unesco.org/.

The percentage of women graduates in STEM subjects has actually declined in some countries of the region over recent years. This means that men and women are not being equitably prepared for the jobs required by the new technological environment and that women are being held back from participating in these opportunities.

In this context, the choices of young men and women regarding the areas they will specialize in are not the result of chance, but are influenced by what they think about their own capabilities, their expectations of success and the gender stereotypes they have been brought up with since early childhood. As a result, education leads to different fields of work and persistent segregation by sex (Rico and Trucco, 2014) (ECLAC, 2016a).

If the emphasis of the working world will be on science, technology, engineering and mathematics, this is a crucial time for women to enter these areas en masse, deploying their intellectual and soft skills in a balanced way.

The narrowing of gender gaps in this area should be a collective effort by both the State and professionals in these fields, teachers and the private sector. In particular, it will be a major challenge for universities, which will have to create knowledge networks across countries in order to build innovation ecosystems aimed at the specific development of women's skills in the face of disruptive technologies.

There is a disconnect between education and female employment in technical and vocational training too, as the current development model and the traditional roles assigned to men and women by society are sometimes reproduced (ECLAC, 2016a).

At present, educational provision for men and women operates as a mechanism that reinforces a gender segmentation model and reproduces it in the production system and employment opportunities. To reduce gender gaps in labour market participation, increase women's autonomy and foster countries' economic development, it is necessary to eliminate gender segmentation in TVET and increasingly tie this in with the production sector (Sepúlveda, 2017).

Thus, although there are no great differences in TVET enrolment between men and women in the region, the inequalities that contribute to the horizontal and vertical segmentation of the labour market can be identified by looking at the different areas they enrol in. For example, in the vocational training specializations chosen in Central America and the Dominican Republic, there is a clear division between those with a greater female presence and those with a greater male presence. Among the specializations preferred by men are mechanics, electricity, electronics and carpentry, while among those preferred by women are handicrafts, beauty and aesthetics, and decoration (ECLAC, 2016a).

There are several factors that influence the vocational choices leading women towards certain types of courses and study programmes. First, the cultural patterns that associate women with certain roles mean that the educational and family environment pushes young women into choosing certain professions and jobs.

Second, the prevalence of gender-based violence in society at large, which education and training centres are not exempt from, limits the participation of some young women in groups where a majority of the students are men. In addition, the urgent need to generate income forces some women from more vulnerable sectors to opt for short courses that will allow them to enter the world of work quickly.

There are also other conditions related to the reproduction of gender roles in the structures of educational and technical and vocational training centres whereby there is a clear concentration of men in leading roles and managerial positions in these centres and low participation by women as trainers and teachers in areas related to courses traditionally regarded as male (Bloj, 2017; Buquet and Moreno, 2017).

The effects of the education system and the labour market for technical and professional workers feed back into each other. Women choose the specializations that normally command the lowest wages, while at the same time the market pays less to women who prefer to specialize in the areas where men are better paid (ECLAC, 2016a).

On the labour market side, there are situations that contribute to the concentration of women in certain specializations. For example, when some women who choose to study traditionally "male" subjects try to penetrate the labour market, they struggle to find jobs in these areas and, if they do finally succeed, are often excluded from the tasks appropriate to the disciplines they studied and relegated to less highly skilled administrative ("backroom"), cleaning or maintenance functions (Buquet and Moreno, 2017).

In some fields traditionally considered masculine, the appearance of women in a male environment is seen as disruptive, so that employers prefer not to accept them. The study by Buquet and Moreno (2017), conducted in Mexico, includes interviews with employers from various institutions who say that it is inadvisable to hire women in areas where they could be injured. This strengthens the idea of men as protectors and women as the weaker sex who cannot perform all types of work. In addition, women are likely to benefit less from lifelong learning and adaptation to the changing needs of the labour market and have fewer on-the-job training opportunities because they are responsible for looking after children or older adults in their care (ILO, 2013). For this reason, it is essential for approaches to change in several areas: in curricula, teacher training, infrastructure and also culturally, in order to put an end to prejudices surrounding the specializations and roles assigned to women. In addition, technical and vocational education should no longer be treated as inferior in quality or prestige and, once these courses have been completed, it should be possible to carry on with education leading to a university degree if desired (ECLAC, 2018b).

C. The economic contribution of women's work

To harness the transformative potential of technological change, it is necessary to address the dynamics between the market and households. Women contribute to countries' economies with their paid and unpaid work. For sustained economic growth to be achieved, more women need to be employed in higher-productivity sectors. At the same time, it is necessary to recognize and take account of the fact that part of the economy is sustained by the unpaid work of women in households. It is imperative for there to be a social reorganization of care so that responsibility is fully shared between the State, the market and families.

1. Women's contribution through unpaid work

According to the ECLAC (2017) approach, the world of work includes work that is done for the market in exchange for an income and unpaid work done in households, and it is recognized that decisions and opportunities for participation in these spheres are closely linked. This approach highlights the different positions of men and women as economic agents and the way unpaid domestic and care work creates the conditions for and underpins the functioning of the labour market and the sustainability of life.

Women's low participation in paid work contrasts with their high participation in unpaid work for their own households. Time-use surveys conducted in Latin America show that 77% of unpaid work is done by women, with care and home maintenance to the fore.[5]

---

[5]   Calculations based on special processing by ECLAC of time-use surveys in the region.

Unpaid domestic and care work contributes substantially to countries' economies, as well as to individual and social well-being. And it is precisely the people who dedicate themselves to these tasks, most of them women, who contribute to the functioning of the economy by doing work that, although productive, is not classified within the production frontier used by national accounting systems. Thus, most of this work goes unacknowledged because it is not accounted for or considered in decision-making. Not only are these people unpaid, but they do not receive the recognition they deserve.

The countries of the region have measured the contribution of unpaid work carried out in households in order to bring it to light and set an economic value on it. These studies put the economic contribution of unpaid work at the equivalent of between 15.2% of GDP (Ecuador, 2012) and 24.2% of GDP (Mexico, 2014). Most of this is done by women, contributing between 11.8% and 18% of GDP, respectively (ECLAC, 2016a).

In many countries, women's economic contribution through unpaid work is actually greater than that of any other economic activity. This is the case in Mexico, where the economic value of households' unpaid work was found to be greater than the individual share of any other economic activity in the country (ECLAC, 2017). In Ecuador, the economic value of unpaid domestic and care work exceeds that of oil extraction (11.3% of GDP) and construction (11.8% of GDP). In El Salvador, the contribution of domestic work is equivalent to 21.3% of GDP, a figure similar to those for the two largest sectors, namely manufacturing industry and the commerce, restaurants and hotels sector (ECLAC, 2016a).

There are many reasons why women are engaged in unpaid household work. The main ones are related to cultural constraints that relegate them to care tasks in a context marked by the unequal sexual distribution of labour. Furthermore, discrimination in the labour market, where women are faced with worse pay conditions than men, discourages them from participating fully. Macroeconomic phenomena associated with the economic cycle are also likely to have an impact.

In recent years, some Latin American economies, particularly in South America, have faced slower growth due to falling commodity prices, which has had an impact on fiscal revenues. In response, several governments have cut back primary spending or slowed the pace of expansion. This has had a direct or indirect impact on households, especially the poorest, which are more dependent on State action. Women have borne the brunt of these adjustments and the consequent reduction of public service provision through their unpaid work.

As already described, women's full participation in the labour market, although a right and a precondition for their economic autonomy, does not automatically transform the sexual division of labour and has increased their total workload, which is on average higher than that of men in all countries in the region. In addition, the unequal distribution of responsibilities for the domestic and care work that falls mostly on women acts as a barrier to participation and reproduces inequalities in the labour market.

Removing structural constraints and making substantive progress towards gender equality requires effective recognition of women's contribution to national economies through unpaid work. Transformative policies are also needed to reduce and redistribute this work more equitably between women and men, as well as between households, society and the State. It is essential to consider these elements at a time of changes in the world of work that, as was seen earlier, may have different impacts on men and women. This will make it possible to design relevant and effective policies to discharge gender equality debts in the labour market and anticipate the risks and differential barriers to access to the new opportunities arising from the transformations now taking place.

2.   Women's full incorporation into the labour market: the potential boost to economic growth

As ECLAC has reiterated, equality is not only an aspiration but a necessary condition for development. For this reason, in recent years it has proposed to the region that equality be achieved through the enhancement of human capabilities, mobilization of the State and growth based on progressive structural change (ECLAC, 2018a).

Despite the major unpaid contribution made by women, the potential economic gains from incorporating them fully into the workplace on an equal footing with men are substantial. They would be all the greater if production structures were changed and female participation in employment in high-productivity sectors were increased.

Greater incorporation of women into the workplace would not only have a significant impact on economic activity, but would also make help to improve income distribution and reduce poverty while increasing women's autonomy, expanding their rights and giving them access to contributory social protection.

McKinsey Global Institute (2015), which assesses the impact of closing divides in labour force participation, hours worked and economic sectors, estimated that fully closing the gaps in these three categories could increase Latin America's GDP by about 34% by 2025 compared to what it would be if the current situation continued.[6] The study also presents a less ambitious scenario, estimating the impact if all countries narrowed their gaps at the same pace as the country in the region that is making the fastest progress, which in Latin America is Chile. This second scenario yields an estimate of a potential GDP increase of 14 percentage points by 2025 (McKinsey Global Institute, 2015). In an econometric study conducted for Chile, Berlien and others (2016) estimate that the impact of closing gender gaps in labour market participation would increase GDP by between 6% and 9% (see box V.2).

Greater integration of women into the labour market on an equal footing with men would not only increase GDP, but would create the conditions for reducing inequality and poverty. At present, a significant part of the region's poverty can be explained by the fact that women in households in the lowest income deciles do not participate in the labour market or do so under substandard conditions, while also having a large number of dependents.[7] This not only reduces the average income per household member, but makes heavy demands of women in terms of time spent on domestic and care work, limiting their chances of finding work in higher-paying jobs.

Social Panorama of Latin America, 2014 (ECLAC, 2014) shows that closing labour market participation gaps would increase household incomes and significantly reduce poverty and inequality. An increase in the female participation rate to bring it into line with that of men at the central ages (between 14 and 65) would increase average household income by between 3% and 4% in countries such as Argentina, Brazil, Colombia, Mexico and Uruguay, and up to 10% and more in countries such as El Salvador, Honduras, Nicaragua and Peru. This would result in poverty reduction of between 1 percentage point in Argentina and Uruguay and more than 10 percentage points in El Salvador and Nicaragua.

According to the same study, "if more women were to enter the labour market it would help reduce inequality, measured using the Gini index, by 4 percentage points in Nicaragua and Panama, and by 3 percentage points in the Dominican Republic, Ecuador, El Salvador, Honduras and Paraguay" (ECLAC, 2014, p. 193). For some countries, the reduction in inequality as measured by the Theil index would be even greater (between 6 and 8 percentage points in Guatemala, Honduras, Nicaragua, Panama and Paraguay) owing to the greater sensitivity of this indicator to changes in the lower segments of the income distribution. It is precisely in these that large changes in income occur when women with lower levels of education enter the labour market.

---

[6]   This result is obtained by assuming that women achieve the same participation rate, work the same hours and are as productive as men.
[7]   In the poorest households (first income quintile), 42.1% of women aged over 15 have no income of their own and are employed on unpaid domestic work (ECLAC, 2016a).

Box V.2
Opportunities to grow by closing the gender gap in labour market participation

Governments in the region have committed themselves to a multidimensional model of sustainable development based on human rights and gender equality, as set out in the Regional Gender Agenda (Bidegain, 2017). Accordingly, women's full participation in decent work is a right and not a means to economic growth. Moreover, as this econometric exercise shows, investing in policies that encourage greater participation by women in employment does not mean sacrificing economic dynamism; on the contrary, it would allow the region to grow more and in a more equal way.

To measure the impact of gender gaps in labour market participation on GDP, a panel database was constructed with information from 1990 to 2016 for 14 countries: Argentina, Brazil, Chile, Colombia, Ecuador, Guatemala, Honduras, Mexico, Nicaragua, Panama, Paraguay, Peru, the Plurinational State of Bolivia and Uruguay. The panel includes the macroeconomic and social variables needed to estimate a growth model with capital, labour and control variables.[a] Results from the estimation were used to make projections of economic growth, measured in terms of the evolution of GDP, taking three scenarios for the behaviour of women's labour market participation rates with a constant male participation rate of 80.2%:[b]

Scenario 1. The trend of the female labour market participation rate remains unchanged until 2030. To calculate the annual increase, the rates for the last five years were averaged out.

Scenario 2. The female labour market participation rate rises by 1% a year up to 2030.

Scenario 3. The female labour market participation rate converges on the male rate by 2030.

The female labour force participation rate would have to increase very rapidly to match the male rate by 2030: around 2.9 percentage points a year (note the change in slope in scenario 3 of figure 1). For this to happen, there will have to be active policies to break down the structural gender gaps limiting women's ability to enter and remain in the labour market.

The results of applying the model to projected female participation rates make it possible to estimate the effects of these movements on GDP growth. Thus, it was estimated that, under scenario 1, the additional annual changes (the effect of greater female participation in the labour market) in per capita GDP growth in the region could potentially range between 0.05% and 0.01%. In scenario 2, the contribution to GDP growth rates could be 0.17%, and in scenario 3 these contributions trend upward, reaching 0.6% in 2030. In cumulative terms, this means additional GDP growth of 2.14 percentage points between 2016 and 2030 in scenario 2 and additional growth of 6.93 percentage points between those same years in scenario 3.

Figure 1
Latin America (14 countries): estimates of three scenarios for the female labour force participation rate up to 2030[a]
(Percentages)

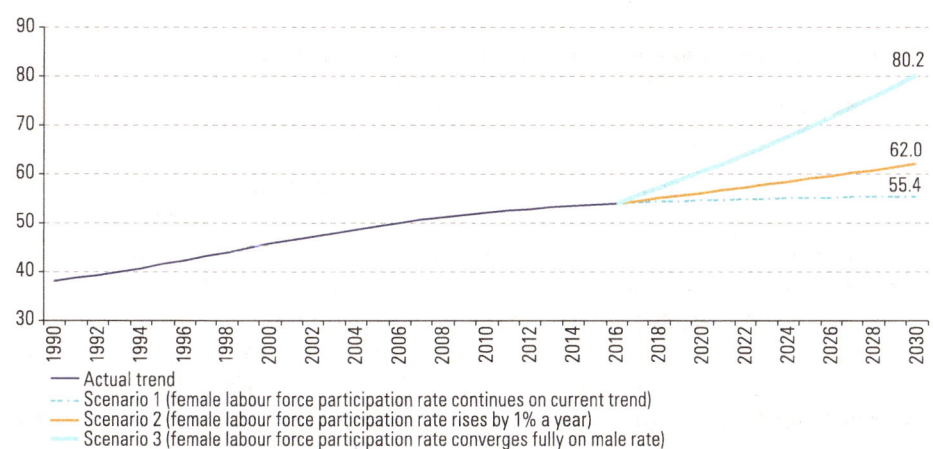

— Actual trend
---- Scenario 1 (female labour force participation rate continues on current trend)
— Scenario 2 (female labour force participation rate rises by 1% a year)
— Scenario 3 (female labour force participation rate converges fully on male rate)

Source: Economic Commission for Latin America and the Caribbean (ECLAC), on the basis of the Household Survey Data Bank (BADEHOG).
[a] The countries included are: Argentina, Brazil, Chile, Colombia, Ecuador, Guatemala, Honduras, Mexico, Nicaragua, Panama, Paraguay, Peru, the Plurinational State of Bolivia and Uruguay.

Box V.2 (concluded)

Figure 2
Latin America (14 countries): estimates of additional per capita GDP in three scenarios
for the reduction of gender gaps in labour market participation up to 2030[a][b]
(Dollars at constant 2010 prices)

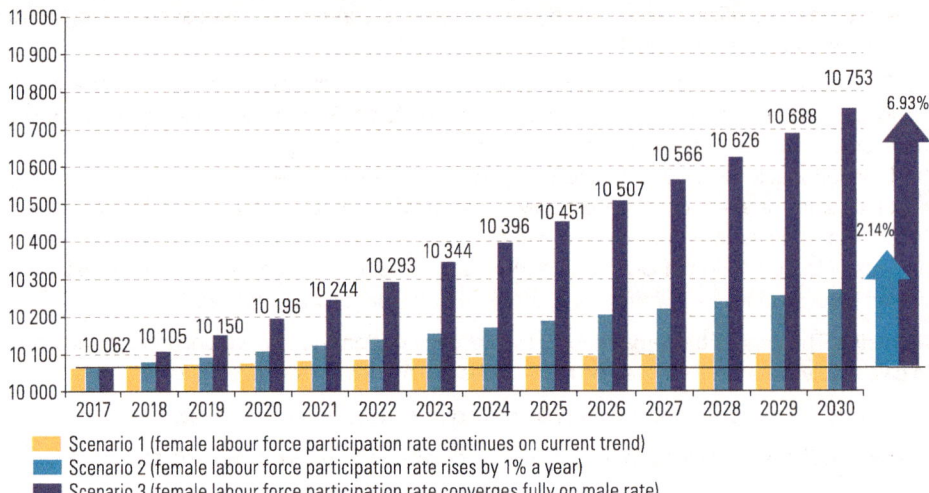

Scenario 1 (female labour force participation rate continues on current trend)
Scenario 2 (female labour force participation rate rises by 1% a year)
Scenario 3 (female labour force participation rate converges fully on male rate)

Source: Economic Commission for Latin America and the Caribbean (ECLAC), on the basis of the Household Survey Data Bank (BADEHOG).
[a] The countries included are: Argentina, Brazil, Chile, Colombia, Ecuador, Guatemala, Honduras, Mexico, Nicaragua, Panama, Paraguay, Peru, the Plurinational State of Bolivia and Uruguay.
[b] These estimates have been prepared on the assumption that all other variables remain constant. Accordingly, the amounts shown in the chart are the additional increase in GDP over trend owing to the narrowing of gender gaps in labour market participation.

ECLAC argues that equalization does not mean sacrificing the value of economic dynamism and growth. On the contrary, it should allow the instrumental role of equality to be harnessed as a driver of sustainable development (ECLAC, 2018a). Thus, the goal of gender equality, far from clashing with economic growth, is a prerequisite for its efficiency. For this reason, it is important for macroeconomic policies to be integrated with policies for structural change in which the gender equality perspective is mainstreamed to create a new model whereby the benefits of economic growth are appropriated more equitably by all productive actors.

Source: Economic Commission for Latin America and the Caribbean (ECLAC), on the basis of the Household Survey Data Bank (BADEHOG).
[a] The figure for male labour force participation in 2016 is from the CEPALSTAT database and does not match that presented in section A of this chapter, which was obtained from data processing by the International Labour Organization (ILO).
[b] The growth model used is based on the neoclassical one proposed by Solow (1956), which establishes that a country's production capacity can be represented by a function of the type Y=AF(K,L), where A represents total factor productivity and K and L represent the amounts of capital and labour in a country at a given time, respectively.

Again, if the monthly income gap between men and women were eliminated (i.e., if they were paid the same when they had the same experience and qualifications), poverty would decline very significantly in countries such as Colombia, Ecuador, Nicaragua, Peru and the Plurinational State of Bolivia.[8] "The Gini index would fall by between 2 and 8 percentage points, depending on the country, and the Theil index would mark an even larger decline in inequality, being more sensitive to the changes that occur in lower income households" (ECLAC, 2014, p. 195). Using a similar methodology, with microsimulations, ECLAC (2018a) analyses what the impact would be if the participation gap were closed and men's and women's wages simultaneously equalized. The effects are considerably greater in this case, with increases in average household incomes ranging from 10% in Peru to over 30% in Nicaragua (ECLAC, 2018a).

---

[8]   In Peru and the Plurinational State of Bolivia, very large percentages of women are in work but not paid. Thus, very significant progress would be made if these women received an income similar to that of men with the same level of education and work experience.

D. Intersectoral public polices to ensure women's economic and social rights

Without appropriate public policies to promote the inclusion of women in STEM areas, prevent them ending up in informal and insecure jobs, increase their participation in sectors with higher productivity and develop shared responsibility for care work while strengthening policies in this area, not only might women not benefit from the jobs of the future, but there is a risk that existing divides and the deficit of decent work currently affecting them might worsen.

1. Labour policies to reduce gender gaps

To deal with changes in the labour market, policies with a cross-cutting gender equality and rights approach are needed to reduce the employment participation and quality gap between men and women, taking advantage of the synergies between equality and growth (ECLAC, 2018a). These policies should promote new opportunities for women that translate, for example, into better situations in terms of labour market participation, wages and social protection.

Labour market policies are important for the equal exercise of rights. For this reason, legislation and programmes should be adopted to facilitate and encourage balance between the employment and family demands of working women and men (ECLAC, 2014), including oversight mechanisms to ensure wage equality between women and men and actions to promote women's participation in the labour market. The inclusion of women in decision-making forums should be encouraged and policies to end horizontal segregation should be pursued with the aim of bringing about equal distribution in professions, occupations and trades.

It is also necessary to ensure the sustainability of the efforts made in recent decades to narrow gaps and be alert to prevent ground being lost. Successive economic crises, demographic change and the emergence of new technologies are just some of the factors confronting today's societies, and their destabilizing effect may imperil hard-won progress with equity between men and women. A comprehensive and sustained strategy of initiatives would have a real impact on gender equality and provide a basis for continued progress in closing gaps, sustaining the achievements made and taking advantage of new opportunities that may arise.

While all these measures are necessary, labour market policies alone are not enough. As has been noted throughout this chapter, policies are also required in related areas to strengthen women's autonomy and involve society as a whole in addressing the care needs of the population.

2. Policies on social co-responsibility for care

This chapter has shown the need to implement public policies that respond to the care demands of the population and take account of the rights of female caregivers, whether paid or unpaid. The situation is made more challenging by the patterns of demographic change estimated for the coming decades, with the outlook being for an increase in the care demands discussed in previous editions of *Social Panorama of Latin America* (ECLAC, 2010b, 2016c and 2017c). In view of the expected ageing of the region's population, there will be an increase in the number of dependent persons (older adults and people with chronic illnesses and disabilities).

It is vital that the programmes designed to respond to this need reflect the fact that the social organization of care is a responsibility that must be shared between men and women and redistributed across the different types of families, social organizations, firms and the State (ECLAC, 2016a). For this reason, the design, monitoring and evaluation of public policies must take into account the relationship between the two spheres of work: paid and unpaid. Women's excess burden of unpaid work often determines their occupational patterns and trajectory in the labour market. It also acts as a barrier to participation in this market.

This situation has meant that in recent years care policies have occupied a prominent place in debates on public policies, especially social protection, in recognition of their important contribution to gender equality and thus to the well-being of societies. They also create employment opportunities and should enhance the participation of different social groups in the labour market. An important area of action is the construction or strengthening of a system of care that, in addition to alleviating the burden of unpaid work, serves to address women's time poverty and improve their participation in the labour force (ECLAC, 2018a).

For these systems to be effective, it is vital that they include the needs of people requiring care throughout the life cycle. The approach here must focus on children, the elderly, people with disabilities and the dependent sick, as well as the situation of those providing care. The experience of the Integrated National Care System in Uruguay is particularly noteworthy in this regard; Costa Rica has the National Child Care and Development Network and the Progressive Assistance Network for the Comprehensive Care of the Elderly; and Chile, Ecuador and El Salvador are also evaluating systems of this type.

For example, early childhood care programmes should cover the full working day to facilitate women's access to paid work. Part-time care services do not allow women to reconcile full-time paid work with the duties they take on as mothers. Thus, care services do not lead to significant increases in female labour force participation, whereas extended school hours programmes do. In Uruguay, for example, expanding the supply of full-time schools has had a positive effect on the labour force participation of mothers of children under the age of 6 (ECLAC, 2018a).

The way these systems are constructed also needs to mark a break with existing structures that perpetuate gender inequalities. As discussed in this chapter, care work undertaken in the market is highly feminized. At the same time, this sector is characterized by low wages and very poor conditions of employment, which affect the quality of care and, consequently, the well-being of its beneficiaries (ILO, 2018b).

At the same time, countries should strengthen legal frameworks and expand State investment to include provisions for maternity protection and paternity leave, parenting provisions and other protective measures that address social reproduction and the different stages of the life cycle, without the whole burden falling on women's time.

These measures encourage women to return to paid work, reduce career breaks and achieve a more harmonious balance between paid work and family life. For example, the experience of applying parental leave to both men and women for just over a year, coupled with recognition of children's right to care and to the protection they need to develop in their first year of life, has led to high female participation in the world of work in countries such as Norway and Sweden (ILO, 2018b).

To move towards greater gender equality, it will therefore be essential to pursue a diverse set of policies that encourage a more equitable division of unpaid work and care tasks between men and women, encouraging a change in attitudes and behaviour vis-à-vis such work. The answer is not just to create care systems, but to ensure that they mainstream the gender perspective from the outset in order to avoid reproducing traditional roles and to play a central part in increasing women's economic autonomy.

3.   Education and capacity-building

For women to improve their position in the labour market and take advantage of the opportunities arising with the technological revolution, policies are needed to break down gender stereotypes and encourage greater female participation in STEM areas, as well as human resources training and technological innovation programmes that anticipate the demands of the labour market, reverse the current imbalance and improve skills and employability.

For there to be progress in this direction, the first step is to adopt policies that address gender biases in formal and technical and vocational education. Accordingly, it is essential that policies related to the education system, vocational training and employment be coordinated to mainstream the gender perspective. Men and women will thus be able to opt for high-productivity sectors under equal conditions and fully exercise their rights (ECLAC, 2016a).

This implies, among other things, a change in the logic of education to overcome prejudices about specializations and roles considered feminine. To this end, it is essential to identify and recognize discriminatory representations and practices in the educational process and to include the community in gender awareness and training activities.

When it comes to the transition from education to work, it is important for educational trajectories to be matched by comprehensive vocational guidance services and the preparation of a vocational career plan. In addition, it is necessary to promote occupational reintegration and retraining policies that allow women to return to the labour market or change jobs or sectors at different stages of their lives, without this severely compromising their career paths.

Policies to encourage greater participation by women in STEM, productive specialization and technological innovation areas are very important and require changes throughout the educational process. It is important to place innovation front and centre from the earliest stages so that children have the tools they need to integrate into the society of the future (OECD/ECLAC/CAF, 2016; ECLAC, 2018b). Later, in the transition from education to work, a twofold adjustment of vocational training systems will be required. These systems will have to provide the fundamental skills needed in the new environment and facilitate dynamic and flexible learning throughout the life cycle to ensure that men and women keep pace with progress (Bertranou, 2018).

Not only will training be linked to entry into the world of work, but permanent, responsive and flexible training systems that are closely tied to the labour market will be required to anticipate the demands for new skills and so that men and women have access to the benefits potentially arising from the transformations that will accompany the future of work (ILO, 2017).

4.   Comprehensive social protection

As discussed in this chapter, women participate less in the labour market and, of those who do enter it, a great many work in informal and insecure jobs. This means that not only are they paid lower wages, but they face greater difficulty in accessing contributory social protection.

To meet these challenges and prevent insecure and informal jobs from widening inequality gaps, there should be policies for universal access to social protection, regardless of how people participate in the labour market. This means making progress both with contributory social protection, accessed by people in formal employment, and with non-contributory social protection, as highlighted in *Social Panorama of Latin America, 2017* (ECLAC, 2018a). Likewise, there need to be mechanisms to protect against unemployment, which, as seen earlier, particularly affects women. It is also important to have arrangements to provide social protection coverage to women whose labour force participation is interrupted because of reproductive demands, alongside the aforementioned strengthening of care systems as a cross-cutting area of social protection.

At the same time, the feasibility of establishing access to a guaranteed basic income as a new human right needs to be considered with a view to promoting and securing sustainable income sources for all household members as an anti-poverty measure. A minimum wage policy combined with access to a guaranteed minimum income would provide a way to advance women's economic autonomy while at the same time helping to improve income distribution in the countries of the region (ECLAC, 2016a).

Moving towards a guaranteed basic income may be important in the context of the technological revolution. Although this will expand production opportunities and allow more goods and services to be produced at lower cost, it poses serious distributive challenges. There is a risk that, with the new technologies, the rate of job creation will not be fast enough to offset job losses. Thus, new mechanisms will be needed to redistribute wealth from those directly benefiting from technological change to those who are disadvantaged. The idea of a universal basic income has begun to be seriously discussed as part of this debate. In the region, it has been suggested that its application will depend on the particular characteristics and conditions of each of the countries and that, if it were to be implemented, it should be done gradually over a long-term horizon (ECLAC, 2018a).

5. Labour statistics with a gender perspective

A crucial area, given the far-reaching changes in the future of work, is the construction and dissemination of official labour market statistics with a gender perspective so that future market demands can be anticipated.

Progress in this direction requires, first, that as many statistics as possible be disaggregated by sex so that the various phenomena affecting both men and women can be scrutinized and appropriate and timely measures taken. In addition, it is essential to carry on incorporating new measurements which serve to quantify dimensions that have been excluded from traditional debates (for example, time-use surveys, which identify the time available to members of a household to carry out different activities) (ECLAC, 2016a).

At the same time, it is important to strengthen measuring instruments and administrative records so that they reflect emerging phenomena in the labour market that have so far gone unaddressed. It is vital to have information that serves to anticipate which sectors will be most affected by automation, which jobs will be destroyed and which created, what new forms of employment and labour relations will emerge, and how women will be affected in these new labour market scenarios. In the absence of high quality data providing a gender perspective, public policies based on information or projections that do not reflect reality could increase gender biases.

In addition, it will be vital to use new technologies as an opportunity to access fresh sources of information that serve as inputs for planning and decision-making. To this end, it is important to strengthen information systems and create new statistics that reflect the evolution of the labour market and of gender gaps.

6.   The need for policies of intersectoral scope

While there is great potential for economic growth in developing countries, there are still difficulties in the way of seizing the opportunities presented by the fourth industrial revolution. A number of questions need to be asked here. What policies will be crucial to prevent labour market polarization and gender inequality from increasing? What policies should be pursued so that countries can reap the full benefits of the current wave of technological change without undermining women's economic autonomy? How can the ongoing technological revolution be influenced to improve the functioning of labour markets and enhance the inclusion of both women and men? What measures should be taken to mitigate the consequences of the destruction of some jobs and the restructuring of others?

In the field of work, the fourth industrial revolution is expanding the scope for an increased variety of employment relationships, which will challenge the design and governance of labour market institutions. Similarly, it will affect the regulatory system and labour market institutions, which will be tasked with ensuring that employment rights and quality are not sacrificed to the productive potential of the new forms of work. This will mean adapting countries' legislation to ensure decent work while at the same time accommodating the flexibility needed for the jobs of the future (Novick, 2018).

Many of the jobs being generated in the fourth industrial revolution are not covered by a regulatory framework that effectively ensures basic employment rights. This situation entails the risk of increasing job insecurity, affecting the quality of jobs and the socioeconomic conditions of workers, especially women in more vulnerable jobs. Confronting this situation means adapting regulations to extend employment rights to all workers, with the adoption of measures that directly address gender inequalities. There is also a need to strengthen social dialogue and collective bargaining mechanisms.

Among other things, a minimum number of hours of protected working time needs to be established, since limiting the variability of working hours can provide safeguards for part-time, on-demand and casual workers. Legislation should also deal with mistakenly (or fraudulently) classified or assigned jobs, restricting some uses of non-standardized jobs to prevent abuses and assign obligations and responsibilities for systems and modes of employment in a way that combines multiple perspectives.

The social protection systems of the region's countries need to be strengthened so that, in addition to a gender perspective, they take a life-cycle approach and offer alternatives to those who are unable to adapt or retrain in the face of changing employment conditions. These would include people who might end up in occupations with very different requirements from those their working careers have prepared them for, especially women employed mainly in low-productivity sectors (such as the service sector), who could be affected by automation and who, because of their stage in life or for other reasons, are unlikely to be able to retrain.

Despite the opportunities afforded by the flexibility of some of the new forms of work, which are attractive to women seeking to reconcile domestic and care work with work for the market, there is also the risk that they will end up in substandard jobs because there are no clear contractual relationships and they are not covered by social protection. It is important to be aware that, while jobs are expected to be more flexible, without more shared responsibility women will have greater flexibility in terms of the working hours of jobs in the market, but their unpaid workload will not be reduced. This will result in even longer total working hours and problems in separating the spheres of work and personal life, creating greater stress for women (OECD, 2017).

Without appropriate public policies to address the issues reviewed in this chapter, women risk not only being excluded from the benefits and opportunities of the jobs of the future, but might find that existing gaps are perpetuated. To avoid these outcomes, it is necessary to create an agenda of relevant policies suited to the regional context that takes account of the production structure, development strategies and interactions with the global economy and, most importantly, that mainstreams the gender perspective and is supported by prospective studies that can generate timely proposals for anticipating and keeping up with change.

Bibliography

Bensusán, G., W. Eichhorst and J. M. Rodríguez (2017), "Las transformaciones tecnológicas y sus desafíos para el empleo, las relaciones laborales y la identificación de la demanda de cualificaciones", *Project Documents* (LC/TS.2017/111), Santiago, Economic Commission for Latin America and the Caribbean (ECLAC).

Berlien, K. and others (2016), "Informe final: mayor incorporación de las mujeres en la economía chilena", Santiago, Undersecretariat of Economy and Small Businesses/Isónoma Consultorías Sociales Ltda.

Bertranou, F. (2018), "El futuro del trabajo y el centenario de la OIT", document prepared for the Sixth National Meeting on Commerce, Santiago, 21 June.

Bidegain, N. (2017), "The 2030 Agenda and the Regional Gender Agenda: synergies for equality in Latin America and the Caribbean", *Gender Affairs series*, No. 143 (LC/TS.2017/7), Santiago, Economic Commission for Latin America and the Caribbean (ECLAC).

Bloj, C. (2017), "Trayectorias de mujeres: educación técnico-profesional y trabajo en la Argentina", *Gender Affairs series*, No. 145 (LC/TS.2017/25), Santiago, Economic Commission for Latin America and the Caribbean (ECLAC).

Buquet, A. G. and H. Moreno (2017), "Trayectorias de mujeres: educación técnico-profesional y trabajo en México, *Gender Affairs series*, No. 146 (LC/TS.2017/35), Santiago, Economic Commission for Latin America and the Caribbean (ECLAC).

Cadena, A. and others (2017), "Where will Latin America's growth come from?", *Discussion Paper*, McKinsey Global Institute, April.

Calderón Magaña, C. (coord.) (2013), "Redistributing care: the policy challenge", *Cuadernos de la CEPAL*, No. 101 (LC/G.2568-P), Santiago, Economic Commission for Latin America and the Caribbean (ECLAC), September.

Eccles, J. and others (1990), "Gender role stereotypes, expectancy effects, and parents' socialization of gender differences", *Journal of Social Issues*, vol. 46, No. 2.

ECLAC (Economic Commission for Latin America and the Caribbean) (2018a), *The Inefficiency of Inequality* (LC/SES.37/3-P), Santiago, May.

_____(2018b), "Educación técnico-profesional en inserción laboral de las mujeres jóvenes en América Latina y el Caribe", G. Mahia (ed.), Santiago, unpublished.

_____(2017a), *El mercado laboral en la subregión de Centroamérica y la República Dominicana: realidades y retos de la inserción laboral desde una perspectiva de género* (LC/MEX/TS.2017/32), Mexico City, ECLAC Subregional Headquarters in Mexico.

_____(2017b), "Políticas industriales y tecnológicas en América Latina", *Project Documents* (LC/TS.2017/91), Santiago, November.

_____(2017c), *Social Panorama of Latin America, 2016* (LC/PUB.2017/12-P), Santiago.

_____(2016a), *Equality and women's autonomy in the sustainable development agenda* (LC/G.2686/Rev.1 - LC/G.2686(CRM.13/3)), Santiago.

_____(2016b), *The new digital revolution: from the consumer Internet to the industrial Internet* (LC/L.4029(CMSI.5/4)), Santiago.

_____(2016c), *Social Panorama of Latin America, 2015* (LC/G.2691-P), Santiago.

_____(2014), *Social Panorama of Latin America, 2014* (LC/G.2635-P), Santiago.

_____(2013), *Women in the digital economy: breaking through the equality threshold* (LC/L.3666(CRM.12/3)), Santiago.

____(2010a), *What kind of State? What kind of equality?* (LC/G.2450(CRM.11/3) - LC/G.2450/Rev.1), Santiago.

____(2010b), *Social Panorama of Latin America, 2009* (LC/G.2423-P), Santiago.

Frey, C. B. and M. A. Osborne (2013), "The future of employment: how susceptible are jobs to computerisation?", *Technological Forecasting and Social Change*, vol. 114.

ILO (International Labour Organization) (2018a), *World Employment and Social Outlook: Trends for Women 2018 – Global Snapshot*, Geneva, March.

____(2018b), "Addressing care for inclusive labour markets and gender equality", *Issue Brief*, No. 3, Geneva, February.

____(2018c), *Care Work and Care Jobs for the Future of Decent Work*, Geneva.

____(2018d), "Global Commission on the Future of Work", Geneva [online] http://www.ilo.org/global/topics/future-of-work/WCMS_569528/lang—en/index.htm.

____(2017), *The future of vocational training in Latin America and the Caribbean: overview and strengthening guidelines*, Montevideo, ILO Regional Office for Latin America and the Caribbean/Inter-American Centre for Knowledge Development in Vocational Training (CINTERFOR).

____(2016), *Women at Work: Trends 2016*, Geneva, March.

____(2013), *Trabajo decente e igualdad de género. Políticas para mejorar el acceso y la calidad del empleo en América Latina y el Caribe*, Santiago, Economic Commission for Latin America and the Caribbean (ECLAC)/Food and Agriculture Organization of the United Nations (FAO)/United Nations Entity for Gender Equality and the Empowerment of Women (UN-Women)/United Nations Development Programme (UNDP)/International Labour Organization (ILO).

INEGI (National Institute of Statistics and Geography) (2018), "Censos Económicos 2009" [online] http://www.inegi.org.mx/est/contenidos/espanol/proyectos/censos/ce2009/.

Manyika, J. and others (2017), *A Future That Works: Automation, Employment, and Productivity*, McKinsey Global Institute, January.

McKinsey Global Institute (2015), "The Power of Parity: How advancing women's equality can add $12 trillion to global growth" [online] https://www.mckinsey.com/featured-insights/employment-and-growth/how-advancing-womens-equality-can-add-12-trillion-to-global-growth.

Novick, M. (2018), "El mundo del trabajo: cambios y desafíos en materia de inclusión", *Social Policy series*, No. 228 (LC/TS.2018/2), Santiago, Economic Commission for Latin America and the Caribbean (ECLAC).

OECD (Organization for Economic Cooperation and Development) (2017), "Going digital: The future of work for women", *Policy Brief on the Future of Work*, Paris.

OECD/ECLAC/CAF (Organization for Economic Cooperation and Development/Economic Commission for Latin America and the Caribbean/Development Bank of Latin America) (2016), *Latin American Economic Outlook, 2017: Youth, Skills and Entrepreneurship* (LC/G.2689), Paris, October.

Rico, M. N. and D. Trucco (2014), "Adolescentes: derecho a la educación y al bienestar futuro", *Social Policy series*, No. 190 (LC/L.3791), Santiago, Economic Commission for Latin America and the Caribbean (ECLAC).

Sepúlveda, L. (2017), "La educación técnico-profesional en América Latina: retos y oportunidades para la igualdad de género", *Gender Affairs series*, No. 144 (LC/TS.2017/13), Santiago, Economic Commission for Latin America and the Caribbean (ECLAC).

Solow, R. (1956), "A contribution to the theory of economic growth", *The Quarterly Journal of Economics*, vol. 70, No. 1, Oxford, Oxford University Press.

Stevenson, D. L. and D. P. Baker (1987), "The family-school relation and the child's school performance", *Child Development*, vol. 58, No. 5.

Tiedemann, J. (2000), "Parents' gender stereotypes and teachers' beliefs as predictors of children's concept of their mathematical ability in elementary school", *Journal of Educational Psychology*, vol. 92, No. 1.

UNESCO (United Nations Educational, Scientific and Cultural Organization) (2016), *Gender inequality in learning achievement in primary education. What can TERCE tell us?*, Santiago.

Weller, J. (2017), "Las transformaciones tecnológicas y su impacto en los mercados laborales", *Macroeconomics of Development series*, No. 190 (LC/TS.2017/76), Santiago, Economic Commission for Latin America and the Caribbean (ECLAC).

Weller, J. and C. Roethlisberger (2011), "La calidad del empleo en América Latina", *Macroeconomics of Development series*, No. 110 (LC/L.3320-P), Santiago, Economic Commission for Latin America and the Caribbean (ECLAC).

World Bank (2016), *World Development Report 2016: Digital Dividends*, Washington, D.C.

Publicaciones recientes de la CEPAL
ECLAC recent publications

www.cepal.org/publicaciones

 Informes Anuales/*Annual Reports*
También disponibles para años anteriores/*Issues for previous years also available*

2018

Estudio Económico
de América Latina y el Caribe
Evolución de la inversión en América Latina
y el Caribe: hechos estilizados, determinantes
y desafíos de política

Estudio Económico de América Latina y el Caribe 2018
Economic Survey of Latin America and the Caribbean 2018
Estudo Econômico da América Latina e do Caribe 2018
Documento informativo

2018

La Inversión Extranjera Directa
en América Latina y el Caribe

La Inversión Extranjera Directa en América Latina
y el Caribe 2018
Foreign Direct Investment in Latin America and the
Caribbean 2018
O Investimento Estrangeiro Direto na América Latina
e no Caribe 2018

2018

Balance Preliminar de las Economías
de América Latina y el Caribe

Balance Preliminar de las Economías de América Latina
y el Caribe 2018
Preliminary Overview of the Economies of Latin America
and the Caribbean 2018
Balanço Preliminar das Economias da América Latina
e do Caribe 2018. Documento informativo

2017

Anuario Estadístico
de América Latina y el Caribe
Statistical Yearbook
for Latin America and the Caribbean

Anuario Estadístico de América Latina y el Caribe 2107
Statistical Yearbook for Latin America
and the Caribbean 2017

2018

Panorama Social
de América Latina

Panorama Social de América Latina 2018
Social Panorama of Latin America 2018
Panorama Social da América Latina 2018
Documento informativo

2018

Perspectivas del Comercio Internacional
de América Latina y el Caribe

Las tensiones comerciales exigen
una mayor integración regional

Perspectivas del Comercio Internacional
de América Latina y el Caribe 2018
International Trade Outlook for Latin America and the
Caribbean 2018
Perspectivas do Comércio Internacional da América
Latina e do Caribe 2018

El Pensamiento de la CEPAL/*ECLAC Thinking*

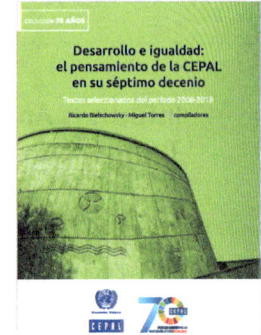

Desarrollo e igualdad: el pensamiento de la CEPAL en su séptimo decenio.
Textos seleccionados del período 2008-2018

La ineficiencia de la desigualdad
The Inefficiency of Inequality

Horizontes 2030: la igualdad en el centro del desarrollo sostenible
Horizons 2030: Equality at the centre of sustainable development
Horizontes 2030: a igualdade no centro do desenvolvimento sustentável

 ## Libros y Documentos Institucionales/*Institutional Books and Documents*

Acuerdo Regional sobre el Acceso a la Información, la Participación Pública
y el Acceso a la Justicia en Asuntos Ambientales en América Latina y el Caribe
Regional Agreement on Access to Information, Public Participation and Justice
in Environmental Matters in Latin America and the Caribbean

Hacia una agenda regional de desarrollo social inclusivo: bases y propuesta inicial
ATowards a regional agenda for inclusive social development: bases and initial proposal

 ## Libros de la CEPAL/*ECLAC Books*

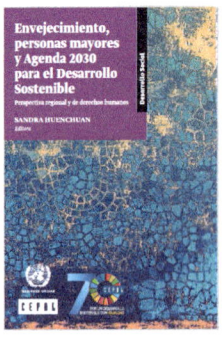

Envejecimiento, personas mayores y Agenda 2030 para el Desarrollo Sostenible:
perspectiva regional y de derechos humanos

La inclusión financiera para la inserción productiva y el papel de la banca de desarrollo

Estudios sobre financierización en América Latina

 ## Páginas Selectas de la CEPAL/*ECLAC Select Pages*

Los cuidados en América Latina y el Caribe. Textos seleccionados 2007-2018

Empleo en América Latina y el Caribe. Textos seleccionados 2006-2017

Desarrollo inclusivo en América Latina. Textos seleccionados 2009-2016

Revista CEPAL/*CEPAL Review*

Series de la CEPAL/*ECLAC Series*

Notas de Población

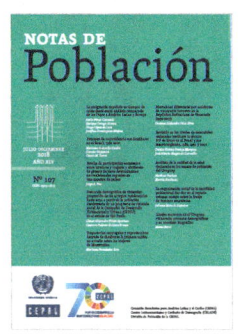

Observatorio Demográfico
Demographic Observatory

Documentos de Proyectos
Project Documents

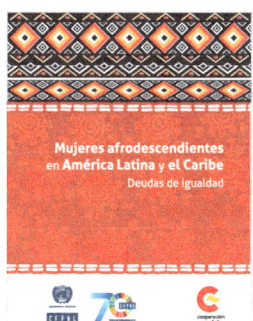

Metodologías de la CEPAL

Coediciones/*Co-editions*

Copublicaciones/*Co-publications*

Suscríbase y reciba información oportuna sobre las publicaciones de la CEPAL

Subscribe to receive up-to-the-minute information on ECLAC publications

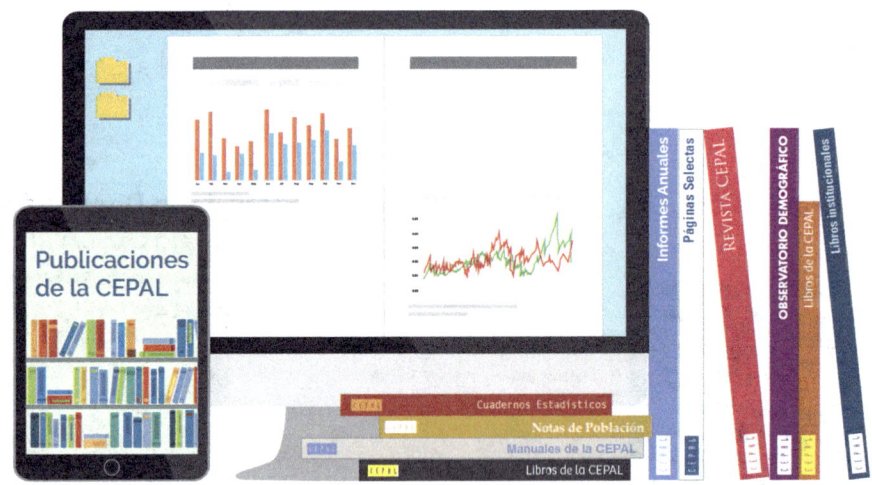

www.cepal.org/es/suscripciones   **www.cepal.org/en/suscripciones**

www.cepal.org/publicaciones

 facebook.com/publicacionesdelacepal

Las publicaciones de la CEPAL también se pueden adquirir a través de:
ECLAC publications also available at:

shop.un.org

United Nations Publications
PO Box 960
Herndon, VA 20172
USA

Tel. (1-888)254-4286
Fax (1-800)338-4550
Contacto/Contact: publications@un.org
Pedidos/Orders: order@un.org